For John and Gerry

PAWN

A Game of Black, White and Red

Donna Poole Mills

This is a historical narrative. Names, places, newspaper article references and incidents are of public record. The author recreated scenes with narrative of reasonable imagination based on recorded facts and oral history. Courtroom dialogue is from actual trial transcripts of Willie McGee vs. State of Mississippi, held in the Mississippi Department of Archives and History.

Grateful acknowledgement for permission to reproduce the illustration of Willie McGee on the cover is given to the Communist Party USA, from the photo collection held at Tamiment Library/Robert F. Wagner Labor Archives, New York University.

First paperback edition of this book was entitled "Road to Laurel" 2016

Book design by Natalia Mills www.nfamousphoto.com

ISBN: 978-0-578-74196-3(paper back)

Published by Donna Poole Mills

TABLE OF CONTENTS

CHESS TERMS USED IN CONTENTS

checkmate – A position in which a player's king is in check and the player has no legal move (i.e. cannot move out of or escape the check). A player whose king is checkmated loses the game.

first board – In team chess, the player who is assigned to face the strongest opponents

gambit – A sacrifice (usually of a pawn) used to gain an early advantage in space or time in the opening.

hanging pawns – Two pawns of the same color (same team) on adjacent files, with no pawns of the same color on the files either side of them. The term is used almost exclusively for two pawns on the same rank (side by side). They can be a strength, a weakness or neutral depending on the position. They are typically an attacking rather than a defensive asset.

trebuchet – A theoretical position of mutual zugzwang in which either player would lose if it were their turn to move.[325] (from French, a type of siege engine)

zugzwang – (from German, "compulsion to move") When a player is put at a disadvantage by having to make a move, where any legal move weakens the position. Usually occurs in endgame.

ACKNOWLEDGMENTS

I could not have completed this book without the patience and encouragement of my husband, John, who withstood, without complaint, a decade of trial and error and frustrations. Thanks to my wonderful and understanding children, Greg, Natalia and Anthony, who managed without me many times in their teens when I was behind the computer. Thanks to my dear sisters, Beverly and Carolyn, were always there for me when I needed support or the filling in of memories. I would have never rewritten the first manuscript into this narrative form without the coaching of Wilson Ellis. Warm thanks to Cheryl Tuggle, who helped with editing, encouragement and good advice. Without the urging of Yohannan and Tessi Abraham, who asked me nearly every Sunday, "How's the book coming?" I may not have crossed the finish line. A tremendous thanks to Alex Heard, who surprised me after I had barely begun – overwhelmed with the findings – with a ton of invaluable research from the writing of his own book, "The Eyes of Willie McGee." He also brought together many "in-heritors" of this story, including Liz Abzug, Della McGee, Bridgette McGee, Jon Swartzfager and others to meet and share our separate experiences. Thanks to Bridgette McGee, who became like family in this interweaving of our own family's stories. A most special thanks to Fr. Moses Berry for being an inspiration and giving me spiritual guidance throughout the time of this writing.

Finally, thank you, from afar, Mom and Dad, for your inspirational love and the weathering of this episode from our family history.

PREFACE

"Pawn" is a tale of the struggle of two men, one black, one white, who were both caught in the crossfire of racial hatred on one hand, and communistic political agenda on the other. They both became used as pawns in the two-sided battle for power over minorities. Although neither man was auspicious by his own merits, the trial by fire fashioned them each to find a higher truth above the fray of the chaos he was a part of. This legacy may be the impetus with which the generation to follow will seek to do the same. In these days when we are facing an uprising against racial injustice, and each race struggles to fully understand the other's point of view, it is important to be aware of the third force, which uses the heart-felt angst of both for purposes of its own agenda. History does repeat itself, and the unresolved griefs of the past that are surfacing in the present and once again fueled by deceptive forces, will accelerate to mayhem and destructiveness all in vain, if history is not understood.

The story of Willie McGee, a black man accused of raping a white woman in Mississippi, which was at that time a crime punishable by death, and my father's defense of him pressed upon me to give it life. In doing so, I was able to see how the thread of the past had woven an inextricable bond not only into my own life, partially told through the Interludes of this book, but also in our societal experience of the present day.

In uncovering this story of my father, John Poole's, experience as he sought equal rights for the black man without the goal of political gain, in a state where it was very dangerous to do so, I wondered what rejection he must have suffered throughout his life from many in his community. Not only was he ostracized – even temporarily disbarred – for his involvement in defending a black man, he was also considered a communist infiltrator for his involvement with the Civil Rights Congress. Willie McGee suffered a terrible death for something that, if it were indeed an affair, would have not gotten a second glance in this generation. He was one of many African Americans who were treated more like beasts than men in our sad history. I was honored during the writing of this book to meet with his grand-daughter, Bridgette McGee, who has also been inspired to write about the story of how the event affected her own family's life.

In my own life as a young adult, I set out to find my path in life and joined myself to a Christian Brotherhood, which terrified my parents in the era of burgeoning cults.

Nevertheless, I found solace for my soul and began my journey to the path of Orthodox Christianity. Fr. Moses Berry, a priest who became my spiritual father in the Church, also had a legacy of the hateful sting of racism. His great-grandparents were slaves who handed down neck irons they were pulled by, now lovingly preserved in Fr. Moses' African American museum in Ash Grove, Missouri. In his own generation, he experienced prejudices that linger, even with those who are seeking to put all judgment aside.

I find that those prejudices exist on both sides of the cultural fence, as my southern accent, along with the fact that I answer "Where are you from?" with "Mississippi," has induced looks of disdain from some with darker complexions or even Caucasians who think "y'all" is a small sailboat.

St. Moses of Ethiopia, a black man and Fr. Moses' patron saint, showed true humility in his life after converting to Christianity. Before his conversion, he led a gang of robbers, who when they came upon a monastery planned to pillage it. Instead, he found in the abbot and the brotherhood there the true treasures that moth and dust do not corrupt. Overcome by this grace and power, he and all in the band of robbers joined themselves to it. It is told that years later when a brother committed a fault and St. Moses was invited to a meeting to discuss an appropriate penance, he refused to attend. When he was again called to the meeting, St. Moses took a leaking basket filled with sand with him, carrying it on his shoulder. When he arrived at the meeting place, the others asked why he was carrying the basket. He replied, "My sins run out behind me and I do not see them, but today I am coming to judge the errors of another." On hearing this, the assembled brothers forgave the erring monk.

Only this kind of humility and forgiveness will heal the division of the races and heal the scars of the past. This Divine gift, the treasures of the spirit, is the third element that will create reconciliation in the way a political movement never could. I dedicate these pages to St. Moses of Ethiopia and pray for intercession for all those who seek forgiveness and reconciliation.

INTRODUCTION

"Donna, come quickly!" came the urgent call. I jumped up, thankful to leave math homework, and ran into the kitchen where I saw a visitor tying a blindfold around my Dad's eyes. Mom put a finger to her lips as she drew out a seat from the small table, urging me to sit across from them.

I watched in anticipation, as I had before attended the Mississippi State Championship tournament where Dad defended his ongoing title, against up to fifteen contenders – all standing in a line behind their chess boards. I observed from a distance, while Dad went slowly down the line, making deliberated moves at every board, punching the time clock, and eventually defeating each player in turn. He went on to win the regional prize. After all that, it was still hard for me to believe that he could do the same without seeing the board at all.

Mom had told me that she had seen him play against three men at a time blindfolded. At that time he won two games and drew the third. This time there were only two, but both were competent players. Dad was situated in between the chessboards, and I set my elbows on the table across from him, head in hands to study the event.

The contenders began their moves and announced them in turn to Dad in chess lingo, such as, "Queen's knight to King's pawn three." I felt the focus of Dad's energy as his forehead wrinkled to submission of the mental effort. He slowly and deliberately, as if placing it in the landscape of his mind, reciprocated with his moves in turn, "King's bishop to queen's rook five." I watched, wide-eyed, as the moves continued. His opponents appeared at first thoughtful, then impressed, and hunkered down for more serious combat.

Once, between moves, Dad reached for the bowl full of peanuts Mom had provided, and I quickly moved it for his groping fingers to find. Gathering some in his hand, he nodded his head slightly towards me and smiled – as a Southern gentleman would – and said sweetly, "Thank you, darling." He then chewed them as peacefully as a cow chewing her cud, appearing to have momentarily dismissed the mental task at hand. When the next opponent called out his move, however, the wrinkling forehead went back to work, calling up the mental image of each board of play in its own time. I remained fixed, fascinated, as the minutes ticked away and the realization dawned on me just what mental fortitude and agility it took to hold the ever-changing games in place and to go back and forth between them. My delight increased with each toss of an opponent's piece.

With swelling pride I watched as these knights with their lances were knocked off their horses, one by one, and my Dad, blindfold in hand, stood poised over them with his sword on their chests, smiling with a conqueror's joy, yet none-the-less gracious, as he in turn to each pronounced, "Check-mate!" I stood and cheered.

Dad's finesse in foreseeing the moves of others also accentuated his later law practice. One judge told our family that time and again he would watch Dad speak kindly and softly to the witness he was cross examining, asking questions that caused the person to engage in what seemed to be a simple-minded and non-intrusive interrogation. He would then say, haltingly, "I believe that's all the questions I have for this witness, Judge," and start back to his seat, but before he actually reached the attorney's table, he would position his fingers to his eyebrow as if just receiving an inspiration and say, "No, I have just one more question, your honor." Then he would play his ace, and ask the big question, catching the witness with his guard down, who would later realize the earlier questions had merely been a set up for the courtroom checkmate.

I imagine he learned a lot from trying the Willie McGee case, and perhaps wished he could have then applied the expertise that later won him the local title, "The lawyer's lawyer." As I grew up, I took quiet pride in the knowledge of my Dad's strengths, but never knew to what extent he had suffered in society, other than random wonderings about why we were always struggling for money.

Dad must have sensed the danger ahead of time with the Willie McGee case. His reasons for taking it on, with the chance of his practice being endangered with a pregnant wife and a toddler at home, must have been inspired by more than mere adventure. He told me once, regarding his practice, that he wanted to try to give the black man in Mississippi the full advantage of his rights under the law. He felt an obligation to his lawyer's oath to serve anyone impartially. I suppose then, in seeing the extreme exigency of Willie McGee, he had set his reasonableness aside.

PART I
WILLIE'S ARREST

HATTIESBURG, MISSISSIPPI – NOVEMBER 3, 1945

"Ticket to Florida, please ma'am."

The bus station clerk peered over her glasses to gaze at the toned muscles of the black man framed in her window. Willie McGee was looking over his shoulder and didn't notice the amorous assessment, "One way," he added hurriedly, turning back.

"In a rush, are you?" she asked, dimpling, reaching slowly for the ticket roll.

Willie glanced up nervously at the eyes of the older white woman, checking for suspicion. Seeing only mild flirtation, he assumed the proper slightly downward look and responded with feigned excitement, "Yes Ma'am, I'm goin' back to see my wife and chillun," he lied. "They's been in Florida, while I been workin'," He shifted side to side in practiced inferior movement. "I been missin 'em bad!" He gave the clerk a big innocent grin.

She looked down her nose, sniffed a slight annoyance at the mention of a wife, and said curtly, "That will be nine-seventy-five."

Willie fumbled his change, barely counting as he threw down his passage on the counter. Raking in the coins, the clerk shoved the ticket through the bottom of the window and said, "Outside, around the corner to the right – bus leaves in 10 minutes – take care, now, hon."

Willie grabbed the ticket, dipped his head and managed a "Yes, ma'am, thank you, ma'am!" while trying to avoid her pointed eye contact and outstretched hand.

He walked casually until he was sure he was out of the clerk's sight, then broke into a run, looking around nervously. As he came into view of the other passengers gathered for their buses, he slowed again, attempting to look relaxed as he scanned

1

the signs for his bus. Then, out of the corner of his eye, he spied the black and white police car with three officers emerging one by one, slamming doors shut behind them.

Perspiration began to roll from his forehead as Willie quickened his pace, but the men overcame him quickly from behind and one grabbed his arm with force.

"What? What you all want?" Willie feigned surprise.

"What's your name?" came the gruff reply from the burly frame. "My name's Willie–"

The blow to the head from a blackjack came before he could finish. Willie reeled in pain.

"You done ravished a white woman at Laurel, you son-of a-bitch! We're gonna break you Negroes up that gone in the Army from coming back here and raping white women."

The policeman jerked Willie up from the ground and shoved him towards the car.

"I ain't been in no army," Willie protested weakly, stumbling and holding his hand to his bleeding head.

"You'll shut up, boy, if you know what's good for you." Another blow to the back of his head rendered Willie unable to protest anyway, as onlookers gasped.

The officer pushed Willie roughly onto the car to handcuff him, then shoved him into the back seat while the others got into the front, and the car pulled away with a screech. Willie's head pounded and his eyes bulged as he heard the officers discussing their plans. The voices dimmed in the foreshadowing panic that overcame him. Through thunderous heart throbs he could barely hear them discuss taking him first to the Hattiesburg jail for examination.

"Hell," one of them was saying, "he's likely to be lynched if we take too much time to get him to Laurel." As Willie slipped into a faint, a vision of his mother replaced the present nightmare. She was wiping her hands on her apron, and looked at him saying, "Why is you so nervous round them white folks, Willie? I've told you what to do. When they fusses at you, you just say – yes ma'am, yes sir. They'll treat you right if you just keep your place. Just don't be lettin' on that you is thinking anything about them at all – that's all. Just play like you havin' a grand ole time, and don't go lookin' at them straight on – they'll leave you be, they'll leave you be." The vision faded as he slipped into unconsciousness.

CHAPTER ONE

FIRST BOARD – THE CHALLENGE

The air in Mississippi is usually thick with humidity – people there say that you could cut it with butter knife and serve it up for breakfast. Although this might turn away the wary traveler, I always felt that it was embracing me as a child and holding me close with its warmth, like I pictured a black Mammy holding her baby, loving it up all the way through its skin and tickling it straight through to its heart to make it laugh. Every part of you opens up in Mississippi, like it or not. You can choose to breathe in deeply the life-giving fragrance of the evergreens and revel in the richness of the magnolias or hold it bitterly at a distance like a strange medicine to be avoided. In order to understand the people of Mississippi, a person needs to enter into that beckoning atmosphere where time goes more slowly and life is savored like a corn muffin slathered with sorghum molasses.

The winter when Dad tried the Willie McGee case was different. Usually, the winter cold that goes straight to the bones is tolerated by the locals only for the sake of Christmas gatherings, New Year's celebrations, and an occasionally rare snow day, where automobiles are abandoned on the side of the road and children celebrate with sleds made of large cardboard boxes until the middle of the day, when wet patches of green emerge to halt the downhill fun. By mid-February the warmth creeps back in and breathes purple crocuses back to life to herald victory over another short cold spell. That winter, the winter of 1948, the chill hung on forebodingly as if it were a grim warning to beware of things to come. Usually friendly passersby now held their hats down low and hurried against the wind, clutching their overcoats. Cats could be heard howling in mournful tones as evening set in. Babies were snuggled in extra blankets, as was the baby girl in the Poole's home. When Gerry heard the cry, it was from morning hunger, not cold. She gathered her up with coos and rushed back into the kitchen, patting her on the back. Checking the percolator, she smiled to see it surge and chug the mud-colored liquid bubbling into its glass knob.

"Almost ready," she announced to John, who was seated at the small breakfast table already dressed for the day and absorbed in reading the morning's news. He tapped his fingers as if in response. Gerry stopped to check her lipstick in the mirror, rubbing her lips together before going back to the stove to flip the sizzling bacon. The baby on her hip protested her mother's rush with a loud cry.

"Baybay, hush, now!" Gerry said, putting her in her highchair with a bottle, which she drank heartily, "Daddy's got to get to work on time." Baybay was the pet name Gerry's mother had given Beverly, the first grandchild, and it had stuck. She was a healthy size and belied her mother's once again lithe figure.

"She's probably protesting all this political bullshit," John joked while flapping the paper into a fold. "Here, let me give her a proper good morning." Swooping Baybay into the air and shaking her gently over his head, he cooed, "You're going to be a big protestor, one day, aren't you?" She grinned widely and he continued, "Oh, you think that's funny, do you? Well, maybe you'll just be one of those new women lawyers, instead. You'd be better doing that, anyway – protestors don't make any money!"

"John – stop it! You'll get the bottle I just gave her all over your suit."

At that thought, John lowered her slowly and cradled her in his arm. "Let's taste some of Mommy's bacon," he said, reaching for a piece put out to drain, while Babay looked on wide-eyed. He grimaced, adjusting himself on his wooden leg and sat down again.

Gerry checked to make sure he wasn't in too much pain, before saying, mostly to herself, "Now, let's see, just what is in the paper?" She glanced briefly at the front page as she set the savory smelling plates onto the table. She poured a cup of coffee and sat down to peruse the paper for herself.

"Fred's column again?" she asked.

John stopped bouncing Baybay on his good knee to say, "Oh, it's just his review on the Dixiecrats and their abhorrence of any real progressive change. If Fielding Wright had it his way, we round up all the blacks and put them into slave quarters again." Without waiting for response, he continued with exasperation, "How is the Democratic party supposed to stay in office if Mississippi keeps it stuck in the mud of the past?"

"You could try running for office again next year," Gerry suggested, calmly spreading jam on her toast. "If," she challenged, "you're serious, that is."

John paused at the comment and handed back Baybay, who was reaching with her whole body for the interesting red substance. "I *am* serious," he said thoughtfully, as he reviewed the argument in his mind against it. He finally shook his head and added, "There's just got to be another way besides politics."

He watched Gerry feed Baybay a fingerful of jam, then as if moved by inward inspiration, he took a last sip of coffee, and shrugged into his coat.

"I've got to get to the office," he said, grabbing a piece of toast and bacon to go. "Love you, darling." He kissed Gerry's cheek and assured Baybay he would be back soon and hurried out the door. Gerry stood and followed him. "Or you could take up preaching again with Mildred! Preachers can move multitudes from the pulpit!"

John flashed a smile as he got into the car. "Couldn't do that! I'd have to give up beer." He waved goodbye and blew a kiss.

Gerry smirked as she stood at the door, patting the now crying Babay. She waved in return and muttered – "Your Daddy sure has his own mind about things!" At Baybay's louder protest, she repositioned her and added, "I know, I know – and so do you!

The day's work filled John's mind as he walked from his parked car, briefcase in one hand and a cigarette in the other. He shuddered against the cold morning, taking in a hard draw from his cigarette. Breath and smoke merged to circle his quickened steps as he sorted out his thoughts. The divorce case he was about to try was really a challenge, and unfair to the woman. A businessman, whose reputation was at stake, had hired him to counter his wife's accusations of multiple affairs and wife-beating. There was no evidence from doctors – she had been afraid to go. John suspected the man was guilty and despised the thought of representing him. As he entered the glass doors of the office building, he began to argue the case in his mind, only to be interrupted by a familiar daily greeting.

"G' mawnin, Mr., Poole!"

"Good morning, Evelyn!" John slowed to a stop. "How do you do this morning?" "I be doing just fine, thank you, Mr. Poole – How's you doing?"

"Fine, fine. It's always a pleasure to see you," he said, with sincere pause. "You, too, Mr. Poole, you, too," Evelyn responded with equal sincerity. "Have a good day, now!" he said with a tip of his hat.

"I will – you do the same!" Evelyn went back to her sweeping, smiling to herself.

John took one last draw from his cigarette, then stumped it out in the sand of a nearby standing ashtray.

"Hey, John!" The greeting came from behind. "Meet at Bailey's at 3:00?" "Hey, Fred. Don't know if I can – pretrial hearing at 11:00, then office work." "We'll be there. Hope you can make it."

"Thanks, buddy," John said with a chuckle and a wave. "I just might need it later."

John came to the door of a modest office weathered by age. He still felt pride at seeing the shiny brass-plated sign on the door that read, "London and Poole, Attorneys at Law." The lights were already on, he noted. Al must have made it before him, as usual. Al had become a sharp businessman as well as a capable lawyer since their days at Ole Miss Law School. He and John had been drawn to each other by their similar intellects – each had a photographic memory – and they both liked to reward themselves at the bar after a day of studying. John had been president of the debate club that Al excelled in, and in those days they had envisioned someday sharing a practice together. Here it was, only a year later, and their dreams had materialized. They both were fresh, sharp, and idealistic.

With Al's connections in the wealthier Jewish community, they had managed to keep afloat so far, but barely. John had even run for State Representative, just to get his name out to the public. He knew that his inexperience would cost him the votes he would need to win. Just the same, he relished going door to door to campaign for his progressive stance, encouraging higher education for women, more benefits for the elderly and greater opportunity for minorities. A one-on-one interchange was his forte, as was the drama of the courtroom. Al's efficient organization and genius in research made them natural counterparts. As he swung the wooden door open to find Al deep in study over his paperwork, John smiled with pleasure.

"Good morning, Al, how's my favorite partner doing?" He grinned and walked with a clump, step sound across the office's hardwood floor.

Al was standing quietly and ignored the obvious invitation to quip that he was John's *only* partner but shuffled the papers in his hand. He looked up with a somewhat stilted smile.

"I'm doing well, John, and you?"

"I tell you, I'll be doing better after I get this case behind me," John said as he shed his hat and coat and hung them on the wooden coat stand.

"Hmm…" Al returned, studying the papers in his hand once again.

"What's got your interest?" John sat down the briefcase, got out a file, and began to search through his own papers.

Al looked up with furrowed brows, adjusted his glasses, then said, "Have you heard about this case out of Laurel – a negro named McGee accused of raping a white woman?

John pulled out the documents he was looking for and set them on his desk, trying to keep interest in his partner's talk while organizing his day's work.

"McGee, yeah, about a year ago – right? They tried to lynch him down there, I heard. Poor fellow. Isn't Dixon Pyles on that case?"

"Nope, he dropped it."

John stopped organizing and looked at his partner. "Oh, yeah? Why'd he do that?" he asked, with more interest.

Al began to pace around their small office, tension showing in his face. "Pyles was getting paid by the Civil Rights Congress, a group that was formed by the merger of the International Labor Union, The National Negro Congress and the National Federation for Constitutional Liberties. They started funding the defense to promote national attention to what they call "legal lynching" cases in the South."

"Yeah, I've heard of that – out of D. C., right?"

"Right." Al walked over to John's desk and stood. "Well, Pyles figured they'd better come up with more money if they wanted him to keep taking the heat. I guess he was getting threats for representing this guy."

"I'm surprised he took it in the first place. You know how he followed Bilbo. And Bilbo hated anything that smelled of Communism. Do you remember when he talked about eating 'nigger steak' for breakfast on that radio broadcast?" Al grimaced, and John felt anger rising at the remembrance.

"So – what made Pyles take the risk?"

"Well, he may have been in it for the money, if there was much. Or then, he *is* feisty, he might have taken on the challenge just as an opportunity to argue against the status quo."

The serious mood broke suddenly as they both chuckled at the thought.

Pyles had been in the army, had a burly frame, and came off to fellow attorneys as a well-spoken bulldog, fully capable of turning on opponents, and enjoyed doing so often in the courtroom.

"He did tell a story, though," Al continued, "that he and Dan Breland, with whom he had associated on the case, were approached by some fellows from Laurel who were worked up because he was trying to move the case for a change of venue. It was obvious a change was needed – the townspeople were itching for a hanging and didn't really care which way their nigger died."

Al leaned against the desk, crossing his legs at the ankles and continued, "One of them called Pyles a son-of-a bitch for representing McGee and told him he had exactly thirty minutes to get out of Jones County. Pyles said he tossed his keys to Breland," Al tossed his hand in the air to demonstrate, "told him to take care of the car, and started running." Al finished with an ironic smile, "He said he ran back to Jackson so fast that he skimmed over the surface of a mill pond, and still has twenty-nine of those thirty minutes left."

John chuckled slowly – the sobriety of the matter held back his good humor – then looked up at Al with serious eyes. "Was there that much of a threat to them, you think?"

"He told me that if he had said the wrong thing in court, he could have gotten them both killed – besides McGee's lynching. It is serious, for certain. Those people were already roused enough by the situation – then when the Civil Rights Congress got involved it became a showdown. Did you know they had 50 National Guardsmen there armed with rifles and bayonets to keep the mob from taking it in their own hands?"

"Hell," John said, "they were putting on a show – you wouldn't need all that just to keep a few guys from acting up." He grabbed his pack of cigarettes and lit one. "And just how are you involved with this, by the way? You're not thinking of us getting our necks into this, are you?" John pointed his hand towards the papers Al had flapped for emphasis.

Al straightened, paused and then leaned over John's desk.

"As a matter of fact, I am." He smiled at John who was taking this in. "This woman came over yesterday afternoon after you left – a lady lawyer from the CRC, named Bella Abzug, smart as a whip, I tell you." He wagged his head for emphasis. "She traveled from New York to find a lawyer who would take up the case. Pyles said he was out," he added with gravity, pausing and looking pointedly at John.

Catching the unspoken drift, John leaned forward, returned the look and nodded his recognition.

"Go on."

Al continued, "She got my name from her brother-in-law, who knew I worked on the Jewish Welfare Board. She's Jewish, herself, and I guess figured I would be sympathetic to a minority cause."

"Well, did you tell her you were?"

Al smiled and said, "I told her I knew someone that might take the case." He walked slowly back to his own desk, giving John time to digest this. He turned around, crossed his arms and looked at John, who was leaning on his fists in thought, and added, "This is your chance, John."

"To get mobbed?" John tilted the wooden desk chair back, balancing it on two legs, half-smiling.

"Your chance –" Al was getting more enthusiastic now, " to do what we talked about in Ole Miss days – a chance to make a difference in the South in race relations; a chance to really stand up for the black man and put an end to this horrid lynching business." Al's voice took on a tone of disgust and passion as he was talking. Looking at John's furrowed brow and knowing he had not quite made his case, he tried a different approach. "Look, I know it would be risky, but Pyles has seen his fighting days – you've just started. Heck, you've handled worse in your life – even if you do meet a few rowdies looking for a tangle, you could just give 'em the old 'one-two, right to the chin.'" Al struck a boxing stance and demonstrated, threw up his hands, and proclaimed, "The winnah! Peg-leg Poole!"

The enactment worked to break the tension created by the thought of such a daunting task, and John, who couldn't resist a joke, sat up with widened eyes, playing along. He pointed outwards. "And there goes his wooden leg, folks! Catch it and get it autographed for the kids!" They both broke out laughing, enjoying the comic relief.

Al leaned back on his desk, laughed again and then sighed. Looking at John, whose image was hazy with smoke, he said, "Well, what do you think, John?"

John went silent. He stumped out the butt of his cigarette with slow certainty, studying the cause with effort. In his mind several thoughts sifted together – the political climate, the frenzy over Communistic infiltration, the long-standing racial injustice, the idealism he and his college buddies shared in imagining their potentials. He recalled saying farewell to those of them going off to war, and how he had to adjust his balance on his wooden leg when he waved goodbye. Then suddenly, a moment from long-ago invaded, and his thoughts swirled together to create a scene.

His new stepmother, who had gotten ready in her finest dress was looking in the mirror to check her lipstick. "Ethel," she called. But before there was time to answer she called again with irritation, "Ethel! Where are you?"

A young Johnny had been watching her with longing, remembering another, more gentle figure, who had also checked her appearance in the mirror not long before. When his stepmother turned to find him standing there, however, she frowned, her overly made-up face showing disapproval, and strode quickly past him.

"Ethel!"

"Yes, ma'am, here I am."

A worried Ethel was wiping her hands on her apron, moving her large body as fast as she could to the command. Mrs. Poole looked pointedly at the Ethel and said with anger, "Those children have not had a bath!"

"Yes, ma'am. They's been playing." She looked slyly at a dirty Johnny and winked. "They's been shoveling out the dirt to make a swimming pool."

Ethel and young Johnny shared a chuckle. He would have gone on to tell his stepmother just how far they had dug, but she cut him off.

"I don't care what they were doing, and I hope to God they haven't done anything that can't be undone" she said in a shrill voice. "They are filthy, and I don't want them sitting on any of this furniture until they've had a bath, do you hear?"

Ethel's eyes were large as she responded quickly, "Yes, ma'am, they's gonna have one right away. I'm jes fixin to draw one up." Smiling, she took Johnny gently with her arm, and turned him towards the bathroom.

"And don't you let them get into that food cupboard again, Ethel. Make sure it's locked up, you hear me?"

"Yes, ma'am."

"And don't you be helping yourself from it either! My children hardly had a supper the other night – if that happens again, you'll go a week without pay. Do you hear me, Ethel?"

Mrs. Poole went back to her studying how her attire draped her lean figure, but shouted over her shoulder, "You know those children have their own food, and they can just do without if anything's missing from that cupboard again." She fluffed her hair, pursed her thin lips, and then smiled with satisfaction at her image before turning to walk out the door.

"I'm going to my meeting, and I don't know when I'll be back. You make sure my children get fed right. I hope you can understand all this Ethel." She said, with pandering disdain.

"I understand, Missus Poole, I understand."

Ethel began to run the bath water, momentarily oblivious to the deep blue eyes of the young boy standing beside her that witnessed the tear well up and drop down her cheek. "Mm-mmh," she said as she shook her head and wiped the tear, then startled to see she was being watched.

"Oh, Mr. Johnny, It's not right what she does to you chillun, it's just not right." She hugged the young boy, and he enthusiastically hugged her back.

"It's ok, Ethel. We don't want to eat anything you can't eat, anyway." She laughed, wiping another tear from her eye.

"Oooh! Look how dirty you is!"

Unconcerned, Johnny said with eagerness, "You should see the hole we dug, Ethel! We've nearly got ourselves a swimming pool!"

She laughed, pulling his shirt off over his arms.

"You is quite the ambitious fellow, yes you is," she said. "One day yous gonna do sump'n real big, I just know it, I just knows it's true."

"John!"

"Hmm?"

"So, what do you think? We don't have much time. Bella is coming back this afternoon. I told her you had court this morning."

Still hunched in thought, John turned to look at his partner. "It's ours to do, Al," he said with quiet resolve. Taking a deep breath, he added, "I hope Miss Abzug knows what she's in for, in Mississippi."

Al nodded and responded thoughtfully, "Probably not. She couldn't be a year or two older than us, and I don't know how much experience she has or how much she really understands about the South. She's enthusiastic for her cause, that's about it. She just needs someone from these parts to try it. She knows that a lady lawyer from the North might not be accepted in trying this case."

John nodded. "It might do more harm than good," he agreed.

They both looked at each other thoughtfully, then John rose up with purpose, grabbed Al's hand with a fist and said with a smile, "Bobashela!"

Al returned the college handshake and replied with a laugh, "Bobashela!"

It was the title of their college yearbook, an Indian word meaning "good friend." They had adopted it in their partnership to symbolize their support for one another. They stood for a moment in the charged and inspired atmosphere of common quest.

Suddenly remembering the time, John ran his hand through his hair. "Jesus! I've got a hearing in fifteen minutes!"

"Yeah, you better call on him," Al returned, "Judge Collins has set this case for pre-trial hearings on the 20th – and you'll be up against Swartzfager."

"The 20th?" John pulled his coat on again and looked at the wall calendar. "Friday?"

"That's right," Al replied with a slight smile at the thought of winning his persuasive argument but slyly saving the details until last.

"Jesus, Al!" John breathed, as he opened the door. Turning back, he pointed a finger at his partner – "You're summarizing the review for me."

"Got you covered." Al replied, now smiling widely. "Good luck now with that divorce," he called down the hallway. "Don't let her take too much from the poor guy!"

Without turning, John waved back, striding with a clump, step, clump down the hallway. Al had closed the door but opened it again to add in a louder voice, "And we have to be in Laurel tomorrow!" John stopped momentarily, shook his head, and walked on.

CHAPTER TWO

QUEEN'S GAMBIT

Bella shook off the February chill and entered the coffee shop, a bell jingling to announce her entrance. The sound rallied the businessman-lunch regulars who sat in groups of two and three around the small tables. Nods, smiles and one, "Mornin'!" went around in Southern style to show they acknowledged her presence, not giving way to their curiosity of the chicly dressed business woman.

"Is it still morning?" she replied, glancing up at a large clock hung over the counter. "I do believe it is past noon. Good afternoon to you." Flashing a smile, she walked briskly up to the counter and said to the waitress, "Hallo, three coffees, and make them to go, if you please."

Muffled conversations then began at the table, followed by low chuckles. The girl, who had been wiping down the counter, looked up, eyebrows raised in surprise at Bella's clipped New York accent.

"Yes, ma'am, sugar and cream?" She replied in her own southern drawl, eyeing with admiration the unique hat that framed Bella's face.

"No, just black, but give me some packs of sugar with it too, will you?"

"Why, yes, ma'am. I'll fix that right up for you." The girl sauntered back to the coffee pot, nodding in answer to a call for a warm-up from a nearby table.

Seeing the server would take more time than Bella was comfortable with in this venue, she occupied her mind with the upcoming meeting. London had told her that he and Poole would take the case, and now all she needed to do was get them shifted into high gear. There would be a lot to cover – the history of the first and second trial, the anger that had been stirred up, and which probable road-blocks the prosecutors would put in front of them. Would these young lawyers be able to stand their ground in the heated climate? She wondered. Boisterous laughter momentarily distracted her. Seeing the waitress engaging in the joke from afar, she continued her inner dialogue.

Poole would need to interview McGee and she hoped the defendant wouldn't freeze up on this lawyer the way he had done with Pyles. McGee had just mistrusted Pyles, for some reason. The fact that he called McGee "boy" probably didn't help. Bella sighed audibly.

"Comin up!" the waitress called as if in response, securing a lid on one of the cups. Bella made no reply.

Judge Collins, she decided, would probably try to rush them into the trial before they were ready. He would love to put the defense in that position – she knew full well his ambitious stance against "Communistic infiltration."

"Excuse me, ma'am."

Bella started, suddenly aware of a towering presence beside her. A tall man in an overcoat, who had just made his entrance into the shop took off his hat and settled into a stool at the counter.

"I see you've come to the famous Mayflower for some of the best coffee in Jackson." He smiled widely, unabashedly sizing her up.

Bella gave him a long, hard look of her own. "Well, it was the closest coffee, anyway," she said, curtly.

"Well, hi there, Mr. Swartzfager," the waitress sang out. "How're you doing today? Are you in town for court?" She came over and set a box-lid containing Bella's coffees on the counter.

Bella recognized the name. Swartzfager was the district's prosecuting attorney. She stalled, fixing her hat pin.

"Well, I'm doing just fine, honey, thank you," Swartzfager returned with Southern style charm. "No, other matters brought me to town this time. Will you please get me a cup of that famous coffee?"

Her cheeks dimpled. "Two sugars and a cream?"

"That's right, hon," he said, smiling. Turning back to Bella, he drawled, "So, rumor has it you're in this fine city looking for an attorney. Is that a fact?"

"Well now, I see news travels fast in these parts." Bella said to the curious eyes of the waitress. She turned back to Shwartsfager, saying, "I'm sure you'd like to know who."

"We-ell, whoever you find, I'm sure he'll do just fine to represent that colored boy."

Bella fixed her eyes on the waitress, wanting to end the interchange. "How much do I owe you?" she asked.

"No, please," Swartsfager said, with a wave of his hand. "I've got this one for the lady."

"Well, all right, then," the waitress said, smiling sweetly at the two of them. "How kind of you, Mr. Swartzfager, to invest in provisions for the defense,"

Bella said with a quick smile, as she balanced with some difficulty the three coffees in the flimsy carrier.

"I'm sure they'll be needing a stiff cup of coffee," he laughed. "Good day," she replied simply, and turned to the door.

"Hell, before it's over, we'll probably all need a stiff drink!" Swartzfager called out, as she walked away.

She turned, smiling. "Maybe that drink will be on the defense." The bell jangled as she went out, and the door banged shut behind her in exclamation.

"A friend of yours?" The waitress asked Swartzfager, placing the creamy coffee on the counter in front of him and wiping her hands on her apron.

"More like an opponent," he said, his smile dropping. Blowing the steam away from the cup, he took a sip and slipped into deep thought.

"John's not back yet? I brought coffee," Bella said, walking unannounced into the law office. Al adjusted his glasses and looked up from his desk and its neatly piled stacks of paper. Taking a cup from the box she held out he said, "Well, thank you, how nice of you. John's still at court – should be back in about fifteen minutes."

"I'm glad you're studying," she said, tapping the documents. "I just met the opposition. He paid for our coffee."

"Swartzfager?" "None other!"

Al sipped from the steaming cup, "I'm surprised he mixed with your kind," he said, chuckling.

"Now, do you mean to imply he doesn't care for female lawyers, Jewish people in general, or just anyone who might support progressivism."

"All of the above," he said, sardonically.

"Well, he was kind enough, really. I'll tell you, I've seen worse in law school." She blew lightly on her coffee and took a sip.

"He's a Southern gentleman when he pleases, but don't you expect that in the courtroom." Al took a packet of sugar and emptied it into his cup.

"I've learned not to expect much from any man who thinks he needs to show superiority. Anyway, where are you on this?" Bella pointed to the trial documents.

Al paused at the warning, then said, "Well, I've read through most of the transcript.

The defense hasn't had much to go on – no witnesses, other than McGee's mother and McGee himself, who couldn't even talk at the time."

"Right," Bella said. "And, the psychological argument was passed over.

There were no black jurors on either of the juries – that fact was swept under the rug and, mind you, during both trials state militia protected him from lynch mobs."

"The extra-marital affair issue wasn't touched," Al added. Just an exploration of 'degree of consent'"

Bella sighed. "If an affair is brought to the table, it would be the dirty laundry that would unearth this area's deepest fears and upset its dearest convictions. No one would be spared in the upheaval." She crossed her arms over her chest and leaned back on the desk. "Do you think you two are up for the kind of heat this case will bring? The affair won't be brought up, but everyone is suspicious already. They've heard the rumors and insinuations." Before Al could respond she added, "This case could be the poster child for a breakthrough on legal lynching, you know."

Al shook his head. "I know, I know. But I'm afraid we'll be stepping into a lion's den." He sat back down slowly, as if already drained by the thought.

Bella leaned over his desk and said, "Listen to me. It's going to get ugly before it's over – I know that already. The prosecution is going to pretend that no one cares at this point, just for the media's sake. You know Mississippi is very worried about image," she said with disdain. "With the connections of the Civil Rights Congress in New York and D. C it's going to be in the national spotlight. That means they will put on a pretty face for show, but will make sure they get their conviction, one way or another.

"I heard that Swarzfager ran for his office on the promise that he would get the McGee execution for the people of Laurel," Al added.

"These people are on fire to preserve their belief that white people," Bella paused, "who aren't Jewish," she interjected dramatically, "are God's gift to the earth. Any man of another color was born to serve them."

Seeing empathy in Al's eyes, she added more quietly, "I don't mean to discourage you. And I want you to realize that you have many good people nationwide, backing your efforts. The nation is interested in Social Justice right now. You can be proud of the fact that you will be spearheading this in Mississippi."

"Hmm. . ." Al mused and looked at her pointedly. "You know that social justice is mostly interpreted as "Red Justice" in this neck of the woods."

Bella straightened, putting off his comment as uninformed. "Some things you can't teach to a culture except through gradual exposure," she said, condescendingly. "The South will be the last to change to the progressive movement, I'm afraid."

Then, changing the subject purposefully she asked, "How familiar are you with Thurgood Marshall's ruling on *Patton v. Mississippi* last. . ."

Before she could finish, the wooden door creaked open to present a bundled figure.

"Well, hello!" John nodded in greeting, swiftly removing his hat.

"Oh, here he is. Hello, John," Al said, visibly relieved to see his partner return. "John, meet Miss Bella Abzug, our Civil Rights Congress representative."

"I am so pleased to meet you. Bella, is it? Such an appropriate description." John smiled warmly, extending his hand.

Bella ignored the compliment and returned his gentle squeeze with a firm, quick shake. "Pleased to meet you, John," she said, briskly. "Al tells me you have decided to take on the McGee case."

"Yes, yes." John set down his briefcase and swung his coat off, draping it over the back of his chair. "Please, tell me more about this."

"Coffee?" Bella reached for the cup and extended it.

"Why, thank you," he said graciously, and accepted her offering.

Al began, "Bella and I were just talking about the Supreme Court and Thurgood Marshall's decision last December. You remember the case?"

John looked as if he was searching for the heading in his mind. "Patton vs. Mississippi? Correct me if I'm wrong – it was won on jury exclusion?"

"That's right," Bella responded. "The NAACP worked with him, otherwise, they might have accepted the inane "ratio" argument of the Mississippi Supreme Court. It reasoned because they had so few eligible black jurors in ratio to white ones it would be statistically unfair for white jurors to have even one black counterpart on a jury."

"There are some prejudices of our State that we are not proud of," John said somberly, looking at his partner.

Al nodded in concurrence as John continued with sincerity, "We would like to help balance that account." He took a drink of the now lukewarm coffee.

Bella's reply was equally tepid. "Well, if further legal lynching could be avoided, at least it would not add to the grotesque debt Southerners owe their fellow Americans." She filled the awkward pause by returning to the matter at hand.

"Patton vs. Mississippi gives us some hope, but this McGee case has heated to a fever pitch, especially since the CRC took it over. That's why your friend Pyles got out." Bella walked to Al's desk and ruffled the paper stack. "How much do you know already about the case?" she asked, looking directly at John.

"I heard about the trials in Laurel, but to tell you the truth, I haven't followed it in the past year. I've been busy trying to establish my practice. And," he added with a laugh, "I just became dad to a spunky baby girl this year. You can ask Al how many times I've come in here just to catch up on sleep." He shared a good-natured laugh with Al, until Bella brought them back to business.

"Congratulations," Bella said, smiling briefly. "She'll be happy you're working for a better future for her." She nodded towards the thick case transcript. "You'll want to study tonight. The indictment is scheduled for tomorrow morning and the arraignment will be in the afternoon. You'll need to make a quick trip to Laurel for that."

"Tomorrow?" John looked at Al in amazement. "We'll have to ask for a continuance – I'll need more time. I've still got a lot of work to do on the divorce case I'm trying. It's set for trial on Tuesday."

"I doubt you'll get a continuance," she said soberly. Judge Collins is not happy we won the appeal, and he has his prosecuting team in lock-step with him. If you're going to sign on to take this case you'll have to know that you're fighting a Goliath, and there's not much time to gather stones. Your aim is really going to count, and you're at more of a disadvantage than David. There's a large group of local Laurel citizens who support the Hawkins. They'll be looking for blood if you even appear to doubt Willette's story."

"So, the defense is expected to not defend." John dryly stated the obvious, packing his cigarettes and drawing one out with his lips. "Al said something about an affair," he added, flicking the brass lighter with his thumb to strike a flame that licked the end of his cigarette.

Bella breathed deeply, as if deciding just how to tackle the matter, then said, "You'll need to meet with McGee and ask him about that yourself. He spoke to Forrest Jackson, one of the first attorneys, about an affair. We have written testimony from him. An investigator, Lawrence Frantz, out of Knoxville, spoke with several people of Laurel. It seems it was common knowledge there was an affair. I'm sure Mr. Hawkins suspected it himself. He's made his own truth, anyway, regardless." She paused to weigh the effect of that statement on the two Southern men before her. Noting only rapt attention, she continued, "After Willie's incarceration, his wife and children left him and moved to California. It was heartbreaking to see the children say goodbye to their father – one of our fellows was with them for protection. Whether they left because they were scared for their lives, or because he was having an affair and Mrs. McGee was fed up, I really don't know. Could've been a bit of both, I suppose." She paused again, pacing the floor between the desks. "He hasn't talked much – didn't talk for the better part of a year after the first trial. We think it's becausehe has been beaten, or drugged, or both. Jackson was the only one he really talked to. He's been in a kind of shell shock, probably from being scared half to death, literally."

"Poor guy," John said thoughtfully. He pulled an ashtray over to tap a rod of ash into it.

"Pyles knew about it," Bella said, "but wouldn't touch it. I don't think McGee trusted him, anyway. See what he tells you, then we'll see if the story has changed. He's very anxious still, as you can imagine." Bella caught the compassion in John's eyes "He'll probably talk to you," she said, but as if wary of not finding genuineness beneath the Southern charm, she did not return his soft smile. "Let me fill you in briefly on what happened at the first two trials," she said quickly, "and what mood we're up against."

Bella laid out the story while Al and John shook their heads and stated their opinions. They bandied about political comments, discussed policies, and in spite of the seriousness, scattered laughter broke the intensity. Sandwiches were ordered and tactics were discussed until the sun went down. By the time the three of them realized John needed to interview Willie before the jail closed, New York and Mississippi had fellows on common ground for the defense of what would prove to be of a greater scope than the trial of one black man.

CHAPTER THREE

FIRST IMPRESSIONS

John picked up the phone and rotated the dial, entering the familiar number, *Fleetwood 3455*. On the other end, a musical voice answered. "Poole residence, Gerry speaking."

"Now that sounds like a fine establishment," John said. "Is that distinguished lawyer John Poole in his quarters? Oh, that must be his child I hear in the background." Babay screeched with delight in the background, and reached for the phone, wanting to be included in the conversation.

"I'm just trying to make it sound like a proper lawyer's home," Gerry answered with feigned hurt in her voice, and bounced Babay on her hip who twirled the curled phone cord around her finger. "After all, I'm practicing to be your secretary one day."

"And you're doing a fine job, but the background music gives away your true occupation."

"Yes, and I could use some help," she said. "When are you going to be home?" "Well, that's why I called," John said, more seriously. "I'm taking on a new case and I have to interview the client tonight."

"A new case?" Gerry smiled at the thought of her husband's business building. "That's good! You take your time, honey. Is it one Al referred to you?" His partner had in the past referred the wealthier Jewish clients his way, which led to much hugging and celebrating if the cases were won. Not knowing where this case would lead or what effect it would have on his new family, John said simply, but not without some guilt of omission, "Yes, Al did refer this one to me."

"Well, just come home as soon as you can and I'll keep supper warm. Love you honey!"

"Love you, too. Kiss Babay goodnight for me." "I will. Bye-bye now."

"Bye-bye" John said, drawing out the last syllable Southern style, as he hung up.

Somberly, he noticed the ashes that had stacked up on his forgotten cigarette and stubbed it out slowly in the small glass ashtray as he thought over the day's events. He looked at his watch with a start, then quickly gathered up his notepad and briefcase — now heavy now with transcript – and donned his hat and coat. At the door, he paused for a moment to look back at the empty office where moments before a story of racial hatred had been laid out, hopes of spearheading a change in the nation had been inspired and danger had been looked at head-on. Now he would meet McGee, a man who had been trapped and wounded in the lion's jaw.

What would it take to set him free?

"It will take a miracle," he said aloud, his inner thoughts taking voice. He turned and walked out the door.

The jailhouse stood cold and hard in the wintry grey. The shiver that went through John seemed to reach the bone. "It should be time we get a little warmer weather," he thought, as he rounded the windy corner that led to the front entrance. He relaxed a bit as he entered the warm entryway, and greeted the guard at the desk.

"Good evening," he said with a nod of his head, taking off his hat.

"Good evening, Mr. Poole," the guard nodded and leaned back in his chair. "Chilly out there!" John shivered again.

"Too chilly, I'd say. Ooo-wee!" the guard answered with a grimace. "We've had enough of this weather, I tell you somethin'!"

"I'd say you're right about that," John said with a laugh. He took off his coat and folded it over his arm, then headed down the hall to the elevator.

The brass doors slid together and the inner iron elevator door opened smoothly to reveal a smiling, black-skinned man with white, wiry hair sitting on the operator's stool.

"Good evenin', Missah Poole."

"Good evening to you, Joshua. How are you tonight?"

"Oh," Joshua laughed a little – a habitual trait – keeping his eyes downcast. "I'm doin' just fine, yessuh, just fine! Heh, heh." Joshua had been the elevator operator for the jail for as long as John could remember. They had built up a cordial relationship over the years, and spoke casually to one another when company allowed.

"And your wife, is she well?"

"Much better, yes, she is. Thank the Lawd, yes she is." Joshua said. "I'm so glad to hear it. Top floor, please." John steadied himself, clasping both hands over his leather briefcase handles.

Joshua first with a large handle closed the heavy outer brass door, then the inner woven iron door, taking obvious pride in the smoothness of his operation.

Alone with John inside the humming confines of the upwardly moving box, he took the liberty to voice his knowledge.

"You visitin' the McGee fellow today, Missah Poole?"

"Why yes, yes, I am. How did you know? Have you seen him?"

"Oh, yes. Oh, yes, Lawd," Joshua said, shaking his head. "A few times, oh yes. I takes them all to the second floor for church meetings. N' I's spectin' you'd be comin' soon."

"Is that right?"

"Yessuh. Heh, heh. 'N that lady from New York come to see him a while ago. She was talkin' to 'nother fellow 'bout Missah London. That's when I knows I see you soon – heh, heh. "

John smiled. After a pause he asked, "What do you think McGee's state of mind is, Joshua?"

Joshua looked up for the first time. "Times he's been plumb scared to death," he said, lowering his voice. "Wouldn't talk to nobody, no suh, mmhuh." He paused, as if to let the hum of the slowly moving elevator give emphasis, then added softly, "Been beat on too much, looks like." Joshua hung his head at this, as if to hide his emotions.

John asked gently, "You've seen him after a beating, Joshua?"

"Yessuh." Then, as the elevator reached its destination he added more quickly, "I'm afraid for him, Lawd." As he pulled on the iron bar and then opened the brass gate, he dutifully and more loudly said, "Top floor!"

"Thank you, Joshua," John said with a nod of his head, and a wink. "Thank you very much."

"You welcome, Missah Poole. You have a fine evenin', now." Joshua smiled, revealing checkered teeth, and then called out, "Goin' down!"

Another man made his way onto the elevator, adjusting his hat. "Ground floor, boy." "Yessuh! Ground floor."

The upper floor of the jail had a dreary stench, as if no fresh air ever washed it clean of the thoughts and tears of its inhabitants. John stopped at the desk to request an interview room and found that there were only a few minutes left before closing. Following the guard down the corridor, he heard the chatter from the cells as the inmates alerted one another to the presence of a lawyer.

Although interviewing clients in jail had become somewhat routine, as he pulled out his tablet and pen and sat at the table to wait, the import of the coming scene settled on him. The inspiration to represent those who could not represent themselves, which had been impressed upon him in law school, came rushing back in a raw, less idealistic form in the reality of the rusty, dread-filled atmosphere of the top floor of the jailhouse.

Unlike the more ornate lower floors, the "mob-proof bull pen" had been added almost as an afterthought, as a place to keep prisoners who needed protection from outsiders. John wondered, as he waited, if indeed it afforded the claim.

The clank of ankle chains and the creak of the heavy iron door announced McGee's entrance. The deputy ushered in Willie McGee announcing, "Ten minutes left before lockdown."

"All right, then. Thank you," John answered, looking up. He searched the face of the surprisingly well-groomed, good-looking figure in front of him, failing to establish eye contact. "We'll take what we can get for now," he said to the deputy, who pointed Willie towards a seat at the table across from John. Willie sat down stiffly, allowing himself a quick glance at his newly assigned representation while the deputy unlocked his handcuffs. He was younger than the last, probably not as experienced. He was more of his own generation, though, looked smart, and had a kind smile. Willie took a deep breath and relaxed a bit.

"Would you care for a cigarette?"

Willie reached across the table to accept the extended stick from the pack. John stood to offer a flame. As their eyes met, Willie's flickered, acknowledging the kind gesture. He drew in the smoke deeply and blew it slowly out his nose, as if savoring its escape from his flared nostrils.

"Much obliged," he said quietly.

John seated himself again, adjusting his body on the supportive wooden leg and began, "Willie, I'm your attorney, John Poole. Miss Abzug, from the Civil Rights Congress, has retained me to represent you in your case. Your new indictment is scheduled for tomorrow afternoon. Were you aware that you would have a new lawyer?"

"They say I was to git one." Willlie said bluntly, looking at the floor. He fought the urge to fully trust another white man.

John paused, reading the haunted face across from him. He was moved to ask, "How have you been treated here, Willie?"

Willie's large brown eyes lifted to meet and study his counsel's. There was a depth about the blue eyes and gentle demeanor that conveyed a shared experience of suffering. He took another draw of the cigarette, to give time to think.

"Much the same as in the beginnin'," he said, finally. Willie held his gaze steady for a moment to convey his meaning.

John leaned back in his chair and said, "Tell me about the beginning, Willie."

Willie took a deep breath and decided it best this time to lay caution aside. In hushed but forceful tones he laid out the story of his capture in Hattiesburg and the beatings with the blackjacks, pointing out the scars he still had from those beatings – one of which was a sizable dent in his skull.

John looked at each one carefully, squinting, as he imagined the pain.

"Damn!"

"They kept hittin' me like they wanted me dead." Willie's eyes went wide with the memory. "I finally passed out."

"What happened when you came to?"

"They say that if I don't confess, they gonna lynch me." "The policemen said they were going to lynch you?"

"Naw, they said other peoples would. They would just give me over." Willie looked up. "Then they took me to this place where a lady typed up what they say happened. Made me sign it."

"They forced you to sign a confession that you had raped Mrs. Hawkins?" John asked, his brow creased.

Willie looked at the floor. "Yessuh," he breathed.

"Willie," John said in a quieter tone, "we don't have much time tonight. Tell me about how you have been treated since you have been here."

Willie conveyed how the beatings were ritual – nightly in the beginning, then every few nights, until every night he sweated and trembled in dread, wondering if they would come this night.

"They like to put me in a hot box, too, until I pass out, usually." He drew hard on the end of his cigarette.

There came a sudden knock at the door and Willie inadvertently jerked. "Two minutes!"

John said hurriedly, "Willie, I want to see you free. I know you have pled not guilty, and claimed you were elsewhere the night of the alleged rape. I want to hear your full story when we have more time. Do you know anyone who can vouch for where you were that night, and would be your witness?

"They's run to Florida." "They're in Florida still?" "I believe so, yessuh."

"Would they come back to save your life, Willie?"

Willie looked up with a desperate new hope in his eyes. "If they had somebody to protect 'em, maybe. I don't want no harm to come to 'em on account of me."

"I'll see that they are protected," John said, pushing a tablet and pen in front of Willie. "Write their names, quickly."

As Willie scratched out names on the pad, John said in almost a whisper, leaning in towards him, "Willie, I need you to be completely honest with me. Did you commit the crime of rape on Mrs. Hawkins?"

Willie looked up somberly, hating the very sound of the word and said with quiet deliberation, "What I did with her, she wanted as much as me."

The two men stared at each other for a moment, then he added, "T'wasn't the first time."

"She was willing? Each time?"

"Wouldn't have happened if she didn't ask for it."

"Are you saying she seduced you?" John asked tensely, his voice barely audible.

Suddenly, the guard was at the door and Willie's face took on its former masked expression.

"Time's up! Lockdown!"

The two stole a glance of heightened awareness of the dangers this liaison could bring and the social boundaries it challenged. As the door swung open, they both rose clumsily, each with his own handicap of movement. As the guard placed Willie back in the iron grip of the handcuffs, John cleared his throat and said, "I'll file motions this week, Willie, and try to buy us some time. The authorities will transport you to the jail in Laurel, for the arraignment tomorrow." John looked meaningfully into his client's eyes, which Willie dutifully lowered in the presence of the guard.

"Yessuh, thank you, suh." Then, bravely, as the guard's hand gripped his arm, he added, "Missuh Jackson had an account of what we's talkin' about."

The guard gave him a shove and growled, "Time's up, McGee!" "Thank you, Willie, I'll check on that."

John watched as Willie was led down the musty hallway back toward the cells, then somberly gathered his blank legal pad and pen into his briefcase.

Mentally perusing their talk, he headed towards the elevator, with downward gaze. His thoughts were interrupted by a raspy voice.

"So, you're representing the niggah boy who raped Mrs. Hawkins, are you?"

John turned to see the small, poorly groomed man who had weaseled his way between himself and the elevator. A greasy smile loitered as he twirled a toothpick in the corner of his mouth.

"And what is your duty in this affair?" John asked, eyebrows raised.

Ignoring the question, the man snarled, "Don't you believe for a minute that he didn't viciously rape that woman!" He lowered his voice then and said more congenially, assuming some camaraderie in culture, "They's plenty of men in Laurel will tell you any story you need to hear about that boy."

"Thank you, sir, but I believe I will take the facts over stories." John sidestepped the man and pushed the button for the elevator, but turned back to say, "It's time for lockdown, you know. Will you be going down?"

The man sniffed and turned his back on John, whistling as he walked down the hallway in the opposite direction. The brass door opened to receive its passenger, as with mock emphasis, the man broke out in song. "Swi-ing loow, sweet chariot, comin' for to carry me hooome." The brass door glided shut on grim faced riders, sealing them from the fate of the bull pen's evening.

CHAPTER FOUR

HIS MAJESTY, THE LAW

"Have you had a chance to read the trial transcript?" Al asked, stirring the sugar into his coffee vigorously.

"That's not your first cup, I see," John teased, as he flipped his lighter open to his cigarette and clanked it closed again.

Al sighed as he sat down at the kitchen table, pushing the paperwork to the center. "Bella called last night to remind me of the precious little time we have."

"It would be ludicrous for Collins to not grant a motion for more time," John said, adding, "I read the transcript, by the way."

Al's brows creased as he pushed his glasses up the bridge of his nose. "It may be ludicrous, but what hasn't been in this trial so far? Besides, Collins doesn't want time for any defense to develop." He tapped the file marked *Summary,* "Pay close attention to the details of what happened just after the alleged rape. It doesn't make sense – her running hysterically to the neighbor's with just a halter top on, and him not following."

"Why would she run to the neighbors' house?" John agreed, sipping his coffee for inspiration.

"She was plumb out of her mind for one reason or another."

"But, why would she run away from her home, unprotected and nearly naked?" John pressed. "She couldn't face her husband because she felt she was disgusting to him after a rape? Or was she afraid of being discovered? He stared off, eyes fixed on the blurred scene in his mind" If it was an affair, like McGee purports, and they had gotten caught, but he managed to escape, she would have been in some trouble that night with the Mister." John rose from his chair and began patrolling the small kitchen and pointing, as if becoming a part of the scene. "Hawkins could have threatened her and forced her to claim it was rape, or...." his eyebrows rose at the thought, "she could have told him it

26

was rape so she wouldn't get a beating. In any case, it would have been smart of him to take the opportunity when she ran out to call the police and say she was raped." John turned to Al, who had a worried look on his face. "Well, what do you think?"

"Well hi, ya'll!" Gerry burst through the door, breaking the focus. She pulled the stroller energetically over the wooden door stop and said, "You made coffee already?

Mmm, smells so good!" She gathered up her cooing baby and deftly relieved her of the warm hooded outfit. "Beverly loves our morning walks!" she offered with a smile, oblivious to the seriousness of the moment.

"Even in this cold weather?" Al said warmly, returning her smile.

"She thrives on it! Gerry proclaimed with feigned seriousness. "But then, that's about all she knows so far. We'll see how she likes our sticky summers this year." She laughed, running her free hand through her long, wavy red hair. Looking at the pile of papers on the table she offered, "You'll have to excuse us girls, we need to freshen up a bit." She turned and walked with the babe in arms, in swift, graceful movements towards the back of the house.

Al looked over at his partner, who was enjoying the flow of his wife's slender frame with hungry eyes. John turned to find he was being studied, grinned sheepishly and sat down, lighting up another cigarette. Al caught the spark in John's eye and said slowly, "You can imagine how Hawkins felt, one way or the other. And – we could be defending a guilty man."

John blew the smoke through his nostrils completely before responding, "We could be."

Al continued, "However, see what you think of McGee's account. I've added that as an attachment at the end. Bella doesn't think it should be included just now, but it might help on a cross-examination. "

"Oh, that must be what Willie was talking about last night. He mentioned that he had told Forrest Jackson about it."

"Yep, I believe Jackson taped it and had it transcribed. You might take it with a grain of salt – it could be just something he came up with to save his neck." John looked at Al questioningly, thumb supporting his chin in thinking pose, two fingers holding the cigarette for easy access.

"Ready to review?" Al asked, picking up the file. "Proceed," John responded, settling in for the study.

Al began, On November 3rd, 1945, Willie Magee, a 30 year old Laurel negro – as the Laurel Leader Call describes him – was arrested in Hattiesburg on a charge of grand larceny for stealing a truck owned by the Laurel Wholesale Grocery where he was employed. The article reported:

'Magee, who is the father of five children, is also being questioned in connection with the criminal assault of a white woman, which occurred at her residence on South Magnolia early Friday morning. Reports that Magee confessed to the assault charge are being denied by officers today."

John jotted down a note – "Confession denied by officers."

Al paused, then added, "Another black man, Floyd Nix, was also being questioned and both of them were taken to the mob-proof jail in Jackson for safekeeping. Evidently, these are measures taken to counter the South's bad press and show that they actually prohibit mob lynching. You know, it has only been a little over two years ago that the negro, Howard Wash, the one who allegedly killed his white employer, had been snatched from the Laurel jail and was hanged from a bridge." "Did anyone get convicted for that?" John asked.

Al grimaced. "I don't think there was much of an investigation."

John recalled the bullpen visitor and the irony of having a "mob-proof" jail. "Too many officers looking the other way," he noted.

Al nodded his consent and continued, "The next report in the Leader didn't come until a week later and said that an affidavit was filed on November 9th as a result of a 'signed detailed confession received by the county attorney from the charged Ne gro.' McGee claims this was coerced through beatings and warnings of lynching, by the way."

John's brow furrowed as Al continued, "The arraignment was scheduled for December 3, and took place after McGee had been escorted back to Laurel by fifty – mind you – fifty Mississippi State troopers. They had rifles, bayonets, submachine guns and tear gas. Armed soldiers line the courtroom and spectators were checked for firearms before entering. The front three rows were kept vacant as a safety measure." Al paused to say, "look at the stark contrast here," then continued, 'As preparations for the arraignment proceeded, Laurel was quiet.'

John shook his head in disbelief and said, "Of course, this was not taking into account the meetings to apprehend and lynch McGee that were going on behind closed doors."

Al smiled grimly with a pointed finger, "Oh, but the News Leader goes on:

'The order...asking for the troops was that the integrity of the courts and the good name of the people of the city of Laurel, Jones County and Mississippi may not be marred by any unseemly interference with the conduct of our courts in the administration of justice.'"

He paused to add, "I think you were right. It was nothing more than a show." "Pretty convincing, I would say!"

"Listen to this," Al continued, reading dramatically, 'Judge Burkitt Collins, who faced the strongest charge of his career, began his address to the jury venire stating:

'The Great War is over, and our country is saved. It is a country of law, governed by law, a law under which all are considered equal. We need bow to none.

The only majesty we recognized is 'His Majesty, the Law.' It is the Law that has given us liberty, freedom, the right to the pursuit of happiness that protects us in our rights, person and property. We owe much to His Majesty the Law, including the protection of our families. But any man who claims these protective blessings has no right to violate the law. He must subscribe to that system of government that says all men are equal. If he claims the right to violate the law, a neighbor has the same right. If we continue to have liberty and freedom and enjoy the blessings of freedom, it will be because we have upheld the law …We must see that the law is preserved.' Turning to the jury, he said, 'Go out and do your full duty.'

"Pompous bastard! John exclaimed, as he smashed his stub into the ashtray.

Al couldn't help but let out a laugh, but said more seriously, "Well, you know the allusion to Communistic influence is hidden to none in this arena. These prosecutors are very aware that the Communist Party has been a leading voice against lynching and are making public the prejudices of the South through the Scottsboro case and others."

John added, "Even with the Anti-Red scare growing, the Communist Party is nonetheless very influential in the northern states."

Al leaned in and spoke more softly, "Did you know that the Civil Rights Congress – our dear benefactor who is targeted as Communistic – was just this year a merger of The International Labor Defense, The National Negro Congress, and the National Federation for Constitutional Liberties – all whom are very suspicious to Southern folk. They have been like eagles watching the developments of these cases. When they funded the defense of this one, this grandstanding of Collins to protect is just a message to the nation that Mississippi is minding its P's and Q's when it comes to its black citizens and trying to win national favor by standing against Communism." Al paused to let this sink in, then added, "An ironic note is that the same newspaper, a few days prior, ran an article lauding the Klu Klux Klan for their "…protection of our laws and of our white women."

"The contradiction is outlandish," John said. "I'm sure no one outside of Mississippi is impressed, nor fooled, by such extravagant attempts to cover the prejudices here. What strikes me is that Willie McGee's fate, at this juncture, is more to these courts than any act of justice. His life and others like him have become symbolic of a battle against the invasion of their territory and culture. They see any progressive movement through "Red" glasses.

Al mused, "If the truth be known, I wonder who we would find wearing white hoods by night."

"Legal lynching rests more easily on the conscience, I would imagine."

Al sighed, "That's right, I'm afraid. To their credit, there were several men who wanted to be excused from jury service, but Collins chided them by saying if their private business was more important than their duty to their government, then they could be excused."

"It wouldn't have been healthy to take him up on that, I imagine," John laughed.

"Most likely not," Al grinned. "Ok, so the trial was set for the following Thursday, and because the attorneys could not get an intelligible statement from McGee, they pled insanity and asked the court for a psychiatric opinion. Collin's, however, decided that since this was a pauper's trial, and a psychiatrist's opinion would be too costly for the state, the jury could just decide whether or not he was sane. The Clarion Ledger even admitted, and I quote,"

'In selecting the jury for the trial this afternoon, the special venire was exhausted, and Judge Collins ordered deputies to go on the street and summon passersby. In this way the last six jurymen were obtained.'

"What?" John started, "Who has ever heard of selecting jurymen by going out on the streets. This could not be within protocol."

"Think of it," Al said, "this pick was most likely made up of those waiting outside, eager to see McGee quickly convicted. " Coincidentally," he added with sarcasm and a nod, "there were no black men available for jury duty."

John frowned, "I wonder if any of Hawkin's buddies got on in this way?"

"I wonder, too, but it says after the final, all-white selection, a sanity hearing was held."

"The defense was purporting that Willie was insane," John reflected. "Right," Al said and began to read again.

'The defendant, escorted into the courtroom by members of the State guard, wore clothing similar to theirs. He was trembling, wide-eyed, unsteady on his feet and jabbered continually and inaudibly throughout the day. He showed no recognition of his mother when she took the stand, and none when she prayed over him before the sanity hearing.'

"It doesn't sound like simple fear," John noted.

"Al nodded and went on, 'Five State witnesses declared that McGee was pretending, and that they had seen him before to be sane. A Captain of the State Guard who took the stand, reported for proof of McGee's sanity that Willie had responded to his command of 'Go to your cell,' and went, as he described, 'like a mule heading for his stall.'"

30

Al looked to John for his reaction. "I'd say there was an ass in the courtroom, but it wasn't McGee," John said with a disgusted look. Al smiled and continued.

"The minister for the jail testified that he had heard him singing when he first came into jail, and described the scene:

'The lady spoke to all of them (that had come to the church service) and they started their service, and she had testimonials from some of the different ones of them, and then they started singing…She had testimonials again and had prayer, and while she was praying, this particular boy over here would bow his head and glance up and look at her, then bow his head and glance up and cast his eyes toward me. On the second song, the song of Swing Low Sweet Chariot – I am a vocalist myself – I noticed the movement of the chords of his throat on his lips as he hummed and sang part of the song.'

"Based on these few observations, the minister went on to answer the prosecutor's question, 'Do you think he is feigning here now?' with, 'I do, it is acting, or horseplay.'"

John tapped ashes into the tray as he responded, "I think it was horse-play by someone else. It sounds to me like he was drugged."

"That's certainly a possibility," Al agreed. However, the selective mutism was not just for the trial, but I'll get there. McGee's mother was the only one who defended him, but it didn't help much, as it says here:

'Willie's mother, who was called by the defense attorneys to help them get the defendant to talk before his trial this morning, also testified at the sanity hearing in response to the question, 'Is he putting on?' with 'I don't know myself.' She believed that her son, 'had just sot in jail, studied and worried and 'bout lost his mind. He's always been easy to get upset, especially when he was scolded by white folks, but I've never seen him in this shape before.'

Al added, "She also said that she had tried to get him to talk with her, but he would only stare off in the distance, as if he didn't see her. Now, with this scanty and unscientific evidence, the jury, who were not qualified in any way to determine sanity, were told to do just that. Fifteen minutes later they returned from their quarters to declare that Willie McGee was indeed sane, and scribbled on a piece of paper their declaration, 'We the jury find the defendant sane.'"

John shook his head as Al continued, "The actual trial got underway mid-afternoon. During the trial The Leader reported Willie as:

'…sitting stiffly in his chair, jabbering, his face averted from the witness stand where thirteen persons took turns in spinning out the story of his crime. Unable to elicit one word from him, his attorneys (appointed by the court and bound by their oath to serve in his defense) declined to put a defense witness on the stand and made no argument at the close of the case.'

"Now, the fact that the attorneys would have been in some danger should they have given an argument in the defense of McGee is implied by the parenthetical addition, offering an excuse for them for even having to be employed in the defense of such a crime. We won't have the same courtesy, you can be sure."

John passed over the comment saying, "A likely reason that McGee was not able to speak intelligibly that day, other than being terrified, is that he had been severely beaten with blackjack blows to the head after being arrested. Either that, or he was drugged."

"If there were any lumps or contusions seen, they were never discussed as interfering with mental capabilities. Of course, they would then have to investigate the source of the injury."

"The panic alone when facing these lying 'protectors of the law,'" John spit out, "which he knew he had no fighting chance against, may alone have led to severe anxiety and mutism."

"Mmhuh," Al agreed, while thumbing through his papers. "There is another interesting article – this one from the Jackson Clarion Ledger – appeared a few days after the hearing. It reported an accounting of some of McGee's cell mates saying that after his arrest and before the trial, he sang the song the minister attested to – "Swing Low, Sweet Chariot" in the prayer service. That was the first and last time they heard him say an intelligible word for close to a year."

"He was probably hoping for a chariot to swing down and get him," John mused.

"You bet. OK – hear this one," 'Willie McGee...four days after the sanity hearing and his subsequent conviction, was not like a normal human being in proper control of his mental faculties. McGee may NOT be crazy, however, if he's sane, he is a great showman and is putting on a master act of prolonged pretending....Willie rolls his saucer pupils with much more effect than a "Popeye" freak show actor, and he doesn't say a word.

This sphinx-like appearance has been going on, his cellmates say, since the Sunday before he was taken to Laurel to answer the capital punishment charge. He hasn't opened his mouth to say a word since then. We called Willie up to the bars to be sure, asked him several questions with no response except for the far-away monotonous stare and the continuous rolling of the eyes. Even our most pleaful puns, coupled with admonitions, failed to get the usual result, gained in such maneuvers in similar cases in the past....Either Willie McGee was CRAZY, or just crazy, like a fox. "

"Did they just ignore the indention on his head? John asked, "Or even think to ask a doctor for advice?"

"If he told Forest about the beatings, it didn't come to light. And, remember, he wouldn't talk for Pyles. He was supposedly able to talk to a former employer Horace McRae, just after the arrest. It was in the trial transcript. Let's see here," Al thumbed through the papers again and pulled out one to read. "Here it is. Horace testified:

'He said he was guilty, and that he had made peace with his Lord…he had his Bible in his hand and had five or six pages out of one of these small tablets where he had copied verses from the Bible – said he had made peace with his Lord, and said he was the right man.'

"McCrae was cross examined and went on to say that when he was visiting with McGee, Hawkins came in and Willie got real excited and didn't take his eyes off him."

John smiled in spite of the scene. "So, Mr. Hawkins was allowed into the jail with Willie during visitation. Wonder what short strings he had to pull for that one?" He paused, as the import of the thought caused him to be more serious. "If he was allowed once, how many other times did he come? Willie claimed that he had been beaten on a regular basis in jail."

"It also makes me wonder why they thought he would have even recognized Hawkins," Al added, then said, "Here's a telling one;"

'After this witness was excused, the court record showed:

By Mr. Boyd: "Willie, do you want to go and confer with us awhile? (No answer)

By Mr. Boyd: "Boy, if you have got any sense, you better be using it.' By Mr. Pittman: We object to that statement.'

"Willie could hear, and could have made some motion, but probably understood that this attorney held him in the same low regard as everyone else in the courtroom and was no more invested in his defense than he had to be by his appointment," Al concluded.

"No witnesses for McGee?" John asked.

"Nope, and his mother's credibility was discounted, but she didn't seem to know much, anyway."

Al started again, "After hearing the witnesses, which took less than half an afternoon, the all-white jury deliberated for two and one-half minutes – minutes, mind you – before declaring him guilty as charged. The judge decided that McGee's punishment would be death by electrocution and set it for January 7, 1946."

"Two and a half minutes to decide a man is not worthy of life. What would the sentence be if this was a white man guilty of rape? A few years in jail? And…if it was the case that a white man was guilty of raping a black woman, would it have even gone to court? Where is our constitution in all of this?"

"Well, the Civil Rights Congress saw it as prejudiced, alright, and flew in to take on the appeal. That was when they hired Forrest Jackson and Dixon Pyles.

They won a Stay of Execution based on the argument that a Motion for a Change of Venue, for reasons of prejudice, had not been properly handled, and on this cause appealed the case to the Supreme Court of Mississippi."

"Yes, I remember Bella saying that," John replied.

"Read this letter from Milton Kaufman, the Executive Director of the Civil Rights Congress then. He sent a letter to the Jackson Daily News in hopes of soliciting funds for the defense from the people of Mississippi," Al said and handed the paper to John.

"More Yankee Meddling," John read the heading with drama. He then scanned the article saying, "He references the lynching in the South then says," 'Every thinking American recognizes that terror against the negro people, particularly negro veterans, is rising in the South today…give as much as you can today toward defense funds for Willie McGee…I assure you that every dollar will be made to count.'

"Oh, and I see Sullens wrote his own opinion for us," John said sarcastically and continued:

'The purpose of the above "shake-down" letter, of course, is to fatten somebody's purse – a purpose much more evident than any desire to see that justice is done in either of the cases cited…we do know about the Willie McGee case in Mississippi, and we do know the rapist is getting all the leniency he is entitled to – and maybe much more…evidence showing the built of the accused offered in the lower court trial at Laurel was conclusive…the jury returned a prompt verdict because the evidence was so conclusive.'

"That Sullens is an idiot!" John shook the paper as if it were Sullen's head. "What conclusive evidence is he talking about? The shorts? The parked truck?

There wasn't even a defensive argument!" John realized he was shouting at this point and sat back again with a huff.

Al readjusted his glasses and said more quietly, "The Mississippi Supreme court wouldn't hear the case but reversed and remanded it back to the original court. Judge Collins was emotionally invested and said that there would be no problem that Willie could have a "fair and impartial trial" right back in Laurel, and denied a motion to change venue that Pyles submitted. Pyles told an interviewer that he would have never taken the case if he would have known ahead of time that his life would be in danger."

"No surprise that Collins would do that," John said dryly. "Did Pyles ever bring up jury exclusion?"

"Well, the reasons given that there were no blacks selected for this jury were that were that in order to serve you have to be a registered voter, and there weren't many blacks who were registered. There were some who they say "elected" not to serve. Bill Hosey – a former mayor – testified that "they would ask to be excused, because they were of that class of intelligent Negroes that didn't want to appear as a juror in court." The s.o.b. actually started to tell a story about how his forefathers used to settle these matters until the judge brought down the gavel."

John laughed, "It would have not have fit with the image he was trying to portray." He thought for a moment then asked, "So, Pyles did try to prove consent by Mrs. Hawkins, isn't that right?"

"Yep, he went from the frying pan into the fire at that point. He claimed that Willette Hawkins may have legally consented to the rape, since she didn't cry out and that she had testified that she 'could take it.'"

"Mississippi law requires that their rape victims struggle against all odds in order to call it such," John agreed.

"Yes, but it didn't fly, partly because it was not to be conceived that a white woman would ever have consented to have sex with a black man, but also because of the mention of threat. Her life and her children's were at stake, the way she told it, and she said that she didn't cry out because she didn't want to arouse her children." Al paused to pour another coffee. "Oh, and they found 'living spermatozoa in her, but claimed they couldn't tell whose it was. Hawkins must have been steaming at Pyles."

"I suppose the gun found on him was the last straw for Pyles before he dropped the case."

"It may have also been about payment. The CRC operates solely on their donations, and Pyle didn't think the small beans worth the danger. I'm hoping there's not going to be a problem with that this time. We'll have to get that clear with Bella, soon," Al noted.

John picked up again, "Even if Pyles had believed the affair story, there would have been no way he would have brought it up in court."

"Oh, no," Al agreed. "He said in an interview afterwards that it would have started a riot. They wouldn't have believed it, and those people couldn't have done otherwise and still lived in that community. Pyles said 'Whenever you charge a white woman in the South with having sexual relations with a nigger in this part of the country, why you better be God-damn sure. We wouldn't have lived to have gotten out of town, then she probably wouldn't have lived, either. They would have killed her.'"

"I imagine that's the truth."

"Think so." Al smiled, "He went on to say that there was no evidence to back up a testimony that the witness wasn't even able to attest to verbally. The only way to have gotten any confirmation from Hawkins would be in cross-examination, and Pyles said if they had done that, 'Why, they would have chewed us up like cotton.'" Al laughed at his own imitation.

John smiled, but went on, "So what was the final argument?"

"Should be in this section." Al flipped through the stack until he found it and read, "In counsel's defense Pyles only pled: 'We don't ask you to turn Willie loose. Send Willie to an institution where he can be guided and do useful work. The defense asks that the jury find Willie not guilty by reasons of insanity."

"Then they deliberated for eleven minutes, came to the same conclusion as before and set the new date of execution – December 20, 1946. What they didn't count on is that this stirred up sentiments to a pitch within the CRC and its sympathizers."

"If you ask me, this case is becoming a showcase for political agendas on both sides, and both the prosecution and defense of Willie McGee will be representative of much greater causes," John declared.

"Buckle up, buddy!" Al returned, then said in a much lower voice, as he heard Gerry coming from the back, "By the way, this account of McGee's would probably start World War III if it got out. Guard it carefully."

"Hi, fellows, ready for a little brain fuel?" she smiled as she walked into the kitchen and tied on her apron.

"You must be an Angel," John quipped.

"I am. I was just sent by God to make you two sandwiches. See the wings?

She flipped the upper strings of her apron in jest.

Al waved his hand in protest. "No, thank you, Gerry, I've got to get going." He looked at his watch and said, "John, let's meet at the office at one, shall we?"

"Sure! Thanks for the review." John rose stiffly with a jerk.

Al slipped the confession on top of the stack, winked at John and said, "See you then," then bid them both goodbye.

John turned back to Gerry, slid his arms around her waist as she stood facing the counter and gently kissed her neck.

"That's the new case from Al?" Gerry feigned interest but was enjoying the affection more. She reached backwards to hold her hand on his head for a bit before spreading mayo on the bread.

"Mmhumh…that's one delicious neck you have." Although he was enjoying the moment, it doubled as a distraction from questions.

"You'd better concentrate, Mr. Poole, or you're not going to get your studying done," she teased, "It's already close to noon."

"Could I get a raincheck?" he asked in mock disappointment.

"Maybe," she said coyly, then added with excitement, "If you promise to take me for a spin later on."

John frowned for a moment, trying to figure out just how much free time he would be able to allow, with the divorce case coming up on Tuesday, and the McGee indictment later this afternoon. He would also need to plan for the Laurel trip the next day. The strain was easy to read on his face, and Gerry turned back to her task dampened, but said reluctantly, "OK – you can be off the hook for now if you promise a Biloxi vacation in the spring! I'm dying to get in a swimsuit again."

"That's a promise – I'm dying to see you in it!" He laughed and kissed her again before returning to his work.

"By the way," he said on his way to the table, "Al and I are traveling to Laurel today for the arraignment and I told him we could grab a bite after the trip, to pay him back for all this work." He turned back to look at her, "You won't miss me too much, will you?" Gerry looked back with concern that she didn't quite understand, herself.

"No...well sure," she said haltingly as she arranged the sandwich on a plate with a pickle. She brought it to the table saying, "Maybe I'll spend the day with Mother. She mentioned she wanted to take me shopping. I could just take her up on that and get that swimsuit!" She managed a smile, wiped her hands on the apron and brushed away the hair off her forehead along with the unsettling feelings.

"That sounds good darling." John answered to appease, already re-immersed into the journey of Willie McGee, hoping she wouldn't probe, and chose another cigarette rather than his food.

As he scanned the papers again, he momentarily became lost in thought. The movement of the Progressive party, although not widely accepted in the Southern school of thought, was talked up in the debate club he had been president of. The defense of women's rights had been forcefully argued by female classmates, as well as himself.

Although it had been controversial, it was only half as incendiary an argument as was the equal rights for blacks brought forth by a brave classmate, yet he had agreed with him. These progressive ideas and debates had inspired him, and today made him glad that there was a female lawyer heading up this case. He wasn't sure yet how he felt about the CRC, but the causes of discrimination were the most important to him, and – hell!

Every good cause seems to be tainted with squirrely money from one source or another. He wondered, though, how acquaintances, friends and family would think of it. What would Gerry's family think of him putting his career on the line when he was already fighting to pay the bills? This case had the potential of showing him to be a pioneer for justice in the eyes of others or...

"Or a dirty rat!" He inadvertently finished his thought aloud.

Gerry had been silently eating her sandwich while looking at a magazine. "Is a rodent the culprit in this case?" she teased.

The laugh she expected did not come. John glanced at her briefly before taking great interest in taking one last draw of his cigarette and stamping it out in the nearly full tray. The thoughts came back to crowd his mind. What would be the possible consequences? If he didn't take it, if it were too dangerous, what regrets would he have in the future for not having tried? What about Hawkins and his cronies – just how angry would they be if he insinuated affair. Forget Hawkins – what about the Klan?

"Where's Beverly?" he found himself asking suddenly.

Gerry paused at his odd behavior, noting his untouched plate, but then submitted to just giving the obvious answer. "She's still asleep, dear."

"That's good, that's good, darling," he faked a smile, attempting normalcy, cleared his throat and rearranged the papers into stacks, as Gerry took a slow and silent deep breath.

CHAPTER FIVE

A WHALE OF A TALE

John had saved reading the attachment after Gerry had been called to duty by the cry from the back of their small home. He pulled it out as if it were a classified document, to read it carefully. Al had typed a note at the top.

"This is the story as told by McGee to Forrest Jackson, who had a transcriber write it down. What isn't included here are some of the more mundane details – he told his story to the transcriber as an autobiography and included where he was born, when his was married, and the places he was employed. He said that he had enlisted in the Army, but was discharged because of 'something on the brain,' which his mother later referred to on the stand as 'erysipelas' and that he was getting shots for it from a local physician. It would be a side note to check if he were part of that government research on syphilis that has gotten some recent attention, and just what kind of shots he was getting."

Although the writing had obviously been dictated, the colloquialisms had remained. John imagined the large brown eyes that had opened up to him, and felt as if they were in conversation once again as it began:

"The first time I saw Missus Hawkin's, it was August of 1944, and it had been hotter than the blazes for way too long that year, it seemed. She was on her porch in a little summer dress, lookin' at me walkin' down the street. I was headed to a job just down the road from her on Magnolia – and she called out to me, sayin,"

"Hi, there Willie, howdy do?"

It made me nervous, y'know, cause we hadn't seen each other since we was children. She was lookin' at me with a big pretty smile – and she had grown to be right good lookin'– kindof caught me by surprise. So, I was friendly and all, but when she asks me to come on in, I told her I had to be somewhere else to do work, and wouldn't have no time, but I was sorry. Then she looks at me, and smiles her big smile again, and asks me to come and do work for her sometime soon. I was thinking I'd better just stay away, but since she was a white lady, and we had known each other before, I just said that maybe I could someday, and it was nice seeing her again. I was nervous, and she could tell, cause she laughed a bit at me. Well, time passed and it weren't too long before she had me in there – guess I passed by her house on purpose a time or two, though I was a little scared, I kindof liked her looking at me like that, y'know? She starts showing me little things here and there that need fixing and asked me how much do I charge. Lawd, I didn't know what to say. I'd never been approached by a white woman to do her work. They usually didn't want to even talk to a black man – only their husbands do, and they call me boy – bossing me round. She smiled real sweet at me, and offered me something to drink. When I was thinking on it bein' strange, I must have been showing it, cause she say, "Seems like you're afraid of white folks, Willie."

"I said, 'Naw, mam!' and tried to look like I wasn't, but I was turning away a little, cause she was getting real close, and I was looking around, making sure nobody was looking through a window, or something, finding us out.

"She said, 'You must be,' then laughed and said again, 'You must be – it looks like you're ready to run. It's like you're doing the jitterbug!'

She laughed again and looked me up and down. That made me laugh a little, and shift back and forth again – you know that's what would make a white man calm down with us black folks – if we act like we's just there for their entertainment. I guess it had just become habit with me. Then she said something that really made me nervous. She came real close to me and said, kindof soft-like, 'I'm going call you my little Jitterbug!'"

"Part of me was ready to run. That part that knew about white men's rules.

That part that wanted to go on home to my wife 'n kids. But there was another part of me that just seemed to be stronger, and it done won out when she caught hold of me and pulled me up to her. No telling what she would do if I backed off. 'Sides, I was pretty excited by then, so I just thought – one kiss wouldn't hurt – that's all she wants – just to see what it's like to kiss a black man. I put my arm around her real gentle like and gave her a good long kiss. That did it. We was both caught up in it and didn't want to quit, it felt so good. Lawd, it felt so good! She pulled me tighter and sort'a whispered in my ear, and said, 'Do you want to love me?'

"I said, 'My, oh yes.'"

"What else could I say to a white woman? Sides, it was true. I tried to not even think of what might happen when she led me back to her bedroom and laid cross her bed, taking her dress over her head. The fan was blowing through the window, and her perfume floated up, making me feel all drunk. She laid down cross the bed and I loosed my pants and got on her. It was real sweet, and she wanted it all. She made me promise to come back, when we was done, and I said I would."

"When I left, though, and started walking down the street, I got my senses back about me. I'd better stay clear away from that white woman and not go anywhere near that place again. I could get a noose round my neck for what I just did. It made me shudder and look around me. All the good feelings just flowed right out, and I was nervous all over again. Problem was, she'd find me, and I couldn't help but want her again, too. Lawd! She even come to my work to say that she needed me to drop in and do more work for her. She'd smile that big smile of hers, and I say, 'Yessum,' just like I supposed to. Had to quit that good job at Newson Service Station after awhile, cause my boss started getting suspicious."

"Then I'd go again, like a fool, go to her house and make love with her while Mr. Hawkins at work and her children either asleep or gone. My wife done caught onto it all once when we both saw her on the street, and she try to call my wife a nigger whore. I had tried to tell Eliza before that I couldn't say no, or it would be trouble for me, but when that happened, I went and told Willette, "This is my wife! She ain't no whore!"

"That was when I finally decided, I'd be better off away in the army, so I on went an signed up an left Laurel behind, and told my Eliza that she and the kids would be proud of me if I was servin' in the army. I think she was glad to see me go, really. But Lawd, it wasn't more than a few months before they told me I has syphilis on the brain. Told me, that's why I's so nervous. That's my luck, I thought. Had to go back to Laurel without even doing no fighting like I ought t'have done."

"Then I tried to lay low, but she seen me working in the neighborhoods, and before long, we was at it again. She really scared me this time by telling me that she was in de family way, and I was the Daddy. Good Lawd! Once that baby came out, there would be some hollering and roping up a tree! What was I gonna do with my own family? She told me if I left again, something bad would happen to me, but she never would say what. She had me come at night, cause Mr. Hawkins usually work till midnight, and the girls would be sleep. Most time, I couldn't' even enjoy it, cause Eliza seems to know when I's with her, staying late and all, but I was afraid to say no, cause she'd get mad awfully easy."

"Then Ms. Hawkins, she starts talking about how much she hates how her old man treats her – calls her names and makes her feel real bad. She said I make her feel special – like a queen. Every time we'd meet up, she told me a little bit more about how her husband is. She told me about times he had hit her in the past or shoved her round, yelling at her. It had made her so nervous, she had to hide 'cause she never knew when he was going to get mad. She said she had to see doctors about her being nervous and was taking some pills. She says it was driving her mad, truthfully, and she'd be happier if he just dropped off dead. She'd then ask me to love her real gentle-like, and I would, but my Eliza was always in the back of my mind. What was she going to do? She had already talked about leaving me, and taking the kids with her."

"Then one day Ms. Hawkins started talking crazy about this big insurance policy her old man had. She wanted me to find some way to kill him, and she'd be sitting pretty and we would be free to love each other all we want. At first I said, naw! Now, that didn't sit right with her – me telling her naw. Then she goes to yelling and telling me that bad things was gonna happen if I left her, or backed out on her plan. Seems she was going plum crazy. Lawd! I was caught in a fix! Then she told me – whispering the whole time – that when Mr. Hawkins comes home at midnight n goes to sleep, I could come in towards morning and stab him with my knife, then leave. She would cover for me, and not call the police till I was safe at home. I'd have to be real careful to wear gloves, and throw way my knife in the river later. It was a dark, dark, plan, and it made me sick to even think about it, but she said if I cared about her, I'd do it. She even said it was like being in de army –fighting against the enemy– just at home. Now I thought about that, because I had felt like I hadn't been able to do my duty, like some of my buddies had.

Maybe she was right. Maybe it would be like fighting for innocent women and children, since she was getting beat, and all. I guess I just tried to talk myself into it, anyways, because she kept going on about it. So, one day I came to ask her for some money, on a Wednesday, and she asked again, when I going do it. I went ahead and told her I'd be back on Thursday night, and I'd do it then."

"Well, now, as I was contemplating this killing, Eliza done up and left me! Came home late one night after seeing Ms. Hawkins, and I guess she'd had about enough. I knew where she probably went – close by in Queensburg, where her sister lives in the project, but if I didn't somehow settle this soon, they'd be gone to Florida, where she's always wanted to go. She has family there, too. Well, that night I started thinking about it all, and asked couple of buddies to go drinking and gambling after I had done delivered my groceries from Laurel Wholesale. If I was to be killing somebody, I figured I'd have to get good and drunk. I got the company truck for the night, and we went out, got a half pint of whiskey from the dealers on South 5th with the money we put together. I had to borrow some, but said I'd win it back, cause I was real good at cards, most times. The card table is where I got the name, 'Black Dad,' because I was always coming up with those spades – outta nowhere. Lawd, I swear, sometimes it seemed like magic. We started gambling, and I did, for sure, win it back before and hour was up. That drink started getting to me, though, cause I was nervous, and drinking more than regular, and I got it in my mind that I wanted to see my Eliza. Damn her for leaving me! She knew what kind of jam I had myself into – didn't she see that? I love her – not that white woman! We'd been together for so long – married for over ten years! I'd go just remind her of that – that's what I do."

"I grabbed my buddy, Bill, to go with me just in case her cousin wanted a fight – there was a few of them, but me 'n Bill could handle them if things got rough. We went driving down that long old bumpy road down to Queensburg for nothing, though, she wouldn't have nothing to do with me with liquor on my breath, even though she seemed kindof happy to see me, all in all. She told me I'd have to show her I'd straighten up for good, and being all liquored up wouldn't be no way to show it. I felt good about it, though, because she made me feel hopeful we'd be getting back. I got it in my head that her Daddy would help me out with her – he always liked me, so I started towards his house, but stopped to get some more liquor first, because he likes a good drink now and then. We went to his house, then, and got to talking and laughing over our drink, and talking about women, and how to make them happy, y'know. Now, he didn't know nothing about me and Ms. Hawkins, it seemed, or he wouldn't have been laughing so much. Anyways, after we said night to him, me 'n Bill went on back towards town, and I got it in my mind that I would stop at her brother, Johnny's house. He'd talk to Eliza for me, and we could share some more of our liquor there."

"Bill was going long for the ride, and the liquor, I suppose. I was feeling pretty generous, and all, since I had won sum money, sides, I wanted to do anything sides what I had to do. Johnny was having some fun of his own with friends, and we sat and drank with him for awhile, before I started feeling sort'a nervous again. He was loving on his wife, and I just wanted things to be back to normal with Eliza again. Lawd, I started feeling so confused in my head, I told Bill I had to get on out and get some fresh air."

"Well, when we got out in the truck gain, I saw my knife in the floor of the truck, and I got to thinking about what Ms. Hawkins had wanted me to do. That seemed ages ago by now. I stopped for one more half pint. Bill says, "Willie, ain't you had enough liquor?"

"But he don't know. I hadn't told a soul about Ms. Hawkins, other than Eliza.

Made a chill go down my spine just thinking about what I was supposed to do that night. I took a big drink an asked Bill if he want to go gambling somewhere else. It was about 2:00 in the morning, and I wanted to put this off as long as I could. They's plenty of gambling houses round Laurel. Well, we hit two more houses, I lost a little, won a little and came out about even by the time we was dun, only I owed Bill a bit, but he wanted go home, so when we left he was a bit short. After I took him home, I downed the rest of that whiskey, and I was drunker than a skunk! It came to me that I wasn't in any shape to be killing nobody. If I was a real soldier, I would have my senses bout me. Fine time to be realizing that! I'd just tell Ms. Hawkins that I would do it tomorrow night. I came up on her street, but parked down the road and walked back. That way I'd be headed inthe right direction going home. Thinking on that made me start thinking of Eliza again, but I tried to put her out of my mind to do what I had to do.

"I snuck up real quiet like to her window n' scratched on it. She was up in a second, like she'd been waiting on me, and motioned that she would let me in the front door. I told her right off that I couldn't do her deed tonight, but that I would love her instead and do it some other time soon. She started to fuss, and said I was lying, that I never would do it – that I wasn't a real fighter. I told her to be quiet, or Mr. Hawkin's goin' wake up n find us here. We had never been together this late at night – when he was here. But they wasn't sleeping together for a long time now. She was mad, but she unbuttoned my coveralls for me, and we got in bed. I nearly fell sleep afterwards, till she wake me. She thought she heard something. I got up real quick, put on my clothes and then remembered what I owed my buddy, and I still was short on what I owed the company, so I asked her for some money. She got angry again, and started raising Sam, said I was drinking and going out with nigger whores, but she went on in the back room anyway n got me $5.50 – four in bills and one and a half in fifty cent pieces. I held her one more time real close and brushed her hair back from her forehead and kissed it before I snuck out. She seem to be happy with that. I was still a little drunk, though, and when I shut the door, it was a little too fast and made a bit of noise. Oh well, I thought, he's still sleep anyways. I run down to my truck and thought I'd just drive to work and park it, then sleep 'till it was time to work."

"The sun was beaming on me when I heard one of the workers saying, "Willie? You sleep? Time to get to work!"

"I rubbed my eyes and looked round and remembered what had happened. Then, thank goodness I look down, 'cause I had blood on my coveralls. Ms. Hawkins must've been bleeding."

"I gotta go home real quick-like. Tell the boss I'll be back soon!" There was a flush of fear going on in me, for some reason and I felt dizzy. A bad hangover, I thought. Then it came to me – Ms. Hawkins must not be in the family way after all! That thought made me a little happier, still, I had a funny feeling that something was wrong.

Wondered if we had made too much noise last night.

When I got home and started changing clothes, I didn't have any fresh underwear. Eliza hadn't been there to do my laundry for me. I rubbed it a little with some water, and it seemed good enough. Then I splashed my face and head with cold water, swished my mouth and spit. I combed my hair back good, then started out to the car, but somebody was knocking at my door. 'That's not right,' I thought – too early for company. Mama was at the door in her housecoat looking awfully worried and holding a handkerchief that had been wiping her tears, looked like.

"Oh, Willie!" she say.

"What, Mom," I says, "what you here for? Why you cryin?" She sounded hysterical and say, "Willie, you better get yourself out of town right now! Them policeman come looking for you while ago, said there's been some trouble. Don't know why he didn't know where you live, maybe 'cause you and Eliza moved out last year."

"Momma, don't you worry none…" I started to say, but she interrupted and say, "Willie, you listen to me now! Here's $10 for you to get a bus ticket. Get on down to Florida now and stay with Charles. I got a bad feeling about this – they looked mighty mad – hanging mad! Now get on out of here!"

"She say this and hugging and kissing me at the same time. I felt her fear – it was real, and I most always took my Momma's advice, 'cause she's got this straight line up to God. I looked around, thanked her, and jumped in my boss's truck, heading for the bus station in Hattiesburg, not thinking twice about it, but trembling all over. Well, now, you know the rest of the story."

The transcript stopped abruptly with no closing notes. John breathed out and leaned back. As he heard the door close to the back room and steps in the hallway, he slid the transcript carefully under his other documents.

"Hey, darling!" he called out as Babay came into the room, dressed up for an outing. She cooed and wiggled as she stretched out her arms to him. He tried to block out his thoughts as he took her from Gerry to laugh and play with her.

Gerry looked at the table at the papers as she put on her gloves and watched the two. Something moved her to sigh, and John looked to catch her worried eyes.

Without really knowing why she was feeling so uneasy, she said quickly, "So, we'll see you later tonight? Mother is on her way."

"Sure, sure," John said with somewhat of a guilty feeling, as if she knew he was hiding something from her. A car horn sounded from outside, and Gerry said, "There she is! Well then, we'd better be going. When will you be back, honey?"

John gave a protesting Babay back saying, "It might not be until late, I'm sorry dear." He gave her a kiss and a deep look that made her wonder, but she smiled quickly and said, "Well, drive safely, and we'll keep supper warm." She hurried out the door with babe in arms towards the safety of the familiar car and her mother's smiling face. After smiling and waving goodbye, John turned somber again and walked slowly back into the kitchen where he took a deep breath, thoughtfully gathered the papers together and slid them carefully into his briefcase. He looked at his watch – How did it get to be so late? It wouldn't be long from now that the prosecution would be gathering for the indictment in front of the Grand Jury in Laurel. How would the heart of McGee pound when served once again his charge from the same judge that twice pronounced him guilty and sentenced him to death? What could be done to turn the tide? How much of his tale was true? John quickly set aside the mixture of emotions welling up inside his own throat as he hurried to get ready for the day.

THE ACCUSERS

They tell me they knew of my guilt – they will prove it with their evidence. Their voices boom and resound in an exaggerated, slow rhythm, like the footsteps of a giant. I am not alone. There are quick-paced, shushed speaking helpers. They are defending me, explaining in quick, light tones what I must say and do. I can't understand, but I know I am entirely dependent on them. Am I guilty, I wonder? I have an ominous feeling that I may be, but it isn't clear. The rhythm of my defenders corresponds in halftime to the rhythm of my accusers, yet the whole pace is quickening. I am shown a car – what do I know about it? It will make a difference. Oh, God, am I guilty? Why is my mind so disturbed? My head aches – the rhythm increases, everything is louder, everyone is larger…

I awake into a sweaty shriek, disturbing the sound and unaware sleep of my sisters who sleep in the same room. My mother rushes in to see what is wrong. I am six years old at the time.

It's approaching – I can tell by the dreaded rhythm. Loud and slow, then fast and soft, again and again. My mind recognizes the familiar sequence and attempts in vain to fight back. I'll never know, will I? The evidence keeps changing. The facts are blurred. I'll never really know if I am guilty or not. I must be guilty. They must be right, or they wouldn't argue so. Where are my defenders? Have they given up? No, but they have been silenced.

The scream comes sooner, with relief. This is familiar enough to my Mother's trained ear. She rises from her bed and enters my room with a sigh to smooth my hair and comfort me, not really knowing how. After all, I'm in high school now.

INTERLUDE I

I was barely reading age, when I accidentally came upon a cartoon of a scowling Krushev and his big red shoe. It was on an anti-communism tract someone had left at our door.

47

"Mamaw, who is this?" It had an ominous look about it.

My Grandmother, who watched out for me while Mom and Dad were at work, looked puzzled, wondering how to convey the political frenzy that boiled with hatred against this philosophy of society to a small girl, especially with the impact it had so recently had on our family with the McGee trial. However she might have tried to modify her answer, I was sufficiently frightened of the man and his big shoe, wanting to "bury" us. The "Red Scare" of Communism came through to me, and Mamaw's assurances of my safety didn't quite cover up the signs of her own worries. She sealed up her stance on the matter to me by letting me know that He certainly wasn't a Christian!

Mamaw, who was a staunch Christian herself, was a great influence on my own spirituality, much to my mother's discomfort, who had rebelled from the strict life she had led while growing up. My first taste of Heaven, however, came while resting my head on Mamaw's lap in Church. The sticky-hot Southern day was shooed away by the relief of her paddle fan that bore a picture of Christ carrying the lost sheep around his neck. I blinked at the sun shining through stained glass depictions of His life, until my consciousness drifted to a blissful sleep. I was awakened to Mamaw gently shaking my arm and calling my name. The entreating plea of the Pastor and the soft singing of the choir filled my ears with, "He-e will save you, He will save you, He will save you now."

"Why don't you go up, darling?" Mamaw soothingly suggested. "O-only trust Him, only trust Him, only trust Him now," the choir added, like angels beckoning me to obey her coaxing. The lure of ethereal sweetness mixed with my curiosity caused me to rise out of the warm embrace of my nesting place and walk the aisle past two or three pews to the front of the church. Still sleepy-eyed, I found myself greeted with adoring smiles, as a big hand reached out to shake mine. I had entered into the realm of the saved, resplendent with their loving welcome. Mamaw had done her duty by God, revealing to me the treasures of Heaven. She was quite pleased until the next week, when I refused to go, a bit afraid of the mystical world I had experienced. The seed had been planted, however, and I would reach for that peace again in due time.

Being the baby, I had the pleasure of spending my pre-school days either with Mamaw at our modest duplex, or with my Mom and Dad in the office. I used to love to play with those little magnetic hair toys. You could dress up the smiling face to be a gruff man with bushy eyebrows, or make it turn into a young girl with pigtails. Then there were the puzzles that you could slide tiles into place to make words or pictures. I considered myself to be quite adept at these because my speed at getting all the tiles in place appeared to fascinate Dad. However, this may have been a ploy to keep me focused on the task at hand. How long these things captured my attention, I'm not sure, but it must have been long enough for Dad to "dictate" kisses to Momma behind the closed office door. Once I would hear my Mom's protesting, "John!" I knew they would be out soon, Dad with a grin on his face, and Mom with a somewhat tense glance in my direction, smoothing her hair, asking me if I was hungry.

On one occasion, my Dad picked me up high and gently shook me, saying,

"We're celebrating and going out to eat! You can get anything you want!" I giggled, and as I gathered my toys, thought about the prospect of "anything I wanted." As we descended the long flight of stairs from his small law office to the restaurant we frequented below, Dad had an extra spring to his step, in spite of the clump, jerk of his wooden leg. His jubilant mood, I was to find out, was because he had won a case in which he had defended a well-off Jewish man in town. The fee could have been as much as five times what he charged the black population he served. I didn't realize at the time, that he was referred the minority cases that his colleagues would not touch. Thankfully, there was a small constituency of wealthy Jewish families, familiar with the prejudices of society, who recognized Dad's worth as a lawyer and were willing to pay him well for it.

Oblivious to the benefactors, I was delighted to eat out with my parents.

When asked my order, I responded with my well thought out selection. "A plate of olives and pickles, please." After a bit of consternation, the waitress finally agreed to some menu-compromising suggestions from my mother, who assured everyone that she would give me some of her fried chicken. I sipped my soda and looked across the table at my Dad, whose clear blue eyes were smiling at me through a swirling wisp of smoke. His one-sided smile lifted his cheeks, full of mirth. As he looked down to stump out his cigarette, he broke into a low chuckle. I couldn't have been more content.

CHAPTER SIX

CHESS AND FRIED CHICKEN

The Chess Club was not actually for playing chess so much as it was for drinking beer, but it left wives with the impression that their husbands were improving their intellects as they shouted their destination from the doorway with their friends. This is not to say, however, that there weren't some intelligent conversations exchanged amidst the smoky clouds and misty smell of ale. There were, in fact, three tables at the back of the Club that each sported a fine imported chess set with wooden time clocks to justify the name. On an ordinary night, John would indulge in several "beat the champ" games, to reaffirm his claim to the title. If there was a lively group, he would tie his long pocket handkerchief to blind his eyes as a handicap and sit not facing the contester or the board. Others would take on moving the actual pieces on the board for the contester to study, and the game proceeded, most always ending with John's smile as he pronounced "Checkmate!" and slid off his blindfold to rousing cheers and lifted mugs of beer.

Tonight, however, he was in no mood for chess nor was there time. John picked a table near the front on the window side to wait for Al as he parked the car. They had just come back into town from the arraignment, where a wide-eyed McGee had looked to them with hope and fear. The prosecution was expectedly smug in reporting that they had set the case for pretrial motions for two days later – the 20th. After that, John, and Al interviewed anyone who would talk with them around to determine the prevailing mood, even a hitchhiker they picked up for a few miles. No one wanted their names used, but everyone so far felt that there was no chance for McGee and were too scared to speak what they thought was the truth, though many hinted at an affair.

Exhausted, the two rode home in silence, but felt the need to have a drink before going home. Al let John out while he parked the car. By the time he walked in and shook off the cold, he found John seated at an empty table, staring out the window.

"What's this, no beer yet?" Al laughed as he took off his coat and interrupted John's trance. "Two house brews!" he shouted over his shoulder to the bartender, who waved back in acknowledgement.

"Sorry, buddy, I guess I was lost in thought."

"Well, I'm thinking I can focus better on this one with a little beer to calm the nerves!"

"You aren't kidding!" John pulled out his cigarettes and packed them down several times on his palm.

"We'll have to stay over tomorrow night, since court is the next day."

"Yes, and I need time to read through the first damn transcript. I have lots of questions." John pulled the string around the top of his pack of cigarettes, tapped it so that three offered themselves in a staggered pattern and precisely pulled out the tallest with his lips.

"Well, that will be a problem, you see, because no one seems to know where the transcript for the first trial is."

John paused slightly while lighting his cigarette, "Is that right?" "Swartzfager said it was available, but Bella said it has been missing. And, frankly, I think those second trial testimonies were coached." Al added, turning impatiently to see where the waiter was.

"That wouldn't surprise me."

"It's going to be hard to win this case without new material." Al leaned back somewhat nervously crossing his arms. John nodded, head in hand, then leaned back as frosted mugs were placed in front of them.

"Here you go, my good fellows!" The intensity was momentarily dropped to thank and greet the familiar waiter.

"Well, hey, Joe," John said gregariously, "Are you treating everybody right tonight?"

Joe wiped his hands on his towel, then straightened condiments on the table, while he said softly, "I'm treating you two right, anyways," and nodded his head ever so slightly backwards. "Not all my customers are family like y'all are, you know what I mean?" In a louder voice he finished with, "What can I bring you gentlemen to eat tonight?"

John caught the insinuation and stole a glance at the table where several men sported white ties – a symbol of the KKK. Assuming nonchalance, he replied in equal tone, "Have you got any of your famous fried drumsticks ready?" "Yes, siree, I certainly do!" Joe smiled with pride.

"Bring us a plate of those, would you? Anything else, Al?" Al waved no in response. "That's it, then, and thank you very much, Joe," John responded.

"The pleasure is mine," he returned meaningfully and turned back to the bar to fill the order.

As John looked sideways again to see who he could recognize, his eyes were met with a significant hard stare. He turned back and took a thirsty drink from the icy mug before saying, "It's not just in Laurel we'll have to contend with opposition." Al adjusted his glasses and leaned in.

"You can bet many of the guys in Laurel wear hoods by night, like these do.

Remember the clipping from the Laurel Leader where, the Klansmen were praised for 'protecting our white women. ' How many times have you seen that as a front page story?"

"I can imagine they are all on alert but are keeping under cover this time around." There was a silence between them as the white tie group began to laugh boisterously.

"Do you know anybody, personally, that lives in Laurel we can talk to?"

"I don't, but Clarence said he has an aunt that lives there who might be able to help us out. I'll see if he can arrange for us to meet with her."

"We've got to keep a low profile while we're doing this, but I want to go into the heart of the black community to find the people who know McGee. He had a wife and children, right? There's bound to be plenty of people that knew him and what was going on between them."

"Well, one fellow I talked to today said they were fighting before this, probably because she knew about the affair. He tried to tell her that he couldn't say no, but that didn't fly evidently, because she knew he's been a lady's man since he knew how to wink. At any rate, they would have been a target for the Klan – that's reason enough to take the children and skedaddle."

John shook his head as he pictured the scene of the children looking at their daddy behind bars, to say goodbye before leaving their hometown forever.

Joe slid the plate of steaming meat on the table, interrupting the vision and proudly announcing: "Joe's special – on the house!"

"Oh, you don't have to do that," John protested, reaching for his wallet. "No, I insist!" Joe said with his palm refusing any other option. In a lower voice he said, "Just so you know whose side Joe is on, eh?" He winked and walked away after patting John on the back.

"Thanks, buddy," John called back to him. He stared at his partner for a moment before saying, "Say, this Civil Rights Congress – is that all they're interested in – civil rights?"

Al looked up with some surprise at the change of subject, "Why do you ask?" He crunched into a drumstick, catching the juice with his napkin.

"Just wondering." John took a few bites and began again. "Something about how Abzug talked. The plight of a black man in the jaws of racism I have a feeling is not the only interest. I'm thinking there's another agenda here." John paused when he saw that there wasn't a reciprocated connection. Al had just lifted his eyebrows and continued to eat.

He continued, "What I'm thinking, really, is how people like Joe, here, are going to feel if this thing blows up and gets talked about up North. If Mississippi gets in the national papers with mud on their face, how does the nation know that not all of us feel the way Collins and his cronies do? I'm not sure the CRC gives a hoot about that, or about McGee, for that matter. I'm thinking that the real goal is not so much to heal racial indiscrimination here as it is about getting people who are down and out to sign on for a new way of government."

Although he didn't use the word Communism, Al knew what he was talking about. He sighed, shook his head and took a drink, rather than express the multitude of thoughts flooding his mind. He wiped his hands and finally answered with a question, "You think the CRC is using McGee?"

"I don't know – just wondering," John said taking another look at the men, whose conversation now was just as hushed as theirs.

He continued, "I just wonder what compassion they actually have for the black man. Hell, I wonder about the compassion for our situation. I'm thinking we all might just be pawns in this matter – easily expendable for the cause."

Al's face went from one of agitation to consternation. Seeing that the topic was overloading his already stressed companion, John changed the tempo.

"Say, is eight o'clock good enough to head out in the morning? By the way, what do we have in the way of an expense account?" He snuffed out his half-smoked cigarette and reached for his coat.

"Expense account? Well, now, I think Bella just said to keep the receipts for now. I'll handle this trip." Al finished his drink and said, "Eight o'clock is good. I know a decent hotel that doesn't cost too much. I'll make a reservation for us," he replied, back in step.

Joe came back to check on them and said, "What, y'all need these to go now?"

"Naw, John grinned and winked, "I'm thinking those men at the other table could use some of those delicious drumsticks." He raised his brows with feigned seriousness, "They need to know what it's like to be family here."

Joe leaned in and replied in a low voice, "Yeah, I'm thinking they need a drumstick to the head."

John chuckled and patted Joe's back, then turned with a slight raise of his hand to the now interested white tie table. No wave returned his, but a slight nod of the head from one of the men let him know his wave had been noted, as a gauntlet thrown.

"Ready?" John asked Al, a new fire gleaming in his eyes.

"Ready!" Al threw coins on the table, and the men walked out together into the brisk night air.

CHAPTER SEVEN

A TEA PARTY CLUE

Early the next morning John and Al headed down the highway, talking over the particulars of the case as they went, and laying out a game plan for their schedule.

"OK – We have a reservation at the hotel for tonight, but I need to go back by tomorrow night. I have other cases to work on," Al said.

"Right, me too. This divorce case hasn't let me get any sleep – the guy called me at midnight, yelling about his ex's boyfriend." John replied as he yawned, "That has to be dealt with somehow, and we need to get this Motion for Continuance ready for Friday. What time is court again?"

"They moved it from the morning to 1:30 – big of them to give us a few hours!"

"Well, we'll need all the time we can get." He sipped his steaming coffee and asked, "Now, for today – we just find who we can on the street?"

"Let's do that in the afternoon, it will be warmer then. Besides, we have a tea party to go to this morning." Al looked sideways and smiled.

"A tea party?"

"I talked to Clarence last night, and he said we could talk to his aunt, who lives in Laurel. He already asked her if we could visit and ask some questions about Laurel's reaction to the case. She's an older lady and has a bridge club that meets every week, which happens to be today." Al grinned. "I think they would be a good source of gossip around town. Clarence will meet us there, but might be late, and we'll split up after that."

"Does she have a maid?" John wondered. "Possibly"

"If we could get in a word to her, we might get a lead into the black population."

"Well, now, I believe he did say she was well off, and is handicapped, so she probably has some hired help."

"If so, try to occupy her while I approach the maid with questions."

"I think I can do that," Al smiled, adjusting his tie, "I'll give her a taste of my Southern charm."

"You mean to say you have Southern charm?" John chuckled.

"I do have the ability to take it out of my back pocket when needed," Al said with mock sophistication.

John became serious again. "I have the feeling we're not going to be met with much Southern charm."

Without waiting for an answer, he continued, "What about that little corner restaurant across from the courthouse? I'll bet the local attorneys meet there for lunch. Let's eat there at noon and see if we can find out what they know."

"Good idea. By the way, Laurent Frantz, an investigator for the Civil Rights Congress, is going to be in tomorrow. If we need any background checking of records and such, he can help us with those things. He's already done some of his own investigating and sent some addresses of Willie's friends for us to check out."

"Not the *friends* who testified against him, I hope." "You can't always trust drinking buddies," Al joked.

"Hell, I'd trust my drinking buddies over some of these attorneys any day." John took a deep breath and looked out the window at the passing pine trees, white clouds, and blue sky. At least they had good weather, he thought. His eyes landed on a shanty in the distance that came into focus to reveal several black children in front playing and tossing sticks for a dog. One little boy stopped and looked at the car with wide eyes, catching John's as they swiftly passed by. The image remained in his mind as he remained silent for a stretch of time.

The first stop in Laurel was Mrs. McMullan's home, the aforementioned aunt, who lived in a vintage home with a wraparound porch in the wealthier side of town. The expected black maid met them at the door, took their coats and hats and led them into a graciously decorated dining area.

"Welcome, gentlemen!" Mrs. McMullan called with a somewhat weak voice from her wheelchair, which was placed by a table laden with tea and fruit bread. "Please do come in and refresh yourselves, I know you've had a long ride and must be tired. Clarence told me you would come. Oh, ladies, these are attorneys from Jackson, Mr. Al London and Mr. , I'm sorry…"

"John Poole, I'm so pleased to meet you."

"Yes, yes, John Poole –," and extended a wilting hand while continuing with a somewhat flat affect, "My nephew, Clarence, the attorney, you know, sent them from Jackson. He's supposed to be here too?" She asked.

Al answered, "He will be along soon, I'm sure."

"Very well, then," she said and then continued, as she addressed the group, "They've come to Laurel to find out what they can about that black boy's case." She lowered her playing cards, looked apologetically at her bridge mates, and took an audible breath as the women all engaged in the normal polite exchanges, with apologies from the attorneys for the interruption of the party. John attempted to make eye contact with the maid, who was filling teacups with a dour expression. It was obvious she was there to do her job and nothing more, although kind comments were made about the provisions and service. She came and went as if she wanted to remain invisible, her silence being louder than any words she may have spoken.

Al started the conversation with hopes up, having fulfilled the expected niceties. "It is so kind of you to want to help us, and we were just wondering…"

Mrs. McMullan broke in with unexpected curtness, feeling somewhat bold with her friends having eyeballed her during the introductions. "I didn't say anything about wanting to help, really." Encouraged by the puzzled looks, she purposefully folded down her playing cards perfectly in a fan on her lap and continued.

"I merely wanted to set the record straight with you two." She paused for dramatic effect and looked them in the eyes as she might two young boys, who were in need of elderly wisdom. "The people of Laurel are not behind any further investigation of this case. The verdict was decided and it is said and done." Another pause ensued as she watched reactions, measuring her effect.

"There was a vicious rape by a negro committed on an upstanding lady of Laurel, and you," she pointed directly towards the lawyers, who backed up a bit from the violent finger wag.

"You, young… lawyers…, inexperienced, come in and think you can make a name for yourselves by breaking through longstanding, good, traditions in our cities. Well, you're just wrong, that's all there is to it, and you'll find no respectable citizen of this community will stand with you!"

John had straightened himself in his seat, but maintained poise as he asked, "And did you find this was so with the attorneys who previously tried the case?"

"You may remember Mr. Dixon Pyles and Mr. Forrest Jackson," Al offered in a lower voice, to soften any unintended arrogance.

It was either the subject matter itself, or the fact that she hadn't fully intimidated the way she intended, that caused Mrs. McMullan's blood to rise to her face and her voice to raise to a pitch as she leaned forward, cards falling unnoticed to the ground, and screeched, "Those lawyers themselves should be shot for having anything to do with the case, for defending the old rascal!" She paused, red and shaking, and took a deep breath to say more, but one of the ladies rose to pat her hand gently and say, "Dear, remember your condition. It's not worth it." She continued to pat as if she could bring down her blood pressure doing so. It appeared to have some success, as Mrs. McMullan finished with a wave of her other hand to the now standing attorneys,

"He is guilty and everybody knows it!"

"Would you be willing to say that in court?" John asked boldly, although Al was leading him towards the door, gathering the coats and hats that the now wideeyed maid had brought.

One of the ladies gasped at the request, but Mrs. McMullan's eyes tightened and she sat upright to say, "I would say that anywhere. It's the blessed truth!"

"Thank you, so much, Mam, for your time," Al managed to say as he opened the door. "Again, we are sorry to have disrupted your game, and please tell Clarence to meet us for lunch at the town café, will you?" He almost pushed John out the door, who was tipping his hat towards one in the group who seemed amused by the incident.

"Good riddance!" was followed by giggles from the tearoom.

"Good day to you," the black maid opportunely spoke as she briefly met their eyes and shut the door.

"Good day," John returned, understanding her unspoken thoughts as he turned into the cold.

"Thank goodness for your Southern charm!" John laughed as they walked swiftly towards the car. Al grunted, shaking off the scene. John put his hands to warm in his coat pockets, then slowed his walk to look at a piece of paper that he retrieved from one.

"Well, what do you know?"

"What's that?" Al asked, getting in his side of the car.

John got inside, slammed the door, then read, "515 Sawmill Road. Ask for Sam." "Sam," Al repeated blankly. "Who the hell is Sam?"

"Well, now, I'm thinking that Sam is a friend of Mrs. McMullen's maid, who just may have some information for us rascal attorneys. Do you know where Sawmill Road is?"

"Straight ahead," Al said as John started the car, "It will be a welcome change from this neighborhood."

The way to 515 Sawmill Road was known as the "K. C. Bottom," a rougher area of Laurel that led through a much different neighborhood. The houses were small, unpainted and worn, their fences in need of repair. Yet some dignity was seen in the rocking chair porches, which were scattered with clay pots that held flowers in warmer days. Springtime would see the area populated with friends and family, greetings and gossip relayed from the vantage point of porch railings. Now, however, the decks were as bare as the surrounding trees, reflecting the scarcity of resources needed to create a full sense of well-being.

John and Al pulled up to the address and walked to the door, not without noticing several wary window watchers from inside nearby homes. At their knock, a small girl with pretty brown eyes and braided twigs of hair standing wire-like from her dark crown appeared and said, "Hallo," as she opened the door and subsequently stuck her finger in her mouth.

"Jessie, who's that you're talkin' to?" came a low voice from the back of the home.

"Hello," John said softly, as he opened his eyes wide, bent down and said, "You sure have a pretty hair-do."

She smiled and giggled, twisting her finger out of her mouth long enough to say, "They's some collectors here, Daddy!" then stuck it back in, opening the door for the men to come in from the cold. A tall dark man emerged from the back, wiping his hands, and said with a worried expression, "Yes, suh, can I help y'all?

"We don't mean to intrude, and we are not collectors," John smiled and offered his hand.

"John Poole, and this is Al London." Handshakes were exchanged as he returned with some uneasiness, "Sam Jackson."

"Pleased to meet you Mr. Jackson, and Jessie?" Jessie giggled and ran back towards a room as a woman's voice called, "Jessie – girl, you get on back here, right now!"

"Mr. Jackson," John continued, "we are attorneys who are working in the defense of Willie McGee. Are you familiar with the case?"

Sam's eyebrows raised. "I's familiar with it."

"I don't want you to be nervous about this, as I said, we are working to defend McGee, and wouldn't ask you to do anything that would compromise your family's safety. We are just looking to see if there are any witnesses that could testify to where Willie actually was that night the rape was said to have taken place."

John paused and Al added, "Or if you have any knowledge that an affair may have been going on between McGee and Mrs. Hawkins." When he saw the dark eyes quickly shifting, John added, "A lady who works for Mrs. McMullen sent us here."

Sam breathed deeply and said simply, "My sister." He motioned towards a small couch whose holes were covered with blankets.

"Won't y'all please have a seat?" "Thank you, kindly."

John and Al took off their hats and sat a bit stiffly on the unaccommodating cushions. "What can you tell us, Sam?" John plied.

Sensing respect in the request, Sam allowed himself to sit just on the edge of an adjacent, rickety wooden chair, and said, "I does want to help." He was interrupted as he saw the figure of his wife and child, who had silently crept to the door of the kitchen to listen.

"I does want to help, but it's dangerous round here to tell the truth." He wrung his hands and nodded towards the kitchen adding, "I'm not just lookin' out for myself."

"We know, that, Sam." John looked with compassion towards his family. "We won't give your name if you are unable to testify, but we need to know the truth."

Sam looked at the two men, weighing the import of the matter, and looked again at his wife.

"C'mon, now Jessie, we need to finish our cleanin'," she said. Jessie took in as much as she could with her back-turned eyes, finger stuck in mouth, as they headed towards a back room. She popped it out to say, "By-bye!"

John waved and smiled, "By-bye now, Jessie." Al encouraged Sam to continue.

"Tell us the story just as you remember it."

Sam got up to close the window curtains more tightly, as if to shut out listening ears, then told the story of that night as it was told by locals. He said Willie and Willette had known each other since they were young. Willie's mother had done housework for Willette's mother, and he sometimes came with her. As they grew older, Willie would do chores around the yard and home, and they eyed each other as they developed into young adults. Knowing the boundaries, the prohibited relationship grew tantalizing through the years.

"When she asked Willie to do her own chores," Sam said, "I tries to talk some sense to 'em. Willie! You better keep your place, boy! Your head's gonna roll clean off, iffn you don't, an you knows that's right. It ain't worth it! But he'd just be cocky, y'know, like he was bigger than all that. We use to call him 'Black Dad,' cause he's a lady's man – good lookin fella, y'know. All the lady folks liked him – he had plenty roses t'pick in his own garden, you know what I mean?" Sam laughed, relaxing a bit through the telling, shook his head and said, "Yeah, mmmh – doggie!

Al and John both smiled.

"Mm,hmm, I think we know what you mean," John said, then continued more seriously, "So, tell us, Sam, do you believe Willette and Willie were having an affair?"

Sam's laughter died down quickly at the direct question. He looked up again and wrung his hands.

"I believe so, Mr. Poole, I believe they was. Talk was she would make it to where he couldn't say no to givin' her favors when he was doin' the chores. A man o' color can't say no to no white woman, no sir-ee! Know what I mean? It don't matter iffn he knows better." Sam looked down as if just remembering the rules of society, himself.

"Sam," Al began.

"Yessuh?" Sam didn't look up.

"Is there anyone else you know that might help us with any other parts of the story – to help us put together the puzzle? We need to know more about what happened in the Hawkin's home that night."

Sam thought a moment, breathing deeply. He finally scratched on a pad names and addresses of others who might help.

"Thank you Sam," John said as he and Al stood. "No one will know about this night unless you decide to testify. It could save his life, you know." He extended his hand to shake Sam's.

Sam looked at the floor, then up at the ceiling with emotion, as if consulting his maker, before finally letting his hand slip away saying, "I-I jes can't chance it."

The last proclamation came out broken, with lips trembling and tears breaking through the strongholds of his lids. John looked sideways at the figure of Jessie, who had snuck back to the frame of the kitchen door, eyes wide open.

"I understand, Sam, thank you for what you have already done. That's plenty for us to go on." He tipped his head to Jessie, smiled and said, "Yall don't worry about anything now, y'hear?" Jessie looked unconvinced, and as the two men left the house she ran to hug her Daddy's legs.

Both men walked in watchful silence to the car. Eyes slipped away from parted curtains in surrounding houses. Once the doors of the car were shut, Al looked at his watch and said simply – "Noon, already."

"Let's head for the café." John said and adjusted his tie.

The men drove in silence, until John finally said, "Damn!" as if a conclusion of his contemplations.

CHAPTER EIGHT

CHECKMATE WITH A PAWN

When John and Al reached the café, there were few parking spaces, and it looked as if the earlier assessment was correct. This was where local businessmen were gathered, taking a mid-day repast. Clarence was already sitting at a table with some other men and called Al and John over to join them. They were welcomed to pull up chairs amidst introductions and orders for the lunch special were given, while iced tea was set in front of them.

"I heard you didn't stay very long at my Auntie's tea?" Clarence asked with a wink.

"Well, we had to be about our business, you know," Al said with a sideways smile. "Charming ladies!" he added as he squeezed lemon into his iced tea. "So, what brings you gentlemen into town?" grunted an older, rotund attorney who sat at the table. "Clarence here says you've come from Jackson."

Al paused slightly and looked at John before saying, "John, Clarence, and I are here on some investigation for a case."

"Is that right? Some investigation," he asked with piqued tone as he spooned an abundance of sugar into his tea. He paused, noting the solemnity. "I hope you're not investigating the subject of Laurel's lawyers' lunchtime lollygagging!" Laughing at his own drawn-out alliteration, he added, "Have our wives hired you two for this investigation?" Canned laughter went around the table, but the façade was understood, as he dropped his voice to say, "You're here on the McGee story, is that right?" and shifted his eyes to look at Al, then John. Clarence shifted uneasily in his seat and looked at Al to answer.

"That's right," Al confirmed and adjusted his glasses. John remained silent as he busied himself to find the nearest ashtray, place his pack and lighter next to it, and then looked upward to find several eyes glaring at him.

"And have you met with any willing candidates for this investigation?" "A few, so far" Al lied.

The other men looked at each other, and throats were cleared. One stood up and said, "You must excuse me, gentlemen, I've got a case to study. Nice to meet you Clarence, Al. Did you say your name was John?" He grabbed his check and coat and with a large smile nodded himself away. Down to three, a second said, "Well, now, you do have my intrigue and I would like to stay for this, but I have to get back to that pile on my desk, or I'm going to be listening to my secretary harping on me." He gave a short nervous laugh, gathered his things and said his goodbyes.

"Did I forget deodorant?" John laughed, feigning a sniff test. Clarence laughed with abbreviation, as he saw the older attorney's now stern face. After an awkward moment, however, he also broke into a laugh, inviting the younger lawyer with a slap to the arm to join in, and they all enjoyed a short moment of comic relief. John then leaned in and said, "This topic of Willie McGee isn't a favorite among your colleagues, I take it."

"We've dropped it – case closed," he returned leaning his chin on his clasped hands, with a pretentious grin. He continued, "What do you think you two will accomplish by opening up this can of worms again?" Without waiting for an answer, he leaned back, cleared his throat, and looked John point blank in his eyes saying, "Do you want to know what I think? I think you've done the craziest thing you could ever do by taking this case." He waved his hand in the air for dramatic effect. "There's no telling what people will do around here. All of the lawyers who were in the case before will tell you the same. That Hawkins guy and his friends mark a big 'X' on anyone who even thought about standing up for that nigger.

Now, don't get me wrong, there are some good Negros in this town, but he's not one of them. Hell, he was young and stupid! Saying she wanted him – that's absurd, and we all know it!" He waved his hand again with dismissal and added with a curled top lip, "What white woman would want to be with a nigger?" They paused as the sandwiches were set in front of them.

"You don't think a white woman would ever be attracted to a handsome, young, muscular man even if he was black?" Al offered, with some nonchalance.

"You're crazy if you think so," came the retort.

"But you said, correct me if I'm wrong, you heard that – it had been said – that she wanted him?" John asked with slow deliberateness.

The older lawyer leaned in, lowered his voice for emphasis and said, "Those towns-people talk nonsense like donkeys braying," waving his hand again. "You can't put much stock in it. Wouldn't you agree?" He turned for support to his fellow attorney, who rubbed his lips together and grunted his consent.

"I would say," the younger attorney started, then paused to gather his thoughts, not wanting to answer the question directly. "I would say that it is correct to say that it would be crazy to try to defend this case again. The last attorneys nearly got themselves a good whipping. Folks were heated up about it." He took a bite of his sandwich, then continued, "It wouldn't have been so bad if this case hadn't gotten all mixed up with the Reds."

"Reds?" Al said, feigning ignorance.

"Well, you know that's who's paying you, don't you?" the older man thrust in. "The damn Communists! If you don't, wise up! The Civil Rights Congress…" he sneered and breathed out in disgust before continuing, "I'd like for the white man's civil rights to be stood up for! We've treated our Negros around here fairly! They've all got good jobs – those of them who will work for a living!" He made a guttural sound from his throat and tore into a large portion of his sandwich. If he was thinking of something else to say, he was temporarily unable to.

The younger lawyer cleared his throat and moved back into the conversation as if to adjust the flow to a rational vein. "The Civil Rights Congress is a front group for the Communist Party – it's a well-known fact. They've paired up with the Federation for the rights of Colored People, or something like that, and it's backed by Red money." Looking at the two faces now affixed on him he reiterated, "This case might not have gotten so much attention if it hadn't been mixed up with them. Now, once and again a Negro has been on trial for such and such, and the juries have found him innocent."

"Well, and that has been true – just recently, in fact," Clarence added, attempting to bridge the gap between them, and had his finger in the air to finish his point.

"Not for raping a white woman!" the older man interrupted. The younger man continued, admitting, "Maybe not for rape, but justice has been lenient for the colored man when the facts show probable innocence."

Clarence dropped his finger and his point. The attorney continued, "You just can't mix the two – coloreds and Communism – and expect it not to get the attention of every God-fearing white man." Seeing the frown that came inadvertently on John's face, he relented with, "What I mean is those Communists are just using the Negro as a whipping boy – they don't care whether or not he is sacrificed for their cause. It will just give them the ammunition they need either way to fight against our freedom to rule ourselves! Social justice to them is taking the States rights away to choose for themselves. It's the Civil War all over again, only this time we're not in uniform."

This caused each man to reflect a moment. The older man, working on another large bite, let out a dramatic "Mmmh!"

Al adjusted his glasses, Clarence crossed his legs and looked out the window, and John lit a cigarette, pushing away his untouched sandwich in favor of the ashtray, and said, "All I wanted to secure for Willie McGee is a fair and impartial trial, regardless of guilt, he deserves that."

"Well," the younger attorney said with an air of washing his hands of the matter, "I do have an appointment to get to, but I hope you two consider what has been said here. It's tough to go against your own kind – and for what? You're just starting your practices, as am I." He called for his check and continued. "If we plan to succeed, you have to listen to what the people want from us. They expect us to stand up for cultural norms."

The older man wiped his mouth to interject a bit more fatherly, "I was idealistic, too, when I was young. You've got to pick your battles. This one is over your heads – you're just pawns in this one."

"I've won many a check-mate with a pawn." The men looked up at the unexpected response and the resolve in John's smiling blue eyes.

"You'd be wise to watch your backs," the older lawyer said with solemnity and rose, throwing on his coat. In good Southern tradition, they all rose, smiled and shook hands with well wishes before parting.

The day's remainder was spent in attempting to snatch interviews with people on the street, both white and black. One older white lady said that she couldn't believe "poor Mrs. Hawkins was going to have to face trial again," and let them know in no un-certain terms what she and others felt about lawyers that would defend such "beasts!" walking off in a huff. A young lady repeated the story that Mrs. Hawkins had run out of her house that night naked to the next-door neighbors' house.

"I can't imagine why she would run out, really, and naked at that, but I did hear that she had some problems with hysteria, you know before then. You know, that's a female problem that sometimes comes with the monthly cycle. And they say she was on her monthly…but now, oh" she looked quickly at her watch, "I'm late." She excused herself, blushing, as she realized what she was discussing with handsome, young lawyers.

An older black man who had worked nearby Willie's employer said that "People's scared to say anthin, y'know. Even the white folks. Mr. Hawkins and his fellas got all riled up after Willie didn't get hung the first time. They was ready to skin some meat, I tell you! I don't think nothing's changed, really – they's just waitin' and watchin'

No one they stopped would say more than a sentence or gave a quick excuse as to why they couldn't talk. All that could be concluded was that most people knew more than they would say.

Clarence met with John and Al as planned, under the streetlights near the downtown library with similar reports from his interviews. The smoke of their breath in the cold air mixed as they shared stories.

"I did get some leads on folks that may be willing to give information but haven't had time to track them down." Clarence said apologetically.

"We'll just have to hope for a continuance," John said with resignation and shifted onto his good leg with a sigh. "Say, let's check in, get warm, and just go over our points."

"Hmm…" Clarence mused, "I'm going to just check on one of these leads that sounds promising before giving up for the night. How about we meet at the courthouse in the morning, and we can ask for a room to draw up the motion then. You guys just relax for the night, how about it?" He turned his face towards Al and winked, having noticed the pain that flashed in John's eyes.

"I'm convinced!" Al said, winking back, and put his arm around John's shoulder, saying, "Let's go, champ – we've done enough for one day. Good luck, Clarence – see you at – what, Eight?"

"Eight it is!" Clarence waved a goodbye and disappeared into the mist.

After the two checked into the hotel, John loosened his tie, sat down on the bed wearily and began to take off the strap that held the wooden leg up against the stump of his own. The grimace on his face let on that he had overdone it, and it was red and sore. Al glanced at him before saying, "Room service tonight?" as he picked up the paper menu left on the desk, next to a Gideon Bible.

"It looks like you're stuck with it, unless you want to go out yourself," John said, rubbing his leg.

"No, I've had enough warnings to curb my appetite for a night on the town.

How about some chili?"

"Sounds good." John lay back on the pillow with his hands folded behind his head and drifted into thought.

Ten years earlier the Jackson Daily News headline heralded, **"Johnny Poole – The Winnah!"**

The article reviewed the Golden Gloves tournament and told the story: "Tugging at the strings that held up his long pants to hide his handicap of an artificial right foot and lower limb, plucky Johnny Poole walks to his corner after acknowledging the official announcer's verdict last Thursday night with the applause of the fans ringing in his ears."

Although he had come close, John had not won the Best Boxer award. He did, however, win the only double award – for popularity in both the novice classes, and received the nickname, "Peg-leg Poole." Only one year after his accident, a similar article had appeared in the paper with the headline, **"Odds Against Smiling Johnny Bother Him Not One Little Bit."**

The photo accompanying the article showed a good-looking young boy with long boxing pants, a cowlick, and a large, dimpled smile along with the caption, **"LaughsOff Handicap."** He was quoted as saying, "I knew the other boys had an advantage, but I felt that if I worked real hard, I could make good."

At the time, the officials were a little worried about his ability to hold his own against the competition, but he proved them wrong by his famous knockout punches, winning straightway the Novice Lightweight crown. They admitted that he had a natural talent, could hit hard, and said that with two good limbs there was really no telling how far he would have gone in the ring.

Yet another article, entitled, **"Young Johnny Poole Packs Wallop**!" read:

"You can't let your hair down and write about the sheer courage it takes for a one-legged boy to step into a boxing ring when the same boy has looked you in the eyes and said: 'I don't think I'm under any handicap, fighting with just one foot. '"

Johnny had told the reporter that he didn't have the support of some of his old friends in the audience since he had changed his ways after the accident. The interviewer invited him to tell the story.

"Take it away, Johnny, and tell about that."

"You see," says Johnny, sipping away at a soft drink he'd chosen even though he'd been taken to a restaurant and offered the works, "I ran around with a pretty tough bunch before I hurt my leg– and I haven't seen much of themlately.

"When it happened, two other boys and me had started for California one summer and gone as far as Dallas before we decided to turn back.

"Joe – he was my pal – and I were waiting for a train on the edge of the railroad yards that night, but we were pretty tired, so I laid down to catch a little sleep before the next freight came along.

"While I was lying there, Joe shook me and called real loud, 'John, John, there goes our train!'

"When I hopped to my feet, I saw it was going too fast, but it seemed like something just made me try for it anyhow. I guess I was still half asleep. I didn't quite get a good hold on the rungs when I grabbed, just enough to jerk me off my feet. It threw me under the box car."

"While his pal hitch-hiked on back to Jackson," the article read, "Johnny lay in a

Dallas hospital for several weeks. When he came back home and was able to get around on crutches, his father decided to send him up to French Camp Academy. 'I guess that's what started me right,' Johnny said in his slow, thoughtful way. 'After I'd been there a while, my father got me an artificial foot. I learned how to walk in three days. '

The interviewer asked about going to shows or dating girls:

"Johnny answers those specific queries with a 'No.' With a grin he admits he'll probably have to start doing a lot of reading soon, because he wants to be a lawyer."

The article wrapped it up by saying, "Before that accident, he ran around with a bunch of tough youngsters, some of whom are in the reformatory today. Now he sticks to his studies and wants to be a lawyer. Before the accident he knew how to fight, but he didn't have a knockout punch until after it…Add that up, and then answer this question: What do you think about Johnny Poole's 'handicap?'"

"Room service!" The call followed a loud rap to the door. Al jumped up to answer it as John woke from his reverie and scrambled for money in his pants pocket. Al settled with the black boy who grinned at the extra dime and said, "Thankee, suh!"

"About to nod off?" Al asked as he shut the door, taking the bowls of chili and crackers to the bedside table.

"Well, just thinking about the handicap we're working with," John said, opening the pack of crackers and shaking it in his bowl.

Al took a large spoonful and let out a "Mmm."

Silence ensued as both ate the steaming meat and beans hungrily.

"When did you say we will get some front money?" John asked finally. "Bella said that she would send some soon. She knew we'd need a travel expense, but wasn't sure how fast it would come in. You remember, they depend on donations." Al glanced at his partner's reaction.

John said frankly, "I could use it, money's tight." "Yep, here, too."

Another period of silence followed as they finished the meal, proclaiming it "Not bad, but nothing like Gerry's!"

John lit a cigarette and both sat back on their beds, pondering the day's events. Al began flipping through the paper for some current news.

John looked over at him and broke the silence with, "Hey, Al."

"Yes?" Al replied as he continued reading.

John spoke slowly and deliberately with mock seriousness, "I'll bet you're jealous of my wooden leg."

Al continued looking at the headlines of the day, a smile creeping up his lips as he said, "I have been, quite jealous."

"You can wear it tomorrow if you want. I won't mind at all."

"Very generous of you champ. I think I'll sleep on that one," Al said as he tossed the extra pillow at John's head.

CHAPTER NINE

THE CRAZIEST MAN
IN THE WORLD

The hurriedly dictated motion that had been drafted only that morning in a room at the Laurel courthouse was neatly typed and placed on their table in court by the time Al and John came into the courtroom. Swartsfager had greeted them in the hallway earlier and offered his personal secretary for their use, smiling at the fact that they were just now drawing up their motion, and commented that they were composing it "just In the nick of time."

They had met with Clarence over breakfast and had decided since no one was willing to take the stand, they would, to testify of the fear of would-be witnesses. They now seated themselves at a wooden table set for the defense. Swartsfager, who was seated opposite, had a look of cool fire in his eyes, and exchanged a joke with his associate, Deavour, who laughed a bit too loudly.

"All rise!" the Bayliff called as Judge Collins entered, donned his glasses and swung his gavel. Collins exchanged a nod of acknowledgment with Swartsfager, and raised his eyes towards the defense as the regular opening of court and announcement of the case was given. The defense team brought forward their Motion for Continuance to the Court, which stated in part;

"…That on or about the 9th day of February, 1948, former counsel for the Defendant voluntarily withdrew from the defense of said Defendant, thereupon leaving said Defendant without counsel…. Defendant was not able to engage new counsel until late on the evening of the 17th day of February, 1948, which time was less than 24 hours before Defendant was indicted by the Grand Jury during the afternoon of February 18, 1948. That, after the arraignment of the Defendant a few minutes after the indictment against him was returned into the Court by said Grand Jury, this case was set for trial at 1:30 P. M. on February 20, 1948. That Defendant's inability to obtain counsel prior to the time aforesaid was due to the prejudice and ill feeling of the public in general and the people of Jones County in particular. That counsel for Defendant have not been allowed sufficient time within which to investigate the facts, interview witnesses, and prepare this case for trial;" and that the defense "needs sufficient time in which to investigate the nature of Defendant's mental condition."

The Motion also stated that the motion for a change of venue in the first trial was reversed by the Supreme Court of Mississippi, and remanded "to a county other than one adjoining Jones County." The second trial had been held in Forrest County, which did, in fact, adjoin Jones County. For this reason, and for the reason that "bias and prejudice still exist in Jones County, and that the same is now worse than before, and that, therefore, a change of venue should be granted at this time; and that defense Counsel need sufficient time within which to investigate the facts on which their motion for a change of venue will be determined." Another point on the Motion brought the underbelly of the prosecution to light, stating that the jury lists "...are not constituted in accordance with both the Due Process and Equal Protection clauses of the Constitution of the United States," pointing to, but not actually stating that the jury lists had been tampered with.

A final point stated, "Counsel for Defendant, in all good faith and in fidelity to their oaths as members of the Bar, are convinced beyond doubt that, unless the continuance prayed for in this motion is granted and sufficient time allowed for adequate preparation of defense in this case, Defendant's constitutional right to be properly represented by counsel, as guaranteed to him by the Constitution of the State of Mississippi (Section 26) and by the Constitution of the United States (14th Amendment), will be denied him by his immediate trial without his being allowed sufficient time within which his counsel may properly prepare his defense… Wherefore, movants pray that this case be continued to the next Regular Term of this Court for the reasons aforesaid.

To all these protests, the Answer of the State merely said that it was an attempt to delay the orderly proceedings of the court and that the two prior trials had given sufficient investigation, which transcripts were readily available for the defense.

London stepped forward and asked the Court for time to file a reply to the prosecution's Answer, to which Judge Collins replied with a flair of caviling, "Well, Mr. London, suppose I continue this case until the next term of court, then your associate and you desire to withdraw from the case, and at the next term of court we have a motion here for continuance, to give counsel time to investigate, there would be no end to it, that just wouldn't do. You may make your record on this. Now, do you want the court to treat this as a motion for continuance, motion for change of venue, or motion to quash the indictment?" The Judge looked over his glasses somewhat condescendingly towards the Defense.

"Your Honor," Al replied, "this motion which we filed is a motion for a continuance, and it is not intended to be a motion to quash the indictment, a motion for change of venue, motion for sanity hearing, or anything else other than a motion for continuance in order to give us opportunity to investigate the case and prepare a defense."

The Judge looked again at the papers, put them down again and took off his glasses to look pointedly at the Defense. "All right, now, do you have any testimony that you want to introduce in support of the facts alleged in this motion?"

"Your Honor," Al began a little hesitantly," it might seem a bit irregular, but the only testimony which I could offer at this time would be that of myself or Mr. Poole, my associate here, for the reason that we have not had time to interview all the witnesses, and at this time we haven't found a witness who would be willing to make an affidavit to support any of the other motions which we mentioned."

"What about the motion for continuance?" the Judge asked with some consternation," Do you want to introduce any testimony in support of the facts alleged there for continuance?"

London adjusted his glasses, cleared his throatand continued, "Mr. Poole and I have personal knowledge of the facts which are alleged in there as being facts based on our personal knowledge. We have certain information and belief on which the other allegations were made. If the Court would permit me, I would offer Mr. Poole's testimony." London waved a hand backwards, ushering in John, who was adjusting his suit coat ready to stand.

The Judge appeared to give in, but somewhat ingeniously, as he said, "Yes, sir, I will hear any testimony you gentlemen want to introduce in support of your motion."

Swartsfager stretched out one leg and leaned back in his chair, scribbled a note and slid it to Deavours who exchanged a smile and nod of the head.

"State your name, please?" Al began. "John R. Poole."

"Are you an attorney in the case, on behalf of the defendant?" "Yes, sir, I am."

"When were you retained in the case on behalf of the defendant" "I was retained on Feburary 17th, at approximately ten-thirty P. M."

"And I will ask you whether or not that was less than twenty-four hours before the time that the indictment was returned against the defendant?"

"That is true."

"I will ask you, Mr. Poole, if you have had an opportunity to interview any witnesses who might testify in behalf of the defendant in this case?"

"Yes, I have."

"How many, and whom?"

"Do you want me to tell the whole situation?" "Yes, sir."

"I have talked with people of Laurel and around Laurel, I have talked with lawyers in Laurel, one of who said this to me, "You have done the craziest thing you could ever do by taking this case…"

Deavours, at a nudge from Swartzfager, stood and said, "Objection! If the Court please, we don't think that kind of testimony is competent here, expressions of opinion, which may be true and may not be true, we don't know."

Judge Collins turned to the Defense and stated bluntly, "That is heresay." London said, "Yes, sir – From the opinion I have in this case, sir, and as we see it, that will be the only evidence which is available to us at this time."

The Judge paused, then nodded towards him as he said, "Continue."

"And I believe that you filed in support of defendant's motion for a change of venue in this case, an affidavit setting forth certain investigations which you carried out with reference to the defendant's motion for change of venue, and I would like to ask you at this time to describe your investigation of the public feeling in Jones County, and tell the Court just how you came to the conclusion as expressed in your affidavit which was filed in this case, and which was read to the Court at that time?"

Swartzfager stood and wagged his head as he said, "We object to the question in that form, because that would be hearsay testimony."

Judge Collins responded "Well, I am going to let him answer it. It isn't in exactly the right form, but I will let him answer it." The Judge nodded towards Poole to speak.

Swartzfager stared at the Judge before slowly sitting down again.

"Judge," John began, somewhat encouraged at the leniency, and spoke with determination, "It seemed necessary to the intelligent and proper preparation of the defense in the case for me to investigate this motion because it was made, I notice, at both former trials, so I not only wanted to investigate it by myself, but I wanted an independent investigator to investigate it, and aid in an investigation.

My investigation consisted of not only questioning people in Laurel, and not even knowing their names, all the time, but it went further, and I would go down into the various parts of the county and did even pick up a hitchhiker and ask him about the case. I would walk down the street and I would meet a man on the street and ask him about the case. I would talk to White men and Negroes. One witness I interviewed said that everybody in the county feels like this, "The lawyers themselves should be shot for having anything to do with this case, for defending the old rascal, he is guilty and everybody knows it." I found the situation so intense in my investigation that I could not get people to make affidavits; that they honestly believe that it would do either them or their business a great deal of harm if they should come up here and testify, or if they should make an affidavit to that effect."

At the pause, Al interjected, "Mr. Poole, I will ask you from considering the amount of time since you have been employed in this case which has been set for call today at one-thirty, if you, in your professional opinion as an attorney, feel that it would be fair to the defendant to put him to trial in view of the brief time within which you have been retained in the case?"

John responded readily, "I feel that to put the defendant on trial at this time is actually to deny him the right of due process of law, to deny him the right of adequate representation as guaranteed by the Constitution of the United States. My oath as a member of the bar is highly respected by me, and I want to always conform to that oath that I will give the best possible services I can when called to represent a person in a case."

After other questions of lack of time involved to speak with the defendant himself, London turned to the Judge and said, "Your Honor, I believe that is all I have to ask Mr. Poole."

On the cross-examination, Swartzfager himself stepped up to the plate, with an air of contention. John's chest tightened as this experience of cross-examination was a new one – as if defending his own innocence.

"Mr. Poole, when is this case going to be set for trial?"

"When is the case going to be –?" John stalled, groping in his mind for a particular answer he didn't actually have – hadn't Al told him it would be sometime the following week? Possibly he just assumed with the motions being heard today.

"Yes, sir."

"I don't know," he replied frankly, swallowing.

"Have you not filed this motion when the case would be set for trial?" Swartszfager's voice was raised, in pretentious unbelieving.

"I don't know." John repeated, some anger brewing in the place of anxiety. "So when you are telling the court here that you haven't had, or don't have adequate time to prepare your defense, you don't even know when the case was going to be set for trial?" Devours tried to hide a smirk as his partner looked at him.

The ploy for the prosecution to prove incompetence played out, diverting the Court's attention from the real matter at hand. The dimensions of logic at hand here became a game, while Swartzfager enjoyed prattling on details that seemingly showed the defense as unprepared. After John said that he had not agreed as to when the case would be called, Swartzfager replied, "Why, don't you know, as a matter of fact that I asked the Court to set this case for call on Friday, instead of Thursday, and suggested there that it be set for one-thirty after conferring with your associate in order that you might have ample time to be ready and get down here?

"You are right, I am sorry, I was mistaken," John replied. What he didn't voice was that this protest was ludicrous. A few extra hours or even days was not the extension they were looking for. Swartsfager continued to question Poole on the details of the exact time he had been given to talk with his client and finished with the assuming question, "And you had ample time to talk with him, didn't you?

John responded with, "That is not necessarily true. I don't know what you mean, in the first place by ample time. I consider that when I am representing a defendant I should be able to discuss fully all the matters with him, I figure he should talk to me sufficiently for me to determine whether he is mentally unbalanced, I feel that he should be able to give me names of witnesses, I feel that he should be able to go into very minute details, into all the facts as he knows them, and I don't consider in view of that that I had ample time to talk with him."

"Well, I mean by that, if you had wanted to stay ten minutes, fifteen, or twenty minutes, it wasn't due to lack of time that you didn't stay longer with him, was it?

John breathed deeply and looked at London, who shook his head slowly. The prosecution continued to badger on petty points, such as they didn't have to go to Laurel together, which could have saved time. John replied to that objection by saying, "We thought it best to remain together, especially in view of the fact that an attorney who formerly represented this boy told us it was very dangerous for us to be down here, and we didn't know, we hadn't been down here before, however, I have found some very, very nice people since I have been here." He thought it best to balance the situation with other observations. The court clerk had been nice and others who had given him interviews on the street.

Shwartzfager took advantage of the positive remark by continuing, "Well, you found that the lawyers here, and the Court and all have been very cooperative with you, haven't you, Mr. Poole?"

Somewhat stiffly but in Southern tradition of polite communication, John replied, "That is very true."

Swartsfager lifted his hand, "You have found that I have been very cooperative with you?" Looking straight into his eyes, John replied, "That is very true, up until now." The point wasn't lost to the courtroom, and Al cleared his throat.

Swartzfager chose to ignore the commentand continued, "And you haven't met a person here since you have been in Laurelthat has said or done anything, and you haven't seen anything that would lead you to believe or indicate to you that you might be the object of any violence, have you, Mr. Poole?"

"I can't answer that question the way you are expecting me to because of what I said while ago –"

Interrupting him, Swartzfager interjected forcefully, "I don't expect you to answer it any way, just answer it the way it is." "Alright," John said, breathing in with more resolve, "I will give you a complete statement of what this lawyer said, as I started to do while ago. A lawyer, a member of the bar, told me in a very honest, frank, sincere tone that I was the craziest man in the world for getting into this case because there is no telling what people will do around here. That was a member of the bar. I told him that all I wanted to secure for Willie McGee was a fair and impartial trial, whether he is guilty or not, that he deserves that."

Swartzfager smiled and winked at his partner.

"Now whether the lawyer was ribbing you, or whether he was serious about the matter, nothing has happened to you, has there?

John admitted, "That is very true, nothing has happened."

"Regardless of what the lawyer said, you haven't seen a thing, and haven't heard a thing that would lead you to believe that any violence might be done to you?" Swartzfager turned halfway to the Judge, as if producing conclusive evidence.

"There was another lawyer that told me that also," John added, feeling a bit chagrined.

"What was that, Mr. Poole?" He turned back. Speaking up a bit, John repeated, "I merely said that there was another lawyer who told me that also."

With mock seriousness, Swartzfager held his ear towards him and lifted his chin, "What was that, Mr. Poole?"

More loudly and with finality he again repeated the point, "There was another member of the bar of the Second Judicial District of Jones County, Mississippi that told me that also.

Deavours, who had been enjoying the banter, could not hold back a laugh and said from the prosecution table, "You can't put too much confidence in these lawyers!"

Swartzfager, took advantage of the setup said with a condescending laugh, "Well, they used to scare me too, when I started out."

Their lack of courtroom procedure, on which the judge remained silent, and Swartzfager's pretentious smile caused John's fighting blood to boil, which made it difficult to continue answering the questions that were meant to distract. The point that the trial had been tried twice was brought up – that should be very helpful to the defense in preparing for the case. Defense argued that it made it more complicated, in light of the fact that there had been interference in both cases that needed to be investigated. There were also other cases to be tried in the meantime. The Prosecution mocked, weren't two weeks enough time to finish his investigation?

John finally said boldly, "Let me state this in answer to that line of questioning. I could try the case today,

I could actually try the case today, but I would not represent Willie McGee adequately under the Constitution and Laws of the United States and under the laws and Constitution of the State of Mississippi, and in all fairness to you as a member of the bar and to the Court as a member of the Court, I must state that I can't adequately represent him today, nor within the next two weeks."

Swartzfager looked at Judge Collins, without a rational comeback in mind and flatly stated, "That is all, if the Court please."

"When do you want to set the case, gentlemen, and do you want to set it for call, for trial, or what? Collins asked.

Swartzfager answered, as if on cue, "Judge, let's set it for call on any preliminary motions that they might have for next Thursday.

The Judge looked at the defense, "Is that agreeable to you, gentlemen?"

Perplexed by this sweeping question that ignored all they had fought for, but understanding that the Judge was in lockstep with the Prosecution London answered merely, "Your Honor, we would like for the record to show that we except to the ruling of the Court in the overruling of our motion for continuance, and that we take exception for the same reasons to the ruling of the Court in setting of the case for call next week."

Ignoring the implications, Judge Collins said with an up-turned chin, "All right, let the case be set for call next Thursday," hit his gavel and rose. "All rise!" came the bailiff's call. The men rose while the Judge walked out, leaving behind two somber and two smirking faces in the courtroom.

CHAPTER TEN

AN UNDERSTUDY WIFE

John leaned his head in one hand, elbow on his wooden office desk, while the other held a cigarette in his mouth. The drive back from Laurel after the hearing had drained his energies. Al, on the other hand, was wound up, had made coffee and was pacing the office, complaining about the lack of time to work on other cases he and John had scheduled for the first of the week, "And how the hell are we supposed to draw up the documents alone for this case in time, much less thoroughly investigate all the cover-ups? He turned to John, stopped momentarily, and pointed, "Another thing, what policeman is going to tell us the truth about the investigation at the Hawkin's house that night?" He threw up his hands and began pacing again. "If this case wasn't a balloon of trouble just waiting to be burst in the first trial, it's three times inflated by now! Everyone has their story, they're sticking to it, and we have no time to prove them liars." He stopped at his desk and began tapping the top of it with his fingers.

"Did you know Hawkins tried to bring a gun into the courtroom in the second trial?" John said somewhat mechanically, his eyes distant.

"Hawkins had a gun?"

John rose up in his seat, took a deep breath and more engagingly affirmed, "Had a pistol stuck in his pants. He had been threatening to kill the defense team, so the police searched him before he came into the courtroom. One of the men I interviewed yesterday told me that."

"It was lucky we made it out of Laurel without any trouble, but Hawkins is warned by now. He knew we were there, talking to folks." Al began pacing again as the possibilities played out in his mind. "If we go back for any more investigation before the trial, he just might gather people or try something himself, and we would have to..." He stopped, searching for a solution.

"We'll have to ask for protection when the trial actually starts," John completed his thought and added, "and it wouldn't hurt to carry a gun ourselves when we go back." John rose to his feet with his customary jerk, heading for the coffee pot. As he poured a cup he continued, "I'm not as concerned about Hawkins as I am the officials involved in cover-up. That Grand Jury had three Negroes on it all right, but I'll bet they were just planted. Otherwise, why were they all so polished? Besides, they would have known that those few couldn't overturn an indictment, anyway, since unanimity isn't required, and I'll bet my life there isn't going to be one black face in the Petit Jury."

"Mmm…You're probably right about that," Al said, rubbing his chin with his hand, "they would have already satisfied 'Patton' by having that many on the Grand Jury."

The reference was to the U. S. Supreme Court case, Patton vs. Mississippi, won by Thurgood Marshall and backed by the NAACP. The decision had finally shown Mississippi's practice of ensuring that no blacks served on a jury with white men due to the lack of qualified candidates, to be in violation of the 14th Amendment's equal protection requirement. At the time, Al and John had celebrated the decision by raising a mug together to toast to "progress," not thinking that they would so soon need to make sure it was applied.

"Even if there were one or two on the Petit Jury," he continued, "it's unlikely they would offer their necks."

"Hell, no!" John laughed, "Would you, in his position?" He broke the mood in mock drama. "For me?" His eyebrows lifted and crossed his hands on his chest. "Would you do it for me, Al? To save my life?" He dramatized to relieve tension, if not to prove a point.

Al threw his hands up. "The last time I checked the lawyer's oath does not require one to go down with the ship. You'd be on your own, partner!"

"Damn! And you know I can't swim with a wooden leg!" John mocked sorrow, then broke into a laugh along with Al's. After a last drink of coffee, John snuffed out his cigarette, and said more quietly, "Let's meet early tomorrow. I'm going home to a good dinner and relax with Gerry before I can think straight again." He began with resignation to and put the papers on the desk into his briefcase.

Al tried to let go of the need to continue analysis of what they faced, without total success. As John set the lock on his case, Al let go of another racing thought.

"You know that the CRC has talked about plans to use Rosalie at some point." John looked up, remembering what Al had told him about a negro woman who had been visiting McGee in jail. She now claimed to be his wife and had been corresponding with the board of the Civil Rights Congress, even asking for money for support of the children they had together. It was a dubious claim, however, since Bessie McGee had said that her daughter-in-law had divorced him and moved to California to be with relatives after the second trial, for safety's sake. If there had been another affair going on, with children that came from it, there certainly hadn't been time for another marriage – other than in jail.

"Use her – In what way?"

"Probably to solicit activists and donations from the North. I can't see what headway she could make here. I just know that Bella has mentioned her several times as a way to stir up sentiment in his favor. She is prepared to say that Mrs. Hawkins seduced him and kept him coming back with the tease that she would cry rape if he didn't." Al looked at his partner's furrowed brow and added the obvious, "It will, of course, stir up a different sentiment here."

John took a deep breath and rubbed the tension of his eyebrows in thought, then looked up to say, "I'm in this to defend the rights of McGee – and to help the cause of the black man in the South – not for any other agenda."

Al bit his lip and offered only a nod and, "Mmm…"

John again gripped the heavy case and lifted it with effort, put on his hat, and finished by saying, "I don't trust anyone or any group who would use deception to accomplish their purposes, however noble their original purposes may be."

Al opened the door for him saying only, "Have a good evening, John. Get some rest."

"Same to you, buddy," came the return with a nod of his head as John made his way out into the dark hallway.

"Hey, Momma!" Willie smiled widely and rose up off his bench as the guard opened the door at the end of the long hallway to present the familiar form that appeared behind it.

"Willie!" The loving call and wave came from a figure clad with a loosely fitting cotton dress that rippled back and forth over her full dark form as she hurried down the hallway past watchful eyes peering through the bars, searching for their own loved ones, to reach the safety of her son's cell door. The hallway became alive with chatter as relatives and friends poured in and called out their greetings to the lonesome souls locked behind their cell doors.

"Oh Lawd, it's so good to see yo' face, Mama, Mmhuh!" Willie chuckled in spite of the aches and pains he attempted to hide from her.

"Willie – my sweet boy!" Bessie rocked herself back and forth, as if she could bend the bars between them with her mother's love, tears welling up in her eyes and spilling out onto her rounded cheeks. Under the watchful eye of the jailer, she simply grabbed his fingers he extended through the bars, kissing them and anointing them with her wet affection. Statements of love were passed between them, ending in "I know, I know, Mmm, mmh!" Tears were shed on both sides and sealed on a shared handkerchief.

After this re-establishing of the mother-son bond, Bessie sat on the stool provided and said more softly, "How they treaten' you in here Willie? You don't look so good," she moaned a bit, her mother's eyes seeing past the cover up of pain and asked, "Is that a bruise on your forehead?"

"Aww, Mom, go on now – it's a jail. They ain't pamperin' me none." He forced another chuckle and distracted her by saying, "Tell me some news."

She leaned in and said almost in a whisper, "I saw where them lawyers was in Laurel at the courthouse this mawnin'."

`"Is that a fact?" Willie drew up a stool and positioned himself on it, looking on his mother with affection.

"Mmhmnh," Bessie said with a nod of her head, "They sure was. What they talkin' bout, do you know?"

Willie sighed and shook his head. "Oh, Mama, I only know theys tryin' to get more time. Maybe to git somebody to give me an alibi."

Bessie squinted her eyes a bit. "An alibi, Willie? What do you mean?"

"If they can git somebody to say I was gamblin' all night, then I got an alibi." "Oh, Missus. Harrison? She don't wan't to get on that stand."

"I know, Momma, that's why she went down to Florida in the first place, probably, but she might do it now."

"Oh, Flawda – Mmhmh…" She paused pensively, then returned, "How they gonna get here?

"I don't know, Mama." Willie's eyes grew a little larger with hope as he continued, " Maybe the Civil Rights Congress going to get them here."

"Mmhmh, Lord have mercy! I do hope so, Willie."

"You sure do look pretty, Mama," Willie grinned, changing the subject. "Oooh, Willie," Bessie laughed and blushed with an obstinate last tear coming out in spite of her delight, "You've always known how to flatter a lady!" Willie smiled then grew serious again whispering, "Momma, I have to ask you to do somethin' for me."

"What's that, honey?" Bessie said softly, wiping her cheek and quickly regaining her composure.

"Do you remember Rosalee?"

Bessie's expression changed to one of consternation, as she said, "Mmmhmn, I remember her, all right."

Willie continued, "Mama, I know you didn't like her much, but she come up here to visit her cousin and sees me and says, "Willie, is that you?" Well, we hit it up again, just like that." Willie smiled largely in expectation.

"You what?" Bessie asked, trying not to picture it.

"Well, Mama, we have feelings for each other still and she says that she has a child of mine."

Bessie shook her head from side to side and said, "Oh Willie..Mmhmnh...I know, I know you want a family, but don't you know she would've told you that long ago if that child was yours." Her look of pity turned into a warm smile – "Now, Willie, you'd have feelings for any pretty woman what you see in jail!" Bessie chuckled at her own insight.

"No, Momma," Willie grasped at the bars intently, "this is more serious than that – and, and – she wants to help me get out." Bessie listened quietly as he continued, "I think she's too afraid to get on the stand – wouldn't help anyway, I don't reckon – but she says she's willin' to say we's married, hopin' it will soften the jury's heart with pictures of children – y'know what I mean?" At his mother's puzzled look he said, "Well, all those chidren aren't mine, but who would know? All the jury's got now is a man whose neck they want to put a noose around. They might think twice if it was a father's neck, don't you know?"

"Might be, that might be true." Bessie hung her head, thinking of the grandchildren she had brought to gaze, wide-eyed at their father between these same iron bars she found herself so sickened by now. How would they feel if they knew other children were replacing them to plead for their daddy? Her jaw twisted to the side with resentment, remembering the argument she had with their mother before they left town. Hadn't she said just that to her? That it would soften the hearts of those white folks if they cried for them to help their Daddy?

How could Eliza just up and run off with them all the way across the nation? Bessie was wounded in heart, thinking she may never see her beloved grandchildren again, wondering if it was really fear or just plain old revenge that had gripped their momma's heart and caused her to run. Still, she sighed, at least they were safe.

"Momma?"

"Yes, child," Bessie was still staring off, but forced herself to emerge from the emotion-packed memory with another heavy sigh.

"I know you miss 'em," Willie said, as if her thoughts had been spoken. "Don't you know I do too?" He reached through to clasp his mother's fingers again and hold them tight. Tears began to stream down Bessie's face once again, only this time she was too heavy in heart to wipe them away.

"Time's up!" The harsh call brought the escape into emotion back down to remembrance of the threatening doom of real time slipping away.

"Ok now, Momma," Willie pulled himself together to reassure her and stood up, "Just be thinkin' about it, cause you'll need to say it's true. Can you do that for me, Momma?" He tenderly touched her face through the bars, "You remember, don't you – I'm alive today cause of that first lie they had me tell when I had to sign that confession. It's no different – this one. It just may keep me alive this time."

Bessie nodded her affirmation but couldn't reply properly. She held her face with her handkerchief for a moment as to forbid errant tears, then sniffed loudly. She gathered herself to stand with a slight grunt and leaned forward to touch and kiss her son's cheek through the bars, attempting to transport the fullness of her unconditional motherly love towards her young son grown into a man's image.

"I'll be back real soon," she said faintly, her hand still on his cheek, which he gripped and kissed in return. She then added, as if an afterthought, "I'll do anything you need me to do, Willie, you know that." "I know, Momma. I love you, Momma."

"Time to leave now, Mam." The guard rapped on the bars, startling Bessie, with a force contrasting the overlay of politeness.

"Take care of yourself, now, you hear me?" Bessie remained obstinately at the bars for a second longer to say anything to regain a sense of normalcy.

"I will, Momma, I will," Willie said accommodatingly with a smile, as if he could.

The figure turned and walked down the hall past the guard, with much less bustle than before, but with an uplifted chin and forward-set eyes, defying the usual stance around white folk.

CHAPTER ELEVEN

HOT POTATO

The time had come to tell Gerry about the nature of the case. After coming back from Laurel, all John wanted to do was forget about the events of the day and enjoy his family. Gerry had seen that he looked exhausted, but that was typical when he had to go out of town for work purposes. She didn't want to weary him further by asking questions and had just let him relax and enjoy the evening at home, hoping he would tell her about it in time. In the morning he began to tell her about the plight of Willie McGee while they both were getting ready for the day. She listened as she slowly brushed her long, wavy hair, as he elucidated the history of the case and the current climate surrounding it.

As he pulled tight the knot in his tie, he finished with, "There'll be some risks involved. There are plenty of good old boys in Laurel who want nothing more than to see me fail, and might be ready to do something about it, if I don't. I took the stand myself yesterday because there was no one in Laurel who was willing to even write down what they knew to present at court."

"Not even any of Willie's friends?" She turned from the mirror.

"Especially not Willie's friends. They would be walking targets in that town if they told what they believe to be true. Only his mother took the stand for him in the previous trials."

Gerry was pensive for a moment, and then asked, "One thing I want to know is, why is Willie able to talk now, when he couldn't in either of the first two trials?"

"That's a very good question, and one I'm not prepared to answer right now," John replied. "I think it may have been a combination of things. He was terrified, had injuries to the head, and his mother talked about him having syphilis of the brain. He could have been getting those treatments from the government we've heard about that

84

might have made his mind sluggish, who knows? On top of that, he tells me that he is still beaten while he is in jail. Men come in randomly now, but in the beginning it was every night. We didn't have enough time to talk about it all, but I can only imagine what they did to him the night before he was ready to testify." He shook his head in disgust and continued with pointed finger, "He's going to be watched by my choice of policeman the whole night before he goes on the stand this time!"

Gerry stood and walked over to put her arm around her husband's neck. "I'm so proud of you for taking this case. I've seen you take too many of your opponents across the chessboard by surprise to think this is too big of a challenge for you. It's time someone stood up for the abuse of the colored man in Mississippi, and I think you're just the man to do it!" She ran her fingers through the dark groomed wave on the top of his head and finished with, "Bring them to a checkmate, Johnnie!"

Although he accepted the encouragement with a laugh and kissed her deeply, a deeper knawing in his belly from the enormous tasks ahead caused him to break away too soon from the embrace to comb his hair back in place, grab his coat, hat and briefcase and say, "I love you, dear. I'll be home by suppertime."

"I'll make dessert!" She waved him away at the door but took a moment to lift up her eyes to whisper, "Lord, have mercy!"

The workday for John was hit and miss for productivity. Al wasn't in the office, making calls from home instead, including one with the CRC investigator to find out how best to use their time in Laurel this next week. John began studying the transcripts of the second McGee trial and lost himself in the actual testimony and drama of the courtroom, making marks and notes as questions came to mind. After he had been at it only a short while, however, he heard at rap at the door as his divorce client showed up unannounced, regardless of it being a Saturday. "Hey, John! I thought I might catch you here."

"Well, hello, Leonard, good to see you." John did his best to sound sincere. "Sit down, sit down."

Leonard drew up a chair to the desk and sat down.

"I've been calling you for the past two days. You're a hard man to catch up with, you know.

"I realize…" John started but Leonard spoke over him.

"You know, I am a man of means and I am willing to refer you to my friends and business partners if you give me your all on this case."

"I certainly…"

"Now, I have done a lot of research for you already – look at this."

He plopped a small suitcase on John's desk and opened it to reveal a mound of small pieces of paper.

"Just look at this, would you?" Before John had time to actually look at them, he continued, "These are proof of my wife's purchases, notes to friends, Hell, there's even a hotel stay in here. I expected it all along!" Leonard got up and poured himself a cup of coffee, talking all the while about his wife's friend, who would keep her secrets, and she was a woman of ill-discretion herself.

John tapped his pencil on the desk, desperately wanting to get back to the transcripts in front of him. His client was oblivious and became long-winded; throwing in stories that he was sure would be helpful in the proceedings. Despite several implications from John that he really just did not have the time today to spare, he stubbornly persisted, telling him that he would be rewarded richly when they walked away with the win he wanted.

Finally, John looked at his watch.

"Oh, my goodness, it's nearly noon! You must excuse me, I have to meet with my wife's parents for lunch," he lied.

Leonard nodded, "Well, my wife's parents think I'm to blame." He looked downcast and immovable.

John finally got his client out the door, with assurances to do the very best he was able and closed it behind him. With a heavy sigh, he turned back to the immense amount of papers that now cluttered his desk. There would be no time to visit with Willie today, as he had hoped. He needed to finish up here and would still have to take home the work tonight. He sat down, lit a cigarette and returned to the transcript, paying no attention to the growling of his stomach.

In Mrs. Hawkins' testimony, she mentioned that she had two doctors, and was taken to an infirmary in Hattiesburg where she had remained a week. The testimony of the doctor did not mention mental health, other than having to give her sedatives, but said that she only had minor scratches to her vagina. Why did he keep her for a week? What mental health issues did she have that were not coming to light? He would have to call to see what they could find out, but interviews take time, which he didn't have, and what chance would they have at an appeal? Mr. Hawkin's testified the electrical wire was cut, but the lights were on when the police showed up an hour later. The last defense team had not even cross-examined Mr. Hawkins. They must have been threatened. Why else would they let the opportunity slip by without any questions at all? Then there was the testimony of Willie's drinking buddy. That was more than likely given under duress, although he had to laugh when reading how Willie was in the hole gambling with $15 of the company lost, then asked to borrow money from a friend and ended up winning almost enough to pay them both back.

"Hope Lady Luck will help you out this time, Willie," John said out loud, then more gravely, "almost enough won't do this time."

After a hearty supper and an apple pie that Gerry claimed "Baybay helped me fix for you," John praised the cooking, proclaiming them to be "exceptional chefs," and played with Baybay for too short a time before setting her in her playpen, as the looming work ahead captivated his thoughts. Gerry resigned herself with a sigh to engaging in domestic tasks once again. She tried to put aside thoughts of the pretty new flowered dress she had hoped to put on after Baybay was in bed, as John set up the creaky old card table he used for a make-shift desk at home and drew up the metal folding chair. A stand-up lamp, given by Gerry's parents, cast a dim light from its yellowed shade onto his work. He adjusted it slightly to get the most advantageous slant, put on his reading glasses and sat down to immerse himself once again in study.

The conflicting reports regarding McGee were racing through his mind. He needed to make a list with just the right questions to make their short visit as productive as possible. As he spread out all his paperwork and notes on the table, he recalled there had been a story he had heard about McGee being the mastermind behind a jailbreak in 1946 with two other prisoners. This was just after the time he was also reported to have been acting like an imbecile. Why would the papers also have claimed that no one heard him speak during this year "despite their most pleaful puns, coupled with admonitions" the Clarion Ledger had reported, other than to have heard him sing once at the jail's weekly prayer meeting. How could he have planned a break and nearly pulled it off without being able to speak? Was it possible the escape was a fabrication to show that McGee was truly in charge of his faculties, and was actually a step above the intelligence of his peers? It was hard to know who was telling the truth throughout this saga. John took a deep breath at the thought of the sporadic beatings. These, along with the accompanying threats would have stoked any man's fear, keeping him in an anxious mental state. Still, it was unlikely it would have kept him speechless for a year. John rubbed the tension in his forehead, and then paused at a thought.

"He must have incurred brain damage at some point from the beatings," John said out loud involuntarily.

Gerry turned from her tidying after putting Baybay bed. "McGee?" she asked.

"He couldn't talk for a year – and during that year he claims they were beating him whenever they damn well pleased!" John didn't lift his eyes from his paperwork and indicated a need to not enter into discussion by turning a page and picking up his pen to underline a date. He added, as if to a team of collaborators around the small table rather than to his wife, "I'll bet they drugged him, too. That would keep him from complaining."

Gerry stared at him for a moment, knowing him well enough to not interrupt his thought processes. She imagined the fury of the men who wanted to smother this defense. She returned to her work, as well, trying to push out the thought of what her mother had said today about the danger her husband was putting the family in. Gerry quickly defended him and their shared values of fighting for the rights of the black population. She had also thrown in a side comment that gave her some battle energy now, "I think anyone who is Christian would want to support this. The people who want the Negroes to stay in their places burn crosses, Mama! It's just like watching the Savior be put on fire to stand by and not say anything, not do anything to stop this." She knew her mother wouldn't resist this stance, but at the same time Cecil Ware had grown up in the old Southern culture where she had been taught as a child that it just might be that God made the white man white because he didn't live in darkness of mind, the way the black man did. After all, Jesus was a white man.

This conjecture showed some ignorance of where Jesus was born and his progenitors, but it was an ingrained picture that so many artists in the Protestant churches had put to their brushes, that it seemed to her to be proof. Cecil had tried to raise her children by the Word the best she was able, making sure they were in church every Sunday morning and each Wednesday night. Geraldine alone rebelled. Her father, Dolphus, a deacon in the church, was embarrassed at times by Geraldine's strong statements. He felt sure her red hair gave her the fiery temper against anything she deemed to be unjust. Both Cecil and Dolphus were wary of this young man going to law school, when their daughter had been drawn into his deep blue eyes. It was true his sister Mildred was a minister and an adept preacher but she was a woman, after all, and this was an abrupt breaking of tradition for them. Why had John turned from his aspirations of preaching the Word, they asked each other? Had it been an evil wind that had redirected his gifts to more earthly pursuits? He did like to drink, too, which was not acceptable. It was all just too much for Cecil to put into words that morning, and all she could manage was a "Humph!" Gerry modestly hid her feelings of triumph over winning a battle with her mother, by assuring her that she trusted in her parents' prayers for them. Another stance hard to argue.

"We will certainly pray," Cecil had said with tight lips as she caressed her granddaughter's forehead, "we certainly will."

Gerry felt the lump in her throat rise again with the memory and cleaned the kitchen much more efficiently than usual as smoke twirled in the light of the lamp while John continued to mutter to himself. Pyle's review of the case had said that "records will show that the defendant is suffering from syphilis of the brain."

It could have been true that Willie had been getting the treatments for syphilis just before the trial had begun. If they were continuing any kind of "treatment" in jail, it might also be a cause of mental impairment. A doctor friend of his had told him that they were discovering the results in some of the syphilis trials that negros were getting worse rather than better, but it was being kept undercover. The medical community had been told to be quiet about the government funded research, which may be using the black community as guinea pigs. He wondered what other drugs they may or may not be feeding McGee in the Bullpen. John grimaced as he thought about the term, "bullpen," originating from the idea that policemen were as masculine and hefty as bulls, managing the cowering criminals inside their "pens." Too many well-intentioned policemen eventually fell into the pride of this position, not keeping values in check, instead loosing what did seem to be their own animalistic cruelty especially against those of color.

John turned back to the transcript of the earlier trials taking in a deep breath, realizing it would be only proven fact, not conjecture or philosophy, which would win this case. He began reading the transcript of the first trial's description of Willie's breaking into the home that night. Allegedly, he had cut the electrical cord and climbed up through the window after Mrs. Hawkins had gone to sleep.

She had not been aware of any of this until she heard someone crawling on the floor. How probable was it to the prosecution, he thought, that a severely intoxicated man would be able to sneak like an Indian – so quietly through a window so as not to wake a woman who had just gone to bed and her children with her, or make any outside noise in the act that her husband in another bedroom would have not heard? If her window was open to let in cool air, it was probable that her husband's window was open as well, and he would have been awakened by any unusual outside sounds. McGee would have had to hoist himself up from a small ledge, after cutting an electrical cord and having no light, to climb into unfamiliar territory. It would have taken someone with great physical skill and balance to have done it so quietly and with such agility, not to mention with less alcohol in their system than McGee purportedly had in his. They did seem to be able to prove, however, that Willie had been there that night – there were several witnesses who had seen his truck parked down the street and leaving early in the dawn. He had even been found asleep in the vehicle later on his jobsite, obviously having stayed out all night, but just what had happened really? Willie's account left room for doubt – even if they were having an affair, why would she have risked making love with him with her husband in the next room? If the story of the Hawkins were true, why would Willette have run from the house and her husband, naked and screaming to the neighbors? If they had been having a fight, after Hawkins had found them together, it would explain some things. Crying rape would be the only way out. John sighed and tapped his pencil on the table.

"Hello?" Gerry had answered without her usual formality at the late hour, thinking it was probably just her mother.

John continued in deep thought. Besides all this, McGee's buddy had said that he was trying to find his ex-wife that night. Did that play into it at all? If Willette had been angered that he had not come earlier, and that he wasn't going to perform the deed after all, she may not have taken precautions the way she usually did – shoot, if she thought he was actually coming to kill her husband, she was clearly out of her mind, anyway – if that had any truth to it. What if they had…

"John!!" Gerry's scream was so high pitched, that he jumped up from the table in terror, just to see her holding the receiver down with one hand and clutching the phone to her breast with the other. Her face was white and tears were beginning to stream down her face.

"Gerry, honey, what's wrong, who called? Gerry!!" He grabbed the phone from her, now in fierce anger and shouted, "Who is this?" to the dial tone at the other end. He slammed it down and grabbed Gerry by the shoulders, who was now sobbing and demanded, "Who was that? What did they say to you?"

"I don't know who – a man," she said through gasps, "it sounded like he was talking through something – I don't know – maybe it was long distance.

Ohh…!" She grasped the counter behind her for support. "What did he say?" John demanded again.

"He said, Oh, John! He said… "If, if your God-damned husband wants you and your children to live, you tell him he had better drop this McGee case like it was a hot potato!"

John embraced her, and started stroking her hair intending to comfort, but instead said, "Son of a bitch!" He broke away and grabbed the phone again off its hook, announcing, "I'm calling the police right now!" As he was dialing, John turned to her and said – "That guy doesn't even know what he's talking about – we only have one child, a baby. Whoever it was, is full of hot air, but I'm going to find that SOB, don't you worry about that…Hello, yes, this is John Poole, I have a phone threat to report."

After questions were answered, the report given, and Gerry had cried some more, they sat in an embrace for a long time and talked. John was willing to drop the case tomorrow, and certainly wasn't going back to it tonight, although something in him didn't believe the caller was going to be a real threat – just wanted to give them a scare. "No one has ever gone so far as to hurt a lawyer's family around here that I've heard of, no matter what the defense was," he said. . But – if this is too much for you, darling, and you want me to drop it, I will – in a second flat!" He stroked the hair off her forehead to kiss it. After seriously considering the thought, Gerry sniffed, blew her nose, and said, "No."

"No, what?" John said as he drew back to look her in the eye.

"No." Gerry said, raising herself up a bit with conviction. "We could have expected this, and then I wouldn't have reacted so. We are going to have to face their hatred at some point – just the way they hate Negros, they are going to hate the ones that defend them." Her eyes looked away from his into the distance as she said, "I used to see my Uncle yell at his hired hands on the farm, they were just young black boys, and then talk about killing them with his shotgun if they tried to mess with any of his things." She turned back to look John in the eyes, "He never would have killed anyone, really, I don't think. I think he was just a little man, trying to be tough."

"You think your caller was just a little man?"

"Trying to be tough," she smiled and nodded, but couldn't help shedding another tear.

"It was scary, though," John said softly.

"Yes," she said as she wiped the final regret away, "but I'm okay now. I want you to do what you're called to do, and we'll just pray that God will protect us."

"Let's sleep on it," John said, and drew her into an embrace. Later, as they lay in bed and John was smoking his last cigarette for the night with Gerry curled up beside him, he thought more seriously. This case is different from the others he comforted Gerry with, saying no lawyer's family had been hurt by protestors. None other had involved in heated national divisions like this one. Would the CRC pay for protection? He would call them in the morning to relay the incident. Bella and others involved didn't have to live in the pot they were stirring. Despite his worries, John drifted off to sleep, emotionally exhausted.

CHAPTER TWELVE

THE BULLPEN

The next morning was a flurry of activity. After insisting that he not lose a minute in preparing for the case yet not wanting to be in the house alone, Gerry assured John that she and Babay would stay with a girlfriend who lived just outside of town near the church while he was gone.

"Gracie always helps me to feel better about things, anyway, and it's been so long since we've spent some time together. Why, she's hardly seen Baybay since she was born. We'll go to out together and have a wonderful time. Don't worry about us." She fluffed her thick red curls in the mirror near the door and corrected her lipstick before picking up a cooing Baybay from her playpen, tying her knit hat on quickly before she could protest. John took the suitcase and baby bag to pack them snuggly into the car with her father, who had come to pick her up. After pressing a finger to her lips to remind of the agreement to not mention last night's incident to her parents, Gerry kissed him and climbed into the car.

"Thanks again for driving them, Dolphus!"

"You betcha!" The smile was sincere from the tall, handsome older man sitting in the family Dodge. "It gives me some time to spend with my daughter and grandbaby. We haven't seen y'all so much over there since you moved to this neck of the woods, but I know you're busy making a living and all now, and we understand."

John smiled, grasping the implication of not being at church, lately. He raised his eyebrows repentantly and said, "We'll be there again soon, Dolphus, I promise. Will you pray for us this week?"

Dolphus looked him straight in the eyes, having heard of the gravity of his present work. "We already are, John, we've been praying for you." He smiled, started the engine and began to back into the street.

"You girls have fun, now!" John waved at Baybay, whose small hand Gerry was manipulating into a wave and instructing, "Say bye, bye to Daddy." Sudden emotion welling up in his eyes angered him, and he turned away before receiving or saying a proper goodbye to Baybay.

His first action was a visit to the police station on the way to visit with McGee, to check on any leads they had as to whom it was that made the call. They had not called soon enough for it to be traced, but the officer at the desk assured him they had a couple of people in mind to alert the Laurel Police of. Some instigators from the last trial would be checked out first. An officer in an adjacent desk leaned back in his chair and said, "Say, Mr. Poole, do you think that nigger is guilty?" He twirled his pen and continued, "I mean, I know you have to defend his rights, an all, but he was the nigger that raped that white woman, donchu think?"

The other officer looked at him pointedlyand said, "He's not going to discuss the facts of the case before trial with you, Lester. He's anattorney!"

"Oh, I know, I know…" he laughed, "I jes thought he might wanna voice his opinion, y'know, so we'd know we's all on the same page." He laughed again at his own cleverness but narrowed his eyes to watch closely for a reaction. John turned to the first officer and said with pronounced sincerity, "I thank you very much for any help you can offer."

Nagging thoughts of not being prepared for his divorce case tomorrow were pushed aside as he rode up the elevator to the top of the jail, trying to go over the questions he had for McGee in his mind. "There you go, Mr. Poole," the crackly old voice said as the lever was pulled and the door swung open to the stale environment of the bullpen floor. "Thank you, Joshua," he said, realizing he had forgotten to greet him or make any small talk.

The meeting with Willie was again brief, but John was able to elicit information regarding Willie's years of silence. He questioned him while Willie chain smoked the offered pack of cigarettes. "Something I wanted to ask you, Willie, that I don't quite understand – why couldn't you speak for all that time, but you are able to now? Willie shifted in his seat, and his eyes rolled back to see if the guard was within earshot. He leaned forward with his arms on his legs and spoke almost in a whisper. "Can't tell you, for sure – they whupped me in the head, and sometimes I's just scared out of my wits. Drugged me, too. I think they put it in my milk, 'cause it'd taste funny, y'know. Told me milk would calm me down before the second trial. I think they got the idea when I was so scared the first trial. It helped when I couldn't say nothin', so they just helped me along with that, I suppose. I stopped drinking the milk – way back."

John took it in with furrowed brow. "What about the beatings – which ones damaged your head?"

"You remember this?" Willie again pointed out the indention on his head, stubbornly remaining as testimony to that terrible day. "And that mark, and this one," pointing to the scarred witness of the blackjacks.

John looked at each one more carefully this time, trying to discern whether any would have actually caused brain damage.

They then discussed in hushed voices his present treatment and what could be brought to trial. Willie interjected, "I met a woman that says she can help me – mebbe testify for me."

"Testify? You met her in jail?"

"She was visiting my cousin in jail, Rosalee's her name. We knowed each other long time ago, but she moved off. We'd been with each other before, y'know, and she says she has one of my babies."

Wanting him to get to the point before their time was up, John motioned with his hand impatiently and said, "So how would that help your case at all?"

"Well, she's willing to pose as my wife, n say that her chillun are mine. It might soften up those folks on the jury, to see chillun missing their Daddy, y'know, and she could even say she knowed about the affair." Willie's tone went from that of excitement to a sullen one, and said, "My Eliza did know – that's why she on and left with my babies." He reached into his pocket and pulled out a worn envelope and took a picture out of it. "These are my babies – all of 'em mine," he said with a note of pride and emotion. John stared at the picture of the lovely black woman with four children. Two of the children had Willie's big, expressive eyes.

"Beautiful children," he said with a smile at Willie, who could not return the smile with sudden emotion. John handed the picture back and took a deep breath, "Well, Willie, we don't want them to catch you in any lies. We need to show your word is good as gold if it's going to be set against the officers. All we need to do is prove that your confession was forced, and I believe you have living proof of that," pointing to his head. If the affair came to light, no Judge in Mississippi would allow it to be proven – especially not this one!"

Willie frowned in thought as a rap came to the door. "Time's up!" A guard emerged with handcuffs.

Willie nodded his head as John instructed him on the time of court and their next meeting, and then watched somberly as Willie was taken down the hallway towards his cell.

Joshua slid open the well-oiled elevator door to the bullpen floor revealing several young students jammed in the small box. Their professor was concluding his elucidation of Mississippi's history of incarceration practices. "This floor, which we aren't allowed to tour, is called the 'Bullpen.' In it are the most violent criminals, rapists and murderers. A criminal here may not see the light of day for his entire incarceration period, for the safety of the citizens."

"Why is it called the Bullpen?" one student asked as John wedged himself into the front corner and the door closed. As he tuned out the explanation and nodded to Joshua, John thought of the big eyes of Willie's children, and wondered what they knew about their Daddy and what may be in store for him. He then realized he had forgotten entirely to ask McGee about the jailbreak.

"Damn!" he exclaimed inadvertently out loud. The professor had just finished a sentence, and the curse had filled the ensuing silence. A student in the back of the elevator giggled.

Joshua smiled widely as he announced, "Fus flawr!"

John turned slightly as the elevator door opened to reveal the light of the open foyer, nodded and said, "Do pardon me." He then walked quickly out the door of the jail into the sunshine, fumbling for his pack of cigarettes, which weren't there. He took a deep breath, shook his head and chuckled at himself as he headed for the corner store.

CHAPTER THIRTEEN

NO COMMIES ALLOWED

Although there hadn't been much rest over the weekend, Al and John hit the road like bloodhounds Monday morning. They had been able to contact Bessie, Willie's mother, and would interview her today. Laurent Frantz had briefed Al on his own investigations and had given them some leads on finding folks who may talk. John would meet with the court clerk to discover Laurel's procedure of creating a jury list, and Al would research Laurel's archives in preparation of the pretrial. There was also the scrawled address that Sam had given them as a lead. There was a spirit of hope driving them that lifted the angst they had felt earlier.

"We should stick together while we are doing our street interviews, wouldn't you say?" John asked Al as they were driving down the highway. "I don't want either of us to be in a vulnerable position. Besides, one of us can write notes while the other talks. I think it makes these people nervous if you're talking and writing at the same time."

"Makes sense. Clarence coming?" Al asked as he flipped through the morning paper he had grabbed on the way out of town.

"He's going to be coming in the afternoon. He wanted to interview Bessie with me. If you want to do your reserach then, that would be a good time."

"Well, now, this is interesting!" Al folded his paper to get a better look, as John looked at him questioningly. "Governors Meet in Closed Session to Ask Retraction Of 'Anti-South' Proposals," he read off the headline.

"Anti-South?" John questioned." Referring to the civil rights bill?"

Al read, "Five Southern governors today demanded the President Truman's 'highly controversial' civil rights program be withdrawn from congressional consideration." He looked further down the page and sarcastically exclaimed, "Thank goodness someone is standing up for our rights to lynch our niggers!"

John added, "No lynching, no discrimination, no poll tax – next they are going to take away our right to call them niggers, take away our separate bathrooms, why – it will never end! Before you know it, they'll be sitting next to us in restaurants!" They both laughed, but knew others thought it serious conversation somewhere.

By mid-morning they reached Laurel and asked directions at the local gas station, which took them into another section of town where the Black folk were segregated to. The lady at the address they were given said that she had known Willette Hawkins when she was young.

"My aunt was a maid for the Hawkins, and she would take me to work with her sometimes. Every once awhile that Willette had terrible nightmares, and she just run around like she's crazy – screaming nonsense. Shoo-ey! I's thinkin' she don't get raped – she's just havin' another nightmare." She referred Al and John on to another home, and on the way they stopped passersby on the street. Everyone had their own slice of the story, but most adhered to the local yarn of the affair. None would make a statement for the court or even give their names to the attorneys. There was no hope that anyone would take the stand for the common knowledge.

They finally left for the courthouse, where John parted to meet Clarence, and left Al to do much of the research, which he claimed to be "much better at than you two bozos, anyway." John pocketed the gun Al slipped to him, scheduled a time to meet up again, and headed for the address of Bessie McGee's home. He parked the car in front to wait for Clarence before going in. As he gazed at Willie's birthplace and imagined him growing up and playing in the yard, he reflected that it wasn't so different a home as the one he had grown up in himself, being from the poorer side of town. This home was wellkept and although it was old, it was one of the better homes in the neighborhood. Glancing around, John remembered his own Nanny, having once seen her neighborhood and had wondered why everyone there was dark, like her. He smiled fondly at the memory as Clarence's car pulled up.

"Why, hello, do come in, do come in!" Bessie greeted the men with a quick smile, then customarily bowed her head, diverting her eyes. "I was just heating up some water in here. Do y'all want some hot tea?"

"Why that sounds very nice, thank you, Mrs. McGee," John said as he swept off his hat.

"Oh, please do call me Bessie," she laughed nervously and said, "I'll be right back with it. Make yourself comfortable! That old couch done lost its spring, but it'll get you offen your feet." Bessie pointed towards a small living room, where a fire was crackling in the fireplace, then bustled back to her kitchen. John and Clarence entered the cozy room, lit only by the fire and a small table lamp. The couch, rimmed with a wooden backing, was old, but stately. There was a small wooden chair to the side of it, and a rocking chair next to the fireplace. Clarence made himself as comfortable as possible on the couch, grabbing for a pillow, while John walked over to the mantle above the fireplace where framed pictures stared in the glow of the fire. He squinted at them, adjusting to the dimmer light, and held his hands down to the warmth of the crackling logs. There was a picture of a younger Bessie on her wedding day, a smaller picture of several children together, one with Willie's wide, dark eyes, and two or three of other family gatherings, in which he discerned the younger and much happier Willie. One pictured him with a lovely lady, who John guessed would have been his wife. Disjointedly laid beside them was a stack of newspaper clippings, one showing Willie beside the bars of his cell. John thumbed through them to see clippings with articles attached, that were a haphazard accounting of the trials, as if putting them together in a scrapbook had been too difficult of a task.

"I been meanin' to organize them." Bessie came in behind them with a tray that she set on the coffee table. She sighed heavily, and continued, "I just don't seem to have it in my heart to 'complish it." She positioned herself carefully on the wooden chair, folded her hands and looked down, as if the energy she had for her guests had just slipped out from her onto the floor. John attempted to lift her spirits by saying, "It is so nice to have a fire to warm ourselves by." Bessie let herself smile and said, "It's nice to have a reason to make it. There's so few visitors anymore." She smoothed her dress and took a deep breath, reminding herself of the reason for the visit. Clarence and John looked at each other, facing the most difficult task in their work, sitting with a mother's grief.

John spoke gently, "Bessie, we are going to try our very best to get your son back home again, but we'll need your help."

Bessie wasn't quite ready to get down to business, and said as if she hadn't heard him, "Willie used to set right there in that chair after dinner, cross his legs and smoke his cigarettes." Envisioning the scene, she smiled and continued, "He," she laughed a bit while dabbing at a tear, "he use to say – Oooh, Mama, nobody can cook like you, nobody! But don't go telling Eliza that." She gently laughed and said, "She was pretty, all right, but her Mama didn't teach her no cookin'. He came here at least twice a week to have some good home cooking, Mmhuh." She became sober before she broke through the emotion to reply, "What y'all need me to do? You know, now, I'd do anything to save my boy. Oh, I forgot my manners. This tea's going be cold." She set the cups out and poured, ceremoniously handing them each a cup.

John stirred in sugar cubes as he said, "Willie told me that there are witnesses that would give him an alibi as to where he was that night – the owners of the gambling house? He said that they left for Florida. Do you have any idea how to get in touch with them?"

Bessie nodded her head in agreement. "Yes, yes, he asked me about that. Willie and Hettie Johnson. Said they moved to Pensacola, and I been thinking, I do believe I can find out how to get ahold of them. Y'know, I sent them a telegram when this trial was in Hattiesburg, but they never did answer it. I think they didn't want nobody finding them then." She shook her head, I don't blame them none for being scared, sho nuf." Bessie frowned, though, and started to wag her finger in protest as she added, "But they knew Willie was there gambling most all night. That's what they told me when I talked with them last, and they say they would help iffun they could, but they got scared off, I'm thinking. Hettie was at the first trial, but nobody done asked her anything. Then she and Willie, I guess figured they needed to just get out of town when all them guardsmen came. I do believe they were just plumb scared out of their wits. Like I said, I sent them a telegram at the second trial and they never answered it, but I was talking to someone while ago that talked like they knew where they was. I believe they would come this time, knowing that Willie might have a chance, particularly since they felt so bad about it before when he got the sentence, mhumn," she mused.

"We'll need an address or a phone number as quickly as possible, because we are pressed for time," Clarence said, sipping his tea.

John added, "The trial may be set as early as next week, Bessie, so we'll need to contact them right away and try to get them fare for the trip. Do you believe they really would put their necks on the line for Willie?"

"Well, now, I know they liked Willie a lot. He was quite a card player, y'know.

Lawd, sometimes he'd bring home enough to spoil us with. He'd say – 'Here, Momma, buy yourself something pretty with this!' Then other times he'd buy me something." She fingered her necklace that had a rose on it that seemed to hold a power over her, because she couldn't hold back her emotions anymore. "Oh, my!" she gasped and the tears started to flow. John put his cup down and reached across the table to clasp her hand. The connection with the strong hand helped her gather herself again, garnering hope from the unusual gesture. She wiped her handkerchief to her eyes with the free hand and after a moment said, "I thank you for taking on this case for Willie. I know it ain't gonna be easy for you, and I do pray the Good Lord for your safety." She squeezed John's hand before letting it go, then stood awkwardly, not knowing what else to do or say.

John handed her a card as he stood and said, "You can call me at the office or at home anytime, Bessie. We'll be waiting to hear what you find out about the Johnsons."

"I sure enough will. I'll try to get hold of that number today," she said, studying the card with undue interest and sniffed, not wanting to blow her nose.

"Good, good. Now, I have another question I want to ask you before we leave, Bessie. What has Willie's mental state been, I mean before the trial – when he was growing up?"

She thought a moment before saying, "He's always been real nervous round white folks. He's seen what they'll do to a black man when they get the itch. Break his leg, put out his eye, hang him, Mmhuh! I'd always tell him the things he needed to do round white folks, to keep himself safe, but Willie wasn't' one to follow anybody's rules if it didn't seem right to him. He resented that he never had enough. Worked hard to get ahead, but never did." She laughed, "That's why he like gambling so much!"

Clarence broke in, "But you say it was just around white folks? He didn't seem to have any kind of nervous problems at other times?"

"No," she started, then thought, "Now, the only thing I think of is when he come back from the service. They let him go, saying he had esryplis of the brain. Gave him shots for it. He seemed just fine, far as I could tell, 'cept since this awful thing happen he just plumb shut down."

"Who was his doctor, Bessie?" John asked with his pen and pad ready. "Dr. Barnes – Dr. T. J. Barnes." She replied.

John looked up from his pad. "Dr. T. J. Barnes?" He repeated, recognizing the name. "Yes," she answered casually, "been seeing him since he was a boy."

"Bessie," John said with some hesitation, "do you realize he was one of the three men who were called to serve on the Grand Jury for the indictment?"

Bessie's eyes widened to take this in, and said slowly, "No, sir, I did not know that was so."

John contemplated whether or not to bother this grief-stricken mother with the affair question, but during the moment of silence, Clarence trumped him asking, "Bessie, is it your belief that Willie committed the act of rape on Willette Hawkins?" Bessie shifted and clasped her hands together tightly. "I believe Willette Hawkins made it to where Willie couldn't' say no. A white woman can do that just 'cause she wants a black man." She steeled her eyes to add vehemently, "And I believe that evil woman cried rape to save her hide. Anybody round here'll tell you that!" Bessie shook her head saying, "Lawd have mercy!" It was unclear whether she was calling upon the Lord for the soul of Willette, or her own, for thinking such things as she wouldn't say aloud.

John felt the need for a smoke, besides, time was slipping away. He pulled on his coat and said, "Thank you so much, Bessie, for your time and for your hospitality. We will be looking forward to hearing from you soon, so we can get to work on getting your son released."

Bessie grasped the outstretched hand and said, "May the Lawd bless you!"

John and Clarence spent the last hour of the afternoon traveling around Laurel, stopping here and there where they saw people walking, white and black alike, continuing to question their views of the Willie McGee case. Many of the white folk, especially the men, told them in so many words what they would do if they saw him walking down the street again. Younger women mostly refused to talk about it, while older women enjoyed a line or two of gossip, relating local yarns. Some did believe the affair was "common knowledge, saying they were sure that Willette ran out of her house naked that night because of the threats of her husband, but no one was willing to give a statement for the record. Others shunned even the idea of a white woman and a black man together, and said they knew, without a doubt, that Willie was a rapist.

"He's been tried twice before!" was the statement that backed their opinion. Two of the white men they stopped insinuated that any lawyer that would represent a nigger rapist, might see a day of justice, themselves. At that, they decided to call it a day and pick up Al, intending to hit the outer lying areas of Jones County another day. Al had an expanded briefcase full of notes and copied paperwork. He walked out onto the lot and climbed into the car as Clarence waved and walked towards his own.

"Got the rules – and found some interesting articles in the archives." He slammed the car door and pushed the lock down. "I asked for the clerk to find out about the procedure for Jury selection, but he was out at the time," his tone piqued with sarcasm. "The women at the desk said we would need to subpoena him for information. I wonder what he's trying to hide."

"Those documents could be 'adjusted' before we see them," John said as he started the car back up, and leaned out to call through the open window "Hey, Clarence, where's a good place to get some eats?"

"Scuze me, suh."

"Oh, what?" John started as the deep voice from behind came in so close to his ear.

"Sorry, didn't mean to startle you none." The hoary-haired black gentleman in a tan work suit smiled from under a wiry mustache.

"That's all right, I guess I'm just a little on edge." John breathed and asked, "What can I do for you?"

He leaned into the car and lowered his voice.

"I've heard some talk, and I just wanted to say that word's got round why y'all are here. It just might not be safe after the sun goes down. Ok, now?" He patted the car and nodded at Clarence's car next to them. "Be aware, now."

"We're much obliged to you, sir," John said, involuntarily feeling for the gun in his pocket.

"Good evening to y'all, now," the elderly man said, with a slight bow of respect and walked away, revealing a hunched back and bit of a limp.

"Follow me," Clarence said through the open car window. "We have time to grab something before we head back, and I know of a place closer to the outside of town that serves a good bowl of soup." Taking the two fingered go ahead from John as assent, he rolled the window up and maneuvered out of the lot.

When they stepped inside the restaurant, the smells of good food helped them to momentarily forget their caution. John, Clarence and Al sat down at the checkered clothed table and took off hats and coats while commenting on how ready they were to eat. A waitress brought over menus, John and Clarence lit cigarettes, and grew silent while studying the options.

Men in coveralls, ruddy colored from the day's work were sitting around the food bar, slurping soup, and talking among themselves. They grew silent, also, as they noticed the men in suits who had just seated themselves. Whispers started and some began to stare. A joke was passed around and the laughter became intentionally loud. John glanced up from his menu at the stir. He nudged Al with his elbow and nodded in the direction.

As one man noticed the attention, he said, much too loudly for conversational purposes, Did y'all hear there's some Commies in town?"

"Is that right?" said another with raised brows.

"Yeah – they must not have seen the sign before they drove in –"he waved his hand to create the picture, "Laurel – the home of decent folk! NO COMMIES ALLOWED!" Amidst the laughter that followed, someone added more slowly, with intent, in a lower voice, "No nigga lovers allowed!" The challenge from the staring faces was unavoidable.

John stumped out his cigarette and breathed, "I don't think this is the right venue for a debate. Let's find a more peaceful establishment, shall we?"

He rose from the table and grabbed his coat. Although his jerky movement showed his handicap, his stance and the vigor with which he threw on his coat gave pause to the on-lookers. His set jaw and straight gaze caused the mockers to fidget and turn to each other for eye-support. Clarence and Al followed suit and the three imposing men headed towards the door of the café. Emboldened with backs turned and the sound of the clump of the wooden leg, one man became overcome with cleverness, saying with flair, "Don't worry, fellas! Looks like those Commies don't have a leg to stand on!" In the rowdy laughter that followed, Al gripped John's arm, seeing his inclination to turn back, and firmly whispered, "Hell, these are just punks – let's just get out!"

On the way back down the highway towards Jackson, the conversation turned to more realistic battles they would soon be fighting – in court.

"We won't be able to use the Florida witnesses unless we are granted the continuance," Al started. "And, if we don't have anyone to put on the stand, they may not even consider it."

"Maybe we could get a letter of intent to travel from them." John replied, "I'm also thinking we need somebody to get on that stand for the Motion for Change of Venue. Out of all those people we talked with, not one agreed to testify." He paused while Al agreed with, "Mmhuh." John paused, then snapped his finger, "What about Clarence's aunt? She said that she would testify to the fact that, 'He's guilty, and everyone knows that!'" Al smirked at the dramatic effect.

"I don't know," he mused, "she's in bad health. Could she make it through a court testimony?"

"If she could, she's a perfect example of the prejudice of the town," John persisted.

"Well, maybe you're right, but just the fact that they couldn't find an attorney before now to take the case says there was a reason to be afraid because of prejudice!"

"You're right, and there's also the fact that the change of venue of the second trial was to an adjoining city, which opposed the ruling of the Supreme Court order," John added. "This case needs to be tried a good enough distance away to where Collins can't get his teeth into it. He's going to want to bypass due process just like he did before. Otherwise, he would have to admit that he did, now wouldn't he?"

Al smiled, and added slyly, "So, you'll be ready to get on the stand Thursday and be cross-examined by Swartzfager again? John turned back in his seat and breathed deeply. Al continued with a challenge in his voice, "I've heard that there are men in Jones County that have backed Schwartsfager with money to get this conviction. He's not going to make it easy for you."

After a moment of reflection, John asked, "Who's going to be cheering for our team around here?" "Only voices in the shadows," Al replied with thoughtfulness.

"Voices in the shadows..." John echoed. "Hell, you're getting poetic about this, aren't you?" He laughed and lit a cigarette before continuing. "If that's what it takes, I guess I'll get on the stand again for those voices in the shadows. Schwartsfager's just a puffed-up dragon – I'll have to pop that ego of his." John held his lit cigarette forward to act out the scene and let out a "Pop! and "Wheee..." to imitate a balloon's reaction.

Al grimaced at his laughter,"Good luck with that!" He continued, pressingly, "So, you're ready for it, champ?"

"Sure, why not," John said with unconvincing confidence. Looking at Al's concerned expression, he continued boldly, "Hell, yeah, – I'm used to working with a handicap!" He straightened himself, took a final hit of his cigarette and finished with, "I'm not staying in the shadows!"

"No, you won't be," Al agreed, "you'll have the light shining right on you. We both will." Moments passed before John pulled his hat down over his face to snooze, while Al stared at the headlights beaming down the road.

CHAPTER FOURTEEN

T. J.'S CHOICE

Bessie burst into the familiar smell of the musty office building, pursing her lips in disgust, yet took to almost racing up the stairs, huffing and puffing so by midway that she did take a moment to gather herself and let out a "Lawda mercy!" She had been up these stairs many times before, but never with such haste and urgency. Quickly remembering her purpose, she regained her resolve and pushed past the fatigue to claim victory over the flights. At the top of the stairs she turned with heavy panting into the dimly lit hallway and pushed through the door that bore an etched brass plate that read, "Dr. T. J. Barnes." She stood inside the foyer of the waiting room just long enough to catch her breath.

"Why hello, Mrs. McGee, how can I help you?" As the bespeckled lady at the reception desk took in the picture of the agitation on Bessie's face, wet with sweat, she looked over her glasses and added, "Are you alright?" The two others in the waiting room glanced sideways with interest at her while holding their magazines still in reading position.

Bessie took a final deep breath and exhaled with, "I needs to see Dr. Barnes right way. I needs to talk with him rite now!" She glanced at the waiting room to check for any signs of emergency then added, "You tell him – <u>rite</u> now, please mam. "The fire in Bessie's eyes somehow conveyed to the receptionist more than her words did, and she found herself almost scrambling for the door to the office within to inform said Dr. Barnes of the urgent nature of the caller.

"Dr. Barnes," she hissed, "Missus McGee is here – needs to see you rite way she say!"

Dr. Barnes peered around the crack of the door and met Bessie's eyes, who were watching for his." Hell-fire," he muttered, involuntarily. He cleared his throat to cover the utterance and then motioned to his receptionist to show Bessie in. He began to slowly clean his glasses as he said with forced casualness, "Well, hello, Bessie, how…"

"You know how I is, donchu try to pretend you don't!" She retorted with a red face.

He finished cleaning his glasses while thinking, put them back on and struck a sober tone. "Now, Bessie, you must be reasonable."

Bessie's patience was spent. "Reasonable? Well, I'll be reasonable! I reason that you betrayed your own kind! You knowed Willie since he was a boy – cumin up here all these years, trustin' in you like a daddy! But that didn't matter none when you was in front of white men, now did it? Feeling all puffed up 'cause you got 'chosen!'" The pitch of her voice reached clear into the outer office, where no one was reading anymore. She gulped in a breath while he closed the door securely with his hand outstretched to her in a stop motion, saying, "Bessie, wait!"

She wasn't about to wait, and continued in a voice just as loud, "I didn't even want to look at those papers that day – didn't want to know who it was that betrayed my boy. Didn't even want to know! I thought it sure wouldn't be anybody who knows him, who cared fo' him, who loved him! How could it have been you?" Bessie was shaking all over with the pent-up anger now being released.

"Bessie, Bessie, "he said, now with equal emotion, "You don't understand – you don't know what it was like! I never wanted to do it, Lord!" He stopped, looked at the ground with force as he gulped back the shame. "If I would have had a choice, I never would've done it!" He looked at her again directly.

Bessie's anger involuntarily spilled over into tears, but she held on to her boisterous tone to release her pent-up grief. "That's just it – you did have a choice – It's my Willie that has no choice now. He might never have no choice ever again because of your choice!" At this declaration she could hold back no longer. The floodgates let down and Bessie begin to sob and shake uncontrollably. Her sorrow was punctuated with mournful wails that caused all who heard from the waiting room to join in empathetically, sighing deeply or sniffing and wiping their own eyes.

Dr. Barnes moved cautiously towards Bessie and offered her his embrace, which she allowed herself to sink into. He murmured continuously "I'm so, so sorry, Bessie. I'm so, so sorry."

At length, Bessie pulled a handkerchief out of her purse, blew and wiped her tears away, then gathered herself up with folded hands and managed to regain some of her former antagonism to demand, rather than ask in a lower, almost threatening voice, "You tell me how this thing happened."

Dr. Barnes pulled a seat for her, and although she meant to refuse it, she felt drained now and took the seat with some dignity. He closed the office door and leaned on the desk beside her to talk in a lower voice. "The attorney that is trying to put Willie down, Mister Pauly Schwartsfager," he paused and adjusted his glasses." Him and some other saucy lookin fellows, 'long with a police officer, came to get me and Claude Arrington and T. D. Brown. I guess they figured we were the ones to lose the most if we didn't comply." Bessie looked at the floor, hardly realizing she was nodding in understanding.

"Bessie, at, at first, I thought we were going to be able to make a difference." He looked up with the memory of how it felt when the men had come to his office, complimenting his work, tapping his framed degree, and saying how they saw him as an asset to the negro race. He decided not to include that part of the story and the pride he had felt at the time but went on. "They told me that it would be the first time negros would be included on a Grand Jury in Mississippi's history," and added with some flair, "and that I should be proud to be picked for such an honor." He looked at Bessie, who had raised eyes that still held some anger, and went on. " Bessie, I thought I had a chance to be part of a team that would help Willie. We thought we might be able to set him free."

He lifted himself up and started to walk across the room. "It was a historical chance for a black man to help another escape from the judgment of the almighty white! Claude, T. D. , and I were proud that day, yes sir!" He paused and dropped his voice to add as he shook his head, "We were fools, – fools! – to trust them." Bessie took a deep breath alongside his own sigh and waited for him to continue. He turned his back to her to look at his framed degree on the wall – shook his head at the past pride and said, "Assets to the negro race – we all became ass-es that day." He turned back to Bessie, wrinkled his nose and said with hot remembrance, "They dropped their 'respect' for us the minute we walked into that courtroom. Mister Swartsfager told us 'boys' to sit in the corner and wait until they told us to raise our hands – like some dumb schoolchildren. He swaggered up to that judge like he was something else, and said," He dropped and shook his head for a moment in shame, then gulped back and continued slowly, "He said to that black-robed man, 'Your Honor, I've found some niggahs who will work with us on this Indictment. ' Then they whispered amongst themselves, y'know, laughing n all. Claude and I started to whisper to each other, too, wondering what we had gotten ourselves into, when that white police officer cracked his stick down on Claude's hand, and shattered it." He paused a moment, with his eyes fixed on the shock of the memory before continuing. "I had to tend to it afterwards – it won't never be the same. " At this point in the story, Dr. Barnes was spent, and besides, he could not bring himself to relate how they were all jabbed and forced to raise their hands, even the bloody one, to sentence Willie to a third trial. He waved his hand and said simply, "Bessie, you knows the rest of the story." He started to pace and wave his hand. "White man threatens his niggahs – if dey breathe a word to <u>anybody</u> dey's dead. Period – dead. End of story."

Bessie found herself looking with compassion upon the slumped figure she had released all her hatred on earlier. She wasn't sure if it was because he lost his polished speech to bond again with those he felt he had now betrayed, or if it was simply because she had already known there had been no way out, and just needed to hear him say it. She raised herself up, clutching her purse and handkerchief to keep herself from reaching out to comfort him, and simply said in a broken voice, "Oh, T. J., what are we going to do? What are we ever going to do?" She turned and walked out, forgetting to voice her forgiveness, and defeatedly passed by the sympathetic eyes in the waiting room without acknowledgement as she headed towards her foggy descent of the stairway.

CHAPTER FIFTEEN

AN OMEN OF THE MOCKINGBIRD

That night and the next day John was running on pure mental energy. Gerry snuck in some of his favorite dishes in front of his stacked papers, but they were left with only a bite or two taken as he either was studying the law, composing documents, or talking out loud to a ghost courtroom. He first had to finish studying and preparing for the divorce trial, which he had lost interest in altogether. The pretrial hearings for McGee would begin on Thursday, and he had to reel in enough convincing evidence to again ask for a Motion for Continuance, a Motion to Quash the Indictment and a Motion for Change of Venue. He hoped that he could at least move the judge to grant the continuance. The Motion to Quash and the Motion for Change would be more for show upon any future appeal.

Tuesday was a bust, as the divorce trial took most all day, ending in a settlement that was not altogether what his client wanted. "It's hard to prove a jackass altogether innocent, especially when he brays too loudly!" he complained to Gerry at the end of the day. "It's no wonder she left him for higher ground." A lawyer's job of defending everyone, regardless of your personal feelings of a client, was not always easy or pleasant. Still, thanks to a narcissistic personality, the divorcee claimed victory anyway, and assured John he would pass on his name to his circle of friends for future business. However, having been given very little compensation due to the lack of assets awarded his client, future business from this sort did not sound appealing. Gerry had gently reminded him of the bills that were due and stacking up on the counter, not intending to put any last straw on his back. However, just after flipping through them he decided instead that it was important that he celebrate the miniscule victory with a shot of whiskey, which led to a second, as he was looking at all that was in front of him. He started feeling such relief and the re-emergence of the lightheartedness that had lately abandoned him that he decided to take another. Predictably, Bella Abzug chose this evening to call and check on progress. John didn't remember a lot about the conversation, except calling Deavours a "weasely son of a bitch," and similar descriptions of Schwartzfager and Judge Collins. He also remembered that she had said something, quite loudly, about how she would call Al, and he should get with him later. "Fine," he thought, hung up, and took another shot which sent him into a blissful and thoughtless sleep in his chair. Gerry sighed deeply as she emerged from putting Babay to sleep and took in the scene. She shook her head, stumped out the still smoking butt in the ashtray and lent her slumped husband her arm and shoulder as she helped him make his way groggily to the bedroom.

Wednesday looked as if it would fare better for him as his mind felt remarkably clear, other than a slight morning headache to pay, but he was keenly aware that it was the last day before the pretrial. Gerry and Babay went once again to her friend's home to stay throughout the length of it. They agreed to call each other at least once a day, in the evening, and embraced with meaning before looking into each other's eyes deeply. Gerry looked down when tears were forming in hers.

"Now, now, it will only be three days at the most," John spoke in a low voice as he brushed a copper curl off her forehead to kiss the fair skin underneath, and added, "I'll miss you, darling." Gerry wiped her eyes and looked up again to say, "I've just been tense lately, I'm all right, really. I'll be praying for your safety," she added. After another embrace and words of encouragement and love, John shut the car door, patted Baybay's capped head through the open window, saying, "I want you to be praying for me, too!" She cooed in response as they waved goodbye, and he watched them disappear before letting his mind turn back to the hurried demands of the day.

Once at the office, the motions were drawn up and dictated by midmorning to the building's secretary. John nearly snatched the last pages from the frazzled typist but paused again to compliment her good work and her pretty new blouse, leaving her smiling while adjusting her glasses. He and Al then gathered the documents into their cases and rushed out to the car to head for Laurel. During the trip Al filled him in on a call he had gotten from Bella last night. She had not been happy that her chosen attorney had been too drunk to talk with her and snipped that they should just focus on getting a new trial in a new venue, where she and other lawyers from the CRC would be happy to step in and take over for him.

"To tell you the truth, I wasn't entirely sober either when she called, but I think she was so agitated at you she didn't notice," Al said, letting out a chuckle. "I just reviewed her on what we planned to present in pretrial."

"Hell, I'd like to see them taking on this defense here without feeling the need to take a break," John returned with some annoyance, and lit a cigarette. He quickly changed the subject to the agenda for the day, not wanting to belabor the affront when energy was needed for more important things. "We need to investigate the actual jury list, to see what clues we may be able to get from that. If they just stuck some hand-picked Negros on there at the last minute, we should be able to tell." Al nodded and added, "You need to also check on the rules of order for selection, just in case you get some hare-brained story about how 'adjustments' were made." "Right," John scribbled on a list while adding, "I also need to meet with the psychologist that will brief me on McGee's evaluation – whenever I can get in. If we need to make any changes in the Motions after that, I suppose we can do it early Thursday morning."

"Then we'll need to rise with the chickadees– " Al said with smirk. "Court starts at 9:00, and Schwartzfager and Collins are going to make damn sure you don't have enough time to find out anything else that could thwart their plans."

"Bessie hasn't called with the addresses for the owners of the gambling house. Why do you think they took off, anyway? Do you think they may have been threatened when it was known they could help Willie in court?"

"By whom – Hawkins?"

"Hawkins or his cronies. I'll bet Deavours knows something about that. I wonder how much they had to pay for him to represent them – and why they thought they needed him with Swartzfager and Collins on their side already."

"With the CRC giving the case national attention, I guess they decided they needed all the help they could get."

The two talked off and on regarding strategies as they traversed the now familiar path towards Laurel. Neither felt terribly confident about these pretrial hearings, and the hope they did have faded as the day passed into the short afternoon hours they had left. As they were coming off the highway into the city of Laurel, however, a mocking-bird swooped just in front of their windshield.

"That was close!" John said, his hand involuntarily swept up, protectively. "A mock-ingbird," Al noted, "a symbol of cleverness – that's a good omen!" "Cleverness? Because it imitates other bird's songs, I suppose."

"I think so, but I've also heard it said that it listens well and then responds – not a bad lesson to remember during this time, wouldn't you say?" Al smiled at John as he pulled into a gas station.

"Hmm…. ," John chuckled and offered, "Well, I guess it's a better mascot than a nit-picking chickadee!"

However, nit-picking was what he did, when John reviewed a copy of the juror's list at the courthouse. Although the supervisor, again was not available for interview, the women of the staff had said curtly, they did obligingly give him a copy of the juror's list. He had read from the previous trials how the jurors were supposedly picked from random, and the slight number of Negros that were registered were the reason that none were picked. The reasons why a black man would be intimidated to not register were not brought to light. Whites even complained, saying that it really wouldn't be fair to let the Negros be included, since the percentage was so slight that even one negro on a jury would be more than would actually represent the whole population of jurors. That case had been overturned by the Supreme Court due to this negligence, citing the Patton case, and required the representation of Negros on a jury deciding the fate of a black man. It was just too suspect that three had been on the Grand Jury for the indictment, where a unanimous vote was not necessary, and none had been there before. Conveniently and suspiciously, none had been selected for the petite jury that would decide the actual fate of McGee. John suspected that the three had been planted, possibly from the white-sanctioned "League of Negro Citizens," who bowed before white rule to get the back page of the newspaper for their own stories. He found that the list itself wasindeed suspect. The pages of names from which the jury was selected was alphabetically arranged, until the last page, where a hand-drawn line separated another short list, not arranged alphabetically other than three names at the bottom, which were spread between the three columns from what seemed to be the "A's" and "B's" of another list altogether. After some investigation, John found that of the owners of these three names were the only negros included in the whole list and were the negros selected for the Grand Jury.

"These were hand-picked and added!" John pointed out to Al what he was referring to after making sure the door to the law library room was shut tightly. "Nothing random about the negros on this list, and besides that, they didn't take a whole lot of effort to cover up what they were doing!"

"So, they thought this would suffice – no one would question? "It's like a slap in the face to the rule of law," Al mused, studying the hand-drawn line and the list below.

"This is legal fraud," John continued, tapping on the paper, "and I am going to say as much in the Motion!"

"Have we found a typist that we can trust not to leak it?" Al asked, looking out the glass door at the clerks who seemed to be watching and gossiping.

"Oh, I forgot – Clarence gave me a name here," John dug in his pocket and produced a folded piece of paper, "Can you call her and see if she will take dictation and type a motion up this afternoon? Otherwise, we've got to trust these local geese. I've got that appointment with the psychiatrist, but I can meet you back here before long."

"Sure!" Al gathered the papers, John his case, and they walked out, energized with the discovery but conscious the clock was ticking. They smiled at the gathering of ladies behind the counter and handed them the documents, asking for copies. No eyes met theirs, as if disdain for their presence reigned, but consent was begrudgingly given.

The morning came all too quickly. The documents had been dictated over a hurried dinner in a corner booth of a restaurant. Clarence's girl came through and promised the Motion would be in court by the morning. She was young and idealistic, and found it adventurous to help in what seemed to be a risky endeavor for her.

"My boss would have a heart attack if he knew," she giggled, "but I have the keys to the office, and can type them up real quick-like tonight – he won't have a clue when he hears about the pretrial that they were actually drawn up in his own office! He wants to see an execution for McGee," she added grimly, as she downed the last of her sweet tea and stood up while looking around with a nervous glance. "I'll have it to you by morning," she whispered.

The Motion was delivered to the hotel room in a brown envelope early that morning. John and Al went over them to check for errors, if not to refresh their minds for the task that lay ahead of them. The most important argument, they felt, and what was sure to be the most controversial was the Motion to Quash the Indictment, which read in part, "...names of the members of the Negro Race have been intentionally and systematically excluded from the aforesaid lists of jurors and persons qualified for jury service...and that such exclusion amounts to and is a legal fraud."

Then, what seemed to be a shoo-in in any other jurisdiction was the Motion for Change of Venue. It was very clear that the local authorities had done whatsoever they pleased, ignoring the opinion of the Supreme Court for changing the venue of the case to a place "...in an atmosphere and with an opportunity that will permit, and will not paralyze such development (of the case)." The second trial had been in Hattiesburg, a city adjoining Jones County, where McGee had been arrested in the very beginning.

Local newspapers and radio stations had followed the case, and prejudice remained high there, as well. The troops that were assigned, by the court, to guard the courthouse during trial certainly had emphasized that fact. The original appeal had asked for a move "to a county other than one adjoining Jones County," but because of the wording of the Supreme Court, they took their liberties, and not only held the first part of the second trial in Hattiesburg, which was actually adjoining Jones County, they even moved the case back with no qualms to Laurel when the Judge in Hattiesburg had mysteriously fallen ill, and Collins had to take over. Now for the third trial they were once again back in Laurel – the hotseat of prejudice – and the motion claimed because of this, "the high feeling and indignation of the people of Jones County, all because of the nature of the crime and not because of the guilt or innocence of the accused, the defendant was immediately taken by officers for safekeeping to the jail at Jackson, Mississippi, commonly known as the 'Mob-Proof Jail.'"

The Motion for Continuance was the final plea – with the addition of the need to procure the witness of Mrs. O. A. McMullen, otherwise known as Clarence Holland's aunt, who had been subpoenaed for her insistence that:

"She was well known in the City of Laurel and had talked with a number of women and other people and that she thought, and that 'everyone agreed' with her, that Willie McGee should be killed and not allowed to stand trial for the crime of which he is accused, for the reason that she said, 'Willie McGee was guilty and that she knew he was guilty' by virtue of the fact that he has already been tried twice before and convicted both times; and the she was not the only one who felt as she did, but that 'everyone I have talked to also feels as I do'; and, further, that …'the lawyers defending Willie McGee should be shot for attempting to defend such a rascal!'"

…so the affidavit read, and the Motion claimed that she was indeed willing to say this on the stand, but hadn't been able to come to the court due to ill health. The other witnesses in Florida were not mentioned at this point, but Al and John both agreed it should be brought up in the argument, as well.

"Ready, champ?" Al asked, putting on his coat and looking at his watch, "We've got fifteen minutes to get there."

John had finished adjusting the strap of his wooden leg, pulled down the pants leg over it, and briefly lifted his head silently, his eyes closed – appealing to a higher authority, before saying, "Ready!"

CHAPTER SIXTEEN

THREE BLACK NAMES

As they approached the door to the courthouse, Al and John noted that the gathering of people for the pretrial was not significant. There were several men, but only one or two women. The balcony held a few Negros, mostly Willie's family. It was obvious at the intake of the situation that the stance of the white male was represented and invested in supporting the prosecution of thiscase.

Pretrial hearings are generally not of such interest to the public, and most of the population of Laurel was ready for the outcome, not the steps leading to it. Mr. Hawkins was there, and men surrounding him with squinted eyes were meant for intimidation.

Had they had a meeting beforehand? The several toothpicks twirled through teeth indicated a breakfast gathering. The looks, throat clearings, and side comments laid the carpet for the entrance of the defense into the courtroom proper.

John laid down his paperwork, adjusted his tie and looked around, waiting for the Judge to make his appearance. His eyes were drawn to the sun coming in the large plate glass windows, where you could see out onto the expansive lawn of the courthouse, and a statue of a soldier riding on his horse stood with his sword in hand. John had seen it before. It was Laurel's monumental tribute to Southern riders of the Civil War.

His attention turned to the creak of the back door of the courtroom that opened as Willie was ushered in by two officers, who seated him next to his attorneys and took off his handcuffs. John took a pack of cigarettes out of his coat pocket and placed them, with his lighter, near the ashtray provided for the defendant. Willie nodded, wide-eyed, and said, "Much obliged."

"All rise!" cried the bailiff.

The first motion presented was the Motion for Continuance. London presented this one, and with his best presence and diplomacy began, "Your Honor, comes now the defendant by his counsel and respectfully moves the Court to reconsider his motion for continuance filed on the 20th of February, and respectfully moves the Court to vacate its order overruling said motion for continuance, and we would like to show at this time why the aforesaid order should be vacated, and why our renewed motion for continuance should be granted."

Before an even natural pause after the request ensued, Judge Collins proclaimed dramatically, "Overruled!" Asking if any further evidence could be heard, defense was denied. John stood up asking for clarification, to which the judge briefly backed up his truncated response by saying that the Court..."cannot waste a lot of time hearing renewal motions. . . where there is no basis for them."

"We would like for the record to note an exception," was the only response that could be given. The murmur in the courtroom acknowledged the approval of the first punch delivered.

The next motion presented by the defense was to Quash the Indictment.

Although time was requested to subpoena witnesses, it was quickly denied and the Court drew upon the personnel available that could give some measure of expertise on the gathering of the jurors. The Court Clerk was sworn in and examined. It came to light as John examined him that the Clerk, in his experience of several years in the position, he had never seen a Negro put on either a grand jury or petit jury. When asked about the drawing for this case, he said that it had been a random drawing, as usual. How curious, then, that for the first time in history Negros had appeared – randomly – on this list, namely Arrington, Brown and Barnes. It was embarrassingly evident that there was no clear reason how this happened. Other witnesses were examined, and the leaning of the prosecution was that Negros hadn't appeared in court because they may have actually been subpoenaed, but not shown up for court. John sighed and thought of the fear of a Negro to state his opinion surrounded by whites. One break came through when John cross-examined a member of the Board of Supervisors, who effectively admitted to keeping Negros off the list. It seemed that the defense, despite handicaps, had delivered a responding blow to theprosecution.

Swartzfager drew himself up from the bench, angered, ready to squelch any prospect of progress to satiate the grumbling of his constituency. His cross-examination offered an out to the clerk.

"I think you misunderstood the question, and I want to ask you this. "He paused for emphasis and drew out his question as to make sure the supervisor got his meaning. "Have you ever consciously kept Negroes' names off the jury list during the tenure of office of twelve years as a member of the Board of Supervisors? "

John stood up to object. "I think we will object. We say he couldn't do it unconsciously." The court reporter stifled a laugh but cleared her throat and quickly regained composure.

Swartzfager frowned momentarily, then smirked and swaggered up to the witness box. "Well, now, you weren't unconscious, were you, during the time you were fixing up the list?"

"No, sir," the clerk returned, readjusting his glasses nervously. Laughter from the courtroom was not admonished by the judge.

"All right, then you were conscious when you did make the list?" More laughter went unchecked.

"Why, certainly."

The witness went on, with greater confidence, to proclaim that the drawing of the list, of course, had nothing to do with nationality or color, and the Judge made no effort to point out the obvious – that the clerk had to have been very conscious when the three Negro names were tacked onto the end of the list.

John recognized that the thin coat of deceptive veneer that was, consciously and intently, laid over the wall of prejudice in the courtroom had to be broken through, but how to approach it was difficult. Willie was silent for the most part, chain-smoking the cigarettes. The only comment he made to Al or John was during the changing of the witnesses to say, "Dr. Barnes – he wuz my doctor growin up."

"Is that a fact?" John remarked with sympathetic tone and looked up to the crowd overhead. "Know anyone here?" He asked quietly.

"Yeah, my boy's heah." Willie motioned with his head to a small boy standing next to his mother. "Fust time I seen him since he wuz a baby."

"Order!" the Judge quieted them as the next witness took his place. Willie, showing no emotion, lit another cigarette.

The arguing of the Motion to Quash, waiting for the calling of the witnesses, and a break for lunch took most of the day, when the Judge finally decided that there was not enough evidence to prove anything, and that the supervisor could make his list any way he wanted to. It was formally overruled, again with a strong exception by the defense for the record, and a recess was called until the morning to hear the final Motion. As Al and John stood up and gathered their paperwork, chatter in the background revealed the mood of the crowd, and they decided to wait until the coast was clear before leaving. As the guard came over to Willie to escort him out, John decided this was a good time to meet with Willie in a side room, giving them time to let the courtroom clear, for safety's sake, and to confer with him privately. Two policemen stood guard at the door.

"Willie," John started, looked at Al for support as he was searching for words, then continued, "The best we may be able to do is to put the burden of proof on the prosecution."

"What you mean?" Willie still showed no emotion. John looked at his eyes keenly to see any evidence of his being drugged, but found none, thanks to a guard he had selected. The local newspaper later reported that "This time around McGee looked much like any other Negro." "Correction" John had commented , "He looked like any other man, black or white on trial for his life, who hasn't been beaten or drugged beforehand!" Willie's lack of emotion was probably due more to a fearful detachment from reality, rather than a true testament of his angst, John thought.

He continued, "Willie, the definition for rape, as it is written in the law, has not been proven yet. By law, a woman has to show some signs of resistance to the sexual act for it to be considered rape." John looked at Willie's now bowed, shaking head, guessing his thoughts. "I know it will be risky to bring it up, but this may be our only chance to win a reversal. Of course, this is only one of the grounds that the Supreme Court could reverse a conviction again – we are going to argue that the venue should be changed, but they are trying their best to pretend that people don't care about this trial anymore, so it may be a wash, unless we can prove otherwise."

Al interjected, "Her argument during the last trial, if you can remember, was pretty weak when she described the rape."

"There was no rape," Willie said softly, but clearly.

"Right, well, the alleged rape, that is." Al shifted in his seat and continued, "She just said that she 'took' it so as not to wake the children." He looked to John to continue.

John searched for just the words she used, "If that is all he wants, well, I can take it," something like that. Willie looked up and let out a grunt in response.

"Willie," John looked at the reflection of the guards by the windows and lowered his voice to a whisper, "you do know that it's risky for us to bring this up – risky to us, your attorneys– do you realize this? If we actually argued that this was an affair, as you tell us it was, and that she wanted her husband killed? I'm afraid none of us would leave that courtroom alive." Willie looked up again into his attorney's eyes for a long moment before he turned his face to the side and said with conviction, "I'm not afraid to die." He gathered himself up and looked forward again. "I've made peace with my Lord bout what I did, 'n no man's law goin' to take that from me." He added more quietly, "I don't expect y'all to put your life on the line on account of me."

John's face softened and acknowledged the bravery of the statement with a solemn nod. "That's all a man really needs – that peace." There was a long moment of silence before he ended with, "We'll just keep going strong with what we've got and see what happens." They stood soberly, shook hands and exchanged partings before alerting the guards that Willie was ready for the escort back.

By now the courtroom had completely cleared, but John still lowered his voice as he said, "This is just the pretrial and the mood is already tense. How are they going to react when we're questioning Mrs. Hawkins?" He looked pointedly at Al. Al only shook his head in response, but said, "Let's order room service again, shall we? I'm not in the mood to experience the atmosphere in the local cafes."

"I'm with you, buddy," John said in a low tone. "My appetite, though, has gone out the window." He glanced towards the door at the back of the courtroom, where Willie had gone, as he lifted the heavy weight of his briefcase. Looking for any other option besides walking out through any lingering crowd outside, he motioned his head back towards the door. "What say we check out this exit?" Al nodded consent and they headed towards the door that led to the hallway between the court and the jail.

CHAPTER SEVENTEEN

CRAWLING ON THE CATWALK

The tainted walls containing the holding cells where prisoners awaiting court were kept smelled rank, with an overtone of cheap cleaning fluid. "Ugh!" Al exclaimed with a hand involuntarily reaching to cover his nose.

"Smells like death warmed over in here," John said in agreement adding, "What do they use to clean these places?" He peered into one of the small square cells, pushing open the heavy, creaking door with its barred window. As he looked around, taking in the stained concrete floor, adorned only with an old wooden chair and center drain to hose down refuse, John's hair prickled on his neck. He could almost hear the moans and see the condemned faces streamed with tears.

"It's inhumane," Al voiced what they both were thinking. "Wonder how many waiting here were black?" he asked rhetorically, as he shook his head. John's attention, however, was turned elsewhere and he started walking down the hall with paced steps, as if following the thoughts of escape that had before echoed in these rooms. Al turned and followed, watching his partner curiously. John stopped just before the window that streamed in the only rays of light to the dismal hallway that connected to the jailhouse just beyond. It was not as high as he had hoped, but he set his briefcase down anyway, and dropped on all fours. "What are you …?" Al started, but then saw John's head turn to see if he could now be spotted from the window's advantage into the elusive route. With only slight hesitation did Al follow the hand wave from John. Dragging his briefcase behind and thinking of the scum on his suit, Al began to grumble, but a "Shh!" from John kept him from further voicing his dissent.

When they were on the other side of the window, which seemed overly wide and too tall for its purpose, John rose up, dusted his knees and whispered, "They are down there watching!" Al sputtered as he rose up and dusted himself off, saying, "Damn sons of bitches! They were waiting for us!" John shushed him again, saying, "Keep it quiet – we don't know what they can hear."

"Well, I don't know that we really need to go to this extent…" Al started again, pushing up his glasses that had slid down his nose.

John cut him off as he helped him with his case and said quietly, "Yes, but we may need this, and I don't want them to suspect we are using it now." They walked more swiftly towards the open door to the hallway of the jail. "Good morning, how do you do," John said with staged warmth to the officer at the desk, who was deeply into his read of the newspaper headlines. Seeing only suited men before him – no cause for alarm – he turned back to the news with a quick, "How do?"

Again, John gave his warmest smile as he asked from behind the spread paper, "Could you kindly tell us which way is the closest exit from here?"

The officer drew his paper down slightly, with some irritation from the interruption, just enough to say and point, "Down the hall, past the men's room to the left – it'll lead you to the stairs." He went quickly back to the interesting read of the Willie McGee case starting up again.

"Thank you so very much," John said graciously. He chuckled under his breath as Al said quietly, "Well done!" and they made their exit out the back door of the jailhouse without further notice. The alleyway fortunately led them onto a side street that they recognized as being a short walk to their hotel.

"We'll have to park the car here from now on." Al noted, seeing his partner's strange jump with his steps.

"It's my stump sock," John explained, "It slipped down when we were crawling."
"Did it hurt to crawl?" Al asked.

"John steeled his gaze forward as he said, "Naw, Not much," not wanting his partner to know how his now sore knee was rubbing against the wooden frame, which he thought may have splintered, as he felt a touch of warm liquid on the stump of his leg.

On the other end of Laurel, Bessie had not yet even taken off her coat, but was rocking a chair on her porch, nervously. The pretrial so far had left her feeling a renewed anger at everyone. Besides that, the attorneys had told her that they would need her to testify tomorrow about the witnesses who ran off to Florida, and she was having a hard time keeping her shaking under control.

Rosalee had decided to visit with her after court "To give her some company," she had said.

"Hmph!" Bessie had thought, "I'd rather be alone, and she's just lookin' to stake her claim that's rightfully my Eliza's." Bessie's heart was feeling all fluttery and confused and this wasn't the day she wanted to give any time towards sorting out those feelings. She yearned to just give herself over to prayer for her Willie.

Each time she thought of him in previous trials sitting in that chair, being questioned and looking the fool, her heart jumped into her throat again, and she would sigh and moan, "Oh my sweet boy, what did they do to you? How's you ever gawn come back home again?" She couldn't focus though, with Rosalee messing around in her kitchen and her boy clamoring for her attention. She had thought that she might escape the crowded feeling with some fresh air. The porch rocking chair had been her consolation for many a day these past years. She took a long breath of the fresh February air, which today had brought in a comforting warmer sun that seemed to kiss her cheeks and hint that Spring was just around the corner. She settled into a rare moment of peace that didn't last long enough, as she heard a call from the inside, "More iced tea for you, Mama?"

Bessie cringed slightly at the address reserved for her beloved daughter-in-law who was now so far away. She yearned to call her but wouldn't while Rosalee was present. Her face involuntarily loosened, however, when the young boy with bright eyes ran out from behind the screen door to her to hand her the tall glass.

"Careful now, son!" came the admonishment from behind. He slowed somewhat and smiled expectantly towards Bessie.

"Mawmaw?" he said, as if questioning again his newfound possession "does you want sum tea?" Bessie couldn't help but smile as she took the glass. She hadn't fully noticed before that he looked so much like Willie when he was young. She couldn't deny any longer that he was her grandson. Familiar tears began to fill her eyes, and to his surprise she pulled him close to her and hugged him to ease her pain.

"Thank you, my dear," she whispered as she kissed him lightly on the forehead. Rosalee looked at the two from the doorway for a long moment with her own glass in her hands. It was the first time Bessie had shown affection since they had been there. It was as if she didn't want to accept any more family into her broken heart. Rosalee knew that Bessie had loved Eliza and her four grandchildren, all Willie's, and she was set in her heart to keep her place assecond – saying within herself that it didn't matter anyway. Didn't she have her own family that cared for her and her children? She had left the others with them. She was here now for Willie, she told herself, and tried to move past any resentment for his sake.

"Awfully warm for a February day," she remarked.

"Mmm-hmn," Bessie managed, as she sipped tea and watched the boy run to the yard, exploring the sticks for one that resembled a gun.

"Sho' feels good, though," she went on. "It does get warmer here sooner than where we from, it seems." Bessie was not open for small talk. She fixed her eyes on the young boy lunging into an attack on an imaginary enemy as he shot with the 'rifle' he had fashioned by breaking a long stick at just the right place.

Rosalee plopped herself into a chair across the porch from Bessie, crossed her long legs and commented to the air, "Willie hasn't met him yet."

Bessie took a long drink of her tea and stared again. Feeling surprisingly refreshed after it, she let herself look at Rosalee long enough to say, "He should have – long ago." Rosalee stared at Bessie, feeling defensive and fighting tears in her own eyes, retorted, "And you wanted me to break up his family for it?" Bessie broke the gaze, staring out again to the yard. Rosalee went own, "I had my own man takin' care of us – Willie couldn't have – he would've tried, but he could hardly care for his own. I knew that." She looked out to the yard herself to say, "Sides, we was so far way, it was better for little Willie to think my man was his Pappy." She crossed her arms to admit, "'Cept, he gone and left us. Probably better if he'd left from the start."

Bessie sighed deeply, and decided the resistance was too hard to maintain. After all, this was all she had of her son's family with her, and this story was all too familiar.

Bessie watched Rosalee flicked the tears that spilled as if she was mad at them, and caught herself smiling at the pretty woman, remembering Willie's words describing her while he was behind bars. Rosalee looked up hopefully at the sign of an opening with Bessie, having momentarily forgotten the reason not to care.

"If they convicts Willie again this time," Bessie said slowly, looking her in the eyes. "If they convicts him again," she repeated deliberately and slowly, "I will say you is my daughter-in-law." She turned her face away from the intensity of Rosalee's expectant eyes to the yard and continued, "An this is my grandbaby – an'all you's." She added the last with a wave of her hand. "Maybe it will soften even that ol' cranky judge's heart!" They both suddenly laughed, and joined with each other in a short, but relieving laugh. "Surely he has chillun," Bessie choked on this, her laughter turning into a gulp and sigh. Rosalee nearly jumped out of her chair to embrace Bessie as the tears began to once again flow from them both.

"I know he does, Mama. You know he does." Rosalee declared as she caressed the bowed head in her grasp. Little Willie's attention had been drawn back to the porch, seeing his mother in a loving hold that seemed most special for them both. He looked down, kicked a rock, then went back to his shooting stance with more vigor. "Bam, bam! Yous dead!" he pronounced, standing tall.

CHAPTER EIGHTEEN

DIZZYING OBJECTIONS

The defense had been able only to summon six witnesses to support their Motion for Change of Venue, which was taken up next in the pretrial hearings.

Two of these were the witnesses in Florida, who were still absent and it was uncertain that they had actually received their summons at this point. One other who was absent was the cantankerous Mrs. McMullan, who would boldly speak her mind regardless of public opinion if her doctor would have allowed it. She was forbidden to participate in these hearings or in any other part of the trial due to the stress it would cause her failing heart. John and Clarence had both submitted affidavits regarding their investigations that would testify to not only her view, but many others, as well. It looked as though they would have to take the stand, once again, in lieu of any other tangible support for McGee.

The witnesses for the prosecution would have put many to sleep had it been a warmer day, as it seemed they had been prepared for the questioning with rote answers, saying basically there was not really anything to get up about regarding this case and most people just weren't that interested anymore.

Regardless of defense prodding, none would admit to any underlying anger or prejudice. Only one, a Mr. Gibbons, the editor of the Laurel Leader newspaper that had displayed many heated articles regarding the first two trials, when questioned about approving the content of his paper, had commented;

"My Lord! Sometimes I don't see the paper until I get home that night. We just have a crew of people we depend on."

"They work under your supervision?" Al asked.

"Well, they get their money from me every Saturday," he replied cockily with a laugh, but denied any personal influence of the inflammatory articles. Later in the questioning, he gave in a bit to say, "Well – people think justice ought to be done, but I haven't heard anybody blowing their top on account of it." Gibbon's seemed to be enjoying himself.

In further cross-examination, Gibbons' answer to the question, "Have you formed any opinion as a result of your knowledge and information and material contained in your newspaper as to the guilt or innocence of Willie McGee?" was, "I think he is guilty." His opinion was based on reports that two trials had found him guilty and that he had made a confession to the crime, but he claimed to not be aware of any general opinion of the case.

Defense then produced for evidence the "Leader" front page headline saying, "Jones County Makes History," showing a picture of the three black jurors who served on the Grand Jury. Swartzfager hurriedly demanded it be withdrawn, saying that it said nothing about the Willie McGee case in particular and "had nothing to do with this case." Gibbons lost a bit of his composure and was peering forward as if it would help him examine the article as well. Defense protested as McGee's name was clearly mentioned early on in the article, but Collins followed the lead of Swartzfager who demanded the picture be cut out, and only the name listed below in the article be presented. While waiting for the conclusion of his cross-examination, Gibbons shifted in his seat, wiped the sweat that was forming around his mouth and appeared flushed. Swartsfager left the quibbling with the article and came back to the stand, resting his arms on the witness seat.

Q. "Mr. Gibbons, of course you said it has been the policy of yourself and others there to suppress excitement and indignation of the people?"

A. "Well, not suppress, but handle it in a conservative way," Gibbons tried to regain calm.

Q. "Truth of the matter, the name of the victim was never used by your paper, isn't that true?" Swartzfager looked at him pointedly.
Gibbons paused – He couldn't remember this actually, even though it had nothing to do with the excitement and indignation of the fact that there had been a rape of any white woman by a negro. He figured it was a distraction that would help him out.

A. "I don't think so." He said more softly.

Swartsfager faced the audience, having effectively slid a smokescreen over the truth, and went on to paint the picture of Gibbon's opinion being based solely on information he was privy to, being a newsman and nothing he actually put in his paper that would rile the public. Gibbons was dismissed after another futile attempt of the defense team to ferret the truth from him.

Al exchanged an angered glance with his partner before standing up and saying, "I would like to let the record show that the defense counsel objects to the modification of the Court's ruling as pertains to Exhibit "D" to Mr. Gibbon's testimony."

"What modification was that, Mr. London? Judge Collins looked down his nose as if he didn't quite recall.

Al stated clearly and directly, "That was your Honor's cutting out the picture and allowing the introduction of only the column as indicated."

Judge Collins looked down at his papers as if disinterested and replied, "All right, you may take exception to the ruling."

It was incredible, John thought, that they would try to say that the two trials before had not stirred the people of the town. Everyone knew that the State Militia had been called in to protect the defendant and quell any riots, which, by matter of fact, the Laurel Leader and Gibbons had at the time liberally reported on. He hoped to get his chance to bring this out with the next witness, a sheriff named Luther Hill, whom he had subpoenaed. After opening questions, John asked:

Q. "I will ask you, Mr. Hill, whether you undertook any action in your official capacity as sheriff to prevent any mob violence?
A. "I did."
Q. "State to the Court what you did?
A. "Well, I applied for assistance to the Governor."

A letter to the Governor was presented for evidence, but the prosecution promptly cut off because it was a copy, not the original, even though the witness attested to its authenticity. The objection was sustained, and again there was another exception by the defense. The opportunity to get it into the record by reading it came when the witness couldn't remember exactly how he had worded it. It was read in its entirety, in part which said, "I believe that we should have a force of at least twenty-five guards or highway patrolmen when he (McGee)is brought back next week. I think they will be needed for only about one day, as I feel sure the case will be transferred to some other County for trial...."

"To which we object," Swartzfager quickly said. "Objection sustained," the Judge replied "Note our exception," Al responded, which was a litany by now all too familiar, and continued throughout the questioning of Mr. Hill, including: "Do people here as a common rule request that the State Militia be sent down for a trial," and "Have you ever requested the State Militia at any other time during your tenure of office as Sheriff?" All were objected to by the Prosecution and sustained by the Court, rendering ineffective any interjection of the reasonable proving of the need for protection from vigilante justice.

After so many officials denying in total the prejudice of the town, John and Al were stunned that the establishment standing behind the prosecution was so unmoving. Notes scratched back and forth between them acknowledged the parallel reality they found themselves in. A final witness, called by the State to again testify to the fact that there was nothing standing in the way of McGee getting a fair trial in Laurel, was the mayor of the town, Carol Gartin. The last note read: "At least the mayor should have scruples!" John's patience had run out, and his blood began to boil after all these men had taken their turn to make a mockery of the truth. Sighs had come often from the crowd in the balcony, and he could see that McGee's hope had given way to stoicism.

John's fighter instinct kicked in, but he attempted to contain himself as he once again adjusted his tie and rose to begin his cross-examination.

Q. "You are mayor of the City?" He queried with as much Southern genteel he could muster.

A." Yes, sir."

Q. "I approach you, Mr. Gartin, with the full belief that you are one of the up-standing citizens of Laurel," he paused and breathed deeply, "one of the most upstanding citizens, and that you want to tell the truth about this thing?" He looked into the steeled eyes of the politician, where he found suspicion and warning.

A. "I hope I am, yes, sir."

Q. "Mr. Gartin, there has been a great deal of publicity about this case, hasn't there?"

A. "Well, in what respect?" John's anger rose at the ploy to divert even the simplest question.

Q. "Well, in the newspapers and over the radio? Don't you think that everybody in Jones County knows Willie McGee?"

A. "Knows Willie McGee?"

Q. "Knows of him?" John found himself huffing at another ploy to divert.

A. "I think they most know of him, yes, sir."

Throughout the questioning Gartin coolly related his opinion that the case was not known any more than any other case in Circuit Court. He had just heard a general discussion of it, and, No, he couldn't recall whether anyone had said whether they thought McGee was guilty or innocent. Finally, with impatience, John asked the previously objected question.

Q "Do you think there is any difference in a Negro being tried for the rape of a White woman and a White man being tried for the rape of a White woman?" By this time there was fire in his eyes, challenging Gartin to state the truth. It was a question that pointed to the bottom line. Everyone knew the cases would be vastly different, as a quick look at Laurel history would prove, but no one would admit to this. The objection came, as expected, but this time Judge Collins sustained it with an admonishment to counsel to quit asking the question.

Realizing contempt of court could be claimed against him, John stopped himself, but a sudden dizziness of built up anger and anxiety, caused him to say, "We beg forgiveness of the Court," adding, "it is just in our nervousness and excitement that we are not properly able to follow the Court's rulings."

John wasn't sure whether the Judge's answer following was sincerely caring, or if it was just another cover, causing the discrepancies to be maddening.

"Now, Mr. Poole, there is nothing here to make you nervous that I can see. If you are sick, the Court will take a recess until you get to feeling better. The Court hasn't seen anything to make you nervous, and I don't want you to feel nervous in this court. You are free to ask any question that is competent under the law, but when the Court sustains...." John tried to focus on what the Judge was saying, but his temples were throbbing, and it seemed that the admonishing judge was far away. "...or persisting in asking particular questions."

"I wish the Court would clarify that particular ruling." John felt his blood pressure normalizing somewhat as he spoke.

"In what respect, Mr. Poole?"

"In regard to what question you were saying we could not ask."

Swartzfager jumped to his feet, as if ready to get the Judge back on his team, "If the Court please, let's see what the question…"

"Sit down, Mr. Swartzfager," came a swift injunction to not let the Prosecution take over entirely. Collins then himself read the record of the forbidden question, which he determined an improper inquiry and not germane to the issue in this case, or its prejudgment against Willie McGee that he cannot get a fair and impartial trial in Jones County.

John's dizziness had subsided. The question was related to prejudgment, and the weight of the scale of justice was, in fact, fully unbalanced with regards to race.

"Note our exception," he replied, and turned back to the eyes of the Mayor which had widened with curiosity.

Q. "Mr. Gartin, you do know that there was some excitement during the first trial of this case, don't you?"

A. "No, sir, I do not," he lied.

Q. "You do know that the State Militia was here?" The mayor would have had to be a part of the approval of such a thing.

A. "No, sir, I don't know that of my own knowledge because I was not in the court room." His eyes steeled again to avoid the truth, hiding behind semantics.

Q. "Because you weren't in the court room?" John was incredulous at the avoidance.

A. "No, sir, I was not, and I just don't know that of my own knowledge." It was a legal way to avoid 'knowing' something if you just heard of it, rather than being there and of your 'own knowledge' seeing something. John felt certain, however, that the mayor had seen – and of his own knowledge – knew of the State Militia's presence – even if it was out of his office window. He was not the kind of man who would not be curious enough to be fully aware of the affairs of his town.

John's eyes relayed disdain as he paused and said, "That is all, Mr. Gartin," and turned with a determined clump, step, clump, back to the attorney's table.

The courtroom was markedly silent, and the eyes of all solemnly watched.

"The Court will recess for a twenty-minute break." The Judge's gavel went down and chatter began again as the population stood, stretched and began to mill around. John and Al took a breather and walked towards the top floor men's room, reserved for staff.

"Thought you were going to pass out there for a minute, buddy!" Al whispered to John in the hallway.

"You and me both! My blood pressure must have risen through the roof. I can't let this facade get to me. I'm either going to start throwing punches or burst." John said, still feeling rattled.

"If we started saying what we were really thinking, we most likely would see punches flying outside the courtroom. You've just got to breathe it out."

After sitting with a cup of coffee, both felt a bit revived. "What do you think about heading home tonight?" Al asked. "I'd rather rest at home than face that dingy hotel room for another night."

"You just don't like the smell of my stump sock, admit it." John said dryly with a hint of a grin.

"Well, now that you mention it – No!" Al wrinkled his nose in feigned disgust. After a quick laugh, he looked at his watch and said more seriously – It's time to be back in the ring!" He patted John on the back encouragingly as he downed the last of the cup and they headed back to the courtroom. The levity dropped as they talked about the next witness that they would call, the ex-sheriff, Mr. Luther Hill, to prove there had been a need for protection.

Mr. Hill, who had just recently retired from the Sheriff's position, admitted to applying for assistance to the Governor to prevent mob violence at the previous trial. His letter to the governor could not be admitted because it was a copy but had been in the record previously. The judge claimed it to be hearsay. Hill claimed he was unable to remember, then John read verbatim:

"Dear Governor: The case of Willie McGee, the negro charged with raping a white woman here last November 1945, will come up again the first week of October…I am sure that you will recall furnishing State Guards at his trial last December. I believe that we should have a force of at least twenty-five Guards or Highway Patrolmen when he is brought back next week. I think they will be needed for only about one day, as I feel sure the case will be transferred to some other County for trial. Thanking you for past favors and trusting you will give this matter your usual prompt attention, I am, Yours very truly, Luther Hill, Sheriff."

Schwartzfager stood, pencil in air, to say, "To which we object."

Collins replied, "Objection sustained."

London turned towards the court reporter with drawn mouth, "Note our exception."

This litany continued as Hill was questioned as why the troops were needed.

"Did you at that time think that public opinion was such that he couldn't get a fair trial here?"

"We object to that." "Objection sustained." "Note an exception."

To the questions, "Do people here as a common rule request that the State Militia be sent down for a trial?" and "Have you ever requested the State Militia at any other time during your tenure of office as Sheriff?" The refrain sounded, "We object to that." "Objection sustained." "Note an exception."

The witness was rendered ineffectual, and mob violence was effectively swept under the rug of the Laurel courtroom.

The Defense put Clarence and John on the stand once again to be questioned regarding their affidavits of investigations of the mood in Laurel amongst the people as to the trial. Both gave testimony witnessing to the fact that their investigations found many, both white and black, who felt McGee could not get a fair trial, and that the general opinion was that Laurel's mind was made up – Willie McGee was guilty as charged. John testified that "…some opinions were expressed that the lawyers should be killed, and that Willie should be killed before the trial and not even allowed to come to trial." No person, however, was willing to even give their names, as one man said, and Clarence quoted, "Just don't mention my name, because I have to live here."

Much less would these witnesses want to appear on the stand to testify, which made the affidavits of little threat to the State. The Prosecution had likewise filed a statement of facts, wherein they denied that Willie couldn't get a fair and impartial trial. With proving this as his goal, Swartzfager questioned John on the stand saying,

Q. "Now, of course, you know that I have lived in Laurel a number of years, don't you?"

A. "I am sorry, I don't – I haven't known that you even lived in Laurel until just now."

Q. "Is that right? Well, I have lived in Laurel here for better than thirteen years, and Mr. Collins has lived in the Second District of Jones County here all his life." He cocked his head to one side." Now who would be in better position, that is, to know the feelings of the people here," waving his hand from John to the defense table, "you and Mr. Holland here who have only been down in Laurelless than a week, or Mr. Collins and myself who have been down here for years?" He turned and smiled at the approving nods from the courtroom floor.

The arrogance angered John into a quick response. "I think I would be in better position to judge, for this reason," Swartzfager turned back, frowning at the response. John continued, "You have probably made no conscientious effort to find out the sentiment of the people. Most of the witnesses introduced said that they had made no conscientious effort to find out the sentiment of the people, and I have. That is why I think I would be in just as good or better position than you." Besides the fact that you're trying to cover it up what you know to be true, he thought.

"Mr. Poole," Swartzfager said in a condescending tone, Don't you know as a matter of law, that a man's general reputation in the community in which he resides is considered good unless you hear something to the contrary? That is a principle of law, a basic law that we all learn, isn't that true?"

John shifted in his seat. "Is this your question?" He asked, trying to anticipate the next move, "That a man has a good character unless somebody hears something to the contrary?"

He responded matter-of-factly, "Yes, that the general reputation of a man in the community where he resides is considered to be good, as a matter of law, unless you hear something to the contrary? You know that as a matter of basic law, don't you? That that is the test of a man's good reputation?"

"No, I may be somewhat chagrined," John replied, "I don't know that as a principle of law."

Shwartzfager continued undeterred. "Well, if it is a principle of law, wouldn't it appear in this case here, that if nothing is said to the contrary," He waved his hand in dismissal, "that is, nothing said about any ill feeling, any hatred or any grudge toward the defendant, Willie McGee, or about any prejudgment, that that would apply here just as well?"

John paused, frowning, "In other words, you are asking me just a hypothetical question?"

"A hypothetical question, yes, sir."

John sat back, "I will object to answering that."

Judge Collins, who appeared to enjoy the drama, interjected, "Well you are on the witness stand, you will have to answer."

The grilling continued with the Judge intermittently overruling the defenses objections. The defense team shared incredulous glances with one another as Swartzfager went on to try and prove that no one was giving Willie a bad name and that most people would consider him innocent until proven guilty. Although John had heard that members of the Mississippi Bureau of Investigation would be present and armed at this pretrial, he could not determine who they were if they were in the courtroom as he scanned the audience during the questioning. Swartzfager chided John as to why he had nothing, such as a list of names, to back up his investigation. John repeated that no one was willing to give their names and stated, that the impression was given that if they were to take part in the trial that they thought they may be forced to leave the State.

Regardless of John and Clarence's testimonies, the Court remained unmoved.

London finally said, "In view of the fact that we haven't been able to get these other witnesses, the ones we consider very important, but haven't been able to get, we are forced to rest at this time.

The Judge then looked over his glasses and asked, "Do you gentlemen want to argue this?"

The prosecution declined. John looked at his watch – six-thirty. If they argued, it would take at least another couple of hours. He rose again with noticeable effort and said, "I realize the Court isn't here on Saturday, and I would like to argue the case, but I am so exhausted now, I don't feel like I can argue it now. If you would allow us to argue it tomorrow morning, we would like to do that, or either Monday morning."

"Well, gentlemen," Collins looked down at his paperwork, glanced at the clock and sighed. "The Court is exhausted, too. I have been holding court now for three months, almost every day, but I will hear you now if you want to be heard. If this Court keeps setting these motions over in this case, and then gives the same amount of time to other cases as it has this case, why the court would never get through, and it won't only be exhausted, it will be dead."

The courtroom's audience had become sparse, as the door had ushered many out into the darkened evening who were saving their energies for the main trial. It seemed that everyone had grown tired of the drawn-out proceedings that held no game-changers. The stale, smoky air gave no refreshment to the atmosphere of discouragement, and John felt that his mental and physical energies had waned. He found himself saying, "I'm so exhausted, I don't feel like I can…" but before he could finish, Judge Collins took advantage of the situation by interjecting, "However, gentlemen, I don't see any use for argument, in view of the testimony here." With what seemed to be a final boost of energy he concluded the day's efforts with:

"The Court finds that the evidence conclusively shows here that the defendant can get a fair and impartial trial in Jones County; that the evidence before this court on this motion is wholly lacking of any credible testimony to the effect that the defendant cannot get a fair and impartial trial in Jones County. For that reason the motion is overruled." The gavel came down to punctuate the ruling as John turned to the reporter wearily and said, "Note our exception."

The Judge said casually, "Now when do you want to set the case for trial, gentlemen?"

John pled for the record that more time was needed to get the witnesses from Florida and to prepare the motions for the case. Without acknowledgment, the Judge turned to the prosecution and asked, "When do you want to set the case, Mr. Swartzfager?" "Set it for Monday morning," he returned sharply.

John interjected, "We want to move the Court for a special venire. We have that motion."

The Judge returned, with no change of expression, "That will be sustained." He didn't want the record to show any lack of compliance on the matter of choosing a jury. There were other ways to deal with the selection. The Prosecution was noticeably silent.

London stood to say, "May I ask the ruling of the Court on Mr. Poole's request for additional time?"

"Yessir – it is overruled," Collins said tersely, stacking his papers loudly, as if to add exclamation.

As the audience was shuffling out, the court reporter noted to the Judge that the date they had set wouldn't actually work with his calendar. Reluctantly, he rescheduled for Wednesday morning.

"Looks like you have had a visit from Lady Luck!" Collins addressed John. "Ample time to get your witnesses!" He smiled largely.

John thought for a moment about arguing the fact that 'ample time' was a gross exaggeration but was somewhat relieved that he would at least have a couple of days to do more investigation and preparation. "We will do our best," was all he said in response.

As they packed up their things in silence, John mused over the fact that they would have had, by the time of the trial, barely two weeks total to investigate and prepare for this significantly prejudiced and one-sided trial that held McGee's life in the balance. He attempted to muster some hope as he looked at Al and Clarence, but they both wore grim faces as well. He said softly, "We've got to get those witnesses, or it's over." Al nodded and followed, as they walked through the doors of the courtroom, leaving behind the jocular talk of the prosecution.

The Judge remained on the bench while the special venire of 200 men was drawn from the jury boxes from which to choose the group to stand in judgment of McGee's fate. Unfortunately, any black man who had attempted to register to vote had been overly taxed or frightened away. Although a few brave souls had still managed to register, only one was drawn, who would later "decline due to illness."

When they reached the hotel room with a bag of sandwiches, John plopped on the bed and wrestled with the straps of his wooden leg, throwing it off as soon as it broke free in order to extend himself on the bed and relax. Al looked at him and stated the obvious.

"Guess we really ought to take a rest before going back to Jackson. Or we could just drive back tomorrow morning."

John had already sunk into a semi-sleep, being truly exhausted, and answered with a grunt.

"Sounds like a good idea to me, too," Al answered himself and loosened his tie, setting aside the sandwich bag.

When the phone rang, the clock beamed the time of 8:30, and roused the two out of a mercifully deep sleep. John leaned over the bed to turn on the lamp, rubbed his eyes and grabbed the receiver. "Hello?" he said, groggily.

Al looked with concern as John sat straight up to say, "When?" After a long and focused pause, he followed with, "Take the baby and get to your mother's house right now! I'll be there by 10:00."

John was struggling to put on his leg while finishing up with, "I love you, too. We will be safe. Hurry up now!"

Al propped himself up and reached for his glasses, prepared to ask as soon as he hung up, "What happened with Gerry?"

A few curse words were forcefully uttered before John was able to tell what Gerry had related to him. She had just settled down to sing her evening lullaby and rock the baby to sleep in the warmth of the living room. Just as she was checking to see if the tiny eyes were fully shut, a rock came crashing in through the window. She screamed, jumped up, and ran to the back room in fright, trying to hush the infant's cries. She had called for the police to the operator with a frantic, hushed voice. Tears streamed down her face as she waited, in fear, behind a closet door. The police had come quickly and made sure she or the baby were not harmed, before searching the premises. They had only glanced at the rock that Gerry then felt brave enough to examine, noticing a note was tied to it with a string. She felt the hair rise in a chill on her neck as she read, "Tell your niggerlovin husband to quit now, or we'll be back with more than a rock." Something had made her wad the note into the pocket of her housecoat and hold back the information from the police, who were telling her to just find a way to board up the window, assuming a childish prank. John was the only person she trusted right now.

Focusing on the road, illuminated only by the car headlights, John vacillated between rage and determination. Al articulated all the things he felt his partner thinking, to help to keep him from doing anything rash. He ended with, "You'll want to leave any correction to the police. If the threats are anything more than foolish attempts to stop the defense from going forward, I would be surprised. I don't see that anyone is going to actually commit a major crime that would show without doubt to the nation that Mississippi is, in fact, very prejudiced about this case." Al looked at John, who was still very focused on the road. He continued, "You have no time to try and discover who did this, yourself, and still defend McGee."

"There are a few policemen I might trust," John finally replied. "I'm going to get Baxter on this. He's not going to bow down to the Klan."

"Right," Al nodded. Baxter would be my choice, too. He could choose deputies to help."

John accelerated around a bend and the two, now wide-eyed, fell silent in thought.

CHAPTER NINETEEN

SECRET MEETINGS

After a frenzied night of calling Baxter to examine the premises, boarding the window shut to keep winter's frigid breath at bay, and relating the day's events to each other, John and Gerry finally fell asleep in a sheltering embrace. Neither wanted to acknowledge the threat for now, in the stronger comfort of one another's arms.

Gerry rose early in the morning and slipped out to fix breakfast. Roused by the smell of the bacon, and soft fussing noises from Baybay, whose crib had been pulled into their room for safety, John sat up and ran his hand through his hair. He was thankful to have the time to be with his family again. Concerns of the night diminished in the rays of the late morning sun that streamed through the bedroom window. He swaddled Baybay in her blanket and said, "Let's see what Mommy's cooking."

After a kiss to "Mommy's" neck, and a sampling of the bacon, he took the warmed bottle from the pan and settled at the table to quiet Babay's hungry cries.

"I'm glad you're here so I can fix you some decent food," Gerry said, adding, "That may be why you got dizzy in court."

"Mmhuh. ." was the only answer, as John was juggling the feeding with opening the morning's paper.

"We need to relax today, and set work aside, before we both have a breakdown." She set a glass of juice in front of him as she continued, "Let's go to church tomorrow, too, and pray for safety,"

John found himself agreeing to it for her sake but made her agree in return to stay with her mother while he was away. That evening, as he was relaxing with a drink, he still scribbled down things to do for the next week. He had to meet with a psychiatrist to attempt to ascertain Willie's mental state at the time, meet again with Bessie to prepare her for being on the stand, and go over with Al the line of questioning for each witness called. He began tapping his pencil on the table, thinking of how else he might locate the witnesses in Florida. Their personal funds were being drained while they were waiting on the CRC to send a check.

Were they just holding out to see if they made headway, he wondered? He ignored Gerry's worried look as he fixed himself another drink, before settling back down again to his notes. He began to sip on it when the phone rang. Of course it was Bella – she had a knack for calling him when he was drinking. She had reviewed the events of the week already with Al but was calling to see what John's perspective of it was. Did they feel they were in danger? Al had mentioned the crawlspace on the catwalk, and it concerned her. He told her of the rock incident. Should they send some support?

"No, no," John protested. "I've got a man on the force watching out for us, we'll be fine." Although he had gone to law school with other women, It was difficult for John to remove himself from a lifelong Southern upbringing that groomed him to protect women from any undue worry, especially when it came to protecting himself. He assured her that there was nothing that he and Al could not handle, and began talking, instead, about matters of the defense that were frustrating in the racial climate, the protest of the anti-lynching law that was side by side the articles of the McGee case in today's paper, and the underlying fear in the area of communistic influence.

"I have a feeling that there have been meetings before the case opened up," John voiced a thought that had not surfaced until now.

"What do you mean," Bella asked, "what kind of meetings?"

"Someone had to have organized that gang of witnesses that showed up to respond the way they did. They were all calm and collected – had the same damned responses – no one showed any interest in the case and claimed that the whole town has calmed down about this. Hell, there wasn't one representative from the guard this time" – John paused for a belch – "which gave the whole thing the appearance that no one much cared anymore about the outcome. Someone had to have schooled would-be lynchers when McGee was being transported."

Bella started with, "What do you…" but John interrupted, continuing with his rant, bringing out the dramatic side of his nature as he painted the picture for her. "Al will tell you – ask him! When we interviewed – what – almost half the town, white and colored alike mind you, everyone was still scared to even talk to us, looking over their shoulder to make sure no one was looking, talking in not much more than a whisper most times." He paused for another sip, and continued, "There was one white man who looked as if he wasn't going to talk to me, but then nearly pushed me behind a building so he could say his mind. Hell! None of them would give their names for witness, or even think about sitting on the stand. The whites are afraid of losing their reputations, and the Negros are afraid of losing their necks! Now, you tell me, is that because every-one is still so damned disinterested?" John usually didn't curse in front of a lady, but the drink had loosened his tongue. Gerry frowned at him from a distance.

Bella had been thoughtful during this discourse, taking in the facts while overlook-ing the intoxicated tones and sound of the ice rattling in the glass. She wondered in si-lence if she shouldn't have sent down someone from the CRC who could rise above the fabric of the culture. Still, she couldn't argue with his perspective, and remembered his passionate nature was what sold her on him in the first place. "Are you certain you don't need us to send support?" She finally asked.

John sat for a moment, watching the ice settling in his glass as he circled it.

He put it down and pulled himself up in his chair, adjusting his weight onto his good leg. "No." He shook his head as if she were there. "No, that would just rile them up." He ran his hand through his hair as he focused and cleared his throat to speak more clearly. "I'm planning to put McGee on the stand. It wouldn't do for people from outside Mississippi to be there at the same time."

This sent Bella off on her own rant. How did he intend to question McGee? Was McGee mentally able to be on the stand and cross-examined? He hadn't been able to even talk in the first two trials – If he wasn't facing lynching at this point, what would be the case after his testimony? Bella sounded anxious, as if she wanted to jump on a plane that night. John sensed her pacing and calmed his own voice. "I had my choice of guard on him last night. He thinks he was drugged the last time so he couldn't talk, but he was ok for the pretrial. He figured they liked that he couldn't speak up for him-self, so they fixed it to where he looked like a dope the second time, too. I don't believe it will happen again."

Bella paused and took a deep breath, as if considering the idea. John took this as a sign to continue and added, "I'm going to prepare him and lead him with questioning. He's wants to tell his side of the story." He paused and added, "Hell, it's better than dy-ing!" John took another swig of his drink.

Bella responded with clear, measured tones, "Whatever the case, make sure you continue to inject the reasons for change of venue into the record so the Supreme Court will look at taking this thing up. I don't think he has a chance in Hell to keep from getting the death sentence again in that den of snakes."

By this time, Gerry had positioned herself squarely in front of John with raised eye-brows and offered her hand for the glass. He submitted meekly and finished the call with a tailored agreement and consent, assuring her that he and Al would keep her up to date. When he finally placed the receiver back onto the waiting hook, he sighed with an inkling of recovered sobriety. He looked up to see Gerry smiling sideways at him as she went to the kitchen, calling back over her shoulder, "So, you still want to support women in careers of their choice?

He chuckled and said softly, "Yes, yes, I still do."

In a deeper part of the State, another conversation was being held regarding the outcome of the trial. Gathered together around a table scattered with mugs of beer in the smoky VFW hall were several men with serious faces, speaking in hushed tones, nodding and exchanging collaborative remarks, one slowly puffing on a cigar, another nervously repositioning himself, until finally another said, "OK, here he comes," and all lifted and straightened themselves.

"Well, well, our distinguished Mr. District Attorney!" The man with the cigar stood up to wave him back to the table and smiled broadly.

Pauly Schwartzfager was tall, broad-chested and well built, and usually looked imposing up against any other man. As he walked into the darkened swirls of smoke tonight, however, his demeanor was one of uncertainty. He had been summoned to the meeting in the middle of a relaxed evening with family and wasn't so much in the mood to don the distinguished district attorney air after the week. Besides, there was an ominous tone to the atmosphere. He took the chair offered, seated somewhat stiffly and tilted his head to one side. "What is this all about, gentlemen?" He gave a stilted laugh and continued, "I thought these meetings were done with while go."

"Now, now, settle yourself down and have a beer with us! Relax!" The older man, another Collins, who was the county prosecutor and would be sitting with him in the courtroom during the actual trial, raised two fingers of his hand and motioned to the waiter to respond. Pauly adjusted himself in his chair and forced a smile towards the others who greeted him. There was a disconcerting mixture of those who were benefactors to his campaign, and others who looked less friendly. He of course recognized Deavours, the cocky attorney the Hawkins had hired and who was already working closely with him, and Hawkins himself. He mused that Deavours had not proved to be as professional as he would have liked – and had more heart for his pocketbook than anything else. Next to him were other characters who he had seen in wealthier circles but didn't offer an introduction.

Carroll Gartin, the mayor, was drumming his fingers as if he had plenty to say. They waited for the beer to be set in front of Pauly, and he obligingly took a drink.

Collins smiled and took charge as if of the opening of ceremony as he began, "Now – we are among friends and of a common mind, are we not, gentlemen?" He waited momentarily to acknowledge the silent nods, as Pauly furrowed his brow but looked straight on each one. "So, to proceed with the reason why we called you to this esteemed gathering, my friend," his smile turned to a look of sinister determination as he continued. "To put it simply, I think we are all in agreement here to say you've got to bust your butt to get this conviction." Collins glanced around the table, waving his hand to include everyone, "There is an investment of our State's Right here and more is at stake than one nigger's life!" His raised voice lowered a bit as he continued, adding a hand gesture to soften the tone. "I know that we are working to include the Negro in such things as good citizenship and keeping their own to a higher standard of living, and we have certainly stretched ourselves in including three Negros on the Grand Jury this time, wouldn't you say?"

Several nods kept him going, although Pauly was remembering the crushed hand of the minister selected for duty who had stepped out of line. He shook off the memory – inwardly chiding himself for the sympathetic thought. He heard

Collin's voice saying, "… stopping once and for all these communistic influences coming in and taking over our right to make decisions within our own jurisdictions!" The mayor burst in with his thoughts that had been held back too long, "Our governor Wright has stood behind this with his meetings. Remember his radio address and his defense of segregation?" There were nods around the table, remembering the words of the governor in his state-wide radio address, saying to the Negro population:

"If any of you have become so deluded as to want to enter our white schools, patronize our hotels and cafes, to enjoy social equality with the whites," he said, "then kindness and true sympathy requires me to advise you to make your home in some state other than Mississippi."

Gartin continued, "Any Southerner who stands in defense of any other philosophy must be silenced! The defense may be young, but that gives them no excuse for this aligning themselves with progressive and Communist policies. Their immaturity makes them just dumb enough to pull these tricks for "equity's sake." They don't give a damn how we are exposed to rest of the nation or to our niggerloving President!" This incited comments from each one, making the table roar with climbing decibels of insults thrown to invisible antagonists.

Finally, a frozen Hawkins stood up spoke out with a trembling that caused the others to stop mid-stream and listen. "It's about my wife, damn it all! Listen now! It's about the vile ravishing of my wife, by that, that…god-damned nigger! I'm not here for any other political purpose!" His lips curled around his words, giving somewhat of a madman's appearance to his spontaneous exposition. He found himself swaying with fury and sweat that had beaded on his forehead was now streaming downward.

Deavours stood up and put his hand on his shoulder and patted him.

"We all are worried about our white women, Troy. That's why we want our rights as a State to make sure there's no intermixing of the blood here." Troy shrugged his hand off his shoulder and snarled his slow response, "There was no intent to mix blood – this was a rape!"

Deavours backed off and Collins interjected with a pandering laugh and said, "And certainly it was. We want to give no more opportunity for such crimes and make an example to all who have the gall to think of themselves able to get away with even thoughts of intercourse with one of our kind. This is what we are determined to prevent." Having satisfied his fury somewhat, Hawkins let himself be lowered back into his chair while Collins continued, redirecting his gaze back to Pauly, who had taken all this in with silence. "So then, you have a large responsibility on your shoulders, Mr. Swartzfager." He paused to draw on his cigar and finished with, "Our State is depending on you to make sure this conviction sees its victory." He leaned in and clarified his intentions with, "We all want to see McGee dead, for once and for all."

"You know, Pauly, that is one reason why we contributed so largely to your election," came a more refined voice from the mustached man who Pauly didn't quite recognize. This caused him to adjust his jacket, clear his throat and declare, "I am intent upon this purpose, as well, gentlemen, and can assure you that I will let no opportunity to squash this arrogant defense slip by. We have already managed to move the case back to Laurel, where the deed was done, and to maintain our appearance to the public as fair-minded. We're not giving any more time for witnesses to pluck up courage to bring in any new testimony. As I see it, the defense doesn't have a leg to stand on." There was first one chuckle, then another from the table at the unintended pun, and Pauly took the opportunity to laugh himself, breaking the pressure of the heated atmosphere somewhat.

Laughter and cryptic comments were washed down with the end of the beer, and one by one the table excused themselves, patting Swartzfager on the back and shaking hands. Hawkins and Deavours finally left together, leaving Collins and Pauly alone.

"Why is it I'm feeling like the criminal here?" Pauly directed his comment towards Collins.

Collins let out a loud, "Ha!" as he circled his cigar head into the ashtray to extinguish the glowing end. "So, my man, you see!" He leaned forward and said more quietly, "The simple fact is, It's his neck – or – it's yours – politically speaking, of course." He broke away from Pauly's stare to raise his two fingers again for the check.

"Of course," came the reply as Pauly shoved himself away from the table and walked out of the hall.

CHAPTER TWENTY

A CORN OF WHEAT

"On a hill far away, stood an ooo-ld rugged cross, The emblem of sufferin'n shaaame." The melody from the man standing next to him had a full deep baritone that took the place of two or more voices around, so John stopped focusing on the hymnal himself and looked towards the pulpit where the preacher was slightly swaying as he sang, as if actually being moved within from the words. A ray of light from the upper window put him in a spotlight that accentuated a mysterious peace in his face.

Something about the scene caused John to shift his view, instead, to the window where straggling church goers were laughing and finishing cigarettes. He blew out an inpatient breath, noticed by Gerry, who was offering up her crystal-toned voice. "I will cling to that Old Rugged Cross!" she declared melodically and more emphatically, while the baritone answered with a deep echo, "Rugged Cross...," "and exchange it someday for a crown."

Although he loved to sing himself, John found himself unable to join in with sincerity after the influence of his college teacher of Religion, who his sister, Mildred – now a pastor of her own church – said had "robbed him of his faith." He recalled the conversation they had when he had tried to convince her with his new-found knowledge that there were Christ-like figures in every religion – why believe only one was the true Son of God? "Of all people," she had said, "John – you know better! You were born with faith." She hadn't said it dramatically or in an accusing tone, but as if opening up to him a forgotten part of himself that required no textbook to understand. He was brought back to a scene in a crowded bedroom, lit only by the gentle presence of a crescent moon and comforted by the sweet night's breeze that stretched the sheer voile curtain, looking like arms held out for a last embrace. John was only seven and shared the bedroom's floor with his siblings, except the older two boys who were in the bedroom adjacent to them. "Cecil?" "Wha...?" came the groggy reply from the next mattress. "Forgive me if I have done anything wrong to you today." "Ok! I forgive you!" The reply was grumpy as she turned over with a thump and fluff of her pillow. "Mildred?" "Yes, John?" The voice was soft, anticipating the nightly request with tenderness. "Forgive me if I've done anything wrong to you today." "I forgive you, John." She waited to hear the rest of the litany as if it were a lullaby that put them to bed each night. "Rose?' Rose, the youngest was already asleep. "Forgive me Rose," he said, anyway. "Leon?" John's thoughts were interrupted by Gerry's hand on his.

She looked back to the front of the church and his gaze followed to see the pastor walking to the podium. Suddenly, without mental effort, the deep round eyes of Willie McGee came to his mind and all the impact of the upcoming trial. He shut his eyes tightly as he heard the pastor's voice booming the Bible verse, "Verily, verily, I say unto you, except a corn of wheat fall into the ground and die, it abideth alone: but if it die, it bringeth forth much fruit."

He excused himself and Gerry from the social hour after church where there were many people, he knew, who would want to ask him about his involvement in the controversial case. There were some who didn't look lightly upon his representation of this sordid deed, and he didn't want to get caught up in their opinionated views.

Besides, he was suspect of everyone, now, and couldn't be sure that someone he would sip coffee with might not be the culprit that threatened his family. He would have to accept the well wishes from afar of those who truly meant to support and use the time more productively.

That afternoon, after going over the new motions with Al, John spent a quiet evening with his family, assuring Gerry that he would not do anything rash, and that he would find someone there to watch out for his and Al's safety. He didn't let her know that most of Laurel's police force would be happy to turn a blind eye to a little "roughing up" of the attorneys who wanted to prove them to be liars.

The next few days did not produce much that he and Al could present for the defense. The psychologist he met with schooled him briefly on the aspects of mental health care treatment. The Court before had only required a psychologist's opinion, which John found out was not sufficient to diagnosis a disease of themind or injury to the brain. He referred him to a psychiatrist, wishing him luck on trying to get an appointment. After managing to get a quick word into the psychiatrist in between patients, bypassing the flustered secretary, he learned that in order to get a plea of insanity, there would have to be further interviews conducted that would take time to discover the causes of McGee's behaviors.

They had also served process for subpoena for the witnesses in Florida and a telephone operator had been helpful in attempting to find them, but to no avail. These setbacks, however, might prove to be the factors that Bella had been looking for to get the Supreme Court to revisit a reversal. Without time to fully present a more solid defense or being able trying the case in a different venue with another Judge, John worried that she was probably right about not having a real chance. Still, the juror's list had evidently been tampered with. There must be some way to reveal that someone had altered it – whether it was the supervisor, himself, or someone else who had done the deed in secret. This thread of hope he clung to, as he envisioned in the coming days having to examine Mrs. Hawkins and having to put McGee on the stand under the hawk-like watch of the time-honored "traditions" of the white supremacy of the South. He reviewed all this in his mind while resting on the bed in the hotel when the phone rang. Al wasin the shower, so John reluctantly left his contemplations and rolled up to answer it, grabbing his pack of cigarettes at the same time.

"Hello?" he said gently, expecting Gerry's lilting voice on the other end of the line as he took a cigarette out of the pack.

"Hey! Is this John?" The raspy voice was unmistakably Dixon Pyles.

John leaned back and smiled, "Why, I think you know who I am, calling my hotel room, and I'll bet I know who this is! There isn't another voice in all of Mississippi as distinguished as yours."

"Well, I'm at least glad to see that you're in good spirits, even if I am the butt of your joke," Pyles laughed good-naturedly.

John laughed himself and then said, "How are you, Dixon? Are you calling to wish me luck in the ring?" He took a cigarette from the pack and pressed it into the lighter's flame.

"Well, that, and just thought I'd add a bit of information you might want to know. Don't know if you want to use it or not, but it wasn't in the papers I gave to Al, and, well, it's just been under my skin and…I, umm. . , "What is it?" John became more serious and leaned in to listen. Al had emerged from the bathroom wrapped in his robe, and took in the scene, wonderingly.

Dixon's sigh was audible as he began, "You know that we haven't been able to locate the transcript of the first trial, right?"

"Right, right."

"Well, there was a fellow who asked me not to mention his name – and let me tell you ahead of time, he will not testify to this fact, but – he tells me that the reason the transcript is missing is because of Mrs. Hawkin's slip up."

"Slip up? What did she say?"

"Seems she talked about the fellow who first investigated her, who got the first story from her. Now, I don't know if this is actually in the transcript of the trial, but I do know she named the first investigator, and my source knows what she told him." Dixon paused.

John waited in focused silence.

"She told him that before McGee actually 'ravished' her, as they say, he went down on her." He paused for that to sink in before he went on. "She also told him she knew at that time that he didn't have a gun or a knife. They coached her to say that one in the next trial. She could have struggled to get away, and made one heck of a noise, if that was what she wanted to do."

"Hmm," was all John offered at the moment.

Dixon continued, "I'm thinking that they intended to scrub that part from the transcript..."

"It would certainly show that it didn't constitute legal rape," John finished. "That's right," Dixon concluded.

"You're right, she slipped up," John said thoughtfully, "because I think she was trying to weave a lie as it was."

"You believe the affair story?" Dixon asked.

"I'm not sure I buy all of the details, but I don't think McGee is making the main affair story up. He knows that it wouldn't do for it to be brought out in court, yet he refers to it without blinking, really. Why do you bring this up now?"

"Oh, I don't know – just thought it might help somehow – might give you more courage when you're up there questioning her. Have you thought about bringing it to light?"

"I've thought about it – not real seriously. Even if we proved it true, he would probably still get a death penalty for it, somehow. Might not be legal, but they would get it done." John took a drag on his cigarette, letting it out through flared nostrils.

"How are you guys doing, by the way?" Dixon interjected, "Any threats from Hawkins and his fellas?"

"Nah, just looks that say what they're thinking, so far," John held his forehead as if he were exhausted already with the task at hand.

"OK, well, you fellas watch out for yourselves, now. They meant business with me, and they're not resting on their laurels now, believe you me." He chuckled at his own pun, but then paused and said more seriously, "They'll see this through, John, mark my words."

"Yeah, thanks. Thanks, Dixon." was all John could muster.

He placed the receiver on the hook and drew on his cigarette in silence. Al sat on his bed and waited. After a moment, John related the conversation, "I wonder what Willette goes through now in her marraige," Al mused. "Well, she has now complied," John pointed out. "Who knows what she went through when it actually happened. Hawkins must have a strangle-hold on the truth, however he knows it, and if anyone tampered with it, all hell would break loose!"

Al nodded his consent, adding, "It's not just Hawkins who would keep it hushed. If Willie's story is true the way he tells it, the neighbors, the police, heck – nearly half of Laurel is involved in the cover-up."

"I would bring the whole mess up if I thought it would free Willie, but I'm afraid we would see vigilante justice on the spot." John ground his stub in the ashtray then looked at Al as if to ask confirmation.

Al stood and paced. After some thought he stopped and said, "There are no guards at this trial. That serves two purposes for them – It makes it look like there is no need because nobody cares anymore, and there is no one to stop them from hurting him if anything is brought up. Clever, if it's planned."

"Clever," John repeated with disgust, "Damned 'White Knights'"...he started, but a thought crossed his mind that made him grab the phone and start dialing.

"Who are you calling?" Al said, somewhat startled.

John looked anxious as he said, "Gerry." Gerry was fine and assured him she was safe where she was, adding that he was overly worried. He had just hung up from her when the phone rang again. It was Bella thistime. After making sure all was well and discussing the call from Pyles, she encouraged him to just keep the exceptions going, and added, "We've got our team ready to go for the appeal, and we're planning to drum up lots of national attention this time to sway it. There are already people riled up enough to travel to Jackson in a group to protest," she said with some excitement, and continued, "I've got Emmanual with me now, He says good luck to you, and we're drawing up plans for it as we speak. There will be a lot to catch you up on, so we'll just fly you out here for briefing when it's time."

John sat in silence for a moment in between two worlds – the agenda of the Civil Rights Congress, in which, at the moment, he was feeling very much like a not-so-useful puppet attached to strings, and the reality he and Al were facing tomorrow when they would be sweating in the pressure of courtroom tension. Should he even mention that he would be putting himself on the stand first thing to fight for a Motion for Continuance; that he was trying to uncover the mystery of the juror's list, which he knew had been tampered with or... "John?"

"Yes, I'm here. Just thinking."

"Oh, I thought we lost connection. Well, again, good luck, and report to us as soon as you can, right?" Her tone was somewhat sharp and slightly suspicious, as if she sniffed renegade thoughts.

"Right, thank you," John said without his usual sincerity, realizing that she was not very interested in his own plan or tactics. "We'll call tomorrow night to update you."

John shrugged off his feelings, as there was a lot to cover before tomorrow morning, and he didn't want the lack of support or any fear of conflict to shadow his own fervor. He drank down ice water sitting on the bedside table and said to Al, who had been watching his expressions and guessing his thoughts, "Ready?" John asked.

"I'm with you!" Al said with double entendre and handed him the Motions for them to review. They studied and mock argued until past midnight, finally resigning themselves to a fitful sleep.

PART II
THE FACES

There were people surrounding me – older people, looking down at me. They had crimped smiles, accusing eyebrows. They bent down and spoke to me with an attempt at kindness that was more like a mixture of pity and disgust. What were they saying? What did it mean? Why did it make me afraid? They spoke to me in one tone, and someone nearby in quite another. Was it my parents they were talking to in lower, demanding voices?

I awoke to the darkness of my bedroom. To my horror, the faces were still there, floating in the black space. As they grew larger and came closer, I realized they were masks. Behind the false faces were animals – wolves and other creatures. They meant no kindness at all. I tried to scream but couldn't. I forced myself back to sleep, and the kind darkness engulfed me.

INTERLUDE II

Any thoughts I had of befriending the blacks who were woven throughout our lives were squelched through a basic lack of opportunity. It surprises me now to realize the population was so large in Jackson, yet I barely noticed them. When I later read how they took on an invisibility around white folks, it made sense that I had grown up oblivious to their tactics of avoidance, based on reasonablefear.

Somewhat of an exception to the rule was Mr. B., who was one of the African American teachers to brave the first year's integration into Murrah High School, which was nicknamed "the silk-stocking school" by opposing football teams since it was on the wealthy side of town. It was the autumn of my senior year when I became more fully aware of the effects of our prejudices. Mr. B. was emboldened by the fact that he had one year left until his retirement, and I suppose he planned to take the opportunity to

149

speak his mind with one foot out the door. He was an unusual character, with large, wise and kindly eyes, a slightly bent back, and arms that seemed much too long for his husky frame. I wondered about this unusual presentation, yet I came to realize that this was his stance in the hallways, around the other teachers who were white. He would sometimes put a thumbed fist to his mouth and the other hand behind his back, as if he were thinking thoughts not allowed to be spoken in the hallways. Once in class, however, he would quit from refraining his thoughts, and taught them as if they were in our Civics textbook. On the first day of school, which was usually just for introduction, he asked us to write what grade we believed we were worthy of. I seized the opportunity to put A+, and afterwards realized it made no difference my answers to test questions – I got the grade I thought I deserved. A precocious friend and I figured out that we could easily skip class by pretending we had important drama practices elsewhere, which he never checked on, but we did have the privilege of being in class to witness several of his infamous speeches. One that seared itself into my memory was an exhortation to apply yourself fully to whatever endeavor was placed before you, no matter how belittling it seemed to be. He raised his chest and declared, "No matter what job is put before you, you can do it to the best of your ability! If you are a ditch-digger, you be the best ditch-digger you can be! If you are a dishwasher, you be the best damned dishwasher around! If you are a whore, you be the absolute best whore you can be!" The minister's daughter quickly looked down at her desk after a gasp of unbelief, while several boys broke out into laughter. He went on, unabashed, "And if people say anything against you, you just say…" and at this point his long arm came swinging around his body to loudly thump his hand on his chest, several times in a row as he proclaimed, "I don't bit mo caaeh! I don't bit mo caaeh!"

My friend and I locked eyes in puzzled amazement, but stifled our laughter, as we both had an inexplicable respect for this highly un-orthodox teacher, who attempted to share his method of maintaining dignity despite oppressive circumstances. For the remainder of the semester, the minister's daughter brought her Bible to read in his class in lieu of the Civics textbook.

On the other hand, the few brave black students that came to Murrah High that year had their defenses up. I became acquainted with the daughter of Medgar Evars, the first African American to become a Mayor in the South, after an assembly fashion show. Styles from the local upper-class boutiques were sported by the most well-known football players and cheerleaders. As the audience was filing out, I turned to a friend and said, "I feel so tacky!" Laughing at my own joke, I turned to face Sheila's searing eyes from her polished black face, as she responded with grave seriousness, "You <u>look</u> tacky!"

This discouraged me somewhat from making any other acquaintances with the small but daunting clique. One exception was Perry, the new star basketball player. He had a quick wit and dignity about him that had won him the respect of the senior boys, and admiration of the girls. He became fast friends with the president of the senior class, another basketball player, and so became an enigmatic representation of acceptance of the black race in this new generation of the South. I was flattered when he asked me to dance at a football victory dance and thought only briefly about the possible consequences. After all, he was such a gentleman and smiled so sweetly. My date, who was also friends with Perry, gladly allowed it, and it seemed to be a natural and gracious interchange, but the atmosphere around us was immediately charged with bizarre curiosity.

In my opinion, the black race wins hands down over the white when it comes to dancing to a beat, and Perry excelled in this area as well. With him as my partner, the rhythmic moving was contagious. It was unclear to me whether it was because eyes were beginning to fix on us, or whether I was enjoying the heightened pace that he challenged me with, but I'm sure I've never been able to dance again like I did that night. Had I known that this was the particular night that the Baptist youth minister had come to check out the victory dance to see if their restricting dancing was a bit archaic, I might not have enjoyed the urging of the music so freely. Coincidentally, it was also the first time an all-black band was playing for our dance. They took advantage of the situation and lengthened the song again and again, as one by one the other couples dropped away to form a circle around us, clapping in time to the music. A quiet panic gripped my heart as I sensed the opinions whirling around the room, but I was more afraid to stop than to go on. Glimpses here and there revealed some nearby faces aglow with approval at the cresting of this new frontier and clapped us on to the beat of the music. Others on the outer rim were stunned, some darkened and very displeased. It felt strangely surreal. My energy began to give out and my smile faded with it, but I couldn't find it within myself to stop and face the volatile situation confidently. The band played on and on.

"What is Perry feeling," I thought vaguely. I allowed my eyes to meet his, which had already been fixed on me with growing concern. He motioned to the band to wind it down. I all but stumbled through the last measures, to hear whoops and cheers from the small supportive group. Perry somewhat awkwardly thanked me for the dance, as we exchanged a worried glance before my date graciously took me aside. We all sensed that unseen boundaries had been crossed that would cost us later. In a state of semi-shock, I asked him to take me home far earlier than was necessary. I avoided my parents when coming in and went quickly to the refuge of my bed while I sorted out my feelings.

The next Monday after school, my old green Rambler puffed as fast as it could towards home. Thankfully, the push-button gears didn't cause it to slip into neutral this time, as it rounded the sharp curve that led to our driveway. I dreaded confronting my parents, but knew I had little time before they would get the call from school with the scandalous report. They had to hear my side of the story first, if I was to be granted any mercy. Thinking to make my confession with a phone call to the office, I gulped when I saw the blue Cadillac in the carport. I opened the door stealthily and heard talk coming from the den. Mom and Dad had, for some reason, come home from work early and were enjoying afree afternoon together. I hated to ruin the day, but it was in my favor that they were in a good mood.

As I unfolded my story with the most repentant tone I could muster, I found them at first sober, then surprisingly receptive to my position as they exchanged sly smiles with one another. I told them that I had been called into the vice-principal's office that day at the urging of the parents of high society in the school district. These were important, affluent families, not to be ignored. They wanted the impudent girl who had the audacity to dance with a Negro student at the football victory dance to be properly warned. The vice-principal himself looked somewhat embarrassed to have this duty, but informed me because of my actions, none of the girls from these families would be allowed to attend the victory dances for the rest of the season. It was 1970, and the first year of integration in schools. No one was quite sure how to lay down the unspoken rules. No one could tell me that it had been wrong to dance with a boy whose skin was darker than mine, but it was made clear that I would suffer socially for my actions. As I became cognizant of my parent's disdain of racial prejudice, in spite of these social mores it became a source of pride for me.

I had experienced the very hub of the wheel of racial conflict, something I had only taken for granted before as popular opinion. Although my parents had always made sure no one in our family ever used the term "nigger," I heard it frequently from others, yet, I never had a friend who was from this rejected category either. Now I had faced full force the heat of this generation who was put to the test of either accepting the society's present beliefs or forming their own.

Had I been born to another set of parents in this Southern state, there would be lectures, shame and restrictions. Instead, I felt such consolation to hear Dad say he was proud of me not to have cared what color of skin my friends had. Mom was compassionate, knowing the humiliation herself firsthand, and encouraged me to be brave in school.

My parents had often expressed disregard for the popular prejudice of their time, yet I was still unaware at this time that the Klu Klux Klan had my Dad on their blacklist.

As I look back, I was one lucky girl that a KKK representative was not also at the victory dance that night, though I'm sure they heard of it.

It wasn't until the incident of my dancing with Perry that I realized that Dad had represented so many African Americans in his law practice, in spite of the popular sentiment of racial prejudice. Yes, I knew of the black man who gave him a Christmas present every year, who Dad said could not really afford it. I had seen the waiting room in Dad's office when Mom would invite me to lunch filled with black men, women and their children sitting on the worn furniture, but for some reason I had not taken note that this was any different from other places of business – especially a law practice. All I knew was that even though I heard that Dad was one of the best criminal lawyers around, we were always struggling financially. I later found out that he charged only what a client was able to pay, and the black man in Mississippi was not able to pay much, if anything at all.

CHAPTER TWENTY-ONE

SOME NEGROS ARE HARD TO FIND

"Order! Order in the Court!" The chatter that had risen to a dull roar quickly dropped at the sound of the gavel, replaced by a quieter shuffling of feet and whispered "pardon me's" as the late comers, dressed in their best suit coats and dresses found their place in the courtroom's floor to settle. The balcony had mostly been gathered quite early on, in order to avoid the polite avoidances or intentional sniffs. Bessie was seated by her preacher, with handkerchief ready for duty if needed, as she watched the action of the lower floor. Willie was led in alongside his attorneys Mr. London and Mr. Poole, and just the sight of him caused the lump in her throat to gain density and her heart to beat more quickly. The "Lord have mercy," that she whispered caused her preacher to reach for her hand and pat it compassionately for fear she may collapse before it had allbegun.

John took a deep breath as he took in his surroundings in the courtroom. The prosecution team, Jack Deavours, E. K. Collins and Pauly Shwartzfager were whispering, waving greetings to some on the courtroom floor, and shaking hands with the Hawkin's family, who sat with pinched expressions, not giving the other side of the courtroom the warmth of even a glare. Willie sat with his head slightly bowed, eyes large, and lips moving as if in prayer. "Order!" Judge Collins said once again, to cover all remaining noncompliance.

After the Baliff's announcement of the case name and judge presiding with grave import, Al stepped forward and called for his first witness Mr. John Poole. The lower floor shuffled and whispered. After swearing in Al began, "I would like to request that the record show that we ask for a special bill of exceptions to clear up the question of facts as to the events which took place on Friday the 27th of February, at which time the factual question is dispute as to counsel..."

Judge Collins interrupted with energy, to say that "to dictate a lot of stuff into the record that the Court thinks immaterial…" would not be allowed, and for the record, as well, he stated that "the Court doesn't mean to get hard in any way, but you can't play with this Court." He adjusted his glasses, attempting to balance outward fairness with the much deeper goal of maintaining sovereignty. He could not allow anything that would return this case back to the Supreme Court.

London responded with consternation, "I respectfully submit to the Court that we are not attempting to play with this Court."

Ignoring the statement, Collins replied, "If you want to introduce testimony, Mr. London, go ahead," emphasizing 'testimony.'

"We feel that this is necessary in fairness to this defendant in order to present the case properly before the Court," London persevered.

Bolstered by the eyes of the floor, Collins responded with cool aggression, "I can't help how you feel about it, the Court is going to rule on it according to law. Go ahead and question your witness." A muffled laugh was covered by coughing.

London attempted to squeeze in an inclusion of all the testimony of the former motion of continuance, to which the Judge promptly overruled. Al politely turned to the court reporter saying, "Note an exception, please Ma'am, to the Court's ruling against us."

Discernibly perturbed, the Judge raised his brows and pressed, "Do you want to ask this witness any questions?"

London complied and began to ask John about the proceedings of the end of the pretrial, when no further time was given to argue their side of the case, regardless of time or exhaustion. It was all just for the record, and both Al and John suspected there would be no mercy given. After John was sworn in, the questioning by London began:

"Mr. Poole, I will ask you first if on last Friday at the conclusion of the evidence on the motion for a change of venue, if you told the Court that you did not care to introduce any further motions at that time?"

John sat straightly and responded, "I did not tell the Court that. I asked the Court on Friday if the Court would allow us some additional time to present other and further motions; that we had not at that time written the motions, and at that time it was six-thirty. We had heard and presented evidence from nine o-clock in the morning, that it was then six-thirty at night, because I looked at my watch specifically to find that out. I know it was six-thirty p. m. when we finished." Swartsfager shuffled his papers.

"Mr. Poole, I will ask you to explain the circumstances of your request to the court for time in which to argue on the motion for a change of venue?"

Swartzfager stood and pronounced, "We object to that. That was taken up before the Court and the Court ruled on it the other night. It isn't competent in this hearing."

Collins returned, "Sustained." Neither wanted anything repeated for the record.

London appealed, asking if there was an issue whether they had actually declined to argue or whether they had been too exhausted to argue. The fact that the Judge had denied to continue the case for even one more day to allow any further motions or argument, had been covered over in the record by an all-inclusive statement that the defense declined to argue, and the pretrial had been closed.

All objections by the prosecution were quickly sustained.

Then whether there had been enough time to adequately prepare for the trial was put to question. London began, "Mr. Poole, I will ask you if you have endeavored to obtain and procure the presence of the witnesses mentioned in this motion for continuance?"

John replied, "Yes, I have. I have used all the diligence that I know how to use. There are two witnesses that have been referred to me by various other people that I have investigated, and Willie McGee tells me, in addition to some of those others, a state of facts by which an alibi can be proven if he can procure those witnesses. They are Negro witnesses, and I have found now that they are residing in Florida. They were residing in Laurel up until – until not long ago, and I got their addresses in Florida, and it took me some time to do that. Then I made a telephone call – I had the operator to attempt to locate these two witnesses, Willie Johnson and Hattie Johnson."

"I will ask you, Mr. Poole, If you have requested process for these witnesses?" "Yes, I have requested process. The operator then called me back and said that she did know where they were, because she had sent a messenger boy out to find them. Now I don't know what diligence she used. I know it must be difficult to locate some Negroes, especially when they are new residents of a place and in a city like Pensacola."

Swartzfager rose with a slight grin, "We object to his explanation about some Negroes being hard to find." The judge quickly sustained the objection, both knowing full well that the poverty of the black race in the South often held them back from having phone service, or even their own place to live. The Johnsons, who hadn't been able to sell their house before leaving town, had not yet been able to afford their own place and were thought to have moved in with others.

John simply answered, "The operator told me that she did locate a place where they were living."

London went on to ask if Poole had time to go to Florida. He did not, nor time to make arrangements for travel. London then brought up that the Court denied that he had not been given ample time to investigate and prepare for the case. John answered that he had not and continued, "...If we are now pushed to trial in this case, Willie McGee will not have that adequate representation by counsel that is guaranteed to him by the Constitution of Mississippi, and by the Constitution of the United States." As for due diligence in investigating the matter of insanity, John denied that it was true that he had failed to use it and declared, "I will tell you what I have done..."

Interrupted by Swartszfager who piped, "We object to what he did about it."

The court allowed him to continue, but another objection came before he got to the fact that the doctor himself needed more information in order to prepare a case of insanity. After a third and fourth objection, wherein the prosecution had John against the ropes for misplaced wording, rather than real content, the Judge interjected finally, "State what you did." John was finally able to state how he gathered information, examined witnesses, attempted to procure special witnesses, and explored the insanity questions, and that there simply had not been enough time to properly prepare for trial.

Swartzfager's cross-examination inordinately focused solely on the subpoenaing of the witnesses from Florida. Had he checked to see if they were found or not? Had he checked to see if they were actually in Laurel?

Al had checked, John thought, but what did it matter? They wouldn't be called until the regular time of trial after the jurors were assigned. Besides, he knew they had not yet been found in Florida. What was he getting at? It finally came to light when Swartzfager claimed that they had been found and processed in Laurel. John looked at Al puzzling, and Al raised his shoulders.

"I was told by the operator, that they are in Florida, and I was told by the operator the specific address at which they are," John stated.

When was he told that? It was yesterday. Why didn't he check to see if they were here? It sounded absurd to John.

Pauly maintained with a sly grin, "So far as the affidavit is concerned, the affidavit falls down, so far as them being in Florida is concerned, when the process shows here that they have been served here and have been found in Jones County?"

London stood, objecting, but Schwartzfager interrupted with assumed authority, "Let him answer my question." Judge Collins agreed, "Let him answer."

"Isn't that right?" Schwartzfager egged on.

"I beg your pardon, what was the question?" John's brow was furrowed. "I say, so far as the affidavit is concerned, the affidavit falls down so far as their being in Florida, because the process here shows that they have been served here and have been found in Jones County?" What he intentionally failed to mention is that two negros, had, in fact, been subpoenaed and were now sitting in the balcony. The sheriff had gotten a good pat on the back for giving them this information, as the prosecution puffed up and winked before the opening of the morning's session. London objected to the conclusion on behalf of the Prosecution, but the Judge overruled.

John pushed back with, "I don't think the affidavit falls down, I think you are assuming a lot if you say that...

Schwartzfager's excitement to push his agenda caused him to begin to interrupt again, but John blocked by saying, "Let me answer, please."

"All right," he conceded, breathing out somewhat heavily.

John continued, "I think the affidavit includes everything, includes everything that our motion is made on."

Pauly waved his hand dismissively, quickly staunching his statement with, "That is...that the 14th Amendment to the Constitution of the State of Mississippi, and the Constitution of the United States of America, and the statutes and laws,...

"No," John stopped him, "the 14th Amendment to the Constitution of the **United States** and the Constitution of the State of Mississippi."

His voice raised, "I **SAID** the 14th Amendment to the Constitution of the United States and the Constitution of the State of Mississippi, and the statues and law, that is about the affidavit all the way through, isn't it?" He shook the paper, as if it wasn't worth his time. "And it is assuming a whole lot when you come down and file an affidavit saying witnesses are in Florida when as a matter of fact they have been served with process, when there has been personal service on them here in Jones County?"

Puzzled, John began, "If they were in Jones County at this time, we will completely ignore that part of the motion which speaks of Willie Johnson and Hettie Johnson, and go forward with the..."

Again interrupting, Schwartzfager used the moment to verbally shove him, "All right, you talk about due diligence all the way through your affidavit, and all the affidavits you filed, is that what you tell the court is due diligence?"

John raised his shoulders and returned, "I think the due diligence I have used in attempting to locate these witnesses on information and belief I have obtained, and find that they are in Florida is as much due diligence as you or any other member of the bar would have used, Mr. Swartzfager."

The back and forth between them regarding the witnesses, where they were, and why Poole thought they were of enough good character to appear, finally ended with, him.

"Why did they leave town, then?"

John paused for a moment, feeling the eyes of the courtroom floor burning.

"I have no idea," he finally said.

Deavours, who had all but put his feet on the table, leaning backwards in his chair grinning, turned somewhat to the crowd, laughed and said, "I wouldn't think so." Laughter only slightly stifled joined in the antics.

Al stood up, "We object to that your Honor."

"I thought you would," Deavours laughed and rocked in his chair, while the courtroom took advantage of the bending of the rules, exchanged comments and laughed a bit louder. The balcony, in contrast, was dead silent.

Collins looked aside to hide his smile, but said as to a favored son, "Gentlemen, let's not have any side remarks. Proceed."

Pauly then proceeded to ask about Willie's knowledge of the witnesses' location.

"Well, Willie didn't know." John replied with dry candor. "He didn't have much time to go out here and find out those things."

"That's right," Pauly continued, "but he has been able to confer with you and your associate here throughout this thing?"

After affirming that he was able to confer somewhat and name witnesses, Pauly came closer to John and asked, "So you don't think a man who is insane would be able to do that?"

John leaned towards him and said with raised brows "I don't know whether you realize it or not, but there are 170 degrees of insanity." He had garnered this statistic in his meeting with the psychologist.

Pauly looked into John's eyes, perceiving an unspoken message. He cocked his head, and said with a grin, "Well, I've got some of them, I think after this." More courtroom chuckles followed.

John related that the psychologist had referred him to a psychiatrist, who actually treats diseases of the mind. The first two trials had not afforded McGee the aid of psychiatric treatment. He delineated this and other steps he and Al had taken to prepare for the case. Schwartzfager pushed him to know why he hadn't even worked on Sunday to prepare, couldn't he have called the psychiatrist then?

John straightened in the chair, and responded, "No, because I wanted to make further investigation and to study the facts, because, as you know, Mr. District Attorney, and most members of the bar know, in order to adequately prepare a case, you have got to study the facts, and study out what arguments can be presented and how the arguments are to be presented, and what they are to be based on etc."

Pauly attempted to avoid this fact by bringing up that the defense had the benefit of having the two previous records of the trial.

John responded, "I have not had the first record. I have attempted to locate the first record in this case, and it has been impossible."

Swartzfager stated that he had the second trial, which should have been enough. Deavours tapped his pencil as he secured in the back of his mind the safety of the first trial transcript in its place of hiding. Noticing London's sideway glance, he cleared his throat and resumed his attention to the questioning.

"Have you had help in Jackson in preparing the motions you bring down here, the several motions, from attorneys either in Jackson or from out of the State or in the State in preparing those motions?"

Answering truthfully as regarding the motions and avoiding the loaded question that sought to unveil the participation of the Civil Rights Congress, John replied, "I have had no help whatever."

Pauly went on to ask questions about what investigators helped him, and who hired him. "Friends of Willie McGee's" wasn't enough, so he persisted, "Who are his friends who hired you?" London objected, as this was not related to the issue, and the Judge reluctantly sustained.

The next person put on the stand was London, who, when being questioned by Poole, stated the facts precisely as to what had happened on that night. The State had denied a desire to present an argument, the Defense had said that it wanted to argue, but was exhausted, and requested extension. The Court made a statement, "...to the effect that the facts themselves were self-explanatory," and overruled the motion for continuance. In effect, he said for the record that the Court refused to give time by simply asking the State if they were ready for trial and setting the date.

On cross-examination, Swartzfager questioned London whether or not he and Poole drove back to Jackson that night. How did they have the energy for that? London recounted that they had eaten, taken a nap, and were then called home for a personal emergency. Al attempted to remain stoic at this point, not wanting to add fuel to the fire by bringing up what the emergency was, saying it was 'personal'. Swartzfager persisted, thinking it may have been a meeting with the CRC, but soon dropped it in favor of questioning why they hadn't driven to Pensacola instead, that weekend.

Regardless of having really uncovered anything significant, he left the examination feeling that he had shown that the Defense had ample time for their investigation. He then called Deavours to the stand to testify to their version of the events – that Poole had declined to argue without asking for extra time to eat and rest before arguing the motion. Deavours recounted it with precision as he saw it. Swartzfager then asked if he had been exhausted himself, to which Deavours replied cockily, "Well, a little bit. I hadn't done much work, you boys did most of the work," He chuckled.

Swartzfager kept his questioning brief, not particularly caring for the fact that he had been lumped together under the degrading term "boys," usually saved for the men of the black population. The defense had no wish, either, to cross-examine.

London then requested the court reporter's records to clear up matters, to which the Court replied, "That request is overruled. The Court doesn't think the testimony in this case shows any cause for continuance whatever. The Court itself was present and knows what happened that night." After recounting the episode from the same perspective of the State, he declared that time was offered and declined by the Defense. He continued saying, "The Court doesn't have to hear argument, and the Court has a right in its own discretion to refuse to hear argument when the testimony is all one way. It would be utter foolishness to take up the time of the court to hear argument on an issue where the testimony is all on one side. The motion, therefore, is overruled."

John stood and looked to the court reporter. "Note our exception," he said somberly.

The Judge announced a recess for lunch as he slammed the gavel and rose in one motion. Willie stood as he was being handcuffed and allowed himself a loving look towards the balcony, scanning for hope in the faces who stared down at him. John and Al spoke silently with their eyes, trying to give one another the same.

CHAPTER TWENTY-TWO

A MOST SPECIAL VENIRE

John and Al spent their lunch in a room in the back of the courthouse, going over the arguments for the afternoon. They would argue the Motion to Quash the Special Venire that was introduced with their other motions this morning. They somehow had to prove what they knew – that the jurors list had been tampered with, and that the special venire, was indeed, especially free from election of the black population, other than the three placed to satisfy the rule established from the Supreme Court's ruling in the "Patton" case.

"It may not have been the Circuit Clerk, himself who went back and changed the list, you know. It could have been a supervisor that changed the list and snuck it back in, without anyone knowing," John had pondered. "Meadors might not want his job jeopardized, but he could have looked the other way while someone else did it,"

"Who knew where the key was."

"Exactly – who was <u>shown</u> where the key was."

"The majority of the names came from Beat One," Al reflected. "Beat One? What locale was that?" John interrupted.

"Oh, you want to know where Beat One is? Well, Beat One takes in the area of a square mile or so right around the Hawkins' house, oddly enough!" Al punctuated the information with sarcasm, "A very 'special' venire."

The motion stated the fact, and also that there had been a "deliberate and systematic exclusion of Negroes from said jury lists"… and that the Special Venire had been altered by placing the names of "…a nominal few members of the Negro Race in an attempt to make a token effort to satisfy the requirements of the Constitution of Mississippi and the Constitution of the United States…" Other wording that would raise the ire of the Prosecution and the Court, was the statement, "That the Board of

Supervisors of Jones County, Mississippi, did not select from the aforesaid registration books the names of qualified persons of good intelligence, sound judgment, and fair character, and list the same for jury service as said Board was required to do by the aforementioned Statute," implying that the Hawkins' friends and neighbors would neither be fair nor nonjudgmental. The fact that they were alleging fraud by the Board of Supervisors, itself, would be enough to shift the sentiment of the court into high gear this afternoon.

"If we can't get the Circuit Clerk, Meadors, to break, there is not much a way to prove it, other than the list, itself," Al said, frankly.

John held his head in his hand, which ached with the gravity of the task and added, "If the supervisors are cut from the same cloth as the policemen around here, no one is going to offer any information that will help us." "Time!" The Baliff announced, opening the door a crack.

"It's mainly for the record and the bill of exceptions," Al added as they walked towards the court, "let's just remember that. Al encouraged John with a hand on his shoulder as he followed him into the courtroom, which was already mostly filled. John took a quick look at the balcony and nodded towards the somber crowd. Bessie braved a return nod.

The Circuit Clerk, Lonnie Meador, was called to the stand, and Al took up the first part of the questioning on details of how many qualified electors were in each beat, and did he make the certification of those electors before this venire was drawn. He then asked where the jury box was kept, and how it was sealed. It was kept in a secure place, sealed with a Yale lock, he had replied. When he was questioned as to whether there was any tape around the slits of the box, Meadors reacted.

"Well, are you intimating that I have been tampering with the jury box?" "No sir, not at all," Al coolly replied.

"Well, I want to get that straight, first," Meadors said, grumpily.

After other detailed questioning on the box and how it was kept, Al asked where it was presently. When Meadors replied that it was in the Clerk's office, Deavours sat up straight in his seat and interjected, "And empty, too, isn't it?" which impertinence was ignored by the Judge.

Deavours started his cross-examination with the same question, which had not much bearing on the actual alleged act and continued to ask a list of tedious questions that merely gave Meadors a chance to say he had done everything just as it ought to have been. London returned to the questioning and asked if he had counted the number from each Beat. He didn't know exactly the count and was excused by the court to count them and return. Meador's wife was then put on the bench to testify that she had actually been the Circuit Clerk at the time of the drawing, but had been ill. Her husband had 'stepped in' to fill her place during the drawing. John and Al looked at each other meaningfully. There was no evidence to question her on, however, and she was excused.

Several circuit-court and county officials were questioned, including a Mr. Orso, who was in charge of preparing the list for Beat One electors. Mr. Orso had been questioned in pretrial and had said at that time that he did not know whether the persons on his list were Whites or Negroes. This time he was asked if he was personally acquainted with the Negro electors on his list, to which he replied, "Yes, I know every one of them."

When the contradiction was brought up to him, he stuttered, saying, "I don't...if I answered the question that way, sir, I was just mistaken."

London moved that the prior testimony be put in the record to avoid repetition, to which the Judge promptly overruled. An exception was noted. Further questioning revealed that each elector was reviewed by the Board to determine whether or not that person was of good character and truly qualified to be a juror. If the man wasn't known, he was just skipped. Al noted this when he said, "And if you didn't know him, well, you just passed him by?"

Orso was pretty well flustered by this time and sat forward. "I am going to ask you a question. Do you think it would be right if I put the name of every one of them on there?"

London turned to the Judge, "We object to the witness asking the attorney questions." Judge Collins had no time to respond if he was going to, before Orso nearly shouted, "I would be very much satisfied, it would please me very much if they would permit me to put every qualified elector in the jury box, whether it was a Negro, Jew, or whatever he was."

Al puzzled at the steamy face across from him for a moment before he looked to the Judge and said, "I don't believe we have any further questions for Mr. Orso, your Honor,"

Deavours, repeating his tactics used with all others, gave Orso a chance to cool down and say that he did everything in his job with prudence and precision, with fairness and impartiality. John whispered to Al during the questioning and Al nodded. Al stepped back to the witness stand for re-direct examination, asking him if his method had been the same during the course of his job, to which he replied positively. Deavours objected. "If the Court please, he can't remember twelve or fifteen years."

"Objection sustained."

London turned to the reporter, "Note our exception."

Deavours wagged his head sarcastically, "Note my exception to his exception."

The defense then asked that Meadors be brought back to the stand. Al questioned him if it was true that the majority of the persons on the special venire were drawn from Beat One, the District in which the crime is alleged to have been committed? He admitted that 69 out of 100 electors were drawn from Beat One. On cross-examination, Deavours pointed out that the majority of "qualified" electors were, in fact, from Beat One. The means by which the electors were qualified were almost impossible to determine, as the qualification process was mostly a subjective judgment call by the supervisors.

John requested that there be an allowance to question whether Negroes have sat on juries in the First Judicial District.

The Judge replied that testimony had already shown that the members of the board had not engaged in fraud or discrimination and concluded by saying, "Now, gentlemen, if you have any witnesses that you want to introduce to show that there was any box in the county left unlocked, or tampered with, of left open, or to which the public had access, or if you have any witnesses that you want to introduce to show fraud in the drawing of this venire, I want to hear it. I want you to present it now." He stared challengingly at the Defense.

Knowing there had been no time to investigate, or that there would be any person who would willingly come forth, John started, "Your Honor, we want to take an exception to your ruling…"

"All right, sir," the Judge cut him off, but John continued, "…<u>because</u>, members of this venire have been drawn from the First Judicial District and we have alleged in our motion that there has been a systematic exclusion of Negroes from the jury list and from the jury boxes in the First Judicial District as well as the Second Judicial District." He spoke frankly and knew it to be the truth.

The Judge exploded that defense had not introduced a "scintilla of testimony" to prove it.

However, the very next witness acknowledged that there hadn't been any Negro jurors for as long as he had lived in the district.

"Now how long have you lived down there in that District?" Al asked. "Fifty-four years."

As the witness was excused, the Judge lifted himself slightly in his chair and announced, "This court is adjourned for the day. We will resume at 9:00 tomorrow morning." The gavel went down.

"All rise!" The Baliff commanded.

Deavours and Schwartzfager took the moment afterwards to shake hands, hear whispered jokes and laugh too loudly over them.

Al and John gathered their belongings slowly as McGee, who had attempted to be as invisible as possible during the last part of the day, now rose for his handcuffs. His eyes shifted ever so slightly towards the prosecution. Willette was standing silently beside her husband, who was asking hushed questions to Deavours. Her cheeks reddened as she felt the glance, and she fumbled to straighten her skirt. John, taking in the scene, drew his attention back.

"Willie, tomorrow will be the juror's selection. We may not have time to get into the meat of the case until Friday." Willie nodded, looking down as he was being addressed in the presence of so many white men. "Try to get some sleep tonight, you hear me?" He attempted to look into Willie's eyes, but Willie just answered quietly, head still bowed, "Yessuh."

After the courtroom floor crowd had dispersed, the balcony began to thin, and Al and John lifted their cases to make their departure. This time John's hand was on Al's shoulder, "You're one cool cat in the courtroom, you know that?" They both allowed themselves a laugh and met the refreshment of the evening air with welcome.

The evening's paper rolled out less than an hour later with the headline, "Willie McGee on Trial a Third Time." It started out by stating that there were new delays as… "Defense attorneys consumed all morning in futile argument for a continuance and this afternoon they had filed another motion seeking to Quash the Special Venire." The article continued for two pages summarizing the first two trials and noted that the new attorneys for the third trial were "young." Not speaking of the crime as alleged only, it painted the scene for readers as, "The young woman who was so brutally ravished on that 1945 November night…is again expected to take the stand for the third time before a jury, to relate her night of horror. During her testimony, she will again be expected to point an accusing finger at the Negro to charge him with the crime for which he faces the penalty of death."

"So, she pointed a finger, last time, did she?" Al shook the paper and looked at John, who had already read it and was untying his shoes. "I thought she said she didn't see him, because it was so dark."

"They all look alike, you know," John said, with a sarcastic grin.

"Ha!" Al continued, "Get this – 'It was Chief Valentine's brilliant deduction and detection that first pointed the finger of suspicion toward McGee. ' And," he continued in feigned drama, "It was that same finger that grabbed his blackjack to plow in his head!"

John smiled slightly. "Have you read the part about today's 'vigorous' cross-examination by Pauly Swartzfager that 'weakened' the defense?"

"Hmm…" was Al's return, as he read on to find it.

"We can't expect this town's paper to give a fair report, or even acknowledge there has been any foul play." John reached for his pack of cigarettes and pushed aside the plate of a half-eaten dinner.

"Nope," Al said. It summarized the situation sufficiently.

CHAPTER TWENTY-THREE

BESSIE TAKES THE STAND

The next morning in court a parade of jurors were questioned as to whether or not they had a fixed opinion of guilt or innocence in the case. The courtroom audience was sparse, due to the tedious nature of selecting jurors. When the first was asked of whether or not he had a fixed opinion, he answered with a hearty, "Yes, I do, yes, sir!"

London requested that the examination be taken down by the court reporter, which request was turned down by the Judge, as "It wouldn't be proper to take down the whole thing."

John protested, "Our point in moving to have the examination taken down is that the answers to these questions have direct bearing on our contention in this case. For that reason we feel it is only fair to allow the record to showthis."

"In what way?" the Judge, already impatient with the process, was ready to get jury selection out of the way.

"Your Honor, in this case of course we have already filed a motion for change of venue, and we want the record to show the general attitude of some of the members of this special venire in the event we would want to renew the motion for change of venue, which we think we have a right to do."

The Judge calculated a moment then said, "The Court will permit you to make a record of all the jurors who get excused because they had a fixed opinion."

"Note our exception to that ruling," John directed towards the reporter. He or London had to manually request for each question they felt was important to be in the record. Already, five prospective jurors had insisted they had fixed opinions. Another question posed by London to one candidate who said he didn't have a fixed opinion was, "Now, Mr. Lowe, this is a case in which a colored man is charged with having committed rape upon a white woman, a jury is going to determine whether or not that is true. We don't know what is true, that is what we want to decide in this case. Of course, under the law every man, white or colored, is entitled to the same consideration. Under the law, if you are accepted as a juror in this case, it will be your duty to give him consideration, regardless of his race or color, can you do that in this case?"

Mr. Lowe looked at Al with tight lips and said frankly, "No, sir." The juror was excused.

Several others were excused for fixed opinions before the Court took a lunch break. On return, the Judge himself decided before he let another one go, to question Mr. Cornett, who stated he also had a fixed opinion. Mr. Cornett was a simply dressed man but stuck his chin out to these impudent lawyers as he spoke, with some pride in his opinion that would support his neighbors. He believed McGee was guilty and should get the chair. Was he fixed in opinion because he was at the other two trials and heard testimony? No sir, he was convinced because of newspaper articles.

"All right, Mr. Cornett," Judge Collins bent over towards him, "the Court will instruct you that in this case that you are to be governed solely by the testimony in this case, and that the fact that he has been twice convicted wouldn't be any evidence of guilt in this case, you understand that?"

Mr. Cornett considered, "Yes, sir." He wasn't that convinced, but this was the Judge that had let his son off easy a couple of years ago. He figured he owed him a favor.

"Would you follow that instruction, and will that weigh with you any at all in this case if you are so instructed by the Court?" Collins pressed.

Mr. Cornett replied positively, not knowing how to do otherwise. At the end of questioning, the Judge felt this juror was clean inside and out.

"All right. I think he is a fair juror," Collins finally declared.

"Note our exception," John chimed, then immediately continued, "Now, Mr. Cornett, if the State should prove beyond reasonable doubt that Willie McGee had sexual relations with the prosecutrix in the case, and the State proved no more than that beyond a reasonable doubt, and then the Court instructed you that there are more elements to the crime of rape than just having sexual intercourse with a woman, under such circumstances would you turn Willie McGee aloose and say he was not guilty?"

Mr. Cornett looked confounded. "I don't know that I under..." he paused.

John spoke a bit more slowly, "In other words, Mr. Cornett, just because a man had sexual intercourse with a woman that wasn't his wife, you wouldn't convict him of rape, would you, just because of that?"

Mr. Cornett's head was swimming. "Well, it's according to how it all come about." "Would you convict him of rape just because he had sexual intercourse with a woman that wasn't his wife, because of that alone?" Cornett gulped, seemingly with a memory.

"Well, no," he said slowly, "I would have to know all the – " Swartzfager interrupted, "If the Court please, we think all that is improper."

The judge took over, explaining the difference between rape and consensual sex and asked if he could judge accordingly. Could he follow that instruction?

"Yessir," Cornett said, taking a breath. He was accepted as a juror.

At the end of the juror selection, after Collins had convinced several that they would, indeed, be impartial in their judgment, the Defense moved to vacate the previous order not to quash the special venire on the grounds that no members of the Negro Race had been selected to be reviewed as prospective jurors, calling it discrimination against the defendant and a deprivation of his rights. The Judge waved it away by saying that there was one Negro selected who was selected but asked to be excused due to illness. A murmur in the balcony was background to the exception.

The jurors having been selected, Collins looked at the clock which read already just past 3:00 p. m. "The Court will take a fifteen-minute break," he proclaimed, satisfied himself with the twelve who would stand in judgment of McGee's fate. Al and John used the break for a cigarette and coffee in the back room of the court, when a messenger boy came in.

"Are you Mr. Poole?" he asked, with his hand already extended, holding a note for him.

"Yes," John said, sitting up and reaching for some coins. "Thank you very much!" he said as John took the note in exchange.

John laughed as he finished reading the note, "Well, well – Ol' Pauly will be interested to hear this one!" and handed it to Al. Al read it and laughed out loud.

Upon resuming court, London began:

"Comes now the defendant by his attorneys and renews his application for a continuance of this cause due to a mistake in identity in the process shown by the records of this Court to have been served on Willie Johnson and Hettie Johnson, who were subpoenaed by the defendant as witnesses in his behalf, and the defendant would show unto the Court that the persons served by the aforesaid subpoena were not the persons for whom process was issued. The defendant would further show unto the Court that Willie Johnson for whom the process was requested was never served, but that one Willis, W-i-l-l-i-s, Johnson was the person served by said process." He continued, "And further that process was issued for Hettie, H-e-t-t-i-e, Johnson, and that the return on this process was on Hattie, H-a-t-t-i-e, Johnson, and the defendant wishes the Court to allow him to offer evidence to substantiate this motion."

The witnesses who had been found by the Prosecution were actually the wrong couple. All the accusations by Swartzfager that Poole had been negligent in finding his witnesses now fell flat.

Swartzfager feigned disinterest, scribbling notes on his pad. However, when the request was made to re-introduce testimony taken on the previous day due to this, the Judge promptly overruled. Deavours, irritated by this newfound fact however, asked that they be able to examine the Constable who served process, I. O. Fowler, whose examination showed the evident mistake. John then took the stand to say for the record every effort he had made to subpoena the correct persons. Swartzfager made an attempt to redeem himself by arguing – How did they even know the witnesses were in Florida? Bessie had told them. Let her be put on the stand. Bessie put her hand to her mouth as she was called down from the balcony to the stand. Her heart began to race as she descended the steps.

"Lawd've mercy!" she whispered into her handkerchief. John smiled compassionately at her, making her feel a bit more comfortable before she was sworn in.

"State your name, please?" John asked kindly.

"Bessie McGee." She was glad there weren't so many eyes from the lower courtroom floor at this point to burn through her.

"You are the mother of Willie McGee?" "Yes, sir."

"I will ask you whether you have ever talked with Willie and Hettie Johnson?" "Yes, sir."

"I will ask you whether you have ever talked with them about this case?" "Yes, sir."

"I will ask you to state to the Court what you talked with them about when you mentioned this case."

Swartzfager objected – it was hearsay. John pled that the only way to show what they knew was by hearsay. Surprisingly, the Judge overruled.

"Do you, Bessie, know of your own personal knowledge that we can establish an alibi by the presentation of these two witnesses?"

"Yes, sir, I believe you can."

"We object unless she knows," Swartzfager interjected. It was sustained.

John took a deep breath and began again, "I will ask you if you know if these witnesses are in Florida?"

Bessie looked up in remembrance. "Well, when I gone down to their house to see them down here on East Oak, why the lady next door – "She stopped – how had it happened? Nervousness was blocking her memory. "I went to this house where she – where they was living at, I went there and knocked and the lady next door told me they wasn't there. Well, I gone over then to her house and asked her could she tell me which way I could find them, and she said, "They done moved now to Florida, Pensacola, Florida." She nodded to confirm her memory was accurate.

"Did she give you their address?"

"Well, she give me an address to find them in Florida." "Did you then give that address to your attorneys?" "Yes, sir."

"Will Willie and Hettie Johnson testify as to the defendant's whereabouts on the night this crime is alleged to have been committed?" John asked with more vigor, hoping for no objection.

"Yes, sir," Bessie said with a note of certainty.

John continued, "Did they tell you what hours of the night they were with him?"

"Well," Bessie looked upwards again. "They say Willie come to her house at two o-clock that night and they gambled there then from that time up until five-thirty next morning."

"And the crime is alleged to have been committed around four-thirty in the morning?" John asked, knowing that at least Mrs. Hawkins had come screaming naked to her neighbors about that time – whatever had made her do that.

"I don't know, sir, exactly what time the crime was committed, but I do know she told me that."

Swartzfager stood up somewhat lazily and said, "If the Court please, we are going to renew our objection as to that. Of course, the Court overruled my objection, and I don't want to be obstinate about it, but,"

Judge Collins, looking interested in the testimony, returned, "Well, I am going to open up the gates and let them testify."

John, looked hopeful and nodded towards Bessie, saying, "That is all." Swartzfager, looking irritated, began to cross-examine Bessie.

"How do you know they will testify to that?" Bessie replied, "Accordin' to what they say."

"When did you talk with them about it?" Bessie didn't like the glint she saw in his eyes.

"I talked with them when they had the first trial in Laurel." And you didn't see my sufferin' then and don't now, she thought.

"They weren't in Florida then, were they?" Swartzfager cocked his head. "No, sir," Bessie wished she could look up at her pastor.

He narrowed his eyes, "Why didn't you use them on the first trial?" Bessie felt panic, but managed, "I did, I..."

John stood up, "We object. She isn't the one to present evidence." The Judge merely stated, "No ruling."

"Well," Swartzfager continued, "did you tell the lawyer who represented him the first time about them?"

Bessie swallowed, "I told Mr. Boyd."

He asked for details, where had they been? When did they leave? She told the story again. They left before the second trial.

"When did you tell these men here," he waved his hand towards the Defense, "they were down in Florida?"

"Since they been had this case on," she said simply.

"All right," he pressed his lips together. "They were hired, I believe they told the Court, on the 17th day of February. When did you first talk with them about it?"

"I wouldn't be to say shore, to tell the truth, what day it was I told these men where she was at." Bessie's heart was pounding steadily.

Swartzfager pressed her to remember the day, but she couldn't. He pressed on, and her nervousness reached a pitch. She scrambled through a dizzy mind to remember events.

"When the paper come out, let's see, from the paper –I think it was Wednesday. I seed it in the paper – the Wednesday paper, I think, if I make no mistake."

John's jaw tightened as he glanced sideways at Al.

Swartzfager pressed on – what date was it exactly, was it before Willie was indicted? No, she remembered seeing the paper on a Wednesday.

"Did you talk with them then that day?"

"No, sir, I didn't talk with them that day." She felt certain of that, anyway. "So, if you talked with them on Wednesday, it would have been the next Wednesday, is that right?"

What he messin it all up for, she thought? "No, I don't understand just – anyway, I talked with them Wednesday. I seed it in the paper Wednesday, I seed these fellow's name in the paper." She blotted her forehead with a handkerchief.

As Swartfager continued to needle her, John stood up and said firmly, "She said she didn't know."

Swartzfager turned to him with raised brows, "I am trying to refresh her memory." Bessie tried again, "I say I don't know exactly when they came to see me.."

Swartzfager didn't let her finish. "How soon after you saw it in the paper was it?"

Bessie paused at her train of thought being interrupted, "…I do know I seen it in the paper."

Swartzfager's impatience was visible, "But how soon after you saw their names in the paper did you see these men?"

Bessie's full lips stretched to a nearly straight line. "I couldn't exactly tell you," she said with finality.

Schwartfager continued to barrage her with questions, and finally persuaded her to say that it was at least two days afterwards, but she still couldn't recall if it was before Sunday, or not.

John stood up again, "She stated she didn't know," he said firmly.

Swartzfager grinned, "I know you don't want her to tell it, Mr. Poole, but she is on cross-examination."

Judge Collins grumped, "Proceed, gentlemen."

Bessie pleaded, "I say I couldn't tell you, and I want to tell the truth." She was serious about this. She had put her hand on the Bible, and she did fear God's wrath much more than this white man standing in front of her, egging her on.

Swartzfager questioned her without empathy – why didn't she make any effort to go down to Florida, herself, to get them?

"No, sir, because I didn't think I ought to went, I thought the lawyers would tend to that." Bessie didn't want to tell him that she had never been out of the State of Mississippi, or that she didn't have money for a trip like that, or maybe she would have gone to Florida, knocking on doors to save her boy. She had, at least, sent a telegram and said so to Swartzfager. He had asked about a phone call.

Didn't he know not everybody has a phone?

"I never did get no answer from that telegram," she proclaimed, "but I haven't sent them nare one in this trial."

The telegram had not come back, so they would have received the first one. She didn't even know that they might testify – wasn't that right? She just believed they would. What made her believe that? She couldn't tell him that her instincts had saved her and her family many a time in the past. Her instinct told her so about this.

"I just believe they would come, that's my belief." "That's all," Swartzfager finally tiring of the effort.

John had a chance to re-directly examine her. "Bessie, contrary to Mr. Swatzfager's statement, we would like for you to tell exactly when it was, if you know, that we talked to you?"

Now she could concentrate a little better. Missah Poole was so much easier to talk to. "I was just studying, trying to get my mind together – now it was –"

John tried to help her out, "Now, Bessie –" but she waved her hand, as if to say she was receiving the information from a distant part of her memory. "All right, go ahead," he complied.

She remembered seeing Clarence and John "if I make no mistake – if I make no mistake, I believe that was on Monday." John sighed.

Finally, Bessie was excused from the chair, and she snuck outside – "for just a spell," she thought – to breathe in the cool air and straighten her mind out.

After calling John back on the stand and grilling him on the same details, Judge Collins took the final stance that evidence was "flimsy" even if the witnesses were found that they would actually come to court. The Court granted no continuance and overruled the motion.

"Note our exception," London directed to the reporter.

John quickly stood and added, "And note our exception also on the grounds that we have not been able to sufficiently prepare this case, by virtue of not having a longer time in which to prepare it, and that to press us to trial at this time will deny to the defendant competent counsel as guaranteed him by the due process clause of the State Constitution," he breathed deeply, "by the clause of the Constitution of the State which guarantees to him the rights to a fair and impartial trial, and by the Fourteenth Amendment to the Constitution of the United States."

The proclamation sounded to the disinterested and nearly empty courtroom was punctuated by the gavel's pound to adjourn and seemed to be said for an audience far from the walls that encompassed them.

CHAPTER TWENTY-FOUR

A MONSTER AND A BEAST

Gerry sipped coffee while her mother rocked Babay in the next room. She took advantage of the opportunity to read the morning's paper, which lauded the fact that "First Grand Jury Containing Negroes Concludes Work." She grimaced at the thought that the Grand Jury "three" anomaly was only for show and influenced nothing. She put the paper down, remembering Court would start again soon. She shouldn't call again. The emotion might show in her voice and take away from the hope John said he felt last night, regardless of the past two days. He had been more worried about her and the baby than himself, but she thought she heard a slight tremor as he talked about tomorrow's task of interrogating Mrs. Hawkins and putting Willie on the stand. Gerry stood and walked towards the window to feel the morning sun's rays shine on her face. The light glinted across her mother's pewter dish that read, "The Lord is My Shepherd, I shall not want." She looked at it thoughtfully, then out the window again. Crocuses were beginning to bloom, scattered like ballet dancers in a random pattern across the still frosty ground.

Gerry tried to embrace the call to life, but her heart felt hard like the stone – with the warning attached.

In Laurel, Troy and Willette Hawkins drove to the courthouse in silence until Willette spied the gathering crowd. She moaned, shook her head, and said, "Why, why, why?" Her voice escalated to a pitch as she turned to her husband accusingly, "Why do I have to do this again? And this time in front of…of everybody! Don't you realize how humiliating this is?" She moaned as if death was knocking at her door, and she sunk further down in her seat. Troy's blood pressure was so high, he couldn't calm her very well. He gritted his teeth and declared, "I'll take care of that two-bit attorney if he even so much as insinuates that you had sex with that nigger!"

Willette silently stared at him, eyes large, her mixture of emotions rendering her incompetent of a response. He looked at her again, eyes darting this time.

"Me and the poker fellows are ready. There's more, too! We'll take care of them if they don't stay in line, don't you worry."

Willette said in a lower, but pointed tone, "Whatever the case, be assured I am never going through this again!" She paused for a moment to take out a pill bottle, shake a few into her hand, and repeated sharply, "Never!" She threw the pills in her mouth and swallowed bitterly.

The jury filed in, one behind the other, having been briefed on their instructions just before court. It was an all-white, all-male jury from several different walks of life. A farmer with weathered skin sat next to the storekeeper. An automobile mechanic, a service station manager, a sawyer for a lumber plant, a manager of a bottling plant, three other farmers, and lastly, a projector for a local theater. There was much adjusting, clearing of throats and nervous gestures before everyone faced the entrance of the handcuffed McGee. Eyes followed, with much interest, his sober, downturned face. They observed the Defense conferring, passing sheets between themselves, and the Prosecution, adjacent, whispering to their clients. There was standing room only – a courtroom packed with solemn faces that ranged from ivory white to pale rust on the lower floor, while the balcony produced a sea of chocolate to black sheen. An occasional pair of eyes darted to and from each crowd, but due to an unseen tension, most kept to their own population. A white collared male in the balcony was seen lifting his eyes upwards in prayer. Muffled comments halted when the Baliff stood and intoned, "In the Circuit Court of the Second Judicial District of Jones County, Mississippi, State of Mississippi vs. Willie McGee, Judge F. B. Collins presiding!"

Mrs. Willette Hawkins, first called to the witness stand, was sworn in with trembling hand. A black suit dress accentuated her tall, lean frame. A black hat adorned with a single black twist had a slight veil tucked ready for use. She twitched tight lips, appearing as a woman attending a funeral. She glanced towards the jury to her side, and quickly to the balcony crowd. It was much different, this trial.

Deavours, chest plumped in a fine suit coat, addressed Willette with a gentle but strong tone, "Your name is Mrs. Troy Hawkins?"

Her eyes fluttered as she answered diminutively, "Yes sir."

Deavours encouraged her to match his tone, "Mrs. Hawkins, speak out loud so I can hear you, and if I can hear you back here, the jurors can hear you." She nodded slightly and he continued, "Mrs. Hawkins, where do you live?"

Willette seemed to want to swallow her voice and disappear. As Deavours asked questions about Troy's employment and the hours he worked, her eyes were locked forward to avoid seeing the table for the Defense. She pressed her arms tightly to her body.

"And he usually got home about what time?"

Willette cleared her throat, "Most always he got home around twelve o'clock, but this particular night it was during the first of the month and he had to work late."

"And what time did he get home that night?"

Troy had come home close to one o'clock, she related, and added that she had been in very bad health at the time.

"How long had you been sick, or in bad condition?

"Well, practically ever since I have been married. I haven't been well all that time, and I have always been thin and nervous." She lowered her eyes a bit as if hiding information.

"Now, Mrs. Hawkins, during that time, about November 1945, tell the jury approximately what you weighed?"

"Less than 100 pounds, about 92 pounds." Murmurs came from the crowd. "Mrs. Hawkins, on this particular night in November – what was the exact date, November 2?"

"This happened on November 2nd," she stated firmly, pressing her lips together. She said that she had gone to bed at twenty minutes to four as her baby had been sick. She had been up rocking and feeding her, but she couldn't get to sleep and was crying. Finally Troy came in and she told him that she would fix a bottle. "So, I got out of bed, or I got out of the room, went through the living room, the dining room and into the kitchen and fixed her bottle and went back in the bedroom and gave it to the baby," It was a practiced description. Deavours asked her the exact location, where she could have been seen from an outsider's point of view, and to describe the location of the bedroom, its relation to other rooms in the house and their windows.

"Mrs. Hawkins, on this particular night state to the jury whether or not you had a light in your room?"

"Yes sir, a small table light."

"What, if anything, occurred to that light during the night?"

"Well, the wind was blowing, and it knocked it off the table, so I just set the lamp on the floor by the bed near the window."

Deavours asked her to paint the picture of the room. It was very small, full of furniture, hard to get around, really, with the baby bed in there, but the baby was in bed with her that night and her two girls were in the room next to them.

Troy had gone to the back bedroom to get some rest because he was so exhausted. She had been terribly tired, too and must have gone to sleep just as soon as she got in bed. Willette paused, as if not wanting to delve into the next scene too quickly.

"Go ahead," Deavours encouraged her.

She took a deep breath and glanced again at the jury before continuing, "Well, I awoke, I heard some mumbling and scratching along by the side of my bed, and of course I thought it was Troy. I didn't know what he was doing there, but that was what I thought it was, and I called him. I said, "Troy, what do you want? What is wrong?" And this thing kept mumbling. Well, I started feeling along by the bed – my light had gone out – and I started feeling along, and felt up the back and got my hand on a bushy head, a kinky negro head, and he began to say, 'Shut your mouth, shut your mouth!'"

The women on the courtroom floor wagged their heads in sympathy, giving her encouragement to continue. "And then, you see, I realized it wasn't Troy. He said, 'Shut your mouth, shut your mouth, don't say a word, don't call him!' And of course I called him but he had just…Oh!"

Willette held her forehead dramatically as if reliving the scene, and finished, "I was just scared, that's all."

Deavours said in sympathetic tone, "Did he make any threats toward you, Mrs. Hawkins?"

She recoiled as if being presently threatened, sounding out dramatically, "He threatened me, he said, 'Don't open your mouth, I will cut your throat. I will cut your damned throat. I will cut your God damned head off. Don't say a word!'"

"Did he make any threats toward your children?"

"Not then, not until he was in bed with me." A guttural sound was heard from the courtroom floor. Willie's head was hung, focusing on his pounding heart.

"Mrs. Hawkins, did you try to turn on the lights in your room?" Deavours prompted her.

"I was lying on my right side, and the baby was over here," she indicated further to her right, "and when I heard this I turned over like this with my left hand," she felt energy at this point in acting out her tale, "and felt him and when he got on the bed, I reached up and tried to turn the light on and he said, "There is no reason for you doing that, the lights are out. I fixed them. I broke them." She began to quiver.

"Now Mrs. Hawkins, what efforts, if any, did you make toward resisting his advances that night?"

"Beg pardon?" Willette looked as if she felt light-headed.

"What efforts, if any, did you make toward resisting his advances that night?" Deavours reworded, as if this was very important for her to relate correctly. "What efforts or method did you use to try to fight him off?"

She shrugged and said, "I begged him not to do anything, I pleaded with him and I pushed him, and he was so big and so rough…he was just a brute, and there was nothing I could do." Willie looked nothing like a brute in the courtroom, as he wasn't a very large man, anyway, and was almost collapsed in on himself. It didn't change anyone's picture of the scene.

"Did he make any threats towards you?" Deavours repeated.

"He said, 'I will cut your throat, don't make any noise, I will cut your throat.' The baby kept whimpering and he said, 'Keep that damned brat quiet or I will cut her head open,' or something to that effect, and during the time I was calling Troy, and every time I said anything, he would shut me up, and all the time he was on the bed he was talking to me, telling me to 'shut up!' and he told me what he came for, and he said he was going to do it with me dead or alive, and the only reason in the world I took such things was for my family." She paused for breath, then proclaimed, "You know mother instinct is something."

Deavours nodded but kept the pace. "Mrs. Hawkins, did you believe he would carry out the threats he made toward you?"

"I did, He would have killed us all," her voice elevated as she spewed, "and I wish to God he had killed me, it would be better for my family all the way around if he had just killed me, but I wasn't thinking of myself, I thought all along he would kill me when he was through, and I thought my family would be protected." Her breath was heavy.

"Mrs. Hawkins, if you hadn't believed he would carry out those threats would you have submitted to him?"

"Never," she said, shaking her head firmly. "Never. From the minute he was there I thought he would kill me. I just prayed and prayed that something would happen that I could get away from him."

Deavours straightened and asked, "Mrs. Hawkins, did he actually have intercourse with you on that occasion?" The courtroom was dead silent.

Willette gathered her strength. "He actually had intercourse with me. He was on me from one moment into the other, from the whole time he was there. He was a beast, a brutal beast." She closed her eyes tightly for a moment.

Deavours leaned in. "You mean by that he actually had sexual intercourse with you?"

"He actually did. He raped me. He came there for that, that was what he said, and that's what he did." She held her arms at the elbows, hoping it would cause her not to shake so. Deavours continued to question her resistance, to which she replied, "I did everything in my power. God only knows how I fought it."

Bessie didn't know where to look. Not at her son, that was too painful. Not at her pastor or friends, she would break down at their sympathy, or rile up if they looked shocked. She certainly could not look at any on the courtroom floor, for fear of sparking retaliation from disrespect. It made her nauseous, though, to watch this white woman practically acting out the scene with her son as the demon. She looked down at her shoes. The ones Willie had given her years ago on Christmas Day. She blocked out all thoughts as Deavours asked how Willie was dressed.

"Yes, he –" Willette searched for acceptable words, "His nakedness was against mine the entire time. The only thing was, he had on an undershirt. I shoved until my arms were so tired, I shoved all I could, and all the time I was thinking about my baby, and her on the bed with him. That was the only thing I could do, push."

John made a note, "only an undershirt," and looked back again at the, indeed, frail woman on the stand. She had a spitfire about her but appeared to be stretched beyond the slight amount of weight on her bones, as if uncomfortable in her own skin. He held the two dramas being played out in his mind, as often he had held two chess games played simultaneously. The one Willie had written and talked about with the same plausibility as the one Willette was now forging on the stand. There was not an inch of common ground. Several men gathered together in a corner of the courtroom caught his attention, distracting him from hisstudy.

They whispered; countenances grim. This was the first time the public had heard Willette tell her story, and it was causing more than just a stir in the minds of the townsmen. John felt a chill.

"Mrs. Hawkins," Deavours was saying, "the man who attacked you finally left, did he?"

"Yes, sir, I had thought and thought all the way that he would kill me. I never thought that he would ever leave without killing me, so I told him," she took a breath, then continued, "I said, 'If you will leave me I will do anything, anything, promise you anything in the world.' And he said, 'Will you do that, Miss?' and I said, 'Yes, I will do anything if you will just leave me.' That was after he had raped he, he was still on me," she explained. "I was referring to the money that we had right in the room, and he said, 'Would you promise never to tell this?' and I said, 'I will never tell it as long as I live, it is between us, nobody will ever know what happened.'"

Willie involuntarily looked up at these words, as if he had heard them before, in a different world.

She continued, "and he said, 'Will you swear to God you will never tell it?' and I said, 'I swear before God I will never tell it,' and he just gave a shove and jumped up and ran out through the front door. He had the front door propped open, and when we went to bed the front door was locked." Willette caught Troy's eyes for a moment in an emotionless exchange. She turned back as Deavours was saying, "Do you know of your own knowledge, Mrs. Hawkins, how he got in the house?" "No, I don't know how he got in, but when I went to bed that night the small window on the west side of the house was closed, but it had just a slight opening in it. I kept thinking, 'I should push that down before I go to bed,' but you know, the baby being sick and everything, I didn't – I just didn't…"

"Mrs. Hawkins, during the time this man was in bed with you, state to the jury whether or not he made you take off your clothes or jerked your clothes off?" "He demanded that I take them off, he was…"

"Did you take them off?"

Willette looked shocked at this question, as if it were an accusation. "I beg pardon?" "Did you unbutton your clothes?" Deavours waved his hand, as if it were no great thing.

"I unbuttoned them," she started, "they were jerked off, oh, I don't remember how it was, but I did unbutton them, and I was stalling for time and he…"

Deavours interrupted, offering an out, "Did you do that because of the threats he had made toward you, Mrs. Hawkins?"

"Oh, yes," she said with some relief, "I was so afraid." "Afraid for yourself and your children?"

"For my family. We didn't even have a gun in the house," she bemoaned. "Mrs. Hawkins, tell the jury whether or not you were menstruating at that time?"

"I was menstruating at the time, it was at the end of my period and I wasn't menstruating a whole lot, but I was menstruating, I had on a sanitary napkin." "Did he make you take that off, or did he jerk it off?"

"No, I took it all off at one time. He told me to." She made her face look angry saying, "He said, 'Get that rag off.'"

Deavours nodded in affirmation, "Did you do that because you were afraid?" he asked.

"Because I was afraid," she nodded.

"…for yourself and your family?" She seemed irritated to have to repeat, and came back with unexpected fire.

"I was afraid, afraid. He threatened me, told me he would kill me and my family, and anybody that was that monstrous, that wouldn't stop raping a woman my age, and those little girls in there, I could just see him doing the same thing to them." She looked steeled not to cry.

"Mrs. Hawkins, after he left, what, if anything, did you do?"

"I lay there a little while, thinking, 'What will I do?' and I was…" she trailed off.

With Deavours' encouragement, she got back on track and told of getting out of bed, walking through the dark house, in the "darkest morning she had ever seen," making sure her girls were all right, before waking up her husband and saying, "Troy, wake up, wake up, the most horrible thing that could ever happen to a woman has happened to me!" Troy had tried to turn on the lights, and felt so bad that it happened. Willette paused in thought. "Go ahead, Mrs. Hawkins."

"Or at least he tried the switch, which is on the back porch, you know, how the old houses have meters on the back porch, and our meter was on the back porch just outside the door leading to his room." John wrote down, "his room."

"Well, he tried the switch, and it was so dark, and he couldn't find a match, and I was so scared, and we walked to the front of the house and the door was propped open, and we went on the front and tried to call somebody, we both called, and when we both called, I went all to pieces. Well, we had our neighbors all along there, all the neighbors looked after me, they all knew I was alone, and I went to one of my neighbors, went to the window and I said, 'It's Billie, I have…'"

London stood up, "We object to the conversation." "Objection sustained," Collins breathed.

Deavours continued, "Mrs. Hawkins, did you go to a neighbor's house?"

"I did, I went to the window and called them and begged them to let me in, let me in!" She described them as the Jensons, who did let her in.

"Mrs. Hawkins, I want to ask you just for the record, whether or not, if at all times during this act you made all the resistance you could?

"All that was in my power," she said with finality. "Did you ever submit to the act at all?"

"Never."

"And did he at all times threaten to kill you and your children?"

"Oh, he used some profanity, and every other word was 'shut your God damned mouth, I will cut your God damned throat.' One thing he said was, 'If you ever tell this on me, I won't just cut your throat, I will cut your head off and they will find it in one end of Laurel and the rest of you in the other end of Laurel.'

"And you say that happened here in the City of Laurel, Second Judicial District of Jones County, Mississippi?"

"Yes, sir," and she added dutifully, "and I was raped."

"That's all," Deavours said to the Judge and walked back proudly to the table.

All was quiet as John rose and walked with a slow step, clump, step, clump to a short distance from Mrs. Hawkins, who was wiping her eyes with her handkerchief, putting off looking at him.

He approached her gently. "Mrs. Hawkins, I know this must be a somewhat embarrassing incident, and I know your talking about it must be embarrassing to you, and I don't want to embarrass you, but I do want to ask you just a few questions to try to clarify for the jury the whole situation." She looked at him with suspicion and remained silent. He began again, "Now, you have told this story, I imagine, about twenty times, haven't you?"

"Beg pardon?"

He rephrased, "You have told this story a great many times, haven't you?" "Yes, sir." There was no way to avoid it.

"To your attorneys and to the court?" "Yes, sir."

"Would you state just about how many times you have gone over it, Mrs. Hawkins?" Devours bellowed, "We object to that."

"Objection sustained," Collins affirmed. It didn't matter – the point was made.

"Now, Mrs. Hawkins, I want to know where your bed was in reference to this door that leads into the living room from your bedroom?"

"As you leave it is to the south, up against that south wall, the head of it was."

"The head of it was?"

"The head was, so that I could lie there and see clear through into the living room, and it wasn't against the other wall, I had it pulled out from the wall." "Now I believe you stated, Mrs. Hawkins, that when this person…" he paused, "By the way, you don't know who that person was, do you?" He looked at her with large eyes.

"I never saw him," she said dryly.

"All you know is that he was a big monster of a Negro, that was what you thought?"

"He was a Negro, and he was a beast," she affirmed curtly.

"…And he was a big old Negro, and as you termed it while ago, a monster…" Deavours stood. "We object. The witness said she did not see him."

"No ruling," Collins replied.

John continued, "Now, Mrs. Hawkins, when he first came into the room, I believe you said you heard him scratching along the bed?"

"Crawling," she clarified.

"Crawling along the bed?" John tried to imagine the noise level of a crawl. "He was crawling along by the bed."

"Did you say you first thought it was Troy?" "I did," she said with certainty.

"Did you smell anything on his breath?"

She spoke more softly, as if remembering. "Not at that time…" Deavours interrupted, "Let her speak a little louder so the jury can hear her."

"Did you smell any whiskey on his breath at that time? John asked again, amplifying his voice to encourage her to do the same.

"Not until he got in my face," she said more loudly, with effort.

"You say you didn't smell any whiskey while he was down on his – while he was crawling?"

"No, not until – Well, he didn't have to crawl many steps to be in my face." Willlete squinted.

"Where was he when you first awakened?" John asked. "Along by the side of the bed," she repeated impatiently.

"And he was crawling at that time – Was he toward the end of the bed?" She sighed, "He was crawling up the front – up to the head of the bed." "I mean when you first awakened, Mrs. Hawkins, where was he atthat time? Was he crawling?" He wanted to clarify what woke her.

Willette became flustered. "Yes, he was crawling on his all-fours or something."

"I will ask you," John began, "was it a usual situation for Troy to be crawling along the bed there?" It was an obvious question to her fallacious conclusion.

"No, but no other man had ever been there, and I thought it was Troy." She stuck her chin out.

"Then you realized it wasn't Troy at that time?" he pressed.

"Not at that time, I didn't. I didn't know who it was and naturally I thought it was him, he was the only person in the house besides myself and the children," she said somewhat indignantly.

John wasn't swayed. "But now, Mrs. Hawkins, you have testified in court about this twice before, haven't you?"

Less confidently she admitted, "Yes, I have."

"And," he continued, looking at a paper he held, "I believe you said on one of the former trials, "That isn't Troy," and then you reached out to feel to see who it was?" This point would show that she hadn't responded with a scream, which would have been normal.

She looked down her nose at the attorney and said definitively, "At first I thought it was Troy, and until I started feeling, I thought it was him." She squirmed and continued, "You know, all this happened in a very few minutes."

Undeterred, John continued, "But now, when you started feeling, you say you knew it wasn't Troy at that time?"

She leaned back and pouted, "I don't remember now just how I felt about that."

"Well, the whole situation, Mrs. Hawkins…"

She cut him off, "It didn't take me but just a very few seconds to realize it wasn't Troy, but by then I was threatened."

John came back quickly. "Didn't you say the first thing he said to you was, "Miss, wake up"?

"Yes."

"Now, that was the first thing he said to you?"

"That's the first thing I remember," Willette crossed her arms tightly. "And you realized it wasn't Troy then, didn't you?"

She nodded. "Sometime within just a very few seconds."

"Now then, you started feeling along," John motioned his hand to revive the image, "didn't you?'

"Yes," she said, suspiciously.

"And you felt a human body?" His eyes widened dramatically. "I did." She remained stoic.

"Then you felt on up the human body," John moved his hand horizontally, "and felt the bushiest hair you had ever felt?"

"Yes," she said dryly.

"And that was the way it happened, Mrs. Hawkins?"

Willette looked trapped. There was something she wasn't getting right here.

Devour's eyes seemed to warn her. She remained silent.

John accepted it, saving his suspicions for the argument. "Now," he continued, "had he said anything to you other than, 'Miss, Miss, wake up,' until you got to his head?"

Willette forced the answer, "He said, 'Don't make any noise, be quiet.'" As John repeated it she added, "He was very hard to understand, though, he was just mumbling, mumbling."

"And you didn't understand everything he said?"

"No, I said he was hard to understand, he mumbled his words."

"And you had to do some straining to understand what he meant, is that right?"

"No, he made plain what he meant," Willette said with conviction, although contradictory.

As he continued to question her, and she answered as she had twice before, Willette looked out towards those looking at her, as if dissociating somewhat. She saw Troy glaring at the attorney, her own attorney searching his papers, and the bushy head of Willie McGee, as he was studying the floor. Her face was pale.

"Now Mrs. Hawkins, I want to go back just a little bit here. You had been in bed with your husband up until about twenty minutes to four?"

She creased her forehead in thought. "I don't remember that he had ever gotten in bed, we had been up and down with the baby. "Well, didn't you test..." John began.

"Well, I guess he was," she interrupted sharply.

"Then from the time that he came in and went to bed until about twenty minutes to four, he was in the bed with you during that time, wasn't he?" John looked as if he were reading from a paper.

Deavours stood and objected. "If the Court please, I suggest that she said she didn't remember whether he was or not."

John looked up towards the Judge, "I believe she said she thought he was." Judge Collins looked at Willette, who looked scared. He said gently, "Mrs. Hawkins, do you remember whether he was in bed at that time or not?"

"No," she simpered, "I really don't remember about that, Judge Collins."

John continued, "Well, then, Mrs. Hawkins, you did testify in one of the other trials that when you got your hand on his hair you said, "Go away. What do you want?" and "Why are you here?" That's true, is it not? He looked at her with wide eyes.

She pursed her lips, "That is the best I can remember, you know it has been quite some time."

"I believe you stated on a former trial and you stated here that you were scared for your children?"

"Well, I am still scared, still scared." She wouldn't let her daughter even look at colored men.

"What I mean," he drew her back, "is you were afraid he was going to attack your children?"

"Yes," she said flatly, but with quivering lip.

John saw the emotion and said compassionately, "Now, I don't mean to humiliate you, I am just trying to bring out the truth, and that was the main thing you were scared of, wasn't it?"

"What?" She looked up.

"That he was going to harm your children in some way?"

She sat up a bit and said, "I was. He was saying he was going to kill me and also them."

"Unhunh…" John studied her eyes, then continued, "Now, Mrs. Hawkins, I want to ask you whether he put both of his hands on you when this was happening?" Willette looked uncomfortable. "His hands?" she asked. "Yes."

She paused a moment, mouth open, before answering, "He used his whole body."

"Did he put his hands around you?" John looked at her quizzically. She grit her teeth and said, "He held me."

John pressed for clarification, "Did he put his arms around you?"

She answered with exasperation, "When he wasn't holding me with his hands he was holding me with his weight and his legs." She was almost shouting.

The questions kept coming, "Now he did put both of his hands on you at the same time?"

Deavours objected. "If the Court please, we submit he has asked that question three times, and we object to it as repetition. He said he didn't want to embarrass the lady," he added contemptuously.

"Objection sustained," Collins said, nodding his head.

John looked back at Deavours and said with sincerity, "I don't want to embarrass the lady."

"Then why are you doing it?" He spit back. John spied the restless wave of heads behind Deavours.

"She is on cross-examination, we have a right to…' he started defensively, but Collins interrupted brusquely, "Proceed, gentlemen."

John searched his notes, then looked up again. "Mrs. Hawkins, he didn't have a knife, did he?"

"No," she said impudently, and added, "He didn't have to have a knife. He could have choked me. That Negro could have hit me one time, and I would have been gone."

"But you said he threatened you?" John returned.

"He did threaten me," she emoted, "he threatened to cut my throat, but he didn't have to have a knife to kill me, not that monster!"

"He was a big man, then?" John entered into her drama. Willie sat scrunched, looking very short and small.

She looked at him disdainfully and snapped, "You don't have to be big to be a monster."

John stepped back, "Mrs. Hawkins, I want to know whether you screamed when you first knew that it wasn't Troy?" It was a sensitive question.

She looked as if searching for words. "I was so scared by then, and at first…" She started again. "This was the way it was. At first, I thought it was Troy, and there was no reason to be alarmed, him being in there, of course I was wondering why he would be there like that, and then…"

"But you didn't scream," John interrupted.

"Let her finish her answer!" Deavours interjected vehemently.

John looked at the Judge and said, without emotion, "I believe she answered my question."

"She wasn't through," Deavours blared. Judge Collins said firmly, "Let her answer."

Willette, looking justified, lowered her voice somewhat and continued, "Then, by the time I knew it was a Negro, he threatened me," her voice rose, "threatened me," she looked at John and repeated as if she were slapping him, "threatened me!"

John remained detached, holding his chin as if studying her, then asked, "But I mean, up until the time you felt his hair?"

"All that time I thought it was Troy!" She snapped.

"Mrs. Hawkins," John puzzled, "you thought it was Troy after you touched his body and..."

She interrupted hastily, "Actually, I don't know just..."

He interrupted in return, "...in feeling on up, and you didn't scream at that time?"

"No," she insisted, "I thought it was Troy."

John pressed, using his hand again, "And after you got up on his head and found out it wasn't Troy, then, Mrs. Hawkins, you asked him," he looked down at his papers and said, "What do you want? Go away. Why are you here?" He looked up again, "That is correct, isn't it?"

It looked as if he were reading a transcript. She responded safely, "As best I can remember, that is correct."

"Now," he continued, "I believe you said the method you used to try to get rid of him, at least, one of the methods that you used was to try to bribe him or something, in other words, you wanted to give him money to leave?"

"Yes, I thought of the money," she answered. Hawkins restlessly crossed his ankles and stretched to look back at the men who supported him, who nodded understanding.

John came in closer and lowered his voice, "Now, Mrs. Hawkins, I want you to answer this question, answer it very frankly, when as you say, he told you what he came there for..." He was interrupted by a hand wave from the court reporter who asked, "Speak a little louder, Mr. Poole."

Deavours added, "Speak out loud enough for us to hear you. I can't even hear you here."

John breathed in and stated more loudly, "...did you or not testify on one of the previous trials, 'Well, if that is all you want I can take it?'"

"You mean that I said that to the Negro?" she stalled. "Yes."

She thought before answering. "I didn't say it to the Negro. I might have testified I said it, but at the time I was just thinking that."

John continued, "I will ask you whether when you were asked the question, 'Go ahead, please Ma'am," you answered: 'Well, this is an awful thing, it is terrible to have happened to anyone – I said, 'What do you want? Why are you here?' and he was on his knees and hands, I could see nothing. That was the darkest place I have ever seen, and he says," John dropped his voice involuntarily, "'Miss, Miss, I come for you, I want your pussy and I am going to have it...'"

Swartzfager rose with a dare, "Speak out, these men can't hear you!" Judge Collins

190

intervened, "Mr. Poole, stand back over there to examine the witness and speak out loud so we can hear you."

John recanted saying, "I would like to just restate the entire question again."

"All right," Collins allowed and added, "go ahead and talk out loud."

John raised his voice and began, "I want to know whether you testified on a former trial of this case when asked the question, "Go ahead, please Ma'am" and you answered," He started to read from the paper, "Well, this is an awful thing, it is terrible to have happened to anyone. I said, 'What do you want? Why are you here?' and he was on his knees and hands, I could see nothing, that was the darkest place I have ever seen, and he says, 'Miss, Miss, I come for you, I want your pussy and I am going to have it!' And I said, 'No, no!' and he said, 'Shut your mouth, I will cut your throat, shut your mouth!' 'Well, I was just scared to death, that's all, not so much for myself, if he had killed me, I never would have felt it, because I was just petrified, but I had that baby, my two year old baby girl in the bed with me, and in the next room my two little girls, one eight and one ten, and one of them awoke so easily I was so afraid she would get up, and I didn't know what he would do to them or what he would do to the baby, and he said, 'Shut your mouth' every time I called Troy. I called him, not loud, because I didn't want to wake the children up in the next room, and I didn't know but what he had already killed Troy, and when I called Troy he said, 'He's back there asleep, Miss.' I said, 'Why did you come here?' and he said, 'I came to fuck you.' 'Well then, I thought, 'Well, if that's all, I can take it.'

Swartzfager interrupted, "She said she thought that and that is exactly what her response was to this question, that she didn't say it, she said she thought it!" John looked at the paper again and realized that he had, in the flurry of trying to grasp everything about this case in so little time, seen the quotes and thought mistakenly that she had said it. He took a deep breath.

Willette had her chance. She glared at him loathingly and asked, "Do you have a wife?

John nodded; his lips pressed together with conflicted feelings.

"That's all I want to know," she said, through tight lips.

He protested, "Yes, I do, and as a matter of fact I realize that the crime is awful, especially when perpetrated as this one is alleged to have been perpetrated, so I approach you, not with the attitude of embarrassing you at all, and I hope you understand that." The sincerity caused her to keep her peace momentarily.

Accustomed to picking himself up from a blow, John picked up where he left off, "Now, Mrs. Hawkins, I believe that you testified also on the former trial that you were interested in finding out something about him, and so you put your hands around his neck?"

She thought, "I might have said I put my hands around his neck, I shoved against him, and my fingers were inside his shirt," She broke away from the thought. "I might have testified that if it is there."

"I will leave that for just a little bit," he said, but intended to leave it altogether until the argument." How far was it from your husband's bedroom to your bedroom?"

"Well," she seemed thankful for a cut and dried question, "the house is a straight six-room bungalow and it is quite some distance back there. There are a lot of partitions in there and the house is sealed with Masonite, and that makes is pretty soundproof." The Masonite factor had been emphasized throughout the retellings, as if it made it a shoo-in.

"Well, now, approximately how far was it?" he pressed. "I have no idea," she answered flatly.

"But you say you didn't scream? In other words, you didn't scream out, because you were afraid, is that right?" John was trying to engage her.

"I cried out," she said with irritation, "I don't know how loud I screamed." John mitigated his tone to keep her mollified, "Now, I want to know, Mrs. Hawkins, how far it was to the next house, on the north and on the south of you?"

Although the several directional questions he asked did keep her from getting more anxious, she appeared to wax very weary. When he asked the age of her children, Willette looked pale.

"Well, it has been two years, I will have, I will have, Ooh...! Deavours stood and asked, "Do you need to take a rest?"

She looked at him thankfully, "Oh, yes, I could stand some rest." She swayed in her seat, and the Baliff rescued her, taking her arm to lead her to the adjacent jury room.

The Court did not take an actual recess, since the jury had nowhere to retire to, so most stayed in place. A few took the opportunity to use the facilities. For those who remained, sobbing from the back room caused the jury to become uncomfortable. The rest of the courtroom population had various reactions. The attorneys tapped their pencils. The balcony shuffled and coughed. Hawkins' jaws tightened and he glared towards the Defense table angrily. Lowly uttered comments were passed among those on the floor.

Al penciled a note to John, "Nothing trumps feminine persuasion." John scribbled back, "She's taking full advantage of that." After what seemed to be a prolonged suffering, the sobs abated and the Judge motioned for the Baliff to bring Mrs. Hawkins back to the stand. Her "rest" had left her looking even more pale and puffy. Her handkerchief was wadded in her hand.

John approached her less compassionately than expected. "All right, what are the children's ages now?"

She sniffed and related their ages, thirteen, eleven and four. They were two years younger at the time. They were asleep in the next room? Yes. You didn't scream loud enough to wake them? They didn't awake. Your resistance to this man was to push him and plead with him? Yes, she pushed until her arms were sore. Did she attempt to bribe him? She just wanted to get rid of him, but she never told him there was money. You kept asking him what he wanted? Yes. It was the darkest night you had ever seen? Yes. Did he threaten to kill the children? The baby who was in bed with her. Did you try to call the neighbors? No, there was no need – when? The swirl of questions seemed to confuse her. John asked more pointedly, "Did you call for your husband?"

"When?" she asked again, sounding confounded.

"When all of this was happening," John said more slowly.

She stopped for a moment then said, "I told you I called, "Troy, Troy, Troy." She began to act it out.

"Is that about as loud as you called?" John asked Willette became infuriated and snapped saying, "Listen, someday your wife

– this might happen to her, and if it does you can ask her all those foolish questions, 'What did she do? How loud did she call?' Or 'What did she say?'

John redirected, "Yes – I am certainly in sympathy with you, Mrs. Hawkins, and your position, but you didn't call loud enough to awaken Troy, did you?"

She sat, breathing heavily." He didn't awaken."

"And I believe you testified that the baby was in bed with you when this happened?"

"Yes, she was."

John kept firing questions, going back now and then to the defense table to pick up notes Al waved him to. What about the door, was it broken open? The door had been propped open when she and Troy had gotten up. She was sick at the time, what was the nature of her illness?

Willette folded her arms." That is kind of a long story." "Did you have a cold?" John offered.

Willette grew quieter with memory." I did have a real bad cold during that time."

"And that was in reality the nature of your illness?"

She looked at him with a smirk." Remember, I only weighed about 92 pounds, and the cold certainly didn't cause that."

John took note with his eyes, then went back to the question of the details of the rape.

"Now you testified, Mrs. Hawkins, that he had both of his hands on you, and he didn't have a knife at that time, did he?"

"I never saw a knife, he told me he had a knife, and he threatened me with it every breath, but I could not see a knife."

"You didn't feel a knife?" He pursued.

She frowned and answered, "I wasn't feeling for a knife, I wanted him to get away."

John looked curiously at her, "What I want to know is, he placed both hands on you?"

She waved her hand, "At one time or another he placed both hands on me, and all the rest of his body. He touched every inch of me. "Willette's height was hard to hide, as was McGee's short stature, but this was not brought up. John just looked at McGee and back at Willette and said, "Now, Mrs. Hawkins, do you know Willie McGee?"

Willette straightened her skirt and replied with a weary sigh, "No, I don't know Willie McGee." She began to sway again.

John looked at the Judge, "I will ask the court to give us a recess and allow her to rest just a little bit."

Collins looked at Willette, remembering the recent scene and asked, "Do you want to rest, Mrs. Hawkins, or do you want to try to go on and get through with it?"

The extra medication she had taken during the break had made her woozy, but she insisted, "I want to get through and go home!"

"All right," Collins said, "let's go ahead with the examination." He pointed to-wards the Defense table and added, "Don't take up so much time, gentlemen between questions."

John continued, "Mrs. Hawkins, did he say that he had a knife?" "He told me he would cut my throat."

"But he didn't say that he had a knife?" John pursued the question.

"He told me he would cut my throat. What's the difference?" She said flippantly. "And I want to get this one thing clear, Mrs. Hawkins, and this will be just about all.

The extent of your struggle with him was trying to push him off? "He looked more directly at her, "That is correct, isn't it, and trying to bribe him?"

"Well, my legs were bruised and everything, " she said with a note of sarcasm and added, "I don't know how I struggled. Ask him, he will tell you." She had lifted her chin towards McGee.

John looked at her with mock surprise and said, "Now, Mrs. Hawkins, you don't know who this was, do you?"

Willette straightened and said smugly, "No, I have never seen him."

"Now, Mrs. Hawkins," John continued, "after it all happened, I believe you said you rushed back in the next room and your first interest then was to look after your children and to make sure they were all right, and that you went through their rooms to see that they were all right, and felt of them –"

"That's right," she interrupted. "…is that correct?"

"That is correct."

John tucked it away for the argument. She had said it had been too dark to even recognize features on McGee, even with the curtain swaying open, yet she could walk through the house quickly and go into the rooms where her children were to check that they were in their beds. He continued to ascertain her testimony, "You couldn't identify the person that was in your house at all, could you?"

"I will never forget the voice," she said, and added, "I have never seen him." "What I mean is, you couldn't see him at any time, could you?"

"No, I couldn't see him, it was dark," she spit back. "And all you know is he was just a great big man?"

Willette wouldn't be fooled this time. "He was not a great big man, I said he was a big monster, a beast, and he is, no matter how big or how large he is." She and Deavours exchanged smiles.

"Didn't you testify on one of the trials of this case that he was a great big old Negro?"

She had told someone that but couldn't remember if it was in court or not. "I might have testified that. If it is there, I said it, but he is not." Her language included McGee as if it were already a fact. Realizing this, she added, "Anyway, he wouldn't have to be big to be a beast and a monster."

John turned to the Judge and said, "That is all."

Willette was visibly relieved as her own attorney approached. He let her relate all of the reasons why she might be confused, or not remember so well. She had been so frightened, had stayed in the hospital a week or two, had a terrible shock and didn't want to live. She agreed and emphasized emotionally, "I don't want to live when I go places and people look at me and say, 'That's the woman that Negro man raped,' and I can hear them say it." It was convincing. She looked drawn and sickly – as if she wanted to die.

Deavours was overly empathetic. "Now, Mrs. Hawkins, from the questions Mr. Poole asked you he seemed to think you could remember…" John objected, but Collins let it continue. "From the nature of the questions Mr. Poole asked you," he repeated, "he seemed to think you could keep all these things that happened in just exactly the order in which they occurred…" Deavours waved his hand upwards as if it were an absurdity.

Willette responded in kind. "No, no!" she began.

"…could you do that?" He asked with his eyebrows raised. "No, I couldn't, I couldn't," she wagged her head.

"Of course, he has never been raped?" He flaunted an insulting tone.

Willette considered it. "Well, if he had a fight with a man, he could never remember exactly what happened, every detail, and tell it over and over and expect it to be done in the very same words, that can't be done,"

Deavours cemented it with, "I believe you testified that he at all times threatened to kill you and kill your baby?"

On cue she came back with, "He threatened me, he said, 'I will cut your God damned throat' and he said, 'Keep that brat quiet, I will cut her God damned throat. Keep that brat quiet.'"

"That is all," Deavours swaggered back to his seat.

John rose for one question. "Mrs. Hawkins," he said, "You did say that you told this story time and time again since it happened, to the grand jury, petit juries and to your lawyers?"

Deavours stood, "We object. We don't think that is material." Collins sustained.

Swartzfager added to nail it in, "And it is repetition." "That is all," John sat again.

Deavours couldn't help but stand back up and walk towards her, as she was looking befuddled on the stand.

"You have told the truth, haven't you?" he offered.

She straightened to proclaim, "I have told the truth, and I think the truth is bad enough!"

"That's all," Deavours said, and Mrs. Hawkins was excused for the third time from the witness stand. She looked stiff and aged.

As she passed by to the side of the Prosecution, London stood and looked towards the court reporter. "Will the Court note our exception to the Court's last ruling?" She nodded in weary affirmation.

CHAPTER TWENTY-FIVE

JEST LOOKIN FOR A WHOOPIN

After a short recess, Mrs. John Jenson, the Hawkin's next door neighbor, was questioned. She testified that she had taken Willette in after she had run crying hysterically, to their house with nothing more than a halter on, saying that someone was going to kill her. Yes, she had been menstruating at the time, because Mrs. Jensen had taken her back to a bed to lie down, and the sheets were soiled. There wasn't much to contest, and cross-examination couldn't show that Mrs. Jensen knew anything prior to the incident. It wouldn't be brought out until another year that the townspeople had heard what they believed was an argument between the Hawkins, and that the "someone" who would have killed her may have been her husband, who didn't perchance to follow her.

The court would not recess for lunch until after Mr. Hawkins' testimony.. Troy Hawkins was shorter than his wife by several inches, but he preceded her by five years, which he felt gave him the edge. He and Willette had been married for almost fourteen years. Their anniversary was only two weeks away, but neither was in any mood to celebrate it. She had been just twenty when they had been married, with romantic dark hair and beautiful eyes. Willette had been quite the catch for Troy, and he was proud of her, not to mention jealous of any man whose eyes followed her graceful hips. For reasons unknown to others, but gossiped about in whispers, Willette had lost so much weight the years following her marriage that she was down to ninety-two pounds, with a height that could have held almost twice as much. Troy did not look well, himself. He had been a hard worker and was respected at his job but lacked joviality. Whether it was because of the illness of his wife, or the illness of his wife was due to any underlying nature of their relationship, was hard to tell. Others came to their own conclusions, while remaining cordial. By now, whatever else affected his character, the strain of the years of the trial and the hatred he had felt during it made him appear hard, drawn and wiry. There wasn't much inner strength to draw on, and it made him feel all the more defensive. He was sworn in and sat in the witness seat with hunched shoulders, clasped hands and elbows pressing hard into the arms of the chair for support. He checked for fellow antagonists in the crowd and nodded his readiness.

Devours initiated the examination, asking routine questions of identity and his repetition of the story that his wife had conveyed. The only discrepancy was that he referred to the bed in the small room where the crib also was, where there was hardly a space for an intruder to crawl, as "our bed where we sleep," and that he had gone into the "back bedroom," to get sleep that night only. Deavours slipped, referring to the room as "your wife's bedroom," but Troy came back with, "That's right, in <u>our</u> bedroom." Devours continued to ask structural questions about the home, which bedroom was positioned where and how far. Troy reported that the window shade had been down, but it was windy that night, and a breeze could have given someone the advantage of a revealing glance into the lit room. A vine on the outside near the window, large enough for someone to climb onto, was found broken the next morning, along with some missing shingles on the roof. He testified further that when he was awakened by his wife, he tried to turn the lights on, but the wire had been cut. He had not run to the neighbors after her because he was afraid to leave the children. He had called a Doctor to come to the house and took her the next morning to a hospital in Hattiesburg, where she stayed a little over a week. Deavours gave leave for the cross-examination.

John started off by asking Hawkins just exactly where it was that Mrs. Hawkins began to scream and run. Although Hawkins complied with questioning, his expression belied his cooperation. John paused to say, "Mr. Hawkins, I know this must be somewhat embarrassing to you. I don't want to embarrass you. I just want to ask you just a few questions." It was said sincerely, though it was obvious that Mr. Hawkins had his mind on what his wife had gone through earlier and wanted revenge.

"Shoot'em!" Hawkins replied sharply through tight lips, as if insinuating a double meaning.

Could he hear Willette as she ran through the house screaming, although she was far ahead of him? Sure. But he hadn't heard her scream earlier from one bedroom to the next. That's right. He found the wires cut? Only one. Did that keep all of the electricity from coming to the house? He imagined it did – he couldn't turn on the lights. John then asked about the time that the police arrived and when the electricity was cut off. Hawkins couldn't say. Was he too disturbed at the time? Yes, he had been too disturbed to notice the time, and, besides, it was too dark in the house to see a clock.

John had previously heard from Pyles of conflicting stories in the beginning. One of the stories from the initial investigations was that the policemen early on had said that when they had come the lights were already on. Now the story had changed – Hawkins said they had helped him find the wire.

"I want to ask you one or two more questions about this back screened porch," John continued. "Now, how far does the wooden part extend on the outside from the screen?"

"I would say it was about a foot or eighteen inches, I don't know exactly." Hawkins folded his arms over his chest.

"Then you would say there was that much of the wooden part of your back screen porch…" John began, but Hawkins interrupted.

"It might be a little more than that, but it's about that."

John began again, "In other words, you could get very easily one shoe, number 12 size shoe on that?"

Hawkins curled his lip and spat, "I don't even know what a size 12 shoe is, mister, don't know what size it is." He repositioned, narrowing one eye.

"Well, you could get a shoe around this long," John sized it with his hands, "on that wooden portion of the porch?"

Hawkins questioned him on just where he meant, saying they might not be talking about the same place. When they became clear on where it was, John asked, "I want to get this clear, Mr. Hawkins. Did you say while ago a man could stand from the floor of your porch and reach up to this wire?"

Hawkins wagged his head vigorously, "No, I sure didn't say that." "Then where would he have had to step to have reached that wire?"

Hawkins breathed in and said,"He would have had to get on the porch, but you can stand on the platform and reach the top, put your foot on that wall and shimmy up. I always do that when I want to get in the attic to put things in the attic. We had a hole in the house and I went up through there."

John asked with furrowed brow, "Is it the supposition that the man who was supposed to have gone in your house went all the way around to the back? And that was where you were sleeping?"

Hawkins looked at him challengingly. "That's right."

"All the way around to the back," John demonstrated with his hand, "and he would have had to go through the process, you say, of climbing to the top by putting a foot on the wooden porch and lifting himself up enough to cut the wire?"

Hawkins then added some detail as to how he thought it would have been done.

John would save for the argument that this person was allegedly drunk, making it much harder to complete the feat without making any noise to wake Hawkins. After questioning how closely the houses were situated in the neighborhood, John asked, "I want to get this clear for the record. It is true that the policemen came there before the lights were fixed?"

"Sure," Hawkins said with as much nonchalance as he could muster.

John asked if Hawkins knew the defendant. No, he had only seen him in court, or may have seen him before, but didn't know him.

John then asked, "Now, Mr. Hawkins, to your best knowledge, could you have heard your wife if she had screamed from the front room?" Hawkins became more impatient.

"No, sir!" he answered with deliberation.

"You don't believe you would have been able to hear her?" John persisted. Hawkins sat up in his seat and said vehemently, "Listen, fellow, I had lost sleep for about three nights and when I went to bed, I was just the same as dead!" He looked ready for a brawl.

John countered, "I understand…"

Hawkins interrupted with a huff, "Well, you should!"

John continued, more diplomatically, "…you must have been quite sleepy. Do you think under normal conditions you could have heard her?"

"Well, I don't believe so, not the way our house is insulated, even if I hadn't been needing rest." He settled back a bit.

John pursued, "You could have heard her if you hadn't been asleep?" He thought a moment, "Yes, I…" then caught himself.

"Quite easily?" John finished for him.

"Well, I don't imagine quite easily, because the house is insulated with Masonite insulation." It was the second time he had brought up the insulation, as if it were a solid crutch for his story.

"Your wife testified that the door to her room was open, would that have made a difference?"

Hawkins had to agree but looked perturbed. "Sure, it would have made a difference."

"Was your door open?"

Hawkins thought, "I'm not positive, but I think it was. I think it was open." He looked contradicted.

John reviewed, "You think your door was open, now there is a distance there of about 25 feet, and both doors were open to the best of your recollection. That is true, isn't it?"

Hawkins breathed out, admitting, "That's right."

"That's all," John said to the Judge. Hawkins glared at the back of the lawyer who walked with a slight jerk back to the Defense table, as Deavours moved the Judge for a re-direct examination. In it he bolstered Hawkin's story to affirm that regardless of how he might have been able to hear her, he didn't. He also wasn't even able to see that she was not dressed, because of the darkness of their home and the darkness of the outside of the house. It was dubious but stated as if commonsensical. Hawkins was excused from the witness stand.

The next witness was the electrician, who had come to fix the wire. It was a small wire, he testified, that could have been broken without pliers and by a stick if it was crystallized. The wire seemed to be crystallized, he said, shaking his head affirmatively. He had mended the wires just before daylight, about 5:00 he said, smiling.

John jotted a note for the argument. Rapist escaped – 4:30, Hawkins woke (deep sleep), followed wife, came back to dark house – phoned police, phoned electrician (found number?) – fixed by 5:00. Impossible?

When court recessed, John decided with unassuming bravado that he and Al should go out for lunch this time. It had been a trying morning, and he felt he deserved a good meal at a restaurant.

"To hell with the opposing crew of locals."

Al agreed, "I could use a hot meal," and pulled on his coat to join him.

They had barely walked out of the courthouse onto the lawn, as John stopped to light a cigarette, when they spied a group of men from afar pointing towards them, motioning to another smaller group standing nearby to join them. Obscenities and threats began to fly as they started walking towards them with clenched fists.

"You son-of-a-bitch, nigger lover!"

"You're jes lookin for a whoopin, aren't you, Mr. Attorney!" "Hey, Mr. Attorney, I hear you have a wife! Has she ever been scared?"

John intuitively struck his boxer's stance, but heard direction in his ear, "We don't want this now, John, head this way!" Al grabbed his arm and turned him towards the alley where they ran for their car parked on the side. They made it inside and screeched out of the lot before allowing a backwards glance.

"There's at least twelve of them!" John announced, breathing heavily, as Al wheeled down the street away from the scene. John turned back around to rub his sore stump.

"Whew!" Al allowed himself after they were a safe distance away and shook his head. "Why in the world did we pick this day to eat out?"

John laughed in comic relief, but quickly sobered up to say, "Not again!" They did manage to find an out of the way restaurant to have a hot meal in peace, but returned to the courtroom, sneaking back on hands and knees through the catwalk as before practiced.

John and Al avoided any eyes in the courtroom, although they heard muttering and muted laughs as they sat down.

The next witness the State brought to the stand was Bill Barnes, who claimed he was with Willie the night of the crime. Bill was awkwardly dressed in a Sunday suit that was a bit too tight on him, and repositioned himself several times, remembering to look down just a bit when being addressed by the lawyers. He tried to look both respectable and subservient, of which he was neither. Willie looked sideways to John and said, "He's no friend." John nodded and pushed a pad towards him. Willie scratched out some notes.

Swartzfager examined Bill, who related how he and Willie had done work for Laurel Wholesale Groceries, made a delivery, and then went out for drinks and gambling along with another fellow named George Walker, using the company truck. They had then gone to his "Daddy-in-Law's" who lived near a town called "Hot Coffee," just as Willie had described it before. He related how they had gone to several places looking for Willie's wife, then to eat something and finally to gamble again. Bill said that he didn't get back home until close to four o'clock in the morning, and when Willie let him off he thought he was probably going back to his mother's house, above the Black Cat Inn, but he looked to be going in a different direction. His testimony put Willie where he could have been at the Hawkin's house around 4:30.

On cross-examination, John asked, "Now, as a matter of fact, Bill, you got kind of mad at Willie, because he wouldn't let you have some money, didn't you?"

"No, sir, I didn't get mad." He forgot to look down and instead stuck out his chin. "I just asked him to let me have some."

"You asked him to let you have some money and he refused?" "Well, he said he was losing." Barnes coughed.

"And you were traveling around with him to all these skin games?" "Yes, sir."

"And you got a little hot with him because he wouldn't let you have some money?" "No, sir, I didn't get hot. No need getting hot with a man about his own money."

Bill squirmed a bit.

After questioning of the details of that night, John ended with, "You were doing that gambling, and that was at Willie Johnson's house and Hettie Johnson's house, that's right, isn't it?"

Barnes looked as if he was getting a warning from somewhere and didn't answer.

He just shrugged his shoulders as if he really had no idea and grunted.

On re-direct examination, Schwartzfager managed to get him to say that he really didn't know whose house it was, and no, neither one of them was really drunk, although he had earlier testified that they had gone through a couple of pints of whiskey.

John rose again to ask, "Bill, how long have you known Willie?"

"I wouldn't say how long I been knowing Willie," he said, with avoidance. It had been most of his life, but to say so would cause him to face his own conscience.

"He never has been in any trouble before, has he?"

"Sir?" Barnes wasn't quite sure how to answer this and looked nervously at the Prosecution's table.

"We object to that, it doesn't matter whether he has been in trouble before or not." Swartzfager protested.

"Overruled." Collin's gave leave for John to proceed. Barnes had to admit that all the time he had known Willie, he had not been in any trouble. John proceeded to ask what street the house they were gambling in was on.

"I forgets all those streets, I couldn't just say right now,"

John nodded slowly, "Willie was just about asleep, I imagine. Wasn't that one of the reasons he wanted to leave?" Barnes admitted that he had drank a good bit, and he was getting pretty sleepy by that time, himself, because he had to go to work. John left his questioning at that.

Swartzfager persistently got back up for further examination, asking if a pint and a half of whiskey was really all they drank. Yes, that was all. Then he came out with, "He asked you whether Willie has ever been in any trouble before," smiling at his own analogy, "Judas Iscariot was a pretty good man until he betrayed, Christ, wasn't he?"

John being infuriated, London stood up and said calmly, "We object to that as leading."

"At the very least," Bessie whispered to her pastor, who nodded his assent.

Although Collins sustained, Swartzfager swaggered back to his seat, looking as though he didn't care a whit about the objection.

London continued, "We want to register an objection to the District Attorney's question on the grounds that it is inflammatory and prejudicial."

Judge Collins adjusted his glasses and said merely, "I have already sustained the objection."

Bill Barnes was excused and walked with disdain past Willie. It was for naught. The balcony crowd had already decided he would no longer be accepted in the community of his peers.

Willette's doctor was questioned next and testified that there were slight abrasions just inside the vagina, and live spermatozoa, but admitted that the sperm could live up to 48 hours, and – no, he couldn't tell whether they were from a white or black male. She had some marks on her, but he couldn't really say they were bruises, and it hadn't been noted that she was menstruating. Other than saying she was hysterical when he saw her, there wasn't a lot to go on from his testimony.

The next witness was George Walker, a taller man, who slouched just a bit to make himself less threatening to the white men in the room. He testified that he was with Barnes and McGee that night, and readily told that the gambling house was owned by Willie Johnson. He had seen Willie the next morning with his suit on his back, looking like he was going to pawn it. He had said, "Willie, If you had come home with me, you wouldn't have to pawn your clothes!" He said that Willie had just answered, "I'll get it," and passed on his way. George didn't think he had been very drunk that night and didn't think he was driving like he was drunk. George's testimony had nothing really incriminating, and he didn't act friendly towards the Prosecution, although they had brought him to the stand.

Several other witnesses had seen early that morning, around 5:00, what seemed to be the Laurel Wholesale Truck sitting where it shouldn't have been sitting, down the street from the Hawkin's house. The owner of the company, Mr. Elliott, testified that the truck that Willie had taken had burned about thirty-some gallons of gasoline that night. He admitted that "That happened lots of time in our business…that some of them take trucks out and get drunk – All of them Negroes." What Willie did was not unusual. Still, there was the problem of the money he owed the company, and when he hadn't come back at all, Chief of Police Wayne Valentine was called, and a pick-up order for McGee was submitted area wide, including the neighboring town of Hattiesburg.

Hugh Herring, a policeman from Hattiesburg, was the next on the stand. Officer Herring testified that he and Officer Harris apprehended McGee in the town of Hattiesburg. He recounted that, "He got awful nervous. He got so nervous that I could see a sweat pop out on him, and he looked like he changed colors." Herring remembered that McGee tried to wrench away, "…and when he did I twisted down on his arm a little bit," he demonstrated with his hands, "and that was about the only thing I did." at him.

On cross-examination, John asked if he or anyone else had slapped him or cursed "No, sir, did not," he said, succinctly.

Knowing it was a lie, John asked, looking at him more directly, "They didn't threaten to hang him?"

Officer Herring half-smiled as he answered, "No, sir we don't have no gallows there." The witness was excused with no further questions.

Chief M. M. Little, the Chief of Police in Hattiesburg testified next that he had kept Willie in his jail until the Laurel officers came for him. Swartzfager asked him, "Did he make any statement to you in regards to what he was being held for?" It was a cue.

"Well, he did." Chief Little adjusted himself and continued, "I went to the jail and opened the cell door and told Willie what we were holding him for, and he swallowed three or four times, and finally said, "Chief, I ain't done nothing," and the sweat popped out on him."

John objected, asking the jury to be excused, so the court could determine the admissibility of his testimony. The jury was excused.

Chief Little continued to testify that when Chief Valentine asked him "if he would mind pulling down his clothes and letting him see his underwear," Willie responded with, "All right," and did so. He further testified that there looked to be a stain of blood on them. London objected to this unless he knew. It was overruled and an exception was noted. Chief Little went on to answer to the State's questioning that there was no force, duress, threats of violence, or even any hope of reward that caused him to drop his pants so readily.

John asked, on cross-examination, how many officers were there that went into the cell with Willie. There were several, although he couldn't remember the number, and yes, they all had guns on them. John went on, asking if he had stayed there the whole time. No, he had gone back to the office.

"Then you don't know whether they had been slapping Willie, or beating him, or telling him they were going to take him to Laurel and let the mob have him?" It was the first time this had been implied, and Chief Little stuck his lip out and said, "Yes, I do."

"How do you know?" John countered.

"Because we just don't do it that way," Little returned slowly with reddened face.

"You don't know of your own personal knowledge, though, that they didn't do that?"

"Yes, I do," he insisted. "How do you know that?"

"Because I have taught the officers not to do that," he said with pride. "Well, you don't mean to tell the Court that they always do what you say?" Little insisted there was no abuse, saying he had never seen it before.

John asked, "He was pretty scared, wasn't he, Chief?"

"Well, I imagine he was after he had done what he did," the Chief said indignantly. John asked with incredulity, "Chief, you don't know what he did, do you?"

Scattered laughter interrupted the proceedings.

Judge Collins sat up straight and declared, "Just a minute. I am not going to have any laughing in the court room. The Court wouldn't like to clear this courtroom, but if you keep that up, I will. I don't mean to be harsh, I don't mean to be arbitrary, but I am going to have order in this courtroom, and if you keep up that laughing, I am going to clear the court room. Just try it."

A pin could have dropped and been heard as the crowd became like school children threatened with no recess. A snicker escaped, but none followed.

The Chief, somewhat chagrined, answered the following questions saying that he could tell from his experience when "someone has been into something."

On final examination after the jury had been brought in, John asked, "When a Negro is being charged with the rape of a White woman that is a pretty serious charge around here, isn't it?"

Little responded, "Well, I thought it was a serious charge."

Deavours interrupted, leaning back in his chair, "Did you really want him to answer that question?"

John turned around, "Why yes." As the Judge made no comment, John continued. "You thought he was guilty immediately, didn't you?"

"In my estimation he had been into something – he was guilty of something," he retorted.

"Yes," John said dismissively, then added, "You didn't advise him that anything he might say or do would be used against him?"

Deavours sat up a bit to say, "That is immaterial." Collins returned, "Let him answer."

Chief Little just stated that he had just told him what he was charged with, and that was all.

Wayne Valentine, the Chief of Police of Laurel for twenty-four years, was the next to take the stand. His demeanor was both professional and authoritative behind a stoic expression. It intimidated many and had won him his long-standing position.

Deavours, giving way to his authority, merely asked him to relate his story. He had been the first to reach the Hawkin's home that morning, about five-thirty or six, he said. The lights were already on by the time he came. He had found the window to the bedroom open and the screen was out. There had been a dirt smudge on the sill, and it looked as if there was a foot mark on the wall where someone had slipped. The fingerprints had not been sufficient to be developed. He then made an announcement to several police departments in the State to pick up Willie McGee. When they had detained him, he went with two officers to pick him up. Deavours then asked a battery of questions regarding the investigation. In no way, the Chief related, was McGee threatened or mistreated. He was not promised anything, but voluntarily showed them the underwear, and willingly pointed out the house to them once back in Laurel. He was not threatened with mob violence. He made his confession without inducement or compulsion. In fact, there was nothing done to make him nervous in any way.

After the State rested, London questioned him. Didn't he have handcuffs on him, and didn't they all have guns?

"Yes, we did."

"Now, Chief, did he appear to be pretty scared about that?" "No, sir," Valentine said, flatly.

"You mean you told him that you were arresting him and taking him up to Laurel charged with rape, and he didn't appear to be scared in any way?"

"No, sir," he repeated, eyes blank.

"Did you tell him that he didn't have to make any statement that might incriminate him, or that he was entitled to counsel before he made any such statement?" London asked, matching his nonchalance.

Swartzfager reacted, however, and objected, saying that it wasn't compulsory to do so. Judge Collins unexpectedly overruled, London took exception, assuming it was sustained.

Swartzfager grimaced at London, "He said, 'Overruled. '"

"I beg your pardon," London said quickly, smiling at his own error, and turned back to the Chief, "Did you answer that question, Chief?"

"Not yet," the Chief adjusted his uniform coat with grim expression.

London paused, then encouraged him. "Go ahead, sir."

"No, sir," he replied, staring at London with steel eyes.

When asked how long he had talked with Willie before he 'voluntarily' gave his statement, the Chief said it must have been about 30 minutes. London then asked, "Chief, before you got any statement out of him, did you ask him or give him opportunity to talk to any members of his family, or friends, or to seek a lawyer?"

The Chief was not ashamed to answer "No." He did not, however, admit to offering him the Jackson jail instead of the Laurel jail if he would confess. None of those in the vehicle with him even laid a hand on Willie, and he was sure about that. No, no report of mobs came over the radio, and Willie showed no signs of nervousness throughout it all.

London was undeterred.

"And you say you had the handcuffs on him?" "Yes."

"Chief, were those plain handcuffs, or the kind that go around your waist with a chain or strap?"

Valentine looked up as if accessing his memory, "I think they were the ones that had a strap on them, you can use them either way, you can take the strap off or leave it on, but I think it had a strap."

"In other words," London said clearly, "his hands were in cuffs, then down against his waist?"

"That's right," the Chief replied with no emotion. "I see, and locked?" London emphasized.

"That's right." Valentine didn't blink an eye.

"And, Chief, you say that he just voluntarily told you where he had been the night before?"

Valentine related that he had simply told McGee that it "was always best to tell the truth." He denied threatening him to confess, and said that, really, he had no trouble in getting him to answer his questions. It appeared to be a honey of an arraignment.

London finally asked, "Well, Chief, from your experience in police work over a number of years, haven't you found that most people are not very anxious to admit that they violate the law, if they did?"

"Well," Valentine replied, with his chin tucked in, "You find some people that readily admit it, and some that won't."

London looked unconvinced. "But you say you didn't have any trouble getting Willie to admit it?"

"No, I…" the Chief began, but London looked at the paper in his hand and interrupted, "Chief, I will ask you whether or not on the first trial of this case here in Laurel, that you answered in answer to the question, "Where did he say he had been?" referring to the night of this occurrence as follows:…"

The prosecution looked at each other sharply. Schwartzfager quickly stood up and interrupted London saying, "I am going to object to that. I asked counsel, and counsel has informed me all the way through this trial that they haven't been able to get hold of the record of the first trial, and I haven't been able to get hold of it. And I want to know now where it is and if they have it."

Poole interjected from the table, "We have a right to ask our question." "But I want to know what he's reading from," Schwartzfager scowled.

London said shrewdly, "I would like to submit, if your Honor please, that I don't believe Mr. Swartzfager can tell whether I am reading or not."

"He said he was reading from the record of the first trial," Swartzfager insisted.

Judge Collins nodded towards London with curiosity, "Go ahead and ask your question."

London started again, relating the answer Valentine had previously given. "He said he gambled here in Laurel until about two-thirty in the morning, that he left Laurel and went to Taylorsville, Mt. Olive, Collins and back to Laurel, and said he reached Laurel just about daylight in the morning?"

Valentine spoke cautiously. "Well, I answered your question, I said that he told me he had been around Mt. Olive, Mize and Taylorsville, covering the same area, and I don't think I said as to what time he was doing the gambling."

"You don't recall making that statement which I quoted for you then at the first trial, do you, Chief?" London repeated.

Swartzfager stood again, "We object to it unless it is shown that this record he is reading from is from the first trial."

John looked at him and said, "We don't have to show it's the record at all." Collins intervened with prudence, "Well, he has answered the question anyway."

John couldn't resist prodding Swartzfager and smiled, saying, "Don't you know that much law?"

Swartzfager turned on him, seething and saying, "Wait until we finish this case, and we will see who knows the law."

Judge Collins did not interfere but watched with interest.

London brought the attention back to Chief Valentine. "Chief, do you deny that you made the statement which I told you just a while ago?"

Valentine sat in silence, setting his jaw.

"Answer the question, please," Collins finally said.

"No, I don't deny that I made it if you have quoted it," he offered, begrudgingly. London then clarified that he was reading from the transcript. Swartzfager let Valentine know, by another interruption, that he didn't think he actually was. When the Prosecution got a chance to have a re-direct examination, there was another back and forth regarding a point on whether or not Willie knew what he was charged with. At this point the attorneys themselves were in a battle of wills, and there was no more to wrest from the Chief. The witness was finally excused.

Montgomery, the next officer to take the stand, repeated in lock-step with the Chief, other than to admit that at times McGee did look nervous. It sounded more realistic to him to say it, and figured it would play in their favor. He didn't keep his story as air-tight, however, as the Chief. When John asked him, "You did tell him you wouldn't let anybody harm him if he would tell the truth about it?"

The officer replied with honor for his occupation, "It was our duty that we would let nobody harm him. That is part of our profession – our job."

"Unhunh –" John nodded affirmatively with supposing approval but added, "You told him that, didn't you?"

"Yes, sir," he confirmed with pride.

"That you weren't going to let anybody harm him if he would tell the truth about it," John repeated for the record, – what else did you say to him?"

"I don't know that I said anything to him," he said, suddenly confused. He was guarded for the remainder of the questioning.

The Judge, looking at the time and wearied with the day, adjourned the court before the direct examination. They could take it up in the morning and have time for arguments before this dang trial was over for good. He wanted to be done in time to rest himself before a celebration on Saturday night. John whispered something to Al, who nodded. They packed up as Willie was being handcuffed and the courtroom began to empty and then followed him out the back courtroom door to the jail. John noticed as they began walking through the catwalk this time that there were several men outside below, lighting cigarettes and looking up, watching the window to see them following McGee and the jailer.

CHAPTER TWENTY-SIX

I'M THE RIGHT NEGRO

Bessie McGee entered the courtroom Saturday morning, filled with trepidation. There were too many fires burning. She had heard about Mr. Poole and Mr. London's narrow escape yesterday, and there was talk around the black community about those so-called friends of Willie's who had testified for the State. What consequences would there be for them, having sold out to the white man?

Bessie sighed. It shouldn't tear apart the black community. They needed each other. Her mind was troubled as she watched the people filing into the courthouse, recalling her meeting last night with Willie and their pastor.

"Now, Willie," the pastor had said. "You know you mustn't fear what man can do to you but fear Him who can cast your soul into everlasting Hell."

"Yessuh," Willie had returned.

"Is there anything you want to get off your chest, Willie?" He looked over at Bessie with raised brows. She took the hint and went out, softly closing the door behind her. It wasn't long before she heard muffled sobs from the room, and although she really was trying not to listen too much, she discerned from bits and pieces that he was making his confession and forgiving those who had brought harm to him. She welcomed the stream of tears that wet her own face, and prayed from the ache in her heart, "Lord, just let Willie find his peace. Let him find his peace with You, Lord, and give him strength to bear this awful trial." She pressed her handkerchief to her cheeks.

⚬╪╪⚬

John and Al had held their own meeting with Willie that morning. Briefing him on the kind of retaliation they could expect, John asked if he was ready to finally get on the

211

stand. He nodded his head almost continually while they bolstered him with an assurance they themselves did not quite own. John pushed the pack of cigarettes towards Willie, who was chain smoking.

"Your story needs to be told, Willie," John said, looking with kindness into his client's anxious eyes. "Not just for you, not for Al or me to gain anything, but for all Negros in the South."

As John finished his sentence, Willie spoke in concert with him, having heard it several times by now. He rubbed his hands together briskly, looked up and said with conviction, "I'm ready for it now."

Al stood with arms crossed, and then began to pace as he went over the questions they would ask. Willie continued to nod and continued to smoke. When Al finished, Willie looked up and said, "I heard ya'll was in trouble, too. There's men out to get ya'll. I heard the jailers talking."

"That's not your worry, Willie," John said, reassuringly. "We can take care of ourselves."

Al nodded. "Don't let that keep you from saying everything you need to on the stand."

John and Al repeated these things to Willie as the bailiff led him into the courtroom.

The atmosphere now was hushed. There was an intensity that seemed to keep the side comments down, as if the audience anticipated a climax. Troy Hawkins sat alone today behind the prosecution desk. Judging by the glances passing amongst the crowd of men behind him, Willette's conspicuous absence had incited their anger afresh.

After the call to court came from the bailiff, Officer Montgomery, who had been questioned late yesterday afternoon, was called back to the stand.

Swartzfager began the examination saying, "Did I understand you yesterday, in response to the question Mr. Poole asked you, 'Didn't you promise him nobody would harm him if he would tell the truth?' What answer did you give to that?"

The officer was on the edge of his seat and had already said "No, sir," continuing, "Mr. Poole made that statement. I don't believe I answered that statement," Officer Montgomery said. "Because the fact was, that he was told it would be better for him to tell the truth."

The officer went on to report, when questioned, that Willie only showed them where he had parked the truck, where Hawkins' house was, and then said that he had raped a white woman in that house. It was a cut and dried confession.

When the Defense had their turn at re-examination, John asked Officer Montgomery, "Now, have you discussed this case with anyone since you were on the witness stand last night?"

"Yes, sir."

"Whom did you discuss it with?" "With the prosecuting attorneys."

"They talked to you after you left the stand?" "Yes, sir."

John, understanding that the prosecution had prompted the witness, asked him questions that confirmed his testimony from the day before, but Montgomery reiterated the propriety story the officers were standing behind. Then, John slipped the witness an unexpected question.

"Mr. Montgomery, even if you had made some threats to Willie, you would be somewhat embarrassed to admit it on the stand, wouldn't you?" Montgomery's mouth dropped opened, but before he could respond, Deavours shot up from his seat and pointed his finger at John.

"You talk about deliberately and determinedly trying to insult an officer of the law, and officers of this court, I never saw a more deliberate attempt at it!" John turned to Judge Collins and said, "Your Honor, I am not." Deavours spit out, "You just asked an officer of the law, "In order to save this case, you get up here and swear a lie!"

Judge Collins looked down at John with cold eyes, "That is an improper question." Deavours couldn't quit, however.

"If you have no respect for yourself, you ought to have some for the officers!"

Judge Collins made no move to intervene. John faced him squarely. "I am going to object to that statement by the Special Prosecuting Attorney, that 'If you have no respect for yourself you should have some for the officers.'"

"Objection sustained," the judge said, with one eyebrow raised.

Deavours loosened his tie as if readying himself for the next round. The muffled comments that filled the air throughout the courtroom without correction from the seat supported the one-two punch from the prosecution.

Although John now had the law on his side, the remainder of his questioning was futile. Montgomery was minding his p's and q's this time. Mr. Horcace McCrae, Laurel's postmaster, was the state's last witness. Swartzfager questioned him as to his relationship with McGee. He related that Willie worked for him, doing odd jobs. McCrae was with the previous prosecuting attorney and Troy Hawkins when McGee had, once again, willingly "confessed" to the crime of rape. Mcrae testified under oath that Willie had even said "hello" and asked how the family was. When Horace had told Willie that he was charged with a mighty bad crime, Willie had said, "Yes sir. I'm the right Negro, Mr. McCrae." According to him, there were no threats of violence nor offers of reward. Willie made a free and voluntary statement. Willie didn't know who Hawkins was at that time, McCrae further said.

Unexpectedly, the defense did not ask for cross-examination, but instead asked for another witness to take the stand, Mr. Luther Hill, who had been the sheriff in Jones County at the time of McGee's arrest. He had gone with the arresting officers as far as Mendenhall before they asked the highway patrolmen to "carry" Willie "to Jackson."

Schwartzfager and Deavours exchanged glances that showed their bewilderment at this maneuver. Hill was to have been their witness. After the preliminary examination, London asked Hill, "And so far as you know, they did carry him to Jackson?" "Yes, I know they did."

"Then I will ask you, Mr. Hill, why you sent him to Jackson? I believe he was in your custody at that time?"

"He was turned over to me at that time, and I sent him to Jackson as a precautionary measure."

London put on a puzzled expression.

"Well, I don't quite understand what you mean there, and I will ask you to explain that a little bit more."

Swartzfager stood up.

"We object to that. I think he understands what precautionary measure would mean."

His attempt to stop Hill's testimony was overruled.

"Well," Hill said, "to save any trouble that..." He stalled, uncomfortably, as if he knew the wording of his answer would have import. "Anyhow," he began again, "well, the man told us there that he raped this woman, and believing his statement to be true, I thought it would be best to send him to Jackson."

"In other words, you feared some trouble might arise over the situation?" "Yes, sir, that's right."

Hill looked anywhere but at the prosecutor's table. After that single admission, however, he answered the questions the same as the other officers had, saying that Willie had been treated properly, with respect, and hadn't so much as been threatened. The man they had described as having been arrested was compliant, contrite, and ready to come clean of his sins. They had just assisted him in this matter. Their testimony had been given twice before and no one had doubted their stories. They were respected in town and had been in their positions for quite some time. The fact that no one had told Willie of his rights didn't really much matter, since they all agreed that Willie's confession had been voluntary.

When London asked Sheriff Hill if he had observed Willie's physical condition, he replied casually, "Well, he looked to be in good physical condition. In fact, he was a lot heavier than he is now, and looked like he was just as strong as an ordinary mule, just to tell the truth about it." It was the second time in the trial process that McGee had been referred to as a mule.

Schwartzfager used his cross-examining to back up the prosecution's stance that no one had mistreated Willie. He helped Hill to clarify his testimony that he hadn't been aware of anyone wanting to hurt McGee at all.

"And nothing had been said or done at that time to put him in fear that anything would be done? Swartzfager asked, in conclusion.

"No, sir, not a thing."

However, on redirect examination, London asked, "Sheriff, I want to ask you one more question. Isn't it pretty generally known around Laurel that a colored man was lynched here about five or six or seven years ago for a killing, I believe, or something of the kind?"

Sheriff Hill, who had been in office when the man in question was lynched, seemed to be caught off guard. He hesitated, then answered stiffly, "I think it is a matter of common knowledge, yes, sir."

"Do you know whether or not Willie knew that at the time he was brought into your jail?" London asked.

"No, sir, I don't."

"You don't know?" London pressed. Not only was the lynching common knowledge, it was an ever-present source of anxiety to the black community. Hill took a deep breath.

"I don't know whether he knew it or not."

"That's all," London said, leaving the matter for the argument. The witness was excused.

Judge Collins, as if ready to wrap up, straightened his paperwork and asked, "Any further testimony in this case?" London looked at John and nodded.

"May it please the court. The only testimony we have on *admission vel non* of the alleged confession is the testimony of the defendant himself. We now offer the defendant for the sole purpose of determining the admissibility of the alleged confession, and for no other purpose."

A collective gasp from the crowd punctuated the statement from the floor.

It was followed by complete silence in the courtroom. In the balcony, necks stretched. Everyone wanted to see the judge's response.

Judge Collins bristled visibly. He was silent for a moment, tapping the bench with his finger, then he said in measured tones, "The only way the court can answer that is, the court will follow the law, and whatever the law is, the court will follow it, but the court wouldn't be bound by promises or –"

He paused long enough for London to interject, "We make this tender of our witness, your Honor."

Judge Collins looked shocked.

"Do you want to put him on the stand?" he asked, incredulously.

"I would like to have the ruling of the court on our tender, as to whether or not the court will allow him to take the stand for the purpose of determining the admissibility of the alleged confession only."

The judge looked sharply at the prosecutors, who were staring just as sharply at him. Then, his eyes scanned the serious faces in the courtroom. He glanced down at his papers as if wondering at the audacity these attorneys were displaying in this climate. He finally looked at Al and said, "The court will be bound by the law on this kind of question. The court will not announce in advance what will be the effect of permitting the defendant to be placed on the stand, and as to how far the prosecution may go or won't go in cross-examining him, and as to what questions the prosecution may be allowed to ask him until the court is confronted with that question." He paused, looked pointedly at John and then Al as he continued, "If counsel desires to introduce the defendant at this time, he may do so and with all legal protection in all legal controversies that may follow therefrom. You gentleman may use your discretion as to whether you want to put him on." It seemed to be more of a warning than permission.

Undeterred, London responded, "Your Honor, we made this tender of this witness subject to the court's ruling as to whether or not the witness may be offered for the purpose for which he is being offered."

Judge Collins set his jaw. "The court has ruled. Now, do you want to put him on the stand?"

"Yes, your honor. Call the witness, please."

CHAPTER TWENTY-SEVEN

HANGING PAWNS

Beaded sweat that had gathered on Willie McGee's forehead formed small streams that laced down his face and neck as he walked from the holding cell into the bright light of the courtroom. Every bench and nook in the place was filled with people, both sitting and standing. An army of well-dressed white folk claimed the courtroom floor. The balcony held a hushed dark-skinned crowd. He thought he saw a handkerchief flutter but couldn't concentrate on it. He wished he could pull his own handkerchief out of his pocket and dab at his neck, but his hands were cuffed.

Even though Lawyer Poole was talking to him softly, offering comfort and reassurance, the other cold eyes fixed on him gave him no hope for vindication. He knew that what he was about to relate would infuriate them further. You never knew what an angry white man would do when his eyes changed from detesting you to looking at you as dead meat. Willie shuddered involuntarily at the thought of one of them turning on him again. His pastor's words echoed in his numbed mind as he crossed the courtroom to the witness stand, "Fear not those that can destroy the body, but not the soul." The words flowed through his spine and he stood taller.

Lawyer Poole was close, leading him up to the seat where the jailer un-cuffed him so he could put his hand on the Bible. It seemed to add strength to strength, putting his hand on the Bible. It was like being fed with the force of the truth. He heard himself swear to tell the whole truth and he prayed silently that the Lord would understand his plight. Lawyer Poole was limpin' a bit, Willie noticed, while he walked over to the table to pick up a piece of paper. He looked like he was hurtin'. Up there, the balcony was full of folks. There was his mother, sittin' aside the preacher. Pastor was wearin' a big cross with Jesus hangin' on it. All of a sudden, he heard Lawyer Poole say, "State your name, please."

Willie felt himself in a strange state, something like a dream. He shook his head a bit to wake himself up out of it.

"Willie McGee," he heard himself say.

The effort to speak brought him back to reality. This was it. Now he would tell his story. He glanced quickly up to the balcony to garner support, but now it was just a blurred sea of faces. He blinked and refocused on Lawyer Poole's kind blue eyes.

"You are the defendant in this case?

"I am." Willie felt in his pocket for a wadded handkerchief and wiped his forehead.

Empathy for Willie calmed John's own anxieties. He was here not just for his client, but for the sake of these downtrodden people, whose many injustices might never be told. He adjusted his stance to straighten and balance more on his good leg and began, "Willie, there is some testimony given that you made a voluntary confession to the crime charged against you."

Before he finished, Willie interjected, "It wasn't voluntary."

Rustles and coughs in the courtroom signaled a desire to silence the witness. "Now, Willie," John continued, redirecting, "we want you to testify to what acts, and only to what acts the policemen committed when they brought you from Hattiesburg to Laurel, and during the time they had you in the Laurel jail. Will you tell the court exactly what happened?"

"I will," Willie said with conviction. He took a breath and began slowly, "I was down in Hattiesburg, I went down there the day before, stayed down there all day. Well," he corrected himself, "I stayed the balance of that day after I got down to Hattiesburg until the next day. I was on my way to the bus station to come back home to Laurel," his eye twitched slightly at this slight untruth, "and I was walking along the street and two officers run up and grabbed me. I turned around and said, 'What you all want?' and they said, 'What's your name?' and by the time I got 'Willie' out, he hit me – Mr. Hugh Herring hit me in the face there on the street, and he said, 'You done ravished a White woman at Laurel,' and he said, 'You son of a bitch. We gonna break you Negroes up that gone in the army from coming back here and raping white women,' and I said, 'I ain't been in no army,' and he took me back –"

"Willie," John interrupted, "we want you to tell what happened in the automobile that you rode in to Laurel."

"Well, they got me –", he paused, "You mean on the way from Hattiesburg up here to Laurel?"

"Yes."

"They taken me out of the jail and started on the way up here with me, and just as we got in the heart of town, Mr. Wayne Valentine told me, 'If you know what's good for you, there's two roads leading out of here, one leads to Jackson and one to Laurel, and the white people in Laurel would be mighty glad to get a hold of you. Fact of the business, all they want is to get their hands on you, if you know what's good for you, you better tell me you done it, so I can take you on to Jackson,' and I said, 'I didn't do it.'"

"At that time did they have your hands tied in any way?"

"Had them stropped down, stropped around my waist, and handcuffs on my hands back of me."

"Did they ask you any questions on the way from Hattiesburg to Laurel?" "From the time they left the jail until they got to Laurel."

The balcony crowd leaned forward as John asked more quietly, "Were you scared, Willie?"

"Yes, sir, I was scared! All of them threatening me said, 'You know what happened to that Negro Howard Wash in Laurel, the same thing will happen to you if you don't tell what you did. '

Willie took a deep, shuddering breath.

John pressed on. "What did they mean, Willie, by the 'same thing was going to happen to you that happened to Howard –?'

"Means they was gonna lynch me," Willie interrupted. "Hang me on a bridge." The prosecution, who had been leaning back in their chairs with arms crossed, began to shift in their seats, glancing into the crowd on courtroom floor. The rising tension was palpable. John maintained eye contact with his client.

"Willie, were you actually in fear of being turned over to a mob?"

Willie nodded as he said, "He told me he was gonna turn me over there." "Were you actually in fear of being lynched?"

"Yes, sir." Willie's eyes began to flit, as if he was in fear of being lynched now.

John leaned in to steady him with his own.

"Willie, did they inform you of any rights you had to have a lawyer?" "They ain't told me nothing, but just kept punching and hitting me in the face and in the side, Willie said firmly as if pushing aside his fear.

"Did they or did they not, Willie, take you to the Hinds County Jail?" "They did, sir."

John gave Willie a reassuring nod and turned to the judge to say, "That's all."

Deavours rose and pulled together his suit jacket, looking like a cocky rooster, as he walked up for the cross-examination.

"Willie, you know Mr. Horace McRae?" Deavours asked with authority, looking down his nose at the witness.

"Yes, sir, I know him." Willie avoided his eyes. "How long did you work for him?"

"I worked – I never worked for him, I worked for Mr. David McRae and Mr. Bennie McRae," Willie said, calmly.

"Do you know Mr. Murdock McRae?"

"Yes, sir, I remember him." Willie's face held disdain.

"Do you remember the occasion when Mr. Murdock McRae came to see you?" "Mr. Murdock didn't come to see me."

Deavours raised one eyebrow, looked down at a paper he drew from behind his back, then continued, "You remember the occasion when Mr. Horace McRae came to see you?" "I remember Mr. Horace McRae coming," Willie said, weakly. He seemed to be almost sickened by the memory, feeling his forehead with the back of his hand. "Who was there that day?" Devours demanded.

"Mr. Horace McRae, Mr. Hawkins and Mr. Albert Easterling."

"Where was the Hinds County jailor? You were in the Hinds County Jail then, weren't you?"

"Yes sir."

"Was the Hinds County jailer there?"

"There was somebody down the hall there, or in the office," "You were there in a room, weren't you?"

"Fastened up in there with them three white men." Willie glanced at the attorney nervously, as if he had not meant to say it just that way.

Deavours didn't seem to take much notice as he said, "All right, and the Hinds County jailer was in there with them?" "No, sir, he wasn't."

Deavours held up a finger, "Just a moment. "He turned to the Clerk and ordered, "Go phone him and tell him to come over here." John rose and spoke from the defense desk, "We want Mr. Herring called, too."

"Mr. Landrum is the one let me out," Willie offered blankly. Deavours ignored that and continued, "You were in the Hinds County jail, weren't you?"

"Yes sir," Willie said, solemnly, "and when Mr. Landrum turned them in there, they whipped me."

Deavours looked up sharply, narrowing his eyes with suspicion. "They did whip you there in the Hinds County Jail?"

"Yes sir, they whipped me in there," Willie said, firmly. "Who whipped you?"

"Mr. Easterling, and Mr. Montgomery, and Mr. Royals, and Mr. Landrum, and Mr. Herring. And they put two Negroes on me and they strapped me and choked me and carried me and put me in the hot box," Willie said, his eyes cast down, nostrils flaring as he slowly enunciated each name.

"They did that in Jackson?" Deavours asked, in an obvious attempt to defer the brunt of any fallout on Laurel.

"Yes, sir." Willie didn't look up.

Deavours looked to the table, indicating to Schwartzfager to write.

Deavours got each name again, as if for verification but unmistakably trying to instill in the defendant a sense of fear at naming in accusation so many white men. Willie appeared unmoved, but when Mr. Horace McRae's name was mentioned he straightened and said, "He wasn't there at that time."

"All right, at the time Mr. Horace McRae was there, what about that?" Willie looked upwards, as if reaching into his memory for another scene. "He come in there and they had me up in a room, talking about killing me." "Mr. Horace McRae?" Deavours asked with disbelief.

"Yes, sir. He hit me, too. Kicked me, too." "What else did he do to you?"

At the table for the defense, John wondered at the prosecution's ploy of letting Willie speak freely. He exchanged questioning glances with Al. "Slapped me."

"Did Mr. Easterling hit you, too?

"Mr. Easterling. . ." Willie faltered. He looked up to the balcony. John followed his gaze. McGee's minister was nodding his head, urging Willie on.

"Mr. Easterling was up there every other day whipping me." "Every other day?" Devours asked, with incredulous tone.

"He come up there at night and pulled me out and whipped me at night." "In the nighttime?"

"That's right."

"And the jailer just let him do those things?" Devours almost sneered, as if there was no way a jailer would be party to a "nigger whipping."

"The jailer would be there in the office." "Did the jailer have anything to do with it?"

"Yes, sir, he let me out and give me to them."

Deavours paused, lower lip protruding, then put his hands in his pockets. "When Mr. Easterling would come up there, who would be with him?"

"I don't know, always three or four with him."

"Always three or four with him," Deavours repeated. "Yes, sir," Willie nodded his head. Deavours turned away, grabbed his glasses and looked at his paper.

The pause in questioning offered Willie a chance to breathe, but not for long.

Deavours began again, "Now, Willie, you were down at Hattiesburg –" "Yes, sir."

"– and you were arrested down there going to the bus station?" "That's right."

"Is that what you told Mr. Poole?" "That's right."

"How far were you from the bus station when you were arrested?" "One block."

After confirming the location of the Greyhound bus station and the destinations of the buses, Deavours asked, "And on the way to the bus station these two policemen, I believe you say, arrested you?"

Willie's expression showed he believed this to be an understatement. "Grabbed me, and started hitting and knocking me right there on the street, right on the streets of Hattiesburg."

"Right on the streets of Hattiesburg?" Deavours asked, casually. "Yes, sir."

"What did Mr. Herring hit you with?" "With his fist, right in my face."

"Hit you with his fist right in the face?" Deavours repeated and crossed his arms in the manner of a schoolteacher listening to an adolescent's tardy excuse.

"Right in the face, "Willie continued. "He hit me right on the nose, my nose started bleeding right on the street."

"Who was with him? Mr. Harris?"

"I reckon so, I didn't know that other white fellow except when I see him." "They put you in jail at Hattiesburg?" "Yes, sir."

"Did they mistreat you more there?" If Deavours was falsely sympathetic, Willie didn't notice. He was caught up in the most terrifying memory of his life.

"I reached in my pocket to get my cigarettes and things and they hit me beside the head."

"What did they hit you with?"

"Some of them had "slap-jacks." Willie's eyes grew larger, and he hunched over in his seat. John leaned forward, in support of his client. "How many of them had black-jacks?"

"I couldn't count 'em. Didn't have time to look."

"How many times would you say they hit you with a blackjack?" "I couldn't count 'em."

"So many of them you 'couldn't count 'em'?"

Willie didn't appear to notice that Deavours had mocked him. "No, sir, I couldn't count 'em," he repeated.

"Did they hit you in the face with a blackjack? Deavours asked, looking at the floor now, instead of at Willie, his hands clasped behind his back.

"All over the head and in the face." Willie seemed to grow bolder without Deavours' eyes on him.

"All over your head and in your face," Deavours repeated, pacing. He looked up suddenly, "Did they break the skin on your face?

Willie pointed to his upper cheek. "See that place there?"

"Uhn huh," Deavours nodded, as he walked in more closely to examine it.

"See that hole in my head up there?" Willie parted his hair to reveal a pit in his scalp.

"Uhn huh."

Willie turned his neck towards Deavours. "See that place there?"

"Unh huh," the attorney said, again, as if not knowing what else to say with what seemed to be incriminating evidence of a beating.

"And there was another place here and another one here." Willie pulled back his shirt to show two more scars. "Five of them."

"They did that to you in Hattiesburg?" Deavours questioned.

John realized that Deavours was trying to at least protect Laurel. "Not in Hattiesburg."

"Where?"

"Up there in the Jackson jail." Willie held his palm to his head as he answered, as if keeping all the memories straight had become a difficult task.

"Well, we are talking about Hattiesburg now. You said they beat you over the head with a blackjack in Hattiesburg?"

"I don't know if it was a blackjack or slapjack."

Devours smiled at this, condescendingly.

"Anyway, they hit you over the face and head with something besides the hand?"

"Every time I looked around it was a lick."

"Did they beat you in the face with a blackjack?"

The repeating of the question seemed to test Willie's patience. "I tell you, they hit me all in the face and on my head."

The rest of the interrogation was focused on the men, Mr. Valentine, Mr. Montgomery and Mr. Jack Anderson, who had driven him back to Jackson in the patrol car. When asked what else happened on the trip, Willie answered, "They jobbed me in the side and face with their fists." At that, an audible groan came from the balcony. "Beg pardon?" Deavours asked.

"Jobbed," Willie repeated, tossing his head back and forth to demonstrate, "in the side and face with their fists."

"How many times did they whip you?"

"I couldn't tell you, my face was all swole and my eyes all closed up." He squinted in remembrance. "I don't know how often."

"You say that was a continuous beating while you were in Hattiesburg and on the way from Hattiesburg to Laurel?"

Willie took a deep breath.

"From the whole time after they picked me up, all after then, they was beating and knocking on me," he said, wearily.

"All right, they beat you all the way to Laurel, and of course when you got to Laurel you were completely beaten up, weren't you?"

"What do you call completely?" Willie asked.

"Well, all over your face. Didn't you say your face was all swollen up and bleeding?"

"My nose was bleeding, and I was beat all up in the face. What you call completely?" he asked again. John understood that Willie did not want to make a false statement. He had sworn to tell the truth, after all.

"All right, that was the condition you were in when you got to Laurel," Deavours said, with resignation, looking down at his notes. "Now, I believe you stated while ago on your direct examination that Mr. Wayne Valentine asked you if you committed this crime?"

Willie lifted his chin and spoke clearly. Immediately, it became obvious that he had been waiting for just this moment.

"'If you don't tell me the truth, that you done this,' he says, 'I ain't gonna risk my neck for you, I'm gonna carry you right up there and let them folks have you.'"

The statement rang true, with Willie sounding almost like Valentine, not the effect Deavors had wanted. He said quickly, "All right, and when he said that to you, you told him you didn't do it, didn't you?"

John stood up. "We object to that. He didn't say that."

"He said that on direct examination," Deavours retorted.

Judge Collins overruled the objection, but John emphatically repeated, "He didn't say that."

Collins ignored John and said, "Let him answer the question."

Willie forgot the question in the ruckus. "What did you say now?" he asked. "Well, now, what <u>did</u> you say to him?

Willie looked at John, who frowned and seated himself, then turned back to Deavours. Humbly he said, "How a man gonna say anything and every time he open his mouth, somebody hit him in the mouth?"

Deavours pressed on, "In other words, you didn't say anything?" Willie looked exasperated and spent.

"You think I try to say something and every time I open my mouth the man hit me in it."

Deavours' look turned cold at this show of impudence. John scanned the grim faces and folded arms of the courtroom in a sideways glance. He felt the temperature rising.

"I just asked you what you said, if anything?"

Willie hung his head more submissively "Nothing for me to do but sit there like somebody tied me down." "So you didn't say anything, is that it?"

Willie said, again, more slowly, "I couldn't say much. Every time I open my mouth he hit me." "All right then, you didn't say anything, did you?"

Willie straightened in his seat.

"I say I did not say anything to that man because all the while he was asking me whether I did it or not, every time I tried to tell him anything so he could try to get the right man, I got hit in the mouth."

"Then you didn't tell him anything about the crime?" "I told him I didn't do it. Told them all I didn't do it."

"In other words, all this stuff you say about there being a mob – that didn't frighten you into telling them anything, because you didn't tell them anything, did you?"

"I told them what I said while ago. I still say I said that. I say I told them in the beginning I didn't do it."

"So, all this stuff you tell then, about turning you out to the mob –" "They did say it!" Willie interrupted, raising his voice.

"– that had no effect on you, because you never did tell them anything?" Willie and Deavours gazed at one another for a long moment, as the truth of the matter echoed silently around the courtroom. If Willie had confessed to the crime in the beginning, they would have taken him to be lynched. There would have been no bargains. Finally, Willie said, "When I thought they was gonna take me to Jackson, when I got to the edge of town, Mr. Wayne said, 'If you don't tell me the truth, that you done this, I am going to let them have you.'"

"I say you never did tell them anything?" "Sure, I told him I didn't do it."

"You told me a minute ago you didn't tell him anything, didn't you?" Deavours said, eyebrows raised.

"I told him after I got in jail."

Deavours drew himself up and turned his head to the side in feigned confusion. "Now, didn't you tell me while ago you didn't tell him anything?"

Willie spoke slowly.

"When I left out from here to Hattiesburg, I didn't tell him anything, I didn't tell anything until I got here to Laurel." Willie did an impression of the sheriff. "He said, 'You know what happened to that Negro Howard Wash –"

"I say, all this stuff about a mob didn't have any effect on you telling anything? Deavours interrupted.

Willie tried enacting the scene again, as if hoping his talent for imitations would convince the court of the truth. "Yes, sir, after I got here and he told me, 'You know what happened to that Negro Howard Wash –'

Deavours stepped squarely in front of Willie, blocking any view of him from the floor. John drummed on the desk with his pen restlessly, hoping to alert onlookers to pay attention.

"All right, you said he told you down there where the roads separate, 'One road goes to Laurel and one to Jackson, and those Laurel people would be glad to get their hands on you –'"

"He told me that in Hattiesburg," Willie said, shifting his eyes away from Deavours. "All right, you didn't tell him anything, then, did you? That didn't have any effect on you, did it?" Devours cocked his head. "Not a bit? And then, when you finally got to Jones County, in the presence of Mr. Luther Hill, Mr. Valentine, Mr. Jeff Montgomery, and Mr. Jack Anderson –"

"When I…" Willie interjected, realizing he hadn't been able to answer the question. "Wait until I get through." Deavours said, with all the authority of a white man sure of his role in a segregated society.

Willie waited, but his look said, "You don't know nothing about white men breakin' you down, bit by bit."

"When you got over there in the presence of those men, then you say you were threatened with a mob, and you told them you did it?"

"When I got in the corporation of the city, when that man told me, threatened me with a mob, that's when I told him I did it, then he said, 'Now will you tell the sheriff the same thing when you get up there? If you don't tell the sheriff the same thing when you get up there,' he said, 'Nigger, it will be too bad for you.' Willie's voice shook, but he plowed on, "I told him when we got to the city limits, I told him –"

Deavours lashed out and Willie froze in his testimony, as if he once again felt the slap of the white man. "You didn't tell me that a minute ago! You told me a minute ago it was when you got up here to the city jail and they told you they were going to make another Howard Wash out of you, isn't that true?"

John's fists clenched seeing Deavours so close to Willie. This was a verbal beating, in front of so many men who were in line to get their turn.

"I told him then and told him again when I got to the jail."

"So, you told it twice?" Deavours asked, his tone accusing Willie of a lie.

"I told you, I didn't tell them between here and Hattiesburg, I told you I told them in the city limits."

"How many more times did you tell them that?"

"I told them at the jail house and after we got in the city limits."

"And you told him at Hattiesburg when he told you, 'The road separates here, one goes to Jackson and one to Laurel –'

Willie tried to rest his head by leaning back on the trunk of his neck. This gave him a peripheral view of the balcony and his supporters leaning forward across the railing. It seemed to offer him some relief, and he interjected, "I didn't tell him I did it over there."

"You didn't tell him that there, what did you tell him?"

"I told him I didn't do it until I got to the city limits, and I told him at the city limits and told him at the jail house."

"And all the beating you got between here and Hattiesburg had no effect on you whatsoever, not a bit?"

"Until I got up here to the city limits and he threatened me he would turn me over to the mob."

"When he threatened you there at the city limits with a mob, you told it?" "That's when I told him."

"Now where do you say the city limits is?"

"Down there where Magnolia and the Boulevard come together." Willie's eyes searched for the defense table. John knew the awful scene of the lit intersection must be flashing through his memory. Shadows he had described to John as creeping like cockroaches, had told him the mob was real.

"And what did you tell them there?"

"I told him –" Willie's voice involuntarily lowered. "When he threatened me with the mob, that's where I told him."

"I say, what did you tell them there?"

"That's when I told him I did it." Murmurs pulsed through the courtroom floor and John knew the white crowd had just convicted Willie on that statement.

Deavours used the momentum, walking towards the courtroom floor audience as he formed the next question. He turned back to Willie confidently, now part of a greater team.

"Now, what did you do between there and town?"

"I just answered questions, whatever he asked, I toldhim – 'Yes, sir, Yes, sir,' that's all I said."

"Did you answer yes to all the questions he asked you?"

"He just said, 'you did so and so,' "Willie waved his fingers in a circle in explanation, "And I said, 'Yes, sir,' and 'you did so and so,' and I said 'Yes, sir.'"

"Now what did they tell you when they arrested you in Hattiesburg?" "Told me they wanted me for rape." Willie's answer was emotionless. "Is that all they told you, what they wanted you for?"

"That's all they told me, the mens that picked me up."

John noted that Willie left out any reference to their curses, spits, and degrading remarks.

"What did Mr. Valentine tell you when he came there?"

Willie sighed, then continued, "Mr. Valentine come and called me out in the hall. They had me in a little old cage in the city jail, and they brought me out there in the hall, put handcuffs on me and a belt around me and brought me out in the hall and he said, 'Get your clothes down, nigger,' and when I was trying to get my clothes down he popped me in the face with his fist. I couldn't get 'em down fast enough."

Groans and murmurs in concert from the balcony hummed like a gospel hymn.

Deavours disregarded the statement. "What else did he tell you about what you were charged with?"

"Said I was charged with rape."

"Did he tell you who you were charged with raping?" "No, sir."

"Didn't tell you that?" "No, sir."

"Did he tell you where the person lived you were charged with raping?" "No, sir," he answered.

"Didn't tell you that?"

"No, sir," Willie responded, mechanically, as if his patience had worn thin. "And you say he didn't threaten you with any mob until he got you to the city limits?"

"That's when he started threatening me." "Willie," Deavours said, "did you see any mob?"

Willie replied, "I can tell you what happened. He called up here and asked how it looked out there."

"What do you mean, 'called up'?" "Called up over the automobile radio."

"Now you were present at the trial the last time, weren't you?" Willie looked toward John, then warily at Deavours and said, "Yes, if I know anything about it, I do." Deavours continued, "That was at Hattiesburg, and you were present at the trial the first time in Laurel?"

"I don't know anything about the first time, in Laurel." This was a true statement, John knew. According to Willie, he had scanned his memory time and time again, and couldn't bring up what had happened during the first trial. It was a vast, dark blankness, but he knew the feeling of it. Willie had awakened many times from a nightmare of that horrible hole in his past.

"You don't know anything about the first time in Laurel?" Deavours looked puzzled. "You were here, weren't you?"

An intuition caused John to look for reactions. He saw one man staring holes in his shoes. John recognized him as one of the jailers.

Willie stumbled, "If I know it...I don't know anything about it." Deavours moved on.

"Now, you didn't see any mob, did you?"

Willie fumbled for an answer, fumbling his hands.

"I was trying not to see nary a one," he said, quietly. "Huh?"

Willie raised his voice slightly.

"I was trying not to see nary a one."

"I know," Deavours answered "but regardless of what you tried to do, you didn't see one, did you?" "Not as I know of."

"Wasn't any mob out there at the jail, was there?" Deavours' voice had taken on a bullying tone.

"Not as I know of, I don't know about that."

"Well, now, you say you remember everything that was done to you when you were arrested in Hattiesburg, is that right? About them beating you up and all that?"

"Yes, sir, I remember it."

"And," Deavours emphasized, "you remember them beating you up on the way to Laurel?"

"Yes, sir, I remember it"

"Did they continue to beat you up when they took you over there to the Hinds County jail?"

Willie looked Deavours squarely in the eyes and said, "When they brought me here, they busted my skull, throwed me back there, and I bled out of my nose and mouth" John pictured the cell where Willie fell with a thump, blood streaming down his shirt.

"I didn't know nothing about what..." Willie continued, but Deavours stepped in with another question to quell the emotional response. "Where did that take place?" "That took place at Jackson."

"Did the highway patrolman that took you from Mendenhall to Jackson continue to beat you?"

"No, sir, no, sir, that was the onliest one." Willie said quickly, obviously glad to be able to witness for the patrolman's kindness.

"The onliest one," Deavours mocked. "But you say when you got to Jackson, they continued to beat on you?"

Willie looked relieved to be able to say, "Every other day, every other night, somebody had me out beating on me."

Deavours desperately needed to prove this otherwise, John knew. He noted that the attorney's hand shook slightly as he wiped his forehead.

"Now when was it they busted your skull?"

"If I know that I could tell you all what happened." "You don't know anything about that?"

"All I know, two fellows threw me back in the hall and told them to go take care of me until I got back my sense."

"Well, no mob got after you, did there, Willie?" "When you talking about?"

"When you were first arrested and brought here to Laurel?"

"I don't know, sir." Willie said, through clenched teeth, showing the first signs of anger.

"You didn't see any, did you?"

"It was that night when they brought me in." Willie's eyes deepened in memory. "Huh?"

"It was that night when they brought me in," he said more straightforwardly. "I say," Deavours waved his hand dramatically as he spoke, as if to brush away the picture Willie had painted, "you didn't see any great concourse of people, or great number of people when they brought you here to the jail?"

"I couldn't say, "Willie replied, meekly. "Well, you were there, weren't you?"

Willie looked straight ahead.

"They brought me here at night and carried me in the jail house." "Well," Deavours said with mock exasperation, "you didn't see any lot of people anywhere here, did you?"

Willie's eyes widened. "I seed people all right."

"Well, you see people on the streets every day in Laurel, don't you?" Deavours chuckled.

Willie was silent for a long time. He seemed frozen. Then, he looked at Deavours straight on and said, "Yes, sir, I see people on the streets."

John wondered if he should intervene. Willie seemed to have exhausted his ability to respond. There was no need, however, as Deavours realized the same and turned to the judge to say, "That's all."

Devours avoided John's gaze as he marched past the defense desk on the way to his seat.

Judge Collins turned to the bailiff to say, "The witness is excused."

The judge pronounced a fifteen-minute recess. Willie turned to the bailiff and offered his hands to be cuffed.

John leaned into the court reporter. "Will you please make a copy of the testimony for the defense?"

"Yes, sir, I'll get it to you after the break."

As John and Al walked to the back room of the courthouse, where the defense attorneys customarily took their breaks, an officer said, "Good day," but leaned in as if he purposed more. John leaned in to hear him say quietly, "Watch out for yourself during these breaks, there's a gang of men out for you." He cocked his head towards Al, "Not so much London as you. John nodded his thanks. Walking on, he felt in his pocket for his pack of cigarettes. Soberly drawing one out, he held it between his lips unlit.

CHAPTER TWENTY-EIGHT

LOOMING LOCALS

Willie spent the entire break smoking with trembling hands, but would not speak, as if he had entered back into the imprisoned mind that had overtaken him before. The distant look in his wide eyes reflected the fire he had seen in the white men's. John looked at Al and shook his head. Willie was a limp figure as he was led back to the courtroom.

As the Court resumed, John sensed a change in the crowd, as if decisions had been made. Sly smiles and nods presaged revenge. An uneasy thought of Gerry and the baby crept into his mind, but he forced his focus back to the present battlefield of court.

Judge Collins asked, with a shade of exasperation, "Anything further?" London stood to say, "Your Honor, we rest with the defendant as a witness, we don't wish to recall him."

Collins drew a breath, as if relieved not to have further contest. "All right, anything further for the State?"

Swartzfager stood and said with a complaining tone, "If the Court please, defense counsel tells me they have other witnesses.

"I thought he had rested." Collins responded quizzically, "I asked if he had any other testimony…"

Poole stood and explained, "We have subpoenaed another witness." It was a witness they hoped would make it to the Court soon. They had sent the deputy out while they were on break. Judge Collins shook his head and instructed the Prosecution to go ahead with the witness they had recalled, Mr. Luther Hill, to ask him what condition McGee was in when he was turned over to him, was he bruised, swollen or beaten? Hill did not blink as he said that there was no sign whatsoever of any beating, and there were no threats of lynching at all. Defense's questions urging him to recall if he had made any special effort to determine if he had been molested in any way resulted in only vapid answers from a drawn face. Prosecution next called Mr. Royals, who was the jailer in the Jones County jail at the time Willie was brought in. He could not recall either, any signs of molestation on Willie at all, nor any threats of violence. Although John objected to his testimony, since he had been in the court the entire time Willie was giving his, it was overruled. John had knowledge of this jailer and on cross-examination he was prepared to test him.

"Mr. Royals, you were the jailer last year?" "Yes, sir."

"It is true, Mr. Royals, that you are now under indictment for having beaten a prisoner?" Royals' eyes dodged his as Swartzfager objected and the judge sustained.

John continued with raised brows, "Have you ever beaten any prisoner?" "No, sir." The answer came from a hard face and tight lips.

"You don't know what happened to Willie between Hattiesburg and Laurel, do you not?"

"No, sir, I do not." He stuck his chin out.

"You didn't make a careful examination of Willie, that is, yourself, after he got over there to the jail, did you?" John asked.

"Well, I saw him," he protested.

"But you didn't make a careful examination of him, did you?" John repeated.

Royals wagged his head, "Well, I didn't get down right on him and make no close examination, no!"

"That's all," John said succinctly, looking at the Judge.

Deavours passed him on the way to the witness, saying, "Mr. Royals, if he had been continually hit in the mouth and over the head with a blackjack, would you have been able to have seen the signs of that?"

Royals lifted himself, and said straightly, "Yes, sir."

"That's all," Deavours had hardly stopped before he turned back again to the table and the shifty eyed witness was excused.

The Prosecution paraded other officers before the court once again to testify that they had seen no evidence of beating McGee, and, in fact, that everyone had been most proper in their handling of them. Mr. Easterling, who Willie had accused of beating him along with Hawkins and McCrae took the stand to say that they didn't even get near Willie at that time, and they certainly did not have two Negroes strap and beat him. As a matter of fact, Mr. Easterling went on to say that he treated Willie, "With all courtesy and kindness." He didn't hear Willie's testimony, but "...if he says he was treated even unkindly, at any time I was there, or by any of the other officers or anybody else that was with me, he isn't telling the truth." He went on to say that, "I was so kind and courteous to that Negro, that I even gave him cigarettes every time I went there to talk with him, then one time I went in when I didn't have any cigarettes, and he wanted cigarettes and I gave him money to buy them with."

"And that's the way you treated him." Deavours stated unquestioningly.

Easterling took the ball and ran with it. "That's the way I treated him, and that's the way he was treated by everyone in my presence."

When John examined him, he asked if he had at one time told Willie to get his friends to get him a thousand dollars, and he would be able to help him. The answer was a firm, "No, sir. If he told you that, he told you another untruth." Easterling went on to say, in a fatherly tone, "Mr. Poole, I'll tell you, here's what you've got here, he is a smart Negro, he writes as pretty a hand as you do. I imagine he has been instructed by somebody to tell you these lies, and definitely they are lies, if he told you them."

John detested the allusion to a 'smart Negro' as one who would also be deceiving. He attempted to get the verbose Mr. Easterling to at least admit that there was much he didn't know, of his own personal knowledge, about Willie's time in jail. Easterling denied knowledge of Willie's time in the hotbox but didn't deny its existence. He imagined the only time Willie might have been struck was when he attempted an escape. He insisted, "they were mighty nice to him there."

On re-direct examination by Swartzfager he was allowed to talk freely, and Easterling painted a picture of half dollars and cigarettes, and generally a good feeling with the fellows in the Hinds County Jail.

It gave John time to contemplate a re-direct examination. He went with the good feeling Easterling was conjuring up, and went on with, "As a matter of fact you told him you would like to help him, didn't you?"

Easterling put up his guard, "No, I never did tell him that."

"What did you tell him when you went up there?" John persisted.

"The first time I went up there, I advised him of his rights," he said with official pride.

John's eyes widened, "You mean you told him he didn't have to testify?" "That's right," Easterling went on, "I told him he didn't have to talk to me or anyone else unless he wanted to." As he said this, Deavours made a remark in a low tone, which the court reporter reported was not heard by her.

John objected hotly, "We want to object to Mr. Deavours continually making remarks in front of the witness."

Judge Collins looked uninterested. "The Court didn't hear it, this is in hearing of the Court, and the Court doesn't know what Mr. Deavours said, so nobody will be prejudiced by it," ignoring the intimidation of the defendant, instructing, "Go ahead with your examination."

London stood to say, rather loudly, "Will the reporter note our exception to the Court's ruling."

The Judge repeated with irritation to John, "Go ahead with your examination."

John glanced back at Willie, who was seated too closely to Deavours, Swartzfager and the pool of unfriendly faces behind him. He returned, "That's all," and went back to sit with McGee.

After several witnesses were re-examined in front of the jury, Devours appealed that they had more witnesses subpoenaed who had not yet shown who would testify as to McGee's appearance during his stay in jail. He proclaimed, "We just want to give the Court everything we have got in this matter."

John stood and said, "I don't think Mr. Deavours understands our position there, your Honor. We think that the Court could rule on the oral confessions now."

Collins replied, "In other words, you have no further testimony then, gentlemen?" "In regard to the oral confession," John clarified.

Judge Collins straightened himself and took a deep breath, looking out over the sea of like-minded fellows, without glancing at the pleading eyes of the upper loft, and said finally with brutish tenor, "The Court holds that every officer who has testified in this case with regard to these confessions, including the Sheriff of Jones County, who was introduced as a witness for the defendant, testified that there wasn't any force, and was no sign on the defendant, and nothing to corroborate what he said, and the Court knows personally every one of these officers, and knows them to be high class citizens." He paused a moment before proceeding with what was, in essence, the third death sentence for McGee. His eyes were not visible behind his narrowed lids as he proclaimed, "This Court believes what they said, and doesn't believe a word the defendant said. For that reason, the Court overrules the motion."

The Prosecution, despite the former ruling of the Judge as to Willie's witness, paraded the Hinds County jailer to again deny any harm done to Willie. Judge Collins finally intervened saying that he had ruled on this already, and that if counsel didn't limit the questioning, we would "not be through until Christmas!" He recessed the Court for lunch.

Al and John went through the back exit quickly enough this time to not be noticed at the window, although by this time, they felt sure their trick was known. They asked a runner to get sandwiches for them, then rested in the jailhouse conference room, as Willie was taken back to his cell. After lighting cigarettes, Al leaned back and rested his eyes, gathering strength for the rest of the day. John couldn't relax though, and leaned forward with elbows on his knees. He finally said, "Judge Collins totally disregarded Willie's testimony, but the Supreme Court won't." Al grunted in agreement. John stumped out his cigarette halfway and announced, "I'm going to attach Willie's testimony as an exhibit and go file it now."

Al opened one eye and said, "You're going out now to file it? After yesterday?"

John put on his suit coat and grabbed the papers, regardless of the warning. "If we don't get it in now, the Prosecution may have it stricken from the record altogether." Al stood to follow, but John raised his palm. "No, we need one of us here if it takes too long, and I'll be careful. No one will be expecting me to be out and about now." He turned to walk down the corridor.

Al knew better to try to talk him out of it at this point, and just shouted, "Good luck!" He scratched his head and began to weed through paperwork to underline points for the argument.

John took the car, which they had parked in an unlikely side lot, to the Circuit Clerk's office. The day was bright, and it felt good to have a break from the stale atmosphere of the courtroom and feel the sun shining through the window. He wheeled into the parking lot just in front of the office, not expecting a need to be evasive here, and started up the several steps to the office. He grimaced, as the stairs always put extra pressure on his stump. Walking inside the building, it appeared mostly empty. He glanced at the closed door of the Mayor's office with some relief. This was no time to face Carroll Gartin. He looked at his watch. The court had gotten out late for lunch. He hoped that this staff would be back now.

"Can I help you?" He heard the voice come from behind. A clerk stepped out of a nearby office, wiping his hands with a napkin. When he recognized John as the attorney representing McGee, there was a stiffness between them.

John replied, in Southern manner, "I'm so sorry to have disturbed your repast. I realize it is still lunch time."

"What can I help you with, Mr. Poole," came the dry reply.

"I… we wanted to file this as an exhibit to our motion," John returned, handing him the paper of McGee's testimony, and smiling cordially. He had hoped to just meet with a friendly secretary. He wasn't in a mood to meet another vengeful attitude.

"I'll give it to our girls," he said, and wanted to say more, but John gave a quick thanks, turned around and walked out, not offering any unnecessary communication.

John had to focus on his stiffening stump as he descended and didn't take notice of the car pulling up. By the time he got to the bottom step, heading towards his car, he saw that the car was packed with male hats and had pulled up next to his. Slowing his steps a bit as he walked to his door, he saw another vehicle pulling up on the other side with several men, faces filled with loathing.

Although his heart began to race, he got into the car, started it, and began to pull away from the curb. Both cars revved their engines and began to pull away, as well.

John looked around to see there were no other cars nearby. Clouds had come to cover the sun as an omen, and the day now felt empty and cold. John's mind raced to find a solution. He could see a face laughing through the window at his dilemma, twirling a toothpick as if it were a weapon. He pulled quickly back to the curb, flew out the door and hurriedly ascended the steep flight of stairs as quickly as he could, numbing himself to the pain.

"Son of a Bitch!" he heard as he felt the eyes burning in his back.

John burst through the office door and slammed it behind him. This time the clerk was in the hallway and saw John, huffing for breath.

"Well, to what do we owe the honor of this second visit?" He asked quizzically. John told him, while trying to catch his breath, of the situation outside and asked, with humility, for him to call for a police escort.

He listened, furrowed his brow, taking in the scene. Then, smiling, crossed his arms over his chest and began to laugh. "Well, now, Mr. Attorney, you are in some fix," he said as he savored the countenance of the compromised man in front of him, then added with raised brows, "I guess you're just going to get what's coming to you." John fought back feelings of panic as he looked into the serious stare and turned through the door to look for another telephone. Hearing female chatter, he followed it to an office not too far down the hall and interrupted a gathering of secretaries to ask permission to use the phone in private.

Noticing the distress, a plumpish woman directed, "Right in there – you can use that one." The chatter died down as attentive ears caught, "Highway Patrol. I need an escort right away, please."

Murmurs announced John's late entrance into the courtroom. He straightened his suitcoat and sat, as the Judge peered down at his whisperings to London. Deavours was entertaining Easterling on the stand, enabling him to tell the whole story, verbatim from his perspective, of Willie's willingly signing the confession. Between notes to each other, and attempting to normalize, Al and John missed the opportunity for objection to the wholly by-passing standard rules of witness examination. Easterling had been given ample time to paint a picture for the jury of his kindly dealing with the contrite McGee. He claimed that he told Willie that he was the Prosecuting Attorney, and that he didn't have to tell him anything, and had a right to have a lawyer, himself. Regardless of that, he went on to "ask" Willie to tell his story and told him that he was going to visit the people Willie said he went to that night, to see if he was telling the truth. He said that Willie had admitted he was drinking very heavily, and that "he was the boy," Easterling caught himself and said, "man, that went in the house." He went on to say that since it was such a serious crime, he didn't ask him to sign a confession that night, but came back the next day and asked him again about it, and reduced it to writing for McGee to sign, saying, "Willie, do you want to sign that?" and he said, "Yes sir, I will sign that because that is the truth." It was a radically different story from what Willie had told. He added at the end as a further embellishment, "Whenever I went in the room to talk with him, I assured him there that I wouldn't let anybody bother him, I said 'Nobody here is going to hurt you, and you don't have to talk if you don't want to.'" He stamped it with, "Willie was assured of that every time I went there."

The Prosecution then produced the written statement Willie had signed.

Easterling said, "I went over it twice with him before I ever went and reduced it to writing, fact of the business, Mr. Swartzfager, I made notes on it."

Swartzfager asked, "Would you mind, in a low tone, for the benefit of the jury, just state what he said?" He was pointing to a sentence in the confession.

Easterling brought his voice down lower, "He said, 'I raped the woman,'" then he looked up, pinching his face and added, "He said, 'I fucked her.'" Waving his hand he went on, "I didn't want to put that vulgar word in the written statement, and I put rape in there."

The written confession was read in its entirety for all to hear, as Willie studied his shoes. It described the night as a drunken lark that had ended in the "forcible assault." It further claimed that he had no remembrance of what was said in the act, as he was drinking very heavy. It ended with, "I make this statement of my own free will and accord, and without any promises whatsoever, and without any hope of reward, and after having been advised of my rights, but desire to make the above statement in order to clear up this matter, and to tell the truth."

John objected and moved that all the testimony be stricken, because it was made in the presence of the jury before being qualified, adding, "At this time we move for a mistrial."

Collins frowned and said, "Overruled." He looked at London and Poole mystified and added, "The prosecution offered all of this testimony and the defense sat here and didn't offer any objection at all up until this time."

John and Al looked at each other searching for a response, as Collins announced that Easterling's testimony be heard outside of the jury's presence, as an ineffective bandaid to protocol, after the jury had already been prejudiced.

Finally, the Prosecution called a Mr. Royals, the jailer, to the stand. Willie was noticeably disturbed by the sight of him. Royals tediously parroted Easterling's testimony.

On cross-examination, John asked if he had heard Easterling tell McGee that if he pled guilty he would see that he got life in the penitentiary. Royals tightened his lips, "No, sir, I didn't hear that." When asked to describe the room they were all sitting in when McGee signed the confession, he said it was about "seven or eight foot square, I would think." He was certain, however, that no force had been used. The State rested after his testimony.

After discussion at the Defense table, Willie's head nodded that he was back to himself, then London rose and said, "Your Honor, at this time we would like again to introduce the defendant in his own behalf on this preliminary hearing as to the admissibility of the written confession, and we want to introduce the defendant solely for that purpose, not in the presence of the jury."

Collins sighed, leaning back in his chair. "All right, let the defendant take the stand."

John led Willie to the stand and after preliminary questions handed him the written confession saying, "Willie, I hand you this piece of paper and ask you if you have ever seen that piece of paper before?"

"I seen one like it," Willie said affirmatively.

"I will ask you if this is your signature down here at the bottom of it," John pointed at the signature, and Willie agreed it was his.

"I will ask you to state to the Court, Willie, why you signed that statement? Give it in just as much detail as you can."

Willie looked straight into John's eyes to say, "Well, the reason I signed it, I was scared of them, that's the reason I signed it."

"You say you were scared?" John repeated. "Yes, sir."

"And would that be the sole reason you signed it?"

"Yes, sir," Willie repeated, adding, "They beat me." The courtroom became stone silent.

John paused a moment then continued, "Now, I want you to tell the Court what happened, if anything, that made you scared, and so scared that you signed this piece of paper?"

Willie drew in a breath, "Well, Mr. Easterling and Mr. Royals and Mr. Montgomery and Mr. Hawkins came up to the jail house next morning, I was carried –" He backed up to explain, "that night I was carried to Jackson, came up there and carried me out and questioned me a long time, then put me in the hotbox."

John interrupted, "You say they put you in a hot box, what is that, Willie?" "That's a place where they put you and sweat you nearly 'bout to death." A cough covered a curse from the balcony. "Who did that?"

"Mr. Easterling had me put in there, the jailer put me in there." Easterling and Royals exchanged glances.

"Now, Willie," John continued, "I want to know whether Mr. Easterling told you you had a right to have a lawyer before you signed this piece of paper?" He held it up. "He didn't tell me nothing," Willie's lower lip quivered in protest of putting this to words. "Every time they come up there, they punched on me and didn't try to tell me nothing, just trying to make me say I did it, and I kept telling them I didn't do it." Willie's eyes began to swell with emotion.

"Who is the Mr. Easterling you refer to, Is that Mr. Easterling who was with the prosecuting attorney?" John turned and pointed towards the frowning wrinkled face.

"Yes, sir, with the prosecuting attorney," Willie exchanged a look with him as he finished, "he told me that." Willie wiped the hot stream off his cheek angrily and sniffed.

John probed, "Willie, I will ask you if he attempted to give you any inducement to get you to sign this statement?"

Willie's eyes went dark with memory as he said, "No more than he just kept punching me, I was scared and he threatened me was the reason I signed it."

"Willie, I will ask you whether Mr. Easterling ever brought any cigarettes, ice cream, candy, gum, etc?"

Willie replied, "He didn't bring me none at all," negating Easterling's testimony with a shake of his head, "I had some money up there…" Willie reached into his pants to demonstrate, "down here in my pocket, and I told him to let me have some means to get my money I had in my pocket down here at the police station." The memory seemed to anger him. They had taken his money, and teased him by smoking in front of him, talking about how nice a good smoke was.

"I will ask you, Willie, whether Mr. Easterling ever offered to get you out of this thing if you would get him some money…"

Deavours objected to the leading of the witness, and it was sustained. John continued, "I will ask you if he made any other inducement, Willie, to get you to sign this confession?"

"No more than he threatened to put me on the gallows up there, put me on the gallows," Willie was becoming visibly anxious at the memory, "threatened – told me they come to take me back to Laurel and turn me over to the mob if I didn't want to sign it, and it would save the State a lot of money."

"Who said that?" John asked sharply.

"Mr. Easterling," Willie proclaimed. Easterling leaned back in his seat and crossed his arms on his chest, trying to save himself with a grin towards his fellow officers. No one joined him.

"Mr. Easterling said they were going to turn you over to the mob and save the State a lot of money? John said, a bit more loudly.

"That's what he said," Willie confirmed.

John came a little closer, "Willie, were you actually in fear when you signed this statement?"

Willie replied wholeheartedly, "I was scared to death way they had been treating me and threatening me, and I was tired of them knocking on me and threatening me."

John looked pointedly at the Judge and said, "That's all."

Deavours walked up slowly to Willie and asked, "Willie, can you read?" "Yes, I can read," Willie said coolly.

"Did you read this before you signed it?" Deavours pointed at his signature dispassionately.

Willie replied straightly, "I didn't read nothing, Mr. Easterling read it." "Did he give you a copy of it too?"

"He didn't give me nothing, just read it."

"He didn't give you anything?" Deavours asked with a tone of disbelief. "No, sir," Willie confirmed.

Deavours tried a different tactic." Did you hear him read it?" "I was in there, yes, sir."

"Well, you were in there, and you heard it, didn't you?" Willie answered that he did, and Deavours moved on to ask him about the room and the jailer that testified earlier.

"You heard him testify, didn't you?" "Yes, sir."

"You heard him testify that you weren't mistreated or abused, didn't you?" Deavours persisted.

Willie pressed his lips together to stop errant exclamations, "Ummmm, Lord have mercy!"

Deavours misinterpreted his exclamation and added, "You heard that, didn't you?"

"Yes, sir, I heard lots of things." Willie said, cryptically.

"All right, now," Deavours looked down at the paper and lifted it back up again as if it were spoils in a victory, "Mr. Easterling came over there and you did sign this paper, didn't you?"

Willie shot back with, "After they done threatened me and beat me up and I stayed in the hot box, I stayed in that hot box, and you stay in that hot box, you sign anything."

Murmurs came from the balcony. Deavours quicky tried to cover them by saying, "Now, who was it put you in the hot box?"

"Mr. Easterling had me put in there."

"And the jailer over there," Deavours pointed, hoping to intimidate Willie by pointing towards the sea of accusing faces, "had you put in there?"

Willie looked straight ahead and continued, "Yes, sir, from Mr. Easterling's order, he told them to put me in there and let me stay until I signed it." He confirmed that Mr. Royals was there, too.

"What kind of thing is that hot box?" Deavours asked, sounding as if with sincere curiosity.

"Well, the box, let's see," Willie complied and showed with his hands, "It's about as big as this chair, ain't long enough to lay down, and ain't nothing in there but just a concrete floor, no more." "What else is in there?"

"Floors – just walls and hot floors," he said, then added, "and hot heat."

Deavours begin to pace a bit, "They heat that up, do they?" He looked unsure of where to go with this.

"Yes, sir," Willie answered, "keep it hot."

Deavours looked back up, "Now that's over here in Hinds County?" At least he could please Laurel by deferring the fault.

Willie answered, "Yes, sir." "Over here at Jackson?" "Yes, sir."

Deavours stopped, crossed his arms and grinned, "Willie, you are talking about the hometown of your lawyer. You don't mean they have things like that over in Hinds County, do you?" It was a weak ploy, but it was all he had.

Willie replied nonchalantly, "He knows it's in Hinds County, he been over there. "

"What's that?" Deavours asked with interest.

"He been over there." Willie looked him in the eye.

Deavours avoided the look and wanted to avoid any recognition that the "hotbox" had been discovered by the Defense. He instead went over the names again, of who was there.

Willie spoke then of Mr. Landrum. "He was not in the room. They had me fastened up in the room, and Mr. Landrum was down there on his work, I reckon somewhere. I don't know, I reckon he was down there on his work." It was the fingerprint room they were in, and Mr. Landrum had come to get him when the men came, turned him over to them and left. He couldn't remember the day, but he could remember how long he stayed in the hot box before he signed the paper.

"All right," Deavours said, "how long?"

"About two weeks," Willie replied, with his lower lip starting to act up again. He heard a gasp from the balcony.

Deavours sounded incredulous, "About two weeks? You mean you lay down there on the floor in a place that wasn't long enough to stretch out in two weeks?"

Willie confirmed, "On that hot floor." "It had walls to it?"

"Yes, sir," Willie answered.

"And had a floor?" These were absurd questions, but Willie obediently answered, "Yes, sir, had a floor."

"Had a top?" Another insulting question. "Yes, sir, had a top."

"And it wasn't long enough for you to stretch out in?" Willie confirmed it wasn't long enough to stretch out in. Where was it in the jail? Fifth floor – the top floor? Yes, where the prisoners were, down below and back from the cell block.

Willie added the fact that there were two or three hot boxes there.

"They really put you through that when you go over there, don't they," Deavours commiserated insincerely.

Willie went on, "Yes, sir, they will put you through, you can ask Mr. Easterling, and he can tell you." The crowd snickered. Easterling, trying to look a sport, snickered, too. He, however, would certainly never admit to the same in court.

Deavours had McGee repeat the time he stayed in, as if to make it sound impossible. Two weeks? That's fourteen days! Fourteen days and fourteen nights, Willie confirmed, with only bread and water.

Deavours turned away from the thought of the torture and went back to the confession he was holding, "So, the first time you saw this paper, you wouldn't sign it?"

Willie had loosened after the remembrance of the hotbox and said in a lively tone, "Listen, when I saw that paper there, I had done took all I could stand, I just read it the first time and told them to go ahead and do what they wanted to." He paused briefly, his tone changing to reflect hopelessness, adding "…and he kept coming back in there ever other day, every other day, maybe a day or so or three days, he would be back up there again." It hadn't done Willie a bit of good to sign that paper.

Deavours broke through his reverie, "And did he take you out of the hot box and whip you when he came?"

Willie responded more slowly, "Pulled me out, I got to where I couldn't walk out, just was able to stand up after they drag me out of there."

"They pulled you out of the hot box?"

"And questioned me." It had been useless to answer the truth. "Questioned you and give you a beating?" Deavours asked.

Willie looked up and asked solemnly, "If you will allow me, I will tell you what happened." Deavours gave way, "All right, just tell me anything you want to."

Willie took in a deep breath then said, "They had two negro trusties up there on the hall and even the trusties got so mean to me they would hit me in the face and beat me around till I wasn't able to get up, and they put me in that hot box."

"Now that wasn't in connection with this paper?" Deavours waved the now seemingly insignificant confession.

"If I wasn't able to come out they would send a trustee to get me out," Willie said with a blank stare, not really answering his question.

After a few more questions, Deavours tried to wash over the picture.

"Willie, isn't it a fact that the only time you got hurt in the Hinds County jail at all was the night you got hurt when you tried to beat up the jailer and escape from the jail, you and two more men?"

Willie answered frankly, "I didn't get hurt at that at all." "You didn't get hurt then?" Deavours was losing ground.

"No, sir, not a scratch, no way." Willie remembered that night the jailer had just been glad to have gotten them back in jail at all and left them to lick his own wounds. Willie had been proud of the one-time fight for freedom but had paid sorely for it later.

"That's all," Deavours said, unexpectedly, feeling exhausted.

Willie was excused, and this time walked uprightly to his seat. He didn't dare to look towards Ms. Hawkins seat to even see if she had been there.

"Any further testimony?" The Judge asked it in a tone that said there had better not be. Both the State and the Defense were finished. The Judge pressed his lips together and wagged his head before declaring, "Gentlemen, I just don't believe any such testimony. I have known Mr. Royals, Mr. Montgomery and Mr. Easterling a long time, and know them to be men of high character, and I believe what they say about it. I believe this is just a prefabricated story, and I don't believe a word of it. The objection is overruled."

London said with incredulity, "Let the record show the defendant excepts to the ruling of the Court."

The Judge brought the jury back in, and Easterling was brought back in to be questioned regarding the hotbox. Swartzfager entered into the subject and allowed Mr. Easterling to say there was no such thing. When the Defense was allowed to question, John described the hotbox and where it was, but Easterling denied knowing anything about it.

"Now, Mr. Easterling, if I told you that I knew that Jackson jail as well as I know this court room…"

Easterling interrupted, "You may know it better, I don't know." "Yes, I do." John looked at him with widened eyes.

Easterling's nostrils flared as he said, grinning, "I would like to have you on the witness stand to see how you know that."

"Well, I don't mind your jesting with me, Mr. Easterling, but you, as a lawyer, should realize that the witness is the one to be questioned." John smiled with disdain and added quickly, "But I still want you to tell the jury over there now if it isn't a matter of fact that you went over there and told Willie to tell his mother to get you up a thousand dollars and you would get him out of this thing?"

Easterling bristled, "If you put that Negro up there to say that, and…" "You just answer my question," John interrupted.

He snorted, "No, sir, I did not, and Mr. Poole" he shook his finger at him, "I don't even like you to intimate that I did."

John turned away from the pointing finger, giving it no heed, asking, "Mr. Easterling, I want you to tell the jury exactly what you told me while ago, just what you told about your giving Willie cigarettes, ice cream and candy?"

"I didn't tell you that while ago," he evaded. "What did you say?" John's eyes narrowed.

"I told you that this morning." The diversion tactic was weak. "I want you to repeat on that," John persisted.

"You want me to tell the whole thing?" Easterling stalled. "Yes, I do."

Swartzfager protested that he only needed to answer questions asked directly, and the Judge waved it away as it had already been gone over. John protested that the jury was not present at that time, but Collins dismissed it as immaterial.

John turned to the clerk and declared, "Note our exception to that, on the ground that if Mr. Easterling began offering Willie McGee, the defendant in this case any kind of reward, began giving him anything, that is grounds why the jury should not believe the contents of the statement to be true, or free and voluntary."

Collins overruled, the Defense excepted, and Mr. Easterling was excused, looking relieved but holding his head a little too straight.

CHAPTER TWENTY-NINE

"I AM NOT AFRAID"

After a short recess, the Defense returned, armed with a motion to exclude the evidence offered by the State and instruct the jury to return a verdict of not guilty for the following reasons:

1. The State has failed to prove by competent evidence, or by any evidence, the identity of the assailant, if any.
2. The State has utterly and wholly failed to prove that the alleged confessions were free and voluntary.
3. That the oral declarations of the defendant are inadmissible in that they are exponents of the alleged signed, written confession.
4. That the confessions, if competent, tend to establish only an association and/or a sexual intercourse, and not rape as charged in the indictment.
5. The State has failed to prove all of the necessary elements required to convict the accused of rape.
6. The State has failed to prove that a rape has been committed, in that the State has failed to prove all of the essential elements of the crime of rape.

"That concludes our motion," London declared.

Judge Collins gave no honor of a glance as he looked at the document and stated far too simply, "Motion overruled." Defense excepted, then called for the court reporter to verify wording of the second trial of Mrs. Hawkin's testimony, which she had not remembered. Swartzfager objected in that she had said she didn't remember what she had said, and that it was unnecessary. After the Judge sustained, John stood up to say, "Your Honor, we would like for the record to show that the prosecutrix in this case was very emotionally upset at the time she was giving her testimony, and that after – The Judge interrupted to say, "Just a minute. Mr. Poole, have you got any witnesses you want to put on about that?"

John replied quickly, "Yes, sir."

"Who are they?" The Judge asked, annoyed.

John smiled back at his partner and said, "We will take Mr. London."

London took the stand and proclaimed that Willette had almost been hysterical and was sobbing within the hearing of the jury, prejudicing the members.

During cross-examination, Deavours took his turn, avoiding the question of prejudicing of the jury, and asking instead about the producing of the testimony. After questioning its admissibility, he stated:

"Those six pages of testimony don't contain the testimony of Mrs. Hawkins, do they, but they contain the testimony of somebody who was purporting to read the testimony of Mrs. Hawkins that was taken six or eight months before that?"

London admitted that but added that it was, indeed, a transcription of her testimony. Everyone knew that the actual trial documents had been missing for unknown reasons. Deavours made clear for the record that he believed it wasn't the original document and then sat down.

John stood to ask London for clarification that the testimony was properly identified by the record, and then turned to the Judge, saying with boldness, "On the basis of this we now move the Court for a mistrial." The Judge looked humored and said merely, "Overruled."

"Note our exception," John returned to the Clerk, then persisted by again addressing the Judge." Your Honor, we would like to now ask for a recess until the next regular day of court.

"Do you have any further witnesses, Mr. Poole?" the Judge asked with raised eyebrows.

John pled with his last bit of energy, "We have moved throughout the trial for continuance, and asked for additional time in which to prepare our defense for this case, asked for additional time in which to secure witnesses that were very important and highly necessary to the defense of this case, and for those reasons we have no other alternative but to rest at this time."

The Judge stated formally, "The defense counsel is now informed that this court is ready to have any witnesses they want called, and the process of this court is available to counsel for the defendant to secure any witnesses that are available to the jurisdiction of this court, and the Court wants to know now if you have any witnesses you want called, or that you want brought here that are within the jurisdiction of the court.

London stood wearily to say, "Your Honor, at this time, for the reasons just given, we are unable to offer any further testimony in this case."

Judge Collins replied with no empathy, "All right, let me have your instructions, then."

London replied, "The defense requests that the Court grant unto them reasonable time within which to prepare instructions of the Court."

"Yes, sir," Collins replied, but called for Court to reconvene later in the day. It was already 4:30, and "reasonable time" was not going to be given. John and Al walked Willie back through the catwalk to the jail. There was no need to crawl this time, since John had asked the Highway Patrolman who had given him an escort to also escort them back to the hotel. First, they conferred with Willie, who was going to spend the time with his mother and pastor, who met them as they entered the jail.

"Now, Willie," John began, not knowing really how to console him, as he knew as well what the outcome would probably be. "Remember that the Civil Rights Congress has said that our main goal here was to get a list of exceptions for our appeal to the Supreme Court. They are hoping to take it to the United States Supreme Court and out of Mississippi altogether!" Willie nodded his head and pressed his lips together, as if silencing thoughts. London took up where John left off, "And, Willie, the arguments we present will also show another Court the evident prejudices!" Willie looked at his pastor and at the swollen eyes of his mother before looking back at his attorneys. He spoke in a low voice.

"I was hearing what those men seys back behind me. They got plans for you, Mr. Poole. I heard 'em whisper bout it." He lowered his voice to a whisper to say, "Don't know if I'd even trust this fellow here. I think he's on their side, too."

John said, "Unhunh, is that right?"

"I've learned not to trust nobody if you want to stay alive." He looked John in the eyes and finished. "I'm not afraid, Mr. Poole. I'm not afraid anymore. You take care of yourself, now." Willie turned away from him and gave himself over to his jailer, who led him back to his cell with his mother and pastor following behind.

The escort to the hotel went well enough, but the attitude of the patrolman showed he wasn't too pleased with his duty, and reluctantly asked when they would need him again. An hour? He would probably be off duty, but he would tell the patrolman on duty to be ready. Al and John entered their hotel room, carefully looking around before locking themselves in. Neither was anxious to start on the preparation of their instructions, and John reclined on the bed to think. Pyles joked about being given thirty minutes to get out of town, but said it had been a real threat. Now there was a gang after him. He and London have angered them more than Pyles ever did. Hell, they almost implied there was an affair, after bringing up Willie to say they were all liars. John looked over at Al, who was staring at the wall.

"Are you thinking what I am?" he asked.

"The arguments won't make a difference to this jury," Al said, on the same train of thought.

John sat up. "If we state that we were too afraid to make final arguments, it may bolster the appeal."

"It would be more effective than if we acted as if there wasn't a threat," Al agreed.

Neither one really wanted to state outright that they were scared for their lives if they were to make a forceful argument. John poured a drink of water and twirled it, forming thoughts before drinking it down.

"We have no friends here," he stated, "but if we leave, neither will Willie." Al shook his head and said, "We're doing the best thing we can for McGee."

He lit two cigarettes and handed one to John.

"Let's tell Collins we're done."

The highway patrol gave escort back to the courtroom to report to the Judge the reasons for no final argument for the Defense. John told him what had happened, and the warning he had gotten. If Collins was pleased, he didn't show it, but wished them a safe trip back, without offering protection. They asked the sheriff for an escort back to Jackson, but he refused, saying flatly that he had no authority to do that. All they could do was leave unexpectedly early, taking the long route back to Jackson.

The Sunday paper would tell the end of Willie McGee's third trial. The jury had deliberated for not quite an hour before coming out. Judge Collins asked McGee if he had anything to say before hearing the sentence. In response, McGee had uttered what others thought was scripture, but was so softly spoken they could not identify the passage. A member of the jury stood and declared Willie McGee was guilty as charged. The judge addressed McGee to once again give him the sentence of death by electrocution. Only those close to Willie heard his response, as he stood straightly and said,

"Thank you Judge. I am not afraid."

Willie's mother and others sobbed behind him.

The radio broadcast the news that night as John and Al stared silently with heavy hearts at the headlights beaming down the road.

CHAPTER THIRTY

FIERY CROSSES

There was a virtual celebration among the white-clad brotherhood of the Klu Klux Klan, and a rallying of State's Rights Dixiecrats following what they believed to be the end of the line for Willie McGee, but, more importantly, the victory over the impinging Communist Party. The Sunday morning's paper in Jackson blazed a warning in the extra-large headline:

"Burn Fiery Cross Here"

Underneath it in bold read; **"McGee Gets Third Date with Death."** The front page hosted a smorgasbord of related articles.

"States' Rights Will be Highlighted at 82 Mass Meetings," which meetings were in protest to President Truman's "so-called 'civil rights.'" There were to be meetings held simultaneously in every county at 3:00 in the afternoon where Governor Fielding Wright would be the first to outspokenly censure the President's anti-Southern recommendations, in a broadcast that would reach the entire state. They were scheduled to be held after the convention of Southern Governors in Washington next Saturday. **"Dixie Delegates Primed to Walk"** reported that if President Truman was nominated there would be a protest from Dixiecrats bused in from half a dozen states, marching in the battle against Civil Rights.

"Cross Burns on East High Street" told the tale of the 'White-Clad Six' who erected a crude cross, constructed of wood on the east end of High Street, the area where the black neighborhood began in Jackson. They set it afire and used kerosene and gasoline to make the flames leap higher. The police "rushed to the scene" but were too late to catch the men who "whooped and hollered" a few times and left in a hurry. Only to the side of the front page was the article that reported that, **"Twice-Spared Convicted Rapist Sentenced Again."**

The execution date had been set for April 9th. The article highlighted the testimonies of Easterling and Valentine, and although it was reported that Willie said he had been kept in a hotbox for 14 days before signing the confession, it ended with the Judge's statement that "he did not believe a word of the defendant's testimony." The next day's paper complained of the costs of McGee's three trials, which was reported to be "Over ten thousand dollars with added costs for keep."

The Laurel Leader Call showed a vivid picture of the Klu Klux Klan meeting in Georgia under a burning cross. A Dr. Green, the "grand dragon" of the Klan was pictured without his hood, addressing the group and was quoted as saying, "The South faced the threat that the government would force social equality between whites and negroes if President Truman's civil rights program was passed."

It seemed as if Willie's plight was secondary to a much greater agenda, and the involvement of the Civil Rights Congress in his case made his life a token to be won in this heated contest between factions that had remained just dormant since the War Between the States, and now were brought to life with the inbreathing of battle.

Although John had escaped what was planned to be a "beating he wouldn't forget," intentions were not forgotten. Despite protest from several family members that he drop the case altogether, especially since payment had not yet come in, John filed a Motion for a New Trial, which stayed the execution for the third time, and did not escape notice of those in Laurel who had been sorely looking forward to the event.

"You need to come," Gerry protested as she checked her dress in the mirror. "Your sister has been working on that gumbo since yesterday, and she hasn't seen Babay for months." John sat on the side of the bed sipping a drink. He hadn't felt like attending any social events since the trial was over, and he was noticeably drinking more. He had had more than enough of people's opinions, whether in conversation or in sneered side comments as he walked through the main streets of Jackson. The paper had referred to him and Al as "lousy and consciousless lawyers," to which he had pondered retaliation to "those bastards' libel."

Early in the morning, he had slipped in to visit McGee to tell him the Motion had been filed, and that he should rest easy for a little while, giving him a consolation gift of several packs of cigarettes. McGee had replied that he had put his hope "not in this world, but in the one to come." Regardless, he had been thankful for the pain-easing smokes and to hear that more was planned by the CRC to garner national support.

"I may not be able to meet with you during the next few months," John had told him anxiously, knowing that this time would not be safe for either one of them. "But rest assured that we will be doing everything we can, as soon as we can, to get this overturned. I hear that Miss Abzug is planning to hold meetings that will spread your story and raise money for your defense." McGee took the encouragement and nodded soberly, thankful that he would still be breathing after April 9, but aware that jail held no promises of change for him. He looked through the smoke circles surrounding them and said, "You watch out for yoself, now," he nodded with seriousness, "that baby is countin on you!" He displayed a rare smile as he recounted seeing his own son who had visited him with his Mommashortly after the trial. His face turned quickly to the side to hide his emotion as he confided, "I want to see him grow. I want to see him grow up to be a man!" Both sat in silence, honoring the desire, ignoring the tears, and hoping beyond hope.

"I need you back, John." Gerry softly broke his reverie, having turned from her mirror to gaze at her despondent husband.

John looked at her, downed his drink and said, "Let's go!"

Settled in his sister's living room couch after dinner, he still felt uneasy and couldn't quite give himself to join into the family gathering. Rose, his youngest sister, had been one of his closest siblings and had always in the past been able to make him laugh, as they had been renegades together as teens. She shared his pitch-black hair and blue eyes, which often sparkled when meeting in sly camaraderie. Tonight, the connection only allowed a reprieve from the necessity to be entertaining. John had a hard time joining in the conversation or even enjoying Baybay's antics. Gerry found herself modulating the talk to break the tension.

Finally, after supper Rose said, "Listen, John, I know it's been a tough week for you, but I've only been able to read the papers and, well, you know Gerry has told me some of what yall experienced, but I need to hear it from you." She paused a bit as he sat silently with his brows raised, stumping out his cigarette, then she impatiently continued, "Hell, you don't have to tell me that the damn Judge has a demon, I know that much!" She puffed up her chest, curled her lip in imitation. "Sittin up there like he really cares about any defending of his nigger-boys who misbehave. Don't you go trying to take away my State's rights to whoop em when they need a good whoopin!" She wagged her head, pointed her finger and aped the judge's speaking so well that John found himself breaking into a laugh, in spite of his somberness. Baybay laughed with him, and he reached down to her to stroke her head. He cooed back to her and handed her a toy she had earlier thrown out of reach. While she gnawed on it, he leaned forward and reached for words to express.

"So, you've got the gist of the atmosphere we were in," he started. While he was deciding just which story to relate, Gerry said suddenly, "What's that?"

Everyone's ears perked up to hear the scuffling noise outside. John leaned backwards and pulled the curtain aside slightly with one finger, carefully peering through the glass and the dimly lit yard. Hooded men! He jumped up, stood to the side of the window, motioned for everyone to be quiet and waved Gerry to take the baby back to the kitchen. As they obeyed, Gerry heard a "Whoosh!" The blaze could be seen through the sheer curtains, and Rose couldn't help but gasp. Flames licked across the arms of the wooden cross, then traveled both upwards and down to the ground, brightly exposing the several ghost-like creatures dancing around it. A chill raced up John's spine. Gerry tried to keep the baby from crying as tears fell from her eyes. Rose's aghast expression reflected the evil glow she was staring at.

After that night John vowed to do what he could to annihilate this terrorism and started moving on the defense once again. After reporting the incident and calling a friend on the police force for protection and to patrol his neighborhood and his sister's, communicated with the CRC about the next steps in the case. Bella told him that the CRC was spending their time this year garnering national support for the case, hoping to sway public opinion to a degree that would force Mississippi's long-standing bigotries to bend under the pressure. She told them they had engaged Willie's mother and wife to appeal to a party of affiliates in New York.

"Willie's wife?" John asked, somewhat shocked, "His wife who moved to California?" Willie had not mentioned any reconciliation with her, or that she would ever be willing to plead on his behalf.

"No, she's living near his mother, Bessie tells me, has some children who would make a plea for their Daddy. I think it will be very moving for public appeal. We're going to get Bessie up here too," Bella said swiftly, but hearing no quick response, moved on to other things on the agenda. "We'll also want you to come to D. C. to meet with Emmanual Bloch, and some others to prepare for our "visit" to the Supreme Court this next year. We're thinking we should meet around October, to avoid the holiday traffic. I'll let you know as soon as I can what that date is, alright?"

"What about Willie?" John asked, not wanting to move so fast away from what was happening at present. "How are we going to prevent his being hurt again in jail?"

"We're sending letters to the governor to have him understand that we are making it known what has happened and that the nation will hear about any future torment that might come to Willie," she announced, as if already speaking to a group.

John was silent for a moment, considering how far removed that was from effecting any real change for Willie. She obviously was not familiar with the Governor's stance on these matters.

"John?" Bella asked with a tone of impatience." Are you still there?" The South in general moved much too slow for her, but in her opinion an attorney should rise above the cultural norms. The CRC was ready to take over this case entirely, but it was respectful to still retain the attorneys, and she was working within the guidelines given her from above – for now. "Hello?"

John was feeling the pressure from within to not enter into an argument with a lady, as he would his fellow male counterpart. He spoke a bit more slowly because of his restraint, which further aggravated Bella.

"Are you aware," he began in his most considerate Southern tone, "that our governor has arranged meetings for all counties in the State of Mississippi to gather to hear his broadcast speech this Saturday on State's Rights? That there is talk he will be asking for a League of Citizens to rally against Communistic influence?" This was the first time he had used the trigger word – Communism.

Bella burst out as if she were a horse let out of the gate for a race, "And are you aware that we have hundreds, thousands! of activists ready to write letters to 'His Honor' to say just what they think about this phony trial and to ask him to consider the consequences of not releasing McGee?" She didn't like to show her anger, knowing it was a weakness, and so added, "I've got to go, John, there's a meeting in ten minutes I have to be ready for. Just keep your family safe, and we will contact you again soon." She paused ever so briefly before saying, "Bye, now."

John held the receiver in his hand to hear the disconnect before slowly placing it back on the receiver.

Gerry, standing nearby, bounced Bay-bay in her arms trying to keep her quiet. She finally asked, "Did she say anything about your payment?"

John shook his head. "No," He looked up at her anxious eyes, and repeated, "No, she didn't say anything about payment." He turned to his makeshift desk to save face and busy himself with what to do next. He penned a note to file a libel suit against the Clarion Ledger and its editor, a Mr. Sullens. He smiled and added, "appropriately named."

The next few months John and Al beat the pavement to drum up work from fellow lawyers but found that nearly everyone was either afraid to associate with them or were straightforward with theiropinions on "Southerners who aligned themselves with Communists." Although he and Al did finally get a small "partial payment" to split from the CRC and were assured that money was being raised to cover the rest, it mostly reimbursed for money already spent. There was included with the check a Letter of Appreciation written for their part played in this "…most important cause for promoting our Civil Rights."

A few cases trickled in from the Jewish society, but more cases came from the poor black population, who wanted to support the lawyers that risked their necks for theirkind. Unfortunately, they could not pay even moderately priced legal fees. John took them in anyway and accepted payment in green beans, tomatoes and corn. It wouldn't buy the milk or pay the mortgage, but as each week passed, he felt a growing sense of appreciation for the culture and those in their penury who could still love, laugh and forgive. They managed to keep afloat, but barely.

Meanwhile, Bessie had mostly forgotten about her son's lawyer in her anxiety over traveling outside of Mississippi. She had been invited, along with Rosalee, by Miss. Abzug to travel to Washington, D. C. to be present at a benefit for Willie's case, and to give a speech. It was true she would do anything for her son, but she was more nervous about being around educated people in the North than having to be in full charge of the Church's Christmas Dinner. She wanted to just forget about everything and sit on her porch for a long, long time. Instead she was busying herself to staunch the pain and was a bundle of nerves. Rosalee and her children had found a place in Laurel nearby, and their constant company did help fill her sore and empty heart, but she found herself sometimes on edge around them.

"Now go and play so your grandmother and I can talk!" Rosalee instructed her three older children, while entertaining her youngest with toys on the floor. "I'll swannee!" She exclaimed as they ran out laughing, "Those kids get so loud you can't no more hear a donkey bray!" Bessie watched with a pained smile. She loved being called Grandma again, and they were sweet children, but she sorely missed her other grandchildren, so far away. It did seem to her that this raucous bunch was much louder than she remembered her own being. She remembered when Willie and Eliza lived with her, and how the little ones would crawl up in her lap, begging for attention. It never seemed to bother her then. She wiped an involuntary tear away quickly, just realizing Rosalee had been talking all along.

"...and we're going to have to do some shopping before we go, so we can be presentable at those meetings. You know, they accept traditional African wear for Negroes up there. Do you know where we could find something like that?" She was flipping through magazines she had gotten in the mail, searching for just the right look.

"Girl, you crazy!" Bessie blew her nose after her exclamation. Rosalee looked at her with large eyes. "I'm not gonno go fixing myself up for nobody! Speshly not any African get up!" She pushed herself up out of her chair and trudged to the kitchen to put on water for tea.

"Well," Rosalee sounded hurt, but still confident in her purpose, "I'm going to go shopping – maybe not for African cloth, but at least a headwrap so I don't have to fix this nappy hair everywhere I go." She turned to fuss with her hair in the hallway mirror. "You know there's going to be important people at those meetings we gone be at."

She looked back at Bessie, who had her eyes fixated on the oven and responded only "Mmhuh – is that right?"

"Unhunh," Rosalee continued, licking her lips and posing for a moment, looking pleased at what she saw. Miss Abzug is going to interview me, so she can print Willie's side of the story to put in a pamphlet, then if peoples want to ask me questions, I can talk about it."

"What all are you gonna make up?" Bessie asked, wiping her hands and putting them on her hips.

"I'm not gonna be makin up nothing!" Rosalee said sharply, then added a bit more contritely, "Except these children ain't all Willie's. He told me everything about what happened with Miss Hawkins," she said, crossing her arms across her chest and added, "I'm just gonna be standing in the place of Liza. She should be doing this, herself!" Her look made Bessie turn back to reach in the windowsill for her tea bags. Rosalee sat down at the table but continued to lay out her justifications. "Somebody's got to tell the true story and not be afraid! Sides, Willie wants his boy to get takin care of, and he hopes that Civil Rights Congress gonna help." She paused a moment, realizing that didn't sound like honest intentions, and then added, "You know, Momma, I feel that this is an opportunity not just for Willie, but for all black people! The Congress, and other groups like them, is workin' to see that we get our rights. Rights to have the same kind of education, rights to have the same kind of houses, rights to live like white people live and not be ruled over by them with these Jim Crow Laws!" Rosalee felt strongly she had a mission to complete, and any means to that end should be sanctioned, even if Bessie didn't see it so clearly for now.

Bessie turned to her, still getting used to being called "Momma" again and dipped her tea bag slowly in and out of her cup and looked at this determined woman at her kitchen table. She couldn't deny she was right in her intent, but still didn't feel right about the way she and the Congress was going about it. She sighed, "I just want Willie to have the right to live." Her composure broke down at this and she lost interest in her tea. She put it down on the table and walked out of the room.

Rosalee pressed her lips tightly together before saying, mostly to herself, "I know, Momma, I know."

Time seemed to pass slowly in Mississippi that year. Spring blossomed new hope as the original execution date came and went unnoticed, except for those who breathed a sigh of relief that the day was just like any other. The sweet warm days turned out ladies in sheer flowered dresses and fragrant gardenia blooms relaxed riled emotions. Spring lazily gave way to the heat of summer that pushed joyful children splashing into cool waters, and inspired talks with iced tea on the porch underneath ceiling fans.

Magnolia trees spread their large blossoms above to give luxurious shade and call lovers to steal kisses underneath.

An intrusion into the serenity came from the national news. "**USSR Tests Atomic Bomb.**" It caused stirs once again to incite fears of Communist invasion. The humid "dog days" of summer sat heavily and persistently upon the people and warmed the once refreshing waters. Tempers began to stir in the heat and the Willie McGee case surfaced in conversations, here and there, amidst circles of men.

Gerry hummed as she hung the clothes on the line. It was a bright and sunny mid-morning in August, the temperature already reaching the nineties.

Usually, she would be complaining of the humidity and avoiding any work in the sunshine that made her freckles pop to the surface, but it wasn't going to dampen her spirits today. She finally broke into song with a lilting soprano, "I'm in love with you, Hone-ey." Her voice dipped and trilled as she bent down for a clothespin. "say you love me too, Honey. No one else will do, Honey, se-ems fu-u-nny, but it's true!" She straightened the damp cloth diaper.

"Loved you from the start, Ho-oney," John's bass voice boomed with comic drama as he opened the screened back door, "Ho-ope we never part, honey!" He stretched his arms out, then placed his hands together over his heart. Gerry laughed with reddened cheeks, embarrassed to be found singing to herself, as he laughed and rose to hug her.

"You're home early!" she said, after a kiss. He tried not to convey his own morning's disappointment. Another case he hoped to get had been referred to an attorney, who had "State's Rights" more in mind, the client had told his friend.

"Just to be with you on this gloriously hot day," he lied, as he took some clothespins out of the basket to hang another diaper.

Gerry didn't stop to think about any other motive. "John," she started. "Mmhumn?" he said, a clothespin in between his lips.

Her voice became hushed, as if she didn't want the neighbors to hear just yet. "The doctor said yes!" She waited with widened eyes for his response.

"Oh, darling!" He dropped the pin in the basket to hold her again and press his lips against her forehead. He would never let her know his angst inside over having to now pay a hospital bill and support two babies without any line of work to count on. "I'm so very happy!" He said instead.

CHAPTER THIRTY-ONE

A KNIGHT ON A WOODEN LEG

It had been a warmish winter that year, without even a light snow. Gerry even asked for the air conditioner to be turned on just before Christmas, because the pregnancy was causing her to run hot. It was fine with John. His irritation level was less likely to rise if his body temperature was cool, and his frustration with his lack of work mixed with Gerry's hormonal swings could sometimes cause a flare between them. The tension was augmented by the societal ostracizing they had experienced even with family and friends. Talks at gatherings would drift back to how would John move forward with this case, with his baby and one on the way to think of? He did realize, didn't he, that getting involved with an agency that had Communism at its roots was dangerous in this day and time?

At the annual Christmas family gathering, some of the men had gathered in the back of the house to talk about Truman's withdrawing of troops from the Korean War, and what that meant for the spreading of Communism, which they suspected was making inroads into America. It was a volatile topic. Well-meaning relatives gave sound advice that John was totally opposed to, but for the sake of the family gathering he held his peace. This gave another reason to drink more than he normally would, in turn causing him to open up and joke, regardless of his underlying feelings. Despite themselves, the family enjoyed a good storytelling from John, whose eyes grew wide in drama, disrupting conversations as others gathered around, while John entertained the whole group.

"Tell us another one, John!" came a female voice after one of his stories. Although Gerry smiled and played with the toddlers nearby, she was a bit nervous with John's drinking, and the tone of the previous talk in the gathering.

"OK – I've got one more," John said, smiling at his sister, Rose, who was pouring another drink into his glass and winking at the others. He began in hushed tones. "Once, in the middle of World War II, there were German soldiers encamped in their trenches not far from the enemy lines, where the Americans also sat deep in their trenches." He crouched, as if in a trench, himself. "It was a starry night, when all the soldiers had rested from their fighting, but were keeping quiet on guard. Finally, this German named Karl got bored with it alland says, "Watch this – I'm going to kill me an American. In every one of these groups there's at least one named Willie Lee." Then he cups his hand to his mouth and yells through the night with this real friendly tone, 'Hey, Willie Lee!'

A head pops up from the other trenches and says, 'Well, hey, there!'

BAM! Willie Lee falls back dead in the trench. Well, the German soldiers get a big kick out of this, and the next night Karl decides to try it again. He calls, real friendly like, 'Hey, Willie Lee!' Another head pops up, 'Well, hey, yall!'

BAM! They all laugh and laugh. Now this got the attention of the General, so he goes to Karl's bunker the next night to watch the scene with the others gathered around. Karl smiles proudly, cups his hand and yells, 'Hey, Willie Lee!' The response through the night air came, 'Is that you, Karl?' Karl, surprised, pops up, **'Yeah, it's me!'**
BAM!"

The dramatic delivery of the end line was priceless, and the room guffawed, all but a few of the men at the back who stood stoically, sensing a deeper meaning within the story.

In the first of the year, John more soberly prepared with Al for their Appeal to the Mississippi Supreme Court, which focused on the exclusion of negros in the jury selection, the need for a change of venue – citing the threats of violence made towards the defendant's attorneys, the testimony of McGee regarding his coerced confession, and the lack of time the defense had to prepare for the case and gather witnesses.

Another point was that Mrs. Hawkins had said herself that she had stopped struggling, and in a previous case in Mississippi the court had ruled that in order to call rape, there must be a struggle to the end. In any other state it may have constituted a solid appeal. Southern judges, however, dismissed all claims. They argued that the fear that Mrs. Hawkins had from the threat of death caused the absence of resistance, and therefore did not preclude rape. Reading into his appeal the abhorrent implication of consensual sex, the judges argued that "This revolting insinuation…finds no proof in support thereof, reflected by the record." The appeal was denied.

Although John swiftly responded with a follow-up appeal, clarifying the point that consensual sex had not been implied, it did not budge the judges' opinions. A new date for execution was set for June 3, 1949. Abzug had told John and Al not to be concerned, they had expected as much. The CRC was planning to get the stay from the U. S. Supreme Court and file for a total review of the case. With surrounding public support, they felt this was the best line of fire with which to approach the appeal. John and Al left worrying about the case once again, until further notice, and went back to the ever-present reality of bills to be paid.

Every now and then John would contemplate visiting with McGee and wondered what his days held for him. A police officer who was a friend had told him that everyone had been on their toes since this thing went public. He didn't think anyone was laying a hand on him these days. John hoped so. If he were to go and visit without a trial necessity, he feared stirring up trouble again. Gerry had bravely stood behind him throughout it all, but she was getting bigger every day, and their second bundle of love would be delivered sometime in the early spring. He wouldn't put them in a compromising state just now. Even a letter to McGee would be read by a jailer and probably several other officials before being delivered to him. For the time being, McGee would just have to be happy to be alive.

That would be threatened soon enough. The appeal to stay the execution had to be done close enough to the date set so that it could not be resolved and thrown away beforehand. The CRC decided to wait until the day before the execution to appeal, making it nail-biting for all involved. On the afternoon of June 2, the U. S. Supreme Court unexpectedly denied the request for a stay, presented by Abzug.

In Laurel, Mississippi, preparations for the electrocution of Willie McGee began. The State's portable electric chair, which was moved from place to place when needed, was being transported to Laurel to be set up in the courthouse. The bustle throughout Laurel was akin to a highly contested football game being held the next evening. It was to be quite an affair, and mothers were asking that the grandmothers would sit at home with the smaller children. The older ones begged to go, and Dads agreed to be in charge of watching them, arguing that it was an historical event. In contrast, the black population appeared to be nonexistent.

Comments regarding the excitement were not held back in public places, and shoe-shine boys, maids and maintenance workers were made to digest the surrounding banter between those who would be vying for the best viewing spots at the occasion.

In Jackson, Al and John awaited the news of the efforts of the CRC to halt the sordid deed. Bella called to relate, desperately, that their efforts had failed.

"We called your Dixiecrat candidate, Governor Wright, to grant us a reprieve pending a clemency hearing, but he wouldn't even come to the phone!" Bella said with derision.

"He's not our candidate!" Al declared, with John listening nearby.

"I know, I know," she breathed, "Well, anyway, his secretary, who he used as his go-between, told us that, 'The governor is a firm believer in letting the courts take their course. The courts have ordered an execution and he's going to do nothing about it.'" Bella was giving her best attempt to imitate the Southern accent, modulating it with her own sarcasm. "He is a very considerate man. He is very diligent in preserving the rights of everyone." In her own voice she added, "Ugh! I wanted to tell her what I thought of him, and her, for that matter, but there is no time for that."

"So," Al was looking at John as he replied, "we have to get an appeal going in Mississippi."

John looked at his watch and said, "No time today! All the offices will be closed." Al related the same to Bella. "All right, then," John heard him say in the receiver, "we'll get it out as soon as we can tomorrow morning. Sure, we'll watch out." Al put down the phone and let out a sigh. John had already picked up the other office phone to call the building's secretary to see if she could come over this evening for dictation. After a failed attempt to contact her, the search began for anyone who could type. An older, retired lady finally agreed to peck it out, but the final document was not ready for service until mid-morning.

John pulled on his suit coat while Gerry was trying to find phone numbers for him to take. He wanted the numbers of two friends he had known in the past who could fight. Al had other business today to take care of, and couldn't go, himself. There was John's friend, Emmett, who had won the statewide boxing championship not too long ago, and another man, Patrick, who had been designated a hero in the war. "Just in case," he had said, but it had caused Gerry to be overly anxious.

"I can't find Patrick's number," she complained anxiously, shuffling through papers on the cabinet near the phone, "I know it's here somewhere."

"I'll just call you later on if Emmett can't go," he said as he grabbed his keys. "Keep looking."

"You will need an escort, too," she insisted.

"Well, just let me get this appeal signed first, then I'll ask about that. I'll call and let you know." He kissed her goodbye but rushed off before his usual kiss and caress to his toddler and new-born baby girl. "Daddy will be back soon," Gerry consoled her toddler, and rocked the other in her arms. "Daddy will come back to us real soon," she repeated, mostly for herself, and went again to look for the missing phone number.

The first task was to try to get into the governor's mansion in the heart of downtown Jackson, to attempt once more to persuade Governor Wright for a reprieve. Although it was obvious from the cars and the personnel going in and out of the back that there were sufficient staff there, no one would answer as John beat the door. He got back into his car and drove to the courthouse to find any judge that would sign off. One secretary after another said, "Oh, I'm sorry Mr. Poole, the Judge is out today," or "I'm not getting an answer from his home phone. I'm just not sure where he is."

John eyed his watch and began to feel a sense of panic. Had everyone communicated to make it their business to not be available today? At last, one of the secretaries admitted to her Judge's location. She thought he could be found on the golf course – yes, just on the other side of town. As he got back into his car to drive to the golf course, he realized sweat was starting to pour. Why had he worn this damn suit, anyway? The car's air conditioner was broken, and the afternoon sun was rippling its waves on the dark hood. He rubbed the stump of his leg, which had gotten irritated in the heat. He happened to glance at the gas gauge, which was even with the empty mark. "Damn!" He exclaimed, as he pumped the pedal and started the engine.

After having to take the time to fuel up and then drive to the city golf course, the attendant informed him that he believed Judge William Roberts, the Acting Chief Justice of the Supreme Court, was on or about the 16th hole. No, all the golf carts were being used, so sorry, but he could show him a short cut. The short cut was long enough, but John lumbered across the greens with the paper in hand, raising his hip to help soften the impact on the side of his wooden leg. At the 15th hole he asked the Judge's whereabouts of a caddy, who pointed onwards. He finally found the Judge about to swing on the 17th hole.

Judge Roberts had not gone golfing today for any other reason other than it was a Friday afternoon and was surprised to see the sweating attorney approach him just before he hit his ball. John motioned for him to continue, as he was panting and needed the time to catch his breath. The Judge positioned himself and struck the ball past the sand pit that usually tricked him.

"How about that one!" he cried. He walked towards John, who gave him the due compliment, shook his hand and introduced himself. He then quickly poured out his reasons for needing a "perfected appeal" to save Willie McGee, who he believed was a wrongly charged man, from dying tonight. He wiped his forehead with his handkerchief while Roberts was reading the appeal. Roberts nodded throughout, then took the pen John offered and scribbled his name. He looked John in the eye as he handed it back and stated somberly, "Thank God you made the effort! I never did believe this fellow was guilty anyhow."

John smiled with relief to find a like-minded Southerner and thanked him in return, but then asked with urgency, "Would you mind to call the Sherriff when you finish your game to let him know that this is indeed your signature? He is not eager to let McGee out of his sights, but I'm headed to Laurel to pick him upnow."

"Sure, sure," Roberts said with a wave of his hand. "I'll finish up shortly and will give him a call in the office. You watch out for yourself, now," he added.

John waved in return as he quickly turned around to make his trek back to the car. Judge Roberts looked thoughtfully at John's back, watching him hobbling back across the course and called, "Say, could you use a lift?" John breathed a sigh of relief as the golf cart turned around to pick him up.

"Yes, yes, I found him on the golf course," John spoke into the pay phone alongside the road. "No, Emmett couldn't go. No, I called the Sherriff and he already has McGee in the Laurel jail. He won't let him go until I come and show him this damned signature in person. He's not going to take my word for it. I have to hurry.

Don't worry, darling. No, I already called the Police. No one there will go. I need Patrick's number, did you get it? Oh, good, Fleetwood 3965? Thanks so much, darling. Don't worry, you hear, now? I can take care of myself. You just stay at home with my girls and keep them safe. Call your dad to come over and get you, if you want. I won't be home until late."

John pressed down the receiver for the dial tone, got another quarter out and fumbled it while trying to look at his watch and grab his lighter at the same time. "Damn!" He reached for another, leaving the fallen quarter on the ground. He dialed the rotary wheel with the numbers, lit his cigarette and drew in a deep drag as he heard the ring sounding. "Hello?" John breathed out the smoke quickly and with relief said, "Patrick? It's John Poole."

The sun was setting on the horizon as they sped down the highway towards Laurel. John explained everything about the situation to Patrick, a muscular man who had brought a gun for each of them, and said he had no fear to use it if he needed to. Although it was a two-hour drive, they didn't dare stop except on the side of the road for relief, to ward off any chance of recognition. John turned up the volume on the car's radio as an announcer broadcast that, "A galvanized iron truck containing the state's portable electric chair has pulled up in front of the courthouse. The chair and the switchboard are now being set up in the second-floor courtroom. Curious on-lookers have already started to gather on the courthouse lawn in anticipation of the State's executioner's arrival. He plans to rev up the motor around 8:00 pm for a test to make sure that this generator is ready to deliver the sufficient load of electricity."

"They're not going to like this," John mused aloud.

To pass the time, the announcer was interviewing a jail official. "Tell us what the last hours of Willie McGee have been like so far."

A scratchy sound came through the speaker as the microphone was being passed. "Well, he just got through eating his last supper, a big one, too! He ordered fried chicken, steak, French fried potatoes, tomato and lettuce salad and extra sweet tea." The jailer stopped to chuckle and then added, "I think they said it would have cost $4.00 in a restaurant." It sounded like a complaint.

"Let's hear now from Pastor Landrum, who says that he has been praying with Willie this evening. Can you tell us about that, Pastor?" A somber voice came across the speaker saying, "Willie has told me he is not afraid to die. He has made peace with his Lord." The announcer added after the short interview that Willie had a visit with his mother and aunt, as well, and was "probably as ready as anyone could be in preparing for a night like this one."

John switched the radio off. "No one is going to be ready for this upset, and it will stir up some tempers," he said in a serious tone.

"Do you think anyone suspects, or …?" Patrick started, when suddenly they saw colored lights flashing behind them. "What's this all about," John said tensely, as he pulled over to the side of the road.

"Mr. Poole?" The Highway Patrolman asked.

"Yes, sir, was I speeding?" John asked with a forced smile.

"No, sir, well maybe, but that's not why I'm stopping you," he said. Patrick looked out back. There was no one else in the car, so he resisted reaching for his gun.

"Your wife called and asked me to escort you into Laurel," he admitted. He half smiled and said, "There was something about the way she was crying and all that just made me do it." He patted the car door and said, "Let's go, fellows!"

John breathed a sigh of relief, shouted his thanks, and waited for the patrolman's car to pull out in front of him before pulling back onto the highway. They had to step on the gas to catch up to him and follow his pace. It wasn't more than fifteen minutes down the road, however, that they were met with flashing lights again, this time coming from the other direction. The patrolman's car slowed to a stop alongside the side of the road, as the other car stopped on the opposite side. Obviously, there had been radio communication between the two, and John recognized the bushy head of dark hair in headlights.

"They've got Willie!" he exclaimed, grabbing the signed appeal and hopping out the door.

Sheriff Brogan's voice was high pitched and annoyed. "I wasn't going to wait and let this brawl start on my watch, and that's just what would have happened if you fellows would have broken up this party they're havin. "He looked at the paper John had in his hands. "I don't have no flashlight with me, we're just gonna have to look at this thing under the headlights. Come on over here," he said as he waved his hand.

John step-clumped carefully along the dark edge of the street until he could take out the paper from its folder under the headlights and show the Sheriff where the signature was. "Did you get a call from the Judge?"

"Yessir, I did, but you can't be too careful, you know." He looked up at John with a forced smile and said, "Anyone can sound like a Judge over the phone." He looked down again at the paper, pulling out glasses from his pocket. "Mmhunh," he said as he recognized the signature. "That's Judge Robert's pen, all right. Guess no one can copy it quite like that." He paused, considering that this could have happened.

John interrupted before he could think on the possibility too long and said, "I guess we'll need to get Willie back before anyone finds that he's missing." Sheriff Brogan's train of thought was broken as he realized John was right. He didn't want to tangle with anyone on the road.

"Okay, boy," he said as he opened the door for the handcuffed McGee. "Yore gonna go with these men here. Looks like they saved yore neck tonight!" He handed the key for the cuffs to John. "Give em to Fred at the desk. He'll get em back to us." He saw headlights coming down the road and turned back to Willie to say, "Hurry up, boy, what you waitin on?" Willie's eyes were round and large as he stumbled out of the car and hurriedly followed beside John back to his car. Patrick stood guard, and the Highway Patrol got back in his car to turn around as a freight truck whizzed past them.

CHAPTER THIRTY-TWO

THE DAILY WORKER

Al read the headlines in the Saturday paper out loud to John as they were having coffee at the kitchen table. Gerry tried to stay within hearing distance while changing a diaper.

"Willie McGee, convicted negro rapist, escaped the electric chair at least temporarily last night, but it was a harrowing experience. The 34-year old negro three times convicted of raping a Laurel, Mississippi white woman was granted a stay of execution just five hours before he was scheduled to die. The stay was signed by State Supreme Court acting Chief Justice William D. Roberts, shortly after 7 pm. The U. S. Supreme Court had, a few hours before, refused a plea for a stay of execution pending the filing of appeal."

"Now, get this," Al interjected, "this next part is set apart and put in bold lettering, just in case you might want to wring Robert's neck!" He continued, flapping the paper outward for effect, "But it became mandatory on Roberts to sign the stay when McGee's attorneys presented the state's high court with a perfected appeal ready for submission to the nation's highest tribunal. It is McGee's first appeal to the U. S. Supreme Court, the action Thursday having been only a plea for a stay of execution pending an appeal."

"So he <u>had</u> to do it, that's what they're implying and for no other reason," John shook his head.

Gerry added from the next room, after taking a diaper pin out of her mouth, "Heaven forbid that anyone thinks he might have gotten an unfair trial!"

"Heaven forbid anyone thinks McGee is anything more than a mule," John added sardonically.

"They even listed everything he ate, and how much it cost the county to give him his last supper, which turned out to be just a free meal for him on their ticket," Al laughed, then added, "Oh – and they quote McGee here–"

"When he arrived at the Hinds County jail here shortly after 10:30 pm, McGee was smiling, but visibly shaken and trembling. 'Faith in God was the only thing that saved me,' the short, big-eyed negro said.'"

"And… a lot of leg work from his attorney!" Al added with a laugh.

John chuckled softly, remembering the ride back to Jackson, when they uncuffed Willie and let him smoke and talk. He was nervous and constantly turning to look out the back window, but had exclaimed, "Wooo-eee! I am so glad to be headed away from that Hellhole! Woo-eee! I'm still alive, yessuh! I'm still alive!

Lawd have mercy! Bless these men, Lawd! God bless you! Wooo-eee!" He had rocked in his seat much of the way back, letting off pent-up terror.

John came back from his memory to hear Al reading again, "Meanwhile, Gov. Fielding L. Wright reported he had been swamped by 'hundreds, perhaps thousands' of telegrams from the north and east demanding that he stay the execution. He said it was apparently an organized campaign to pressure him into commuting the sentence. Several of the telegrams, the Governor said, were signed by 'The Communist Party, the Progressive Party, the American Labor Party,' and numerous civil liberties organizations. But the Governor said he would 'let the law take its course.'"

Al skipped down a bit – "Hmm…just the case details here," he said, then lifted his voice and went on, "Accompanied by three negro ministers, his mother and her sister returned to the jail after McGee finished eating. The condemned man, his relatives and the ministers prayed and sang spirituals for half an hour. McGee spent his last hour and a half in the death cell writing letters. In a note addressed to Sheriff Brogan, the condemned man thanked him for his kindness and penciled, 'I hope to meet you in heaven.'"

John looked up from a pensive hold on his coffee cup, "I guess old Brogan had a change of heart last night, seeing a man at death's door." His eyes twinkled as he added, "The angel on his right shoulder won that battle!" He gulped the rest of his coffee, not feeling any more energy from it. He was plain exhausted. He asked Al weakly, "What do you think about filing a Writ of Habeas Corpus, on the grounds that McGee was denied due process in all three trials?"

At this point, Beverly tugged at his pants legs to gain access to his lap, and he laughingly complied. "Hello sweetheart," he said and gave her a teething ring left on the table to gnaw on.

"I think she wants to chew on that idea for awhile," Al laughed.

Gerry walked to the table holding the other baby girl, Carolyn – named for the meaning, "beloved one." What do you think about giving the case a break for at least this weekend," she pled. I think we could all use a drive to the lake, and it's such a beautiful day outside!" She bounced the happy "beloved one" on her hip and smiled. John didn't have the will to protest.

Al nodded, put down the paper and said, "We've won some time. Let's use it wisely!" He downed the last of his coffee and said goodbyes, patting John on the back with a "Good work, soldier!" It was a phrase that touched John more than he could say, and the emotion left him able only to nod and smile.

The next morning, in a similar kitchen scene in New York, steam from another coffee pot was rising as Bella was reading to William Patterson, the secretary of the CRC, a copy of the "Daily Worker." They had already digested the news yesterday through the Jackson's Saturday paper, which was being delivered regularly now to her office and were eager to see a less prejudiced take on the drama. "'Jones County Sheriff Luther Holden refused to honor the order by telephone even after a conversation with Justice Roberts. He insisted on personal delivery of the order. ' Didn't the Jackson paper say it was Brogden?" she puzzled.

"Well, it was probably the two of them making that kind of decision." Patterson conjectured." You know, their necks would be at stake down there if they showed any clemency or were being tricked by the attorneys."

"Hmm…you're probably right on that." She continued, "Now here's something the Jackson paper didn't bother picking up –"

"**Mrs. McGee Collapses** – Before the last-minute intervention, Mrs. McGee had collapsed, convinced that her husband would go to the chair. She was notified late last night by the CRC that lynch justice had been averted for a third time in this case."

"Bessie told me that Rosalee had collapsed earlier that evening, and was in bed, being watched by a friend while Bessie and her sister went to the jail to see Willie for what they thought was the last time," Bella added, "but the Worker adds here the letter she had sent to us last week."

"Read it," Patterson urged.

"It starts, '**Please Save My Husband'** and "To the Civil Rights Congress: I am the wife of Willie McGee who has been behind iron bars since November, 1945. We have four children and no one to help me with them and I have been very quiet until he got this last sentence in April. '

"Fact is," Bella paused to say, "We're pretty sure this wife, Rosalee, has been 'added' to help Willie out. I think his real wife and children fled to California during the first trial. It doesn't really matter. I've already contacted them to help us to create a more sympathetic picture of him, for the work. Maybe one of her children is his. As I hear it, the colored women in the South will pretty much get anyone they can to support their children. They can pop them out like hotcakes," she laughed.

Patterson refrained from laughing and waved a finger to keep her reading." Let's hear more from our Mrs. McGee," he encouraged.

"I am a poor colored woman and I need my husband with these four kidsto help me, having to send two away to Nebraska. And I want to know, will he go to the chair on June 3? Please save him for me. I feel deep down in my heart that he is innocent.... I don't have any money.... my oldest child had to be taken out of school to work for a living. Please let me hear from you all at once.... Thanks for the help."

"The article goes on to talk about the mob violence causing the attorneys to have to use the catwalk," Bella said, adding with a laugh, "I guess that won't work in the future, now that they are on to it. Well, what do you think?" She pushed the paper in front of Patterson so he could read for himself.

"Does it include anything about all the letters that were sent to the Governor?" he asked.

"Yes, that's on the second page," she flipped it for him and added, "The Laurel paper emphasizes that several of them were from civil liberties organizations, so that will just serve to anger the South."

Patterson read in silence for a few moments, then folded the paper and set it aside. He thought for a moment before saying, "They weren't all from civil liberties groups."

"No?" Bella asked, brushing a black curl from her forehead. She waited as he pulled out of his briefcase a folder full of letters.

He spoke slowly as he explained, "I have copies that were sent to me from regular citizens who were very sincere in their pleas. They certainly heard of the trial and our support of it from our papers, but they write as individuals. May I read you a couple of these?"

"Please," she answered, with a nod of her head.

He cleared his throat and began, "This one is from a Miss May Grant from Los Angeles, California. She says,

'Dear Sir:

I see by the papers that the South is about to have another legal murder on its hands. Why is it possible in this fine, free, young country of ours to have the same old-world injustice that our founding fathers fled from years ago? Please, Governor Wright, stay the execution of the latest victim of Southern justice, Willie McGee. Who knows? You might go down in history as a governor who was not afraid to do the right thing in the face of opposition from the lynch-minded men who apparently rule the South according to their own selfish interests.'"

"Ha!" Bella laughed, "She apparently has no idea of the Governor's political leanings! Oh, well, at least she wrote her opinion."

"Here's another," Patterson began, looking over his glasses, "from a Mrs. Gustafson in Bremerton, Washington. She writes, 'My dear Governor Wright,'"

"Very proper," Bella interjected. He smiled and began again, "My dear Governor Wright:

As a white woman brought up in the south…"

Bella interrupted, "Ah! I could have guessed it! They're either illiterate and use 'ain't and y'all' or else are very eloquent and personable to a fault in the South. There is such distance and division in the classes there," she mused.

Patterson hesitated to go on but did not offer concurrence with her opinion.

After a moment he began again, "As a white woman brought up in the south, I am writing you my most vehement protests against the slated execution of Willie McGee. There was a time when I would have condoned such a 'murder' because I was stupidly and blindly prejudiced against Negroes. Now, every time I read of such happenings, I become more and more ashamed of my background. You know as well as I the only rape of white women which goes on in the south is done by white men. I have known of 'planted' prostitutes who were supposedly raped by Negroes, but they are even rare. The Scottsboro Boys, the Martinsville 7, and McGee are all of the same pattern. There is no such thing as justice for the Negro in your courts – I know whereof I speak. If you allow this execution to proceed, I hope you never spend another decent night. As a member of the human race and one who considers himself a Christian, it is time for you to behave like one. It is within your power to restore my faith that there is some hope for the south. There is none if murders of innocent people continue to be legalized. "

Patterson looked up and said, giving his fist a pound on the table, "This woman speaks the truth!"

"She does bring up some good points," Bell conceded, adding, "and it sounds like she knew more than she actually was willing to say. Read another!"

"Well, there are many, of course, that are just the forms we sent out for people to sign, and no personal letters are attached to them, but here we are – from a New York gentleman."

"Let's see what he wrote," Bella urged. Patterson began, "'Mr. Governor:

The entire world cries out for justice in the case of Willie McGee, an innocent man condemned to die, as a sacrifice to bigotry. It is in the power of your high office to save this man from death, to release him from unjust imprisonment, and thus to reclaim the fame and honor of the American tradition of justice, decency and morality. If

Willie McGee dies, the horror which will attach to the name of our great land, in the eyes of the people of the entire world, will create a burden not lightly to be shaken by your children and mine, and by their children in generations to come.'"

"He signs it – **Urgently**, Milton Forster Roseman"

"I think I recognize the name," Bella said, taking the letter to look at it.

They went through several more letters as their cups were filled by the housekeeper. Patterson selected another letter from a Negro woman which read in part,

"Both my sons, one 22, the other 19, are eligible for the draft. They are good Americans – the best. What do you think they feel when the read of the position that this country has taken – their country – on the question of Negro rights and justice? How can they feel proud of their country and defend it when the feel that those who would set the example, are themselves open to rightful criticism of 'democracy? ' For whom is our democracy? Not for the American Negro, not for the young men who are sent to be killed without being asked whether they agree with our National Policy. Men who are not convinced don't make good fighters "

Patterson thought aloud, "Someone could use this case against us to demoralize our troops."

"Let's hope no one does," Bella replied quickly, then urged him on with a wave of her finger, "please, read the rest of it."

He lifted his eyebrows and refocused to continue, "Criticism is running high in America, and it will run higher as the time goes on, unless some of our leaders begin to understand that they are dealing with humans." He paused, taking in the impact of what that statement meant in his own personal life, being a black man in this country, then sweepingly finished with, "She goes on to say that he should free McGee and align himself with men of America of whom we may all be proud."

Patterson put down the paper, took off his glasses and sighed, adding, "That 'bout says it all." Bella politely ignored his wiping the emotion from his eyes. She stood up, fueled for action, and begin to pace.

"We have to keep these letters coming, to show the 'Good Governor' how the rest of the Nation views his constituencies' stuck in the mud, damnable State's Rights. That's all he is using McGee for, you know. Otherwise, someone would have "slipped" by now and released McGee to that mob." Bella turned back towards Patterson and continued, "Before we make our presence known in Jackson, we've got to have the solid backing of the nation to show to him. We should get Grossman to activate all our groups. They can make flyers that will be pasted all over the streets of the cities and t-shirts that say, 'Free Willie McGee.'" She swept her hands to paint the picture, then continued, not missing a beat, "Of course, Rosalee and Bessie can give speeches, and we can put their story into a pamphlet to distribute." She paused thinking briefly, then continued, "We should send out petitions for everyone to sign, like before, only at the groups, write up a sample letter for others to personalize, and get it all covered in the newspapers." She added with excitement, "I can get John Popham to put it in his column, as an ongoing theme in the New Yorker, not just in the Worker. If the South wants another Civil War, we'll set the stage for it before we go to Mississippi and show them we are ready to pull out all our stops and put State's Rights back in its place like it has been done before!" Bella paused again to think, as Patterson was watching her with raised eyebrows, nodding, then she wagged a pointed finger and exclaimed, "That's it, Lincoln's birthday! If the new execution date is set past then, and it probably will be, we'll use Lincoln to remind people that emancipation has not yet reached its ultimate goal. We could get our people to gather at his memorial in D. C. !" She stopped to take in a breath and placed both hands squarely on the stack of letters on the table. "These letters are just tremors indicating that it's time for a social upheaval to bring in the new, progressive era we've hoped for, William!" If William were as inspired as she was at the moment, he didn't show it. He had a faraway look of grave caution that confronted her spirited energy. "What are you thinking?" She urged, with a note of impatience.

Patterson's mother had been a slave. She had let them know that tyranny was not far from their doorstep, and freedom was worth fighting for to keep. It had inspired him to become a fiery speaker for the rights of the under trodden minorities, but he was all too familiar with the suffering that it takes to stand up against the "sacred" norms of society. He spoke slowly "What the Jew was to Germany, the Negro is to Fascist-minded Americans."

Bella recognized the quote from his speech to a Communist party gathering and nodded in agreement. He continued, "Mr. McGee may never see a day of our 'new, progressive – our new, communistic era.'" He tapped the newspapers from Laurel. "Willie McGee, and those Mississippi lawyers who defend him, are caught in the cross-fire here. Do you remember the other article from earlier on where they were berating those lawyers?" He shook his head, "Their livelihood, their family's status in the community is ruined," he swept his hand, "already! I predict they will be penniless before this thing is over with." He stood, taking his hat from the table in his hand and fingering its rim, "Willie McGee, and his attorneys, may just be the ounce of flesh that buys our 'new era,' but we must understand what sacrifice will be demanded." Patterson put his hat on his head and folded the newspaper under his arm. As he walked towards the door, he finished, shaking his head and saying, "War is never bloodless."

"And we're fighting for his freedom!" Bella shouted the reminder at him from behind. She sputtered, "And the lawyer's rights to defend whomsoever they choose!"

Patterson turned back to her to say, "You are so right, Mrs. Abzug, but you must remember first and foremost, we are fighting for our Communist party and its principles. We must be realistic. If we are not clear about just what our goal is, we **will** lose." He opened the door to go out and said, "Good day," closing it behind him.

CHAPTER THIRTY-THREE

STICKS AND STONES

Gerry wanted to go to church that morning, but the call from Bella prompting John to get a ticket for the next plane out to Washington had them packing and preparing for his time away. The CRC attorneys had plans to submit an appeal to the U. S. Supreme Court as soon as possible and needed him to confer on it as well as to plan for any future action if the appeal fell through. John insisted that Gerry and the girls go to her parent's home while he was gone.

"But Perry will be alone," Gerry protested. Perry was the new parakeet Gerry had bought to entertain the girls and herself while John was so busy with the case. She had insisted that it was worth the money they spent, because not only would a parakeet be entertaining, it would warn them of any intruder. She had proudly demonstrated his ability to repeat the phrases she had taught him, and he knew both the girl's names and had practiced "Happy Birthday" in preparation for Carolyn's first. John was doubtful that Perry the parakeet would actually realize the call to duty if someone did enter the house unawares, but it seemed to comfort Gerry, and he was, in fact, quite entertaining. He had perfected the phrase, "Daddy's home!" and so had won his heart.

"You can get the young girl next door to come and feed him, he'll be fine," John said, adding somewhat impatiently, "I need to call Al to brief him." He picked up the receiver energetically and dialed the familiar number. When Al answered the call and listened to John's briefing, he stalled a moment before answering.

"Look, John, I need to tell you something," he started. He took a deep breath and continued, "I've given this a lot of thought, and knew some action would be taken soon, so I would need to make a decision." He paused again, anticipating his partner's inner reaction to what he knew was coming. He said it quickly. "I'm dropping out of the case." John's silence forced him to continue. "I have a few faithful, not to mention wealthy clients," he gave a short laugh at including the fact, "who have let me know that they would have to drop all support if I become entangled again with a Communistic agenda." He sighed and added, "It would mean certain death for my career, and I just can't afford to lay my neck out like that. You know my family has already suffered for this. I know yours has, too." He stopped, thinking he may have said too much.

John had taken it in, flinching slightly at the implied question of why he was continuing. "I understand," John said simply, and added with a half-hearted laugh, "Anyway, I'll need someone who is still accepted here to forward me some work."

"Oh, I most certainly will! Absolutely!" Al assured him whole heartedly. In the brief silence that followed they both intuited that he probably couldn't follow through on it. Al reached through the rift to say, "Take care of yourself, now, John.

You know the crowd in Laurel is pretty mad that they didn't have their show, and I would bet they won't take this sitting down."

John placed the receiver back on its hook after Al's goodbyes and well wishes, feeling the full weight of the undertaking sink into his gut. He blinked, fighting back the emotions that came from the loss of the camaraderie, and returned to his preparations, with a honk into his handkerchief.

"Happy Birthday!" Perry squawked.

John had gotten his family safely settled before driving himself to the airport. It was a hot morning already, and the suit coat and tie he wore felt heavy and stifling. He accepted help from the Negro attendant with his suitcase and parked the car. On his way back to the airport entrance, he spotted familiar faces, packed in a familiar car, and quickened his pace. Just before the entrance, he heard the "Commie!" shouts, and thrust himself through the door, telling the attendant that he needed protection. The crowd in Laurel either had an informant or had just figured out what John would be up to next. There weren't many flights that were scheduled for Washington, D. C. from Jackson.

Seeing the men in the lot coming forward, the attendant said hurriedly to John, "Come this way."

A long, closed corridor led them to the maintenance room of the airport.

He stayed there huddled, smoking one cigarette after another, waiting on a plane bound for Washington to pull in, while the attendant made the necessary arrangements upstairs for his ticket. When he finally heard the call from an attendant on the ground, "Come this way, Mr. Poole, you'd best run, iffun you can." John took off, aiming for the steps that led to the plane. Halfway there, he heard the strange clatter on the concrete pavement of rocks and sticks that he realized were being pelted towards him. He braced himself as he ran, pulling his suit coat over his face just in time to cushion one well-aimed strike, but not another that grazed his forehead. John took the ascent to the plane two steps at a time, distancing himself from the fence that held back his aggressors.

Once he safely arrived, the meeting with the CRC was brief, but intense.

The two attorneys, Samuel Rosenwein and Arthur Silverman, who would take the case to the U. S. Supreme Court wanted a full description of the trial, its tone, and the threats of violence he was subject to. Rosenwein had been the defense attorney in cases in the recent past that involved Communist infiltration.

Silverman was a member of the National Lawyers Guild. They planned to give a full summary of the case to the high court and state their claims that McGee's confession had been forced, violating the Fourteenth Amendment's guarantee of due process; that there hadn't been sufficient evidence linking McGee to the crime; that the local prejudice, hostility and hysteria warranted a change of venue; that counsel could not represent McGee effectively due to lack of time to prepare and threats to their well-being; and that there had been a systematic exclusion of negroes from both the Grand and Petit Juries. Emmanual Bloch, who had also been working with John from afar, helped to fill in details he had gained from his conversations with him and Holland during the time of the investigations. Bella briefed him on what their steps would be to give more exposure to the case for nationwide support, should the appeal not be accepted. John's work was done for the time being, unless the request for a new trial was not accepted, then there may be more action in Mississippi.

"We wish we could provide protection for you," Bella offered, when they were finished. "I'm hoping that this crowd you met at the airport will simmer down for now, with the execution date still set and far away. We can probably expect to hear from them again when next year's date rolls around. Do you plan to press charges?"

"No," John replied, with a vigorous shake of his head that caused him to readjust his bandage. "I didn't get a good enough look at the crowd to see everyone involved, but the faces I did see were those I saw in the courtroom. I'd just like to lay low for now, and not stir up anymore ire. I'm avoiding visiting with McGee right now." He paused, seeing the concern in their faces and added, "You know, my family's safety is at stake here."

A silent but exchanged acknowledgment caused Silverman to lean forward and ask, "What else can we do for you, John?"

"I could sure use a drink," he said, with a laugh.

The autumn season proved to be a difficult one for the CRC. With the heightened national scare of Communism seeping into the country, there was agitation in more areas than just the South. In a fund-raising concert that featured a CRC speaker, anti-Communist protestors smashed car windows and beat up those attending, causing a great number to be injured. Bella was hit by a rock on her chin, which left her with a permanent scar. Whether it was the outside influences that colored the judges' decision or truly a lack of finding error, the best efforts of Rosenwein and Silverman, couldn't put Humpty together again, as the Federal Court decided, without comment, to not accept the case. It was returned to the Mississippi Supreme Court, where another date for execution was promptly set for July 27, 1950. Despite the discouragement, the CRC huddled together again to come up with a game plan to interfere with the prosecution's intentions. This time, they communicated only by phone with John.

The nations' skeptical mood was exacerbated in the first part of 1950, when Wisconsin senator Joseph McCarthy began making it public that there were Communist infiltrators everywhere within government and the major industries, such as filmmakers and actors in Hollywood. The world was seeing a Communistic takeover, and cartoonists egged it on, picturing the red Communist sickle and hammer ready to snatch your freedom and beat you down. Even those not that interested in politics heard of "red fever" and were warned of its contagion. A story whose inception was in February, and burgeoned out, spooking the red scare to a pitch, involved the arrest of two U. S. Citizens who were charged with being involved in espionage to leak Atomic Bomb secrets to the Russians – Julius Rosenberg and his sister, Ethel. The organization to contact for legal support was, of course, the Civil Rights Congress. Emanuel Bloch was assigned to be his lawyer and had to split his time and efforts away from the McGee case, which fact was not missed by those who watched the papers.

In Jackson, John had been active on his own front to save his reputation in town and, in turn, his livelihood. He had filed a libel charge against the Jackson Daily News, which touted itself under its title as "Mississippi's Greatest Newspaper." The editor, Fred Sullens, who was a long-time upholder of State's rights and the protection of the South's white women and was equally known for his cockiness and fighting temper, had called John and Al "lousy and consciousless" lawyers during the trial. John determined to sue for a large sum of money that would cover the time he had not been able to get work due to his sullied reputation. Sullens, in turn, had countered and sent out interviewers to question him about his involvement with an agency with Communist ties. Sullens' temper flared against him further when John denied knowing anything about the Communistic influences surrounding the funding of the case in the interview.

Although Sullens managed to staunch the suit against his newspaper with top-dollar attorneys, he still wanted revenge. He had in mind to engage the Prosecution team to help him in bringing about total destruction to John's career and arranged a meeting to talk about the prospect.

"Get a list of his clients in cases he lost or didn't win so much for. I'll bet a dollar 'till Tuesday that you'll find folks that will want to complain for a fee!" Deavours winked, as he twirled his cigar in his lips.

"Hell," Swartzfager added, "Every lawyer out there cuts corners. Most of us are just smart enough not to get caught in it," he laughed. "We can dig up something on him," He added, shooting down the brandy Sullens had offered. He paused and looked up with slanted eyes. "The way he spoke to Easterling and the Chief, should be reason for disbarment alone. Then bringing out that Nigger to contradict them and say he was beaten daily!" He sat back with lip pouted out in disgust, "Damned disrespectful upstart!"

Sullens had his men interview former clients of John's to note any infractions of the attorney-client relationship and, as Deavours suggested, gave a sum to anyone who was willing to share details.

Another front Sullens was ready to battle was on the advent of the appeal. Sullens knew the stage was set for the talk around town to flourish as the expectation that "Communist interference" would be coming to town soon, and he had the venue to fan the flame. On Thursday, May 25th, he was obliged to run the article that "Attorneys Will Make New Effort to Save Negro," which read that John R. Poole, Jackson attorney representing McGee said Thursday that future action on the Negro's behalf would be outlined in an answer to the Attorney General's motion for a new execution date." By the time Saturday's paper came out, he was prepared, and first ran an article on the Klan that showed three hooded men on the front page, smoking cigarettes, entitled **"Only thing that burned at Klan rally."**

They had been forbidden by the police to burn a cross within the city limits due to city ordinances, but the Imperial Emperor, Dr. Lycurgus Spinks, claimed, "The Governor and industrialist leaders aren't doing enough in the fight for State's Rights.... because they are beholden to the Federal Government's purse strings." He continued, "They are hollering for state's rights and then panhandling the federal government for all the money they can get!" His Grand Dragon, who was robed and mounted upon a horse, led fifty-six other robed Klansmen, whose faces were daubed with white and red grease paint, and paraded around the unlit cross, in protest. Another photo of the Grand Dragon was pictured on the second page, next to the continuation of the Klan article and curiously set just above the article entitled, **"Seek Hearing for Fourth Trial for W. McGee."**

It related that the "Attorneys for McGee indicated they would seek a new trial on the grounds that new evidence, just discovered, revealed that McGee allegedly was the object of attempted mob violence during the course of the third trial." An adjacent article read that **"FEPC is as Dead as the Dodo Bird."**

The FEPC, or the Fair Employment Practices Bill, would have forbidden racial or religious discrimination in employment. The paper was organized to portray the message – any of you who will stand up for the rights of the colored man or the Jew in Mississippi, beware!

Meanwhile, the Daily Worker was fomenting its own political dissent from afar, using every angle they could to stir up the passion of the base. Rosalee had been frantically writing to the CRC that she and Willie were worried sick about the Federal Court's decision to send the case back to Mississippi. Although they had both before been communicating in letters their gratitude to the CRC, having gotten gifts of money from time to time, they complained that they hadn't heard from their lawyers in Mississippi, despite efforts to contact them. The correspondence showed that they knew what was happening in the case, but also that they believed that "Lawyer Poole" was no longer representing them. They were both assured by return letters from the CRC that all that could be done was being done, and mollified Rosalee by inviting her to come again to speak on Willie's behalf. Bessie stayed at home this time, not wanting to "fool with getting all gussied up on account of white folks," and dedicated herself to praying with the church.

Rosalee was beside herself, excited by this new level of life and, dressed in her finest, spoke at the "One Hundred Cases" dinner gathering for a delegation of the Civil Rights Congress leaders and others that would be supporting the cause of civil rights cases. After that, The Women's Committee of the Harlem Trade Union Council invited her to a reception to speak, and she was interviewed by the "Daily Worker" and others. Cameras flashed around her, taking pictures for use in articles and for pamphlets to be distributed. One paper described her as "A strikingly attractive young woman" She was quoted as saying, "I don't have any faith in that judge. He would just as soon kill Willie as not. We've got to do something." In another article she pled, "Please don't let him die. I need him so much to help me. I am not giving up. I am praying every day that some good may turn up…"

It was a tender appeal from a pretty young woman who said she had been married to McGee, who had fathered their four children. Although there was no mention of the affair at this time, the CRC not willing to put it in the mix just yet, the articles instead berated the court system for the unfairness and prejudice of the trial proceedings. The fact that Willette had never openly identified McGee as the rapist was a point that was pressed, and that her story of not wanting to wake the baby or other children with a scream just did not sound logical. The CRC urged organizations and individuals to flood Governor Fielding Wright of Jackson, Mississippi with telegrams and letters, urging him to save the life of Willie McGee.

The Worker stated, "The entire labor and progressive movement must be immediately aroused over this fascist attack against the Negro people…. Let America cry out: McGee shall not die!"

Meanwhile, Emanuel Bloch had called John to relate to him what tactics they would use when he came. "Patterson and Abzug will be traveling with up to 75 delegates from the CRC to help us plead the Governor for clemency.

There's another delegation from California that says they are coming, too. We'll need to block out some hotel rooms."

"Better stay in Jackson," John warned." Locals in Laurel wouldn't allow that on their turf. I'll call the Heidelberg Hotel. It should be big enough to give some anonymity, but I would suggest spreading some people out to other places, too. Now, what about this writ of habeas corpus?"

"Yes, we want to file that, as well as a writ of Error Coram Nobis," Bloch threw out the name seeing if John would recognize the almost obsolete writ. John's eyes searched his memory and responded quickly with, "The error before us. It's an old English plea, let's see, that a case be reopened on grounds of incompetence or fraud in earlier trials. Correct?"

Bloch was impressed, "You retained your studies well. It's hardly ever been used, but it also maintains that error is caused when evidence has been suppressed, as is certainly the case here. Bella came up with it, but it was called obsolete when someone tried to use it in a case twenty-five years ago. We're hoping that Mississippi judges won't discover that fact. Anyway, the underlying premise applies."

John agreed and said he would arrange for office space and a typist for any last-minute changes they may need. He wished a safe trip to Emanuel, who promised to brief him more upon arrival, and then hung up the receiver with an ominous feeling. He looked up at the calendar tacked on the wall. It was Saturday, May 15th. In less than two weeks, McGee was scheduled to be electrocuted. He must take the chance to visit with him. He decided to go on Sunday afternoon, when the "regulars" were off. Willie showed a mixture of feelings when he saw him, trying not to put too much hope in this man who hadn't visited him for a year after saving him from sure death.

"Hello, Willie," John said with sincere warmth and stretched out his hand to shake Willie's "I wuz hopin' you would come," was all he managed to get out, moved to not complain to the only white man who would shake his hand.

Anticipating his thoughts, John started, "You know it hasn't been safe for me to visit." Willie nodded soberly and he continued. "Have you been told, Willie, that many, many people are traveling from across the nation to protest in your behalf?"

Willie's eyes opened with hope. Rosalee had sent him a letter telling him all about her visit and speeches, but she hadn't known exactly what their plan was. If she had written it, it would have been first read by the jailers, so she had to be careful to not give details.

"What they gonna do?" he questioned.

"They are planning to protest for the Governor to grant you clemency," John smiled.

"Clem-uhn-see?" Willie repeated.

"That means to grant mercy," John explained, "to release you even though you have been tried and found guilty."

Willie tried to let it sink in. It had happened when he was little. He remembered the preacher paying for a sweet roll he had been caught stealing and let him go without telling his Mama, just as long as he promised to be at church for a month of Sundays.

He couldn't quite imagine the white governor doing the same, no matter how many other people asked. He drew in on the cigarette and fingered the pack John had brought him. "Whut if it jes makes em mad?" he finally asked.

John shifted in his chair. He hadn't expected McGee's analysis, which was similar to his own. "Well, we're going to try other legal moves as well, appealing on the grounds that the first three cases were fraudulent and squelched…, that is, kept information from being shown," he offered.

"You mean our relations?" Willie asked "Relations?" John asked quizzically.

"Me and Missus Hawkins – our relations," Willie clarified.

"Oh! No, well, that's not what we would be claiming. We would be claiming that the witnesses who could say where you were had been intimidated into not coming forth." John said simply.

"I was there," Willie said bluntly. He looked at John in the eye and continued, "Those witnesses, even if they comes all the ways from Florida, would be lyin if they were to say I wasn't. "

John nodded an acknowledgment, then raised his eyebrows with exasperation and sighed." I know, Willie, but if we bring that up there will be no legal argument." Looking into the questioning eyes he added, "If we bring up your affair, there would be no need for any further legal proceedings, because we would probably both be either shot or hung."

Willie decided not to protest further. The CRC was interested in bringing out the affair, by what Rosalee told him, but Lawyer Poole wasn't so interested. He understood. He lived in these parts – they didn't. Willie blew smoke rings.

John felt estranged from his client. He felt the whole thing was slipping away from him, as he didn't have much confidence in the protestors, as well-intentioned as they may be. He didn't tell Willie that he was afraid it would do him more harm than good. He changed the subject.

"How have you been treated since I saw you last?" He had noticed that Willie actually looked healthy and well-groomed.

"Haven't been beat," Willie responded. "Not at all?" John sounded pleased.

"Well, they shoves me when they get a chance, but they's all on their P's and Q's since I've been writing the Congress," he showed his teeth in a smile. "And perhaps because of what we brought out in your last trial regarding your treatment?" John added, reminding him of the reason he was even able to write to or receive letters from the CRC.

"Now, thas true enough," Willie admitted, nodding his head. He shared a laugh with John as they recalled how hot the Prosecution team was when they read from the first trial for Chief Valentine's testimony. When Willie's expression turned sober again, John added, "It wasn't right that the Judge refused to even consider your testimony, Willie."

"Thas okay," Willie said, nodding his head in agreement. "Thas okay, cuz I have another judge who hears both me and him."

John gazed for a moment into the eyes that seemed much deeper than he remembered them before answering, "That's right, Willie, that's right."

Once John was outside again, the sun was warm and welcoming even in its final hour. He took off his suit coat and lit a cigarette, thankful for a delicate breeze announcing evening's advent. He looked around at the peaceful streets, empty of all but one or two walkers, hurrying back to their homes under the golden and rose-colored skies. What would it look like with troops of strangers eyeing the citizens with disdain? He began his labored walk to the parking lot.

'Hullo, Mister Poole," came a call from behind the building. He recognized a friendly guard who had helped him out in the past with McGee." How are you doing these days? We don't see you much around here anymore," he added.

John smiled warmly, "Well, hello Ed! No, I've been keeping my distance," he laughed. He began again quickly before Ed decided to commiserate. "And how have you been? How's your wife, Marybelle?"

As Ed began a story of how his wife had started leading the Girl Scouts and went from there to his learning how to thread a needle to help her with a project, John laughed heartily, finding refreshment in a friendly interchange with a fellow Southerner, that he had had so little of this past year.

Ed interjected into a moment when John was lighting a cigarette, "You know, John, there are plenty of us out here who respect you for your courage." John's eyes darted up as he breathed in the smoke and let it back out again. It gave Ed the moment he needed to continue. "It's no mystery that he is being railroaded, and, well, we're just glad someone had the courage to stand against Collins and his cronies." John was moved and was glad the dusk was settling to cover his emotion. He stayed past dark, sharing opinions and laughter with Ed, before putting his suit coat back on and heading towards his car, checking his watch.

PART III
THE AWAKENING

I find myself in a tall office building with many windows surrounding it, letting the light flood in over the very close clouds. The office workers are not at their jobs, but are moving around sporadically, talking wildly, with fear in their voices – the invasion is coming and is very close. There is no time for escape and death appears inevitable. Panic spreads contagiously and strikes deeply into my heart.

But suddenly, I am also endowed with a calm insight, as if a message of hope is being impressed within my soul. I have to speak, though I have no authority. I climb on a desk and shout – "I know what to do! I know what to do! Everyone listen!" The crowd momentarily stops their clamor and in the hush I begin to speak cautiously. All we have to do," – the room stills to a rapt but nervous attention, and I speak slowly and steadily, "… is open our eyes. Open your eyes!" I repeat more loudly, again and again.

Each person seems to understand and attempts to open their eyes. I stop exclaiming and turn inward to do the same. My eyes do open, and I am in a different reality. I awake to the morning streaming light into my bedroom and sit up in wondrous relief. I never hear the rhythm of the accusation again.

INTERLUDE III

I surprised the family in my young adulthood by making a 180 degree turn and committing my life to spiritual discipline. It looked as though the seeds of influence planted by my grandmother had somehow survived and taken root, saving me from the road to perdition I had earlier started on. I converted to Orthodox Christianity and joined myself to a church whose African American Priest, Fr. Moses, I greatly admired. I prided myself on the lessons learned from my Mom and Dad, and I believed myself to be non-prejudiced. Ironically, the small congregation was mostly white, as was Fr. Moses' wife. The differences in the color of our skin made no difference to me, but I ran into trouble with one of the few black ladies in the church.

Shelia had a propensity for getting under my skin, as she seemed to have a chip on her shoulder and would engage me in conversations with what I considered a cynical and opinionated view. I wondered if her attending an all-white women's college in Mississippi precluded her cynicism, or it had been inbred through a family who desperately wanted to infuse self-esteem into their intelligent girl, who would otherwise have been vulnerable to the lack of opportunities she would find for herself in the society of the South. Whatever the case, I must have symbolized to her the privileged Southern white girl, and it may have been hard for her to see me as anything different.

I went to Fr. Moses to confess my irritation and lack of ability to love my sister in the church. He kindly suggested that we go out together and have some fun – just get to know each other. Easy enough, I thought. However, Sheila was not delighted at the prospect of getting to know me. Either she didn't think I was really worth the time or money for a frivolous outing – she was a single mother with tight funds – or she was as timid about what the intimacy might bring to light as I was. Then there was the deciding of what we should do. Watching a movie together sounded non-threatening. She suggested Spike Lee's new movie – "Do The Right Thing." Thinking I would be caught up in a heated racial discussion, I hedged. I offered to see "Dead Poet's Society," only because of my admiration of the comedian, Robin Williams. Her equally oppositional reaction to seeing a movie about a rich white boys' private school took me by surprise. Both offended, we decided to put the outing on hold. After some time she called back, possibly after talking to Fr. Moses herself, and we agreed to go to a local Indian concert she had seen in the paper.

Along the way, we chuckled as we realized that we didn't know if we were going to a concert of Native American people or folks from India. The issue was cleared when we saw the women in their beautiful saris and the sitars carried under their arms, I felt somewhat awkward and out of place as those dressed properly for this event paused at our jeans. Sheila was used to being a minority, however, and returned my nervous glance with a stoic one of her own. We eventually found our way to the auditorium and took our seats. After a brief welcome and introduction of the musicians, the room darkened. The first performer, a young woman, walked on stage and seated herself on a pillow. With sitar in lap, she began to play to a hushed audience – one string at a time.

The reverberation of the music seemed to stun the crowd and as we heard deeply felt utterances from the people around us, we glanced sideways at each other to catch some understanding of what everyone seemed to be so in awe of. Sheila shrugged at my questioning eyes, and we turned our attention back to the performance. Although we were used to listening to flowing music with a little action and melody, we attempted to open our senses to the mystical sounds of this strange instrument. Truly, there was beauty in the sounds, but when the crowd once again began to ooh and ahh in amazement at the twang of a single string, Sheila and I again looked at each other for a clue of what we should be amazed of. She was the first one to let a laugh slip, and I, too, failed when attempting to conceal mine. We were instantly corrected by the frowns of those seated in front of us, who turned to see who could be so impudent. We silently mouthed an agreement after a few more compulsive chuckles to leave after the performer had finished the set.

The laughter and conversation that followed brought Sheila and I closer together than we had ever been, though we never really acknowledged that this bond came about through our mutual lack of understanding of yet another culture in our midst. At least we had learned an unspoken lesson together of what it is like not being able to relate to another race outside the mere black/white split. We understood that being a part of our cultures alone had a great impact on our inability to communicate another culture's "language," no matter if our words were the same, or if we both bought our groceries at the same corner store. There were generations behind each of us whose cultural nuances were unconsciously carried in the makeup of our thoughts as well as our genetics. There were values and goals that had their own familial roots, traditions and foods which might seem strange to others. How would we learn to be truly unprejudiced?

In the book "Black Boy," written in 1943 by a native Mississippian, Richard Wright, about his life as an African American raised in the South, he bemoans the fact that the white culture experiences such different day to day life from the black. He wrote that white culture has no idea how the black man has to adjust his nature to fit in. From his perspective, while he had "All my life...done nothing but feel and cultivate my feelings," the white youth had "all their lives done nothing but strive for petty goals, the trivial material prizes of American life. We shared a common tongue, but my language was a different language from theirs." It was true that he had suffered in certain ways, while it appeared that they no suffering at all. In fact, it may have been true that the shallowness he saw in their souls, which he described as "...like the syllables of popular songs," was an accurate comparison of their experience compared to his – a life filled with hunger and disappointments, a life of fear and unwarranted reproach. As a young adult, Wright joined the Communist Party and felt that it had the answers for living in peace in this nation. Even there, however, he found himself to be misunderstood and finally, an outcast. After finding himself utterly alone, watching a Communist march he had been thrown out of, he wrote:

"My thoughts seemed to be coming from somewhere within me, as by a power of their own: It's going to take a long and bloody time, a lot of stumbling and a lot of falling, before they find the right road. They will have to grope about blindly in the sunshine, butting their heads against every mistake, bruising their bodies against every illusion, making a million futile errors and suffering for them, bleeding for them, until they learn how to live, I thought."

Wright spoke of a spiritual blindness and hoped that his words would "...create a sense of the hunger for life that gnaws in us all, to keep alive in our hearts a sense of the inexpressibly human."

Fr. Moses, whose great-grandfather was a slave, taught our congregation that the fathers of our Church spoke of suffering as the way to follow Christ, to win the freedom, peace and joy our souls hope for. He also told us that the old gospel tunes the slaves sang held a deep spirituality that came from their suffering. He displays in his African American Heritage Museum in Ash Grove, Missouri, an iron neck clamp that had been passed down in his family, as well as slave dogtags, in remembrance of the cruelty that once took place.

Yet, the Socialist or Communist approach, which seemed to promise suf-fering for none and appeared to champion minorities, in the end yields only empty surfeiting and enslavement to its system. I puzzled, as my Dad must have, to determine how to find the "True North," until I found the saving Grace of faith.

Attempting to convey the substance of this lesson to my children, I read to them from "Roll of Thunder, Hear my Cry," by Mildred Taylor. They cuddled beside me to hear a nightly chapter of the tale of a black family in Jackson, Mississippi, whose children walked to a school just down the way from my elementary school, both named "Jefferson Davis Elementary," but one was for black children and one for white, who were privileged to ride the bus. My three children found it hard to understand why and wondered at the family's plight. Words of wisdom from the family's mother gave perspective:

"Baby, we have no choice of what color we're born or who our parents are, or whether we're rich or poor.

What we do have is some choice over what we make of our lives once we're here."

CHAPTER THIRTY-FOUR

I'M MOVIN' ON

"COMMUNISTS COMING HERE"

So read an editorial in the July 19th edition of the "Jackson Daily News".
Sullens had written it, not trusting anyone else to give a thorough berating to the agitators, and not wanting to miss the opportunity to do so himself. It enticed his readers by beginning:

"On the 25th of July there will be an invasion of Jackson by some very undesirable persons. According to William Patterson, secretary of the Civil Rights Congress, from thirty to forty members of that body will be here to appear before Gov. Wright, ostensibly for the purpose of seeking a commutation or postponement of the death sentence of Willie McGee, thrice-convicted rapist."

A brief description of the case followed, underlining the fact that the U.S. Supreme Court had refused to interfere with Mississippi's decision. The article then continued:

"Rev. N. D. Harris, Negro, who proclaims himself chairman of the Civil Rights Congress at Dallas, has issued an inflammatory statement saying that 1,000 members of that organization have been ordered to mobilize in Jackson, 'to demonstrate against the electrocution of Willie McGee.' This is no doubt a gross exaggeration by a loose-lipped Negro.'This is not just a fight for the life of one Negro, but a fight for thelives of fifteen million Negroes,' says Harris."

"Truly spoken!" Gerry interrupted as she was reading it out loud to John. "Go on," John urged, waving his hand, wishing he had gotten to the paper first.

Her lips pouted, but she continued reading, "Our first best piece of advice to this loud-mouthed racial agitator is this: 'Jackson will be the finest place on earth for you to stay away from next Tuesday. For sublimated gall, triple-plated audacity, bold insolence and downright arrogance, this proposed invasion of the Capital City of our state by a gang of Communists truly passes all comprehension. These invaders are just as much enemies of the United States government as are soldiers fighting under the Communist banner in Korea – fighting with Russian arms and ammunition!"

"Oh, John!" Gerry gasped, with a hand to her mouth, "They are comparing them to Russians!"

John took the paper from her impatiently, saying, "Let me see this."

He read on, "These invaders are sworn enemies of law and order and the proper administration of justice in Mississippi. They are members of the Civil Rights Congress, an organization that has spent not less than $30,000 during the past five years trying to save from the electric chair the brutal rapist of a white woman. The one thought in the minds of these persons, both men and women, is not the mere saving of Willie McGee from a deserved death, but to overthrow all semblance of law and order in our state and nation, and to make easy our conquest by Communist Russia."

"Why are they comparing them so much to Communists?" Gerry demanded to know.

John ignored the question and kept reading, "There may be members in the party who do not carry cards showing them to be members of the Communist Party, but their visit is inspired by the Civil Rights Congress, which is a notorious Communist organization."

"John, is that true?" Gerry interrupted.

"Let me finish," he complained and continued, "The Daily News does not believe Gov. Wright intends to interfere with the death sentence of Willie McGee, or that he can be persuaded to do so by these enemies of our government. The Governor will be acting quite properly, and in accordance with overwhelming public opinion if he slams the executive door in the faces of these impudent and lawless invaders and tells them this – 'Get the hell out of here!'"

"Furthermore, if any hotel in Jackson furnishes shelter for this motley crew during their brief visit in Jackson – and it should be made mighty brief – then that hostelry should have the rooms they occupy thoroughly cleansed with the most powerful disinfectants. Carbolic acid and concentrated lye, combined with DDT, will hardly be adequate for the purpose."

John shook the paper as if it were Sullen's neck. "You imbecile!" he retorted. "This is a ranting of a frustrated old man, that's all." He threw the paper on the couch as if it meant nothing, although the emotion defied his words. Both babies began to cry at once, hearing their Dad's voice booming with anger.

"John!" Gerry started, but she held back any other words, afraid of her quavering voice. She picked up the youngest, Carolyn, and satisfied Beverly with a pacifier and a hug to the legs. She waited a long moment while John sat, smoking to calm himself, before saying, "You might need to call Patrick again."

He looked up at her and said with honesty, "I've known all along that the CRC had some backing from the Communist Party, but I suspect now they are more enmeshed than I thought. Bella just didn't say certain things." He paused, clenching his jaw and remembering when he realized the connections after traveling to Washington and seeing Communist papers and brochures in the office. He felt duped, as if he and Willie were both just puppets, playing out an act that was being manipulated by a much greater set of hands. He finally shook his head before finishing with, "I guess she didn't think it was necessary." His eyes took on an inward look. "Now with all this national attention, and just when McCarthy is beginning to lump all progressive thinkers in with Communists," he got lost in the enormity of what he was talking about, shook his head again and looked at his girls clinging to the safety of their mother. He finished with a question, "Do you want me to pull out, honey? I know Al's wife had a lot to do with his…"

"No," Gerry interrupted, putting out her hand for him to stop "I don't want you to drop out now." She lifted her chin to say, "I didn't marry a man who was afraid of obstacles." She patted a wide-eyed Carolyn on the bottom as she said, "We girls are sticking by you to the end, aren't we?" She grabbed Beverly's outreached hands and nestled one on either side of her hips, finishing with, "After a nap, we'll be packing for Mother's."

John watched her walk back to the bedroom before clicking on the radio to soothe his nerves. He stood up with the paper and paced, looking for any other pertinent articles. There was one that highlighted the "Warring Ku Klux Klan Heads" who both wanted to be in charge of the "Mississippi Empire" at this time, as he listened to the tail end of a song just abrasive enough to fit his mood. The lyrics shouted,

"Well, I feel, yes I feel,
Feel that I could lay down oh, time ain't long
I'm gonna catch the first thing smokin,
Back, back down the road I'm goin Back
down the road I'm goin
Back down the road I'm goin
Sure 'nough back, sure 'nough back…"

"And that was Muddy Waters, with "Rollin Stone!" the DJ announced, then continued,

"Now, in the news today, we hear from a Dr. Grayson Tucker, pastor of the First Presbyterian church in Laurel, Mississippi. He claims he was approached by two people who he says were members of a Communist group called the Civil Rights Congress."

John rushed to put his ear closer to the speaker and turned it up a bit.

"Dr. Tucker, tell us about your meeting today."

"Why, sure," he started. "I couldn't say who they were, but they wanted me to intercede with the Governor, Governor Wright, you know, to help them get a stay of execution for Willie McGee."

"Now, you must have been very surprised, Dr. Tucker, what did you say?" "Yes, well, yes, I was, but, you see, I denied their request right away. You see," he continued, "I am a member of the Negro Legionnaires and we are of the disposition that Negros have opportunity to do well here in Mississippi if they put their mind to it, and I would be proud to be a part of a delegation that stands up for our rule of law here for Negros. This man was convicted three times, and I do believe he is deserving of this sentence. Yessir, I believe it to be true. I don't want no involvement with any Communist Group, no matter who they say they stand for. That's right, and this man, McGee, will be no better off for their involvement, I will wager on that. And…"

"Thank you, Dr. Tucker, for your insight," the announcer interrupted and continued, "It was also reported that one of these Communists talked to a woman in Laurel, who wishes to remain anonymous, but said that the Communists 'strongly accused' the ravished young mother, Mrs. Hawkins. It is reported that they were immediately told to leave. Others who have visited houses in Laurel have claimed they were friends of John Poole, the young defense attorney. We're talking here about the case of Willie McGee, who brutally ravished a young white mother of three children five years ago. He is scheduled to die in the state's portable electric chair on July 27. Now, let's hear a song about lost love from Hank Snow called, "I'm Moving On.""

"That big eight-wheeler rollin' down the track
Means your true-lovin' daddy ain't comin' back
'Cause I'm movin' on, I'll soon be gone
You were flyin' too high, for my little old sky So I'm
movin' on…"

John had sworn when his name was mentioned and turned up the song when hearing rustling in the hallway. He didn't want Gerry to ask why, and pretended to be singing along all the while,

"That big loud whistle as it blew and blew
Said hello to the southland, we're comin' to you When
we're movin' on, oh hear my song
You had the laugh on me, so I've set you free
And I'm movin' oo-on…"

He quieted himself when Gerry motioned to him with a finger to the lips, as she had just put the girls to sleep. He shut off the radio and ran his fingers through his hair to help his thoughts right themselves. Where did he stand? Not with Dr. Tucker, who was satisfied with his delegated portion of life, but again, not with the Communist Party delegates who claimed him as a "friend." He abhorred the bullish techniques and didn't want to be lumped into the group that carried this mindset. Pictures flooded his mind of family and friends, workers that exchanged friendly greetings, and friendly faces in church. All from his beloved Southern town that wouldn't allow winter to linger on. He then remembered Willie's deep brown eyes and the reflection of his own family within them.

In his deepened thought, John involuntarily flashed back to a scene from his youth. The new friend, a rich boy who had tempted him with his money to catch the train and run away from home for an adventure, had slept on the bare floor in the hospital until John had regained consciousness. He pictured his face, as he, awakened by John's groan, looked at his missing leg and wiped the tears streaming down his cheeks. "I didn't mean for you to come to any harm!" He had said, and thrown his head on John's pillow, repeating, "I didn't mean for you to come to any harm!"

John dabbed his own eyes, resting his elbows on the table where he had once again settled, as if carrying a heavy weight inside. Emmanuel and Bella would be coming in soon. He would need to focus on the legal process. That was his mission in this chaos – nothing else. He reached for the rotary phone and mechanically dialed the operator for a long-distance call. Sharing the news would help him to focus. After a half-hearted greeting, he related the media's coverage of the delegates' visit.

"I'm not worried about the citizens here, they may be argumentative, but they are mostly harmless. What I'm worried about is the Klan. I'm sure they are planning an intervention."

It didn't mean much to Emmanuel, who seemed to thrive on the excitement they were stirring up, and assured John that they were prepared to cover all bases.

"We'll tackle this on two fronts," he began, as if a general preparing for battle, "you, Bella and I will be filing our appeals wherever we can get a break – in the state Supreme Court, the Circuit Court, and, if we have to, back to the High Court. Grossman will be heading the delegation to ask the governor to grant clemency. He's got a couple of women who head the Progressive Parties in their states to come with him, along with some of their delegates. I know we've counted over a thousand heads of people who have said they wanted to go, but if they hear of the ruckus stirred up already, they might bail. We've got a girl here that will arrange our flights for whatever is necessary, and I guess we could just drive to New Orleans where the Circuit Court is." He barely paused before asking sharply, "Any questions?"

"Yes, one," John started, "where will all these people stay? The papers have already given their warning to any hotels that open their doors to them."

"I don't know about that, I guess they could go to neighboring towns and drive in for the hearing. I'll alert Grossman about that. Anything else?" He had urgency in his voice.

John took a deep breath and answered, "No, I've started work on my part of the Writ here, and I'll finish it up today."

"Do you have protection?" Emmanuel asked with truncated compassion. John smiled sideways before answering, "My right-left punch."

Emanuel laughed, "I'm counting on that! See you tomorrow."

CHAPTER THIRTY-FIVE

NO ONE TO TRUST

The next morning's paper in Laurel cried, "Civil Rights Congress Warned by Governor of Mississippi to Handle McGee Case Under Law." Governor Fielding Wright warned that "Mississippi can handle its own affairs and we intend to do so." It called the CRC outright a Communist organization, giving the Justice Department as its source. The quote from the Governor continued, "We will not tolerate a wild-eyed, howling mob of Communists and sympathizers, gathered by the Civil Rights Congress to stage a demonstration in Mississippi." He went on to say, as if to the rest of the nation, that he would grant a hearing to a reasonably sized delegation "in an orderly and sane manner."

The Police Chief was reported as to have cancelled all vacations and days off for the date of the demonstration, July 25th. The Governor claimed he would "expose this gang" at the proper time and to prove they tried to "mislead the people and create a false impression of the administration of justice in Mississippi." Later on in the article it was reported that representatives of the CRC were continuing their "invasion" on Laurel "to free the rapist" and again referred to them as "friends" of John Poole. It ended with the report that the State Commander of the V.F.W., E.K. Collins, alerted all members and the public to report immediately any suspicious persons or actions in connection with the forthcoming execution date of Willie McGee.

The same edition of the Laurel Paper reported in another article on Communists who had invaded Birmingham for similar purposes, who had been given 48 hours to get out of town and that the City Commission there had made an ordinance that made it a misdemeanor to have a membership in the Communist Party, punishable by 180 days in jail and a fine of $100. The measure was introduced by Police Commissioner, Eugene "Bull" Connor, who had run for the Democratic nomination on a "white supremacy" platform." If this doesn't clean them out," he was quoted as saying, "we'll try something else."

Heads were shaking and discussions flared in cafes and barbershops about what Laurel and Jackson were going to do to with these infiltrators all around town. Word spread fast and everyone was watching what would happen next, as they heard of more Communists pouring in. Underlying messages were given from men with white ties to meet for organizational purposes. Those in the "Negro America Legion" protected themselves with an article that stated their convictions:

"Whereas, we are firm believers in our Southern way of life and customs, and upholders of law and order and especially conscious of our duty to protect our women folk from depraved and ruthless criminals, "Now Therefore, be it resolved by us that we condemn and repudiate all such subversive and communistic individuals and that we further offer our services, individually and as a Post to serve in any capacity selected by our governing authorities to the end that justice shall not be obstructed in said premises."

It was printed in the back of the paper, where two pages were reserved for the "Colored Section" of the news. Couched on the second page was the surprising fact that the McGee Lawyers had already filed a Writ of Coram Nobis in the Circuit Court in New Orleans, "…seeking a new trial for the condemned-to-die, 34-year old negro rapist"

"If you didn't think Mississippi's mind was already set against any kind of appeal, just look at this wording," Gerry complained to her mother. She had to get most of her information from the papers, as John's calls to her had been abbreviated and secretive. "It looks like they went to Hattiesburg right afterwards to present it to Judge Collins," she mused and scanned forward, "Oh, dear," she said, worriedly, and turned to her mother, who was rocking the baby to sleep, raising her eyebrows questioningly. Gerry continued, "It is believed here that Poole is basing his writ for a new trial for the negro on such a claim that he will further claim that McGee met and knew the ravished woman long before the night of the rape." Gerry pressed her lips together and let the paper drop onto the table. Tears forced their way out of her eyes before she turned to her mother and said, "There are people who would kill him for that." They both sat in silence, rocking.

What the paper wouldn't report until the following day was what happened when Emanuel and John went to Laurel to present their argument for the Writ before Judge Collins. With the added bold voice of the CRC integrated into the court document, it claimed that the first three trials had been nothing more than a pretense of justice, listing the reasons of the coerced confession, an all-white jury and the tampering with the jury call-list, the mob-like atmosphere, and final threats that caused the defense to leave town before argument. An inflammatory passage insinuated that the "complaining witness" knew that she was not raped and gave false testimony. They had filed the Writ in Jones County at 11:45 but were informed by the clerk that they would have to deliver it themselves to the Judge who was not in Laurel, but in Hattiesburg.

They got back into the car to leave for Hattiesburg, with eyes planted on their backs, and arrived an hour later at their destination. There they were informed in a curt manner by an older receptionist that Judge Collins had taken a late lunch that day and wouldn't be back until 1:30. They could wait, if they would like.

John had stumped out his cigarette in the standing copper ashtray next to his seat in the waiting room and was stretching out his good leg. Emanuel stood pacing, hands clasped behind his back, studying the framed pictures on the walls of past Mississippi dignitaries. The silence was broken by a young secretary coming through the door behind the desk and clearing her throat.

"I'm so sorry to tell y'all this," the secretary said, as she took off her glasses to reveal interested eyes and addressed the stately Emanuel. "But, the Judge has been compelled to leave the office," she paused to take in the reaction, then continued, "and he… he will not return until tomorrow morning." She paused, smiled sweetly and finished with, "Could I arrange for y'all to stay at a hotel here in town?"

Emanuel's narrowed eyes looked back at John, who was pushing himself to a stand with temper showing in his. Emanuel turned back, donning a false pleasantry to say, "No, Mam, please, don't bother yourself. 'We all' have to get going." He smiled sweetly to wash away the sarcastic tone, turned on his heels and left with John. The trip back to Laurel was at a faster pace.

"Do the police around here stop for speeding ten miles over?" Emanuel asked.

"I think they are all in the cities," John answered, but checked his rear view, anyway. He slowed as he reached the city limits and noticed a gathering of trucks at the V. F. W. Hall. One man looked their way, causing a trickle of heads to turn. "I'm not sure they'll really use the police for anything but show," he added.

Emanuel put a case on the floor of the car that held a gun. "You tell me when you think we need to start carrying this."

"Now might be good," John said as they drove towards the courthouse, noting the glares along the way.

The same steps to the Clerk's office of the Court seemed harder to ascend in the heat of the day. John had broken a sweat by the top, quickening his pace to keep up with Emanuel's longer stride. Emmanuel opened the Circuit Clerk's office door with energy and John followed to explain to the clerk that they needed to file their writ and inform the Judge that they had done so. The clerk, without commenting, dialed a number and shoved the phone towards John, "Collin's home," he said simply.

With no apologies, the Judge replied to John's explanation, "Yes, well, I will hear your petition tomorrow. No, I will be in Laurel, that's right. Be there at 9:00." Collins hung up the receiver and turned back to his table where Deavours was seated, smiled and said as he lit a cigar, "We'll be glad to have our showtime with these Commies!" He laughed and added, "In our own time!"

John had turned back to Emanuel and said simply, "9:00 in the morning." "Well, then," he returned, shaking his head.

John turned back to the Clerk, gave a colorless thanks and walked out. They were discussing what to do with the remainder of the day while descending the stairs, when Emanuel noticed an angry man walking across the courthouse lawn at a fast pace. "Who's this?" he asked John.

"That's Hawkins!" John said sharply, as they stepped onto the pavement, "Let's get to the car."

The oncoming figure threw off his hat as if an invitation to battle and ran towards him. "You dirty son of a bitch!" he imploded as he came in towards John, lunged at him and threw his fist towards his jaw. He was no match for John's side-steps, despite the handicap, but John was not going to engage in a fight that would call on any more of a gang in this atmosphere. He and Bloch both managed to get into the car, with a steaming Hawkins planning his next move. It was to run to get into his car that was parked on a street perpendicular to them. John saw Hawkins back up his car just as they did.

"It doesn't look like he has anyone else around right now, but they could be waiting just around the corner," John said as he pulled the car back up, attempting to divert him." I don't think he would try this all alone." Hawkins pulled his car back into position and waited.

"Let's try to get some of that police protection," Emanuel directed, as he palmed his gun. He added, "You know he just got word of you saying his wife lied. This man is on a rage!"

John pulled the car back out again and sped off for the police department. They made it there before Hawkins could catch them, and hopped out of the car to go in.

"Yes?" The desk sergeant asked as he looked up from the paper and recognized who was standing in front of him.

"We're being chased by Troy Hawkins and need an escort out of town. I don't know how many people he's going to get to follow him," John said, panting for breath. Emanuel stood beside, nodding his head and added, "He's mad as Hell – tried to plant a good one on John at the courthouse, and would have if he didn't have a good duck!"

He laughed, in spite of himself, thinking they were now safe. He added, more seriously, "We're going to need an escort tomorrow morning, too."

The sergeant and a Highway Patrolman who had also come into the office looked at one another. The sergeant stood and said merely, "You boys wait right here a minute." As he left the office, the Highway Patrolman shifted his stance.

"You're down here from New York, are you?" He looked at Emanuel who nodded, still digesting the fact he had been called "boy."

"I hear some of your people are stirring up the town a bit," he said.

Emanuel looked straight at him and said, "There are people who have come from many different states to protest this push-through execution of a man they believe has not gotten a fair trial here."

"Shee-w!" the patrol man exclaimed. He laughed and crossed his arms as he added, "I guess you **will** be needing some protection." The sergeant came back in, along with the Chief of Police, Valentine, who looked at John with cold recognition but said politely, "Please, come into my office." He escorted in the two just to say, "I'll be with you in just a minute," and left again. John and Emmanuel sat, uncomfortably, across from the Chief's desk and passed the time with twitches and passing comments about what was being discussed, was the car safe, and when could they make a call to anyone in the CRC. Valentine returned suddenly and ordered, "Come this way, please." They followed him down the hallway to the Mayor of Laurel, Carrol Gartin's Office. John had a foreboding that this would do no good, and he whispered the same to Emanuel.

Gartin sat back in his chair, tapping his pencil on his desk, responding, "Mmh – Unhumn!" to John's articulation of the day's events, that Hawkins was out to get him and that they needed protection. He looked at the Chief, who remained standing to his side, then back again at the two and said with a sneer, "I wouldn't believe you on a stack of bibles, Mr. Poole!" He looked at him with disgust and said, "I don't believe you were ever assaulted or threatened by Mr. Hawkins or anyone else in this fine town. Now, I know it would make a good story for your Communist publications, but I haven't seen anything but cordial treatment for you since this trial began."

Emanuel stood at his full height and said, "Then you'll believe me if I make that same charge, won't you?"

"Hell, no!" Gartin replied from his seat, "You, nor any of the minions of your Communist party! You can use the same road to get out of Laurel as you used when you entered our city." The vehement statement seemed to hold an ominous clue. He shouted towards their backs as they both turned to walk out the door, "You'd best be going now, that's a good idea! You and all your ilk!"

Hawkins had followed them and was waiting, the exhaust streaming alongside his running car. He pulled his car away from the curb just as they did.

"There's got to be someone else in this God-forsaken town who has some sense!" Emanuel exclaimed.

John sped around a truck, losing Hawkins temporarily." I'm trying the Courthouse!" he almost shouted as he swerved around the corner and down the street pulling up into the courthouse parking lot. Hawkins had been slowed up by the truck and laid on his horn before passing it and chasing after the car now in the distance. It gave John and Emanuel just the time they needed to run into the building and the Clerk's office. John started out, panting, "We need protection…an escort…to leave town." Emanuel began to explain the situation to the puzzled clerk, who wasn't sure what to make of it, while John whipped out his handkerchief to wipe his forehead. County Attorney, E. K. Collins, who stepped in during the explanation from his office, looked at the two and moved the blinds aside to look out the window and see Hawkins stretching his head out of the still-running car, looking back at him. He said to the men, "Stay here for a moment," and walked with squared shoulders down the hall and out the side door. All three men left in the office gathered to watch out the window as Collins sauntered out to Hawkins'car, leaned into his window and talked with him.

Hawkins threw his hand up in the air, the attorney nodded and talked some more. Hawkins finally backed his car up and screeched out of the lot. When Collins came in he said, "The coast is clear for now."

"We are much obliged to you," John said.

Emmanuel and John took back roads, circling the long way around Laurel back to Jackson. The ride was mostly silent after Emanuel had sounded off his opinions of Gartin. They pulled up to the Heidelberg hotel after dark, where Grossman was also lodged, and Emmanuel bid farewell to John for the evening.

"I'll tell Bella what happened," he said through the open window of the car after getting his briefcase out of the back.

"And I will call Judge Collins in the morning to see if we can argue this in Hattiesburg, or anywhere but Laurel," John agreed. "Watch out for yourself," he added, as he pulled off headed towards home.

CHAPTER THIRTY-SIX

AGITATOR'S ARRIVE

The next morning's call to the Judge gave John no sympathetic ear. "I can assure you of protection within my courtroom in Laurel. There will be no need to direct this to any other courthouse."

John set his jaw firmly and asked, "Will you also assure me of protection outside your courthouse in Laurel, Judge?"

The Judge repeated concisely, "You will have protection inside the walls of the courtroom, and that's the extent of the power I have to protect you." He added, "I will be in the courthouse until noon, if you decide to come, but this is a Saturday, and I'm not staying a minute past that." He hung up the phone, giving a loud "click" to John's ear.

"Son of a bitch!" John exclaimed, glad that no one was at home to hear him, other than Perry, who squawked disapproval. He lit a cigarette and drew in deeply with thought as he scanned the options in his mind. "Governor Wright! He's my last chance," he said aloud and grabbed the receiver again, dialing frantically and scaring Perry into jumping around his cage to land on his swing which took him backwards and forwards at a manic pace.

"Governor Wright's residence," a deep voice answered slowly. "Just a moment, please."

Although he doubted the Governor's actual support, John knew he would be pressured by the national attention he was sure to get, one way or another. John made his plea to the Governor, stating his experience with Emmanuel and his fear of returning to Laurel without protection. Governor Wright, whose mail had been inundated with continuing letters and telegrams, did, in fact, see this as an opportunity to state his position on the matter.

"Be at my office in half an hour, and I'll give you a hearing on the matter," he said, and turned to his secretary as he hung up to say, "Get the hearing room ready, and call for the Clarion Ledger photographer! We have a welcoming party to attend in thirty minutes." He took another drag of his cigar and smiled.

John threw on his coat after calling Bella and Emmanuel to tell them he would pick them up. He looked around for his pack of cigarettes and found them empty. As he angrily crushed the package, Perry squawked, somewhat coherently, "Son a bitch!" John moaned, "Oh, no," then laughed instead as he shook his head and walked out the door.

Bella had come in overnight and accompanied Emanuel to John's waiting car." We have ten minutes to get there," he rushed. They spoke briefly along the way. Bella adjusted her hat pin as she asked questions about what they might expect from a Dixiecrat Governor in the first place.

"I'm hoping that he will 'adjust' his stance, knowing that whatever he says may go public," John replied.

"I hope you're right," Emmanuel said and added, "He could be pivotal, but I'll wager he will instead use this as his platform to speak to all his constituents that are fighting for State's Rights."

Before the conversation was finished, they found themselves at the Governor's Mansion and hopped out of the car, at the same time a lady with a pad under her arm hopped out of hers.

"Well, Good mawnin," she offered, with a wide smile from shiny cheeks, and stared with interest at the large floppy hat that Bella wore.

Bella returned her greeting with a forced, "How do you do," and attempted to ignore the stare, wondering why everyone here looked as though they had oiled their faces in the morning.

They entered the Governor's Mansion and were escorted to a large office, where they found themselves in the midst of a gathering of people. The Governor was at a desk on a raised platform, with the large emblem of the State of Mississippi enshrouding his back. The Attorney General and his assistant, a photographer, and two stenographers, were joined by the smiling lady who had greeted them. The three petitioners were shown where to sit as there was chatter for a moment about strategic placement for photo coverage.

"Good day to you all," the Governor finally greeted them from his seated position. After a brief introduction of persons, during which the stenographers all were busily scribbling, the Governor said, "Now, if you please, state your purpose in this hearing." He waved his hand for them to stand.

John stood to lead the group, stating all that had happened the day before and asking that they simply have a protected escort to and from Laurel. Bella rose at the same time as Emanuel, but before his open mouth gave utterance, she explained that the defense had before in this case needed protection and was then refused. Her voice carried a challenge as she continued, "I'm sure the proud State of Mississippi would not want to refuse protection to its visitors, especially those visitors who are here on legal business."

Emanuel quickly added, "I did accompany Mr. Poole on the various trips he spoke of from yesterday and can assure you that the tone that we were met with was as he described. Mr. Hawkins was hostile and determined and was only persuaded to give us temporary leave. We have reason to believe that if we had taken the normal way out of Laurel, he and a score of men with him would have been waiting for us."

Governor Wright took a deep breath, stood, and as if giving a speech to multitudes started, "Let it be known that the proud State of Mississippi," he looked over at Bella with meaning in his eyes, "does, indeed, welcome visitors to enjoy its riches." He paused for dramatic effect and then began a litany on Mississippi's wealth of prolific foliage, distinguished residents, hospitality, and pleasant temperatures. "Except maybe in mid-July," he said with a chuckle. Bella made a strong effort not to roll her eyes.

"However," he said more seriously, "These gifts we have to share are for well-meaning visitors. Those who come with ill-intent to disparage our state and its peoples, and their way of conducting their own personal business, do not ask in good faith for our neighborliness." He stopped, addressing each of them in turn, "Miss Abzug, Mr. Bloch, and Mr. Poole, Mississippi will not harbor foreign policy makers, nor protect any Communist groups in their endeavors." He paused, then smiled as he said, "You just want me to furnish you protection so that you can say, 'Yes, even the governor, himself, recognized the danger!'" He rose his chin and declared, "We are not driving you out of our city as they did in Birmingham, nor are we charging you with a misdemeanor or placing a fine on you, but I'll be damned if anyone under my authority will offer you any protection!"

The stenographer looked up from her writing to offer a look of surprise at the Governor, then compassion towards the three staring petitioners. She saw the proud Miss Abzug turn on her heels, leaving the Governor to stare at her back, and then both men to follow in turn. She couldn't help but smile at her opportunity to witness the event, until the Governor looked at her sharply. She went quickly back to her scribbling of the last words, "I'll be damned...."

The three returned to the Hotel Heidelberg where they decided that John would send a telegram from there to Judge Collins, making him aware of the denial and requesting that the "matter be presented as though I was present, the Writ be deemed submitted and the Petition granted."

Brushing it aside with what he called a "lack of prosecution," Judge Collins dismissed the petition and believed Poole was making up the whole matter to make Laurel citizens look bad. The war of the media was on.

At the same time, while John was conferring with Bloch and Abzug on another written appeal to be filed with the Supreme Court on Monday, a petition was being filed in the building of the Mississippi State Bar Association. Carrol Gartin, Paul Swartzfager, Albert Easterling and E. K. Collins completed their petition to have John Poole, Attorney at Law be disbarred from the law profession in Mississippi for consorting with "subversive and Communistic elements."

The evening's paper printed the whole saga, with leads tossed to reporters to get into the stories by print time. The headline, "Writ of Coram Nobis Petition for Willie McGee Dismissed When Defense Fails to Appear" was situated just above "Disbarment of McGee's Lawyer Asked." The latter claimed, "The petition charges that Poole, by his own admission, is aligned and employed by subversive and communistic elements; that he is unscrupulous in his practice in that he has knowingly made false accusations against other attorneys and members of the Mississippi Bar Association; that he is guilty of subrogation of perjury and guilty of conduct unbecoming a member of the Mississippi State Bar Association." The actual petition, which was printed in its entirety, stated, "We further charge that the said John R. Poole has caused to be filed in the Circuit Court of the Second Judicial District of Jones County, Mississippi certain pleadings and petitions in court containing information that he knew or had reason to know was false and without reasonable foundation, and is therefore guilty of subrogation of perjury."

John had spent the night with Gerry at her parent's home. No one wanted to talk about the news, and no one felt like attending church the next day. While breakfast was being prepared, Dolphus turned on the radio to hear the church's broadcast sermon.

John sat out on the porch to smoke and watch Beverly play with the kittens. He was situated on a bench near the screened window, taking in the savory smells from the kitchen and listening to the gospel choir singing.

At the end of "Amazing Grace," the preacher urged, "Turn in your Bibles with me to Matthew 5:44-45 and follow along. He cleared his throat and began in a louder voice, "But I say unto you, Love your enemies, bless them that curse you, do good to them that hate you, and pray for them which despitefully use you, and persecute you; that ye may be the children of your Father which is in Heaven; for He maketh his sun to rise on the evil and on the good, and sendeth rain on the just and on the unjust."

As the preacher began his sermon, John's thoughts became more prominent. He felt he was right in what he was doing. That was the driving force that helped numb him to the hostility waged against him. He could appeal the disbarment, although it may be years before work in Jackson would be available. Maybe he could move with the family to his friend's house in Texas for a while after this whole thing was over. Another thought nagged him in the back of his mind. The rectifying of a culture's wrongs couldn't be coerced from the outside by antagonists, as Willie's false confession had been gained. It had to be done from the inside, by someone who loved the culture for its intrinsic good qualities. He held his head in his hand, continuing his contemplations, until Beverly brought a fuzzy kitten and dumped it in his lap. He laughed over its protest and small sharp claws bared in defense, and stroked it, making "ooh" sounds to Beverly who delightedly slapped his legs.

"Mr. Poole?" John looked up to see a young man who had quietly walked up to the house.

"Yes?" John instinctively put the kitten down and picked Beverly up.

The man smiled and said apologetically, "I'm very sorry to bother you on a Sunday morning, but your neighbors told me I could probably find you here." He stammered a bit before continuing, "I – I'm a reporter," he paused as if he were apologetic for saying it and decided to add, "a junior reporter, and I just wondered if you might say a few words about the disbarment petition filed against you."

Gerry opened the screened door to call everyone into breakfast, but stopped wide-eyed, on seeing the young man. He continued nervously, waving his hand at Gerry. "Don't worry, Mam, nobody else knows you're here, I don't believe." He shuffled his papers a bit before raising his pad to write and said with all the fortitude he could muster, "Mr. Poole, do you have a statement?"

John smiled at him and nodded, saying, "I'll give you a statement for your story." He gave Beverly to Gerry, adjusted his stance to his good leg and said thoughtfully, "The petition for disbarment filed against me and the alleged charges therein," He stopped to the scribbling reporter who motioned that he wasn't quite keeping up and repeated, "alleged charges therein."

They read the story the next morning that continued, ".... are unfounded and untrue. Its effect is to impair the fundamental duty of an attorney to represent a client, regardless of his station, creed, race or the popularity of his cause, without fear of reprisal. If I permitted myself to be intimidated, I would be dishonoring not only myself, but the entire bar of the State of Mississippi." The article went on to say that "Poole also said that if the Supreme Court refused to issue the writ of error Coram Nobis he seeks, he will seek action staying the execution in either the U. S. District Court here, or the U. S. Supreme Court. He said he will charge that McGee has been deprived of his constitutional rights to a fair and impartial hearing on the petition."

Another story in The Laurel Leader painted a more sinister picture. A County Court jurist countered the charge that Poole had been attacked with another story altogether. He claimed to have seen Hawkins pass by each other on the courthouse grounds.

"It appeared to him, the jurist said, that the husband failed to recognize the attorney, but that Poole threw up his hands in a protective gesture to pretend that he was about to be assaulted."

The same newspaper had in its Colored section a one-page ad, taken out by the "Southern Leadership Institute," President, Rev. W. H. Lewis. It was said in the front of the paper that the SLI was "A negro organization of good repute." In large bold letters was written,

"EMERGENCY CALL – DEFEAT OR BE DEFEATED – DRIVE THE AGITATORS OUT!"

"You cannot adjust by remote control those delicate and intricate problems that always rise when groups of different cultural, economic and racial identification and background are thrown into the concourse of daily relationship. The South must solve its problems for itself."

In a room of the Heidelberg, Grossman read the article over breakfast. "This is ludicrous! Even the oppressed here can't see that we are on their side." He continued, "Rosalee tells us that even the "Advocate," a local paper of the Negro community here, wrote that the CRC is not going to do any good for the case of Willie McGee, and it would be just as well if all the delegates planning to come to Mississippi would stay at home."

"They've been scared into submission for centuries," Emanuel said casually as he combed his hair in place, looking in the mirror. "You can't be too worried about their protests. They're just afraid it will be worse for them if the pot is stirred. They need education. That's the problem." He straightened his suit coat and tightened his tie as he turned to Grossman and said, "When we bring the appeal before the Supreme Court here this afternoon in front of Judge McGehee, we may have that chance to give them some education before the next trial."

Grossman look at him and shook his head, looking back at the paper, "I'll be surprised if you have any luck. He's a bigoted fool, just like they all are." After another bite he concluded, "You're going to have to take this battle outside of this backward thinking town, mark my words!"

"And you suppose you're going to have better luck in your hearing?" Emanuel asked, with one eyebrow raised.

Grossman looked up with concern in his voice, "Well, I did hear from Patterson that one of our contingencies decided to stay in the Gulf Coast because of the hype up here. Didn't feel safe." He wiped his mouth. "I'm wondering if we're going to have people dropping out before the time of the hearing. The more numbers, the more I believe Wright would take a real look at the issue. I know he has been inundated already with letters and telegrams, but he writes it off as radicals trying to take away their State's Rights."

"Are you concerned for yourself?" Emanuel asked, adding, "You have more women than men, it seems, and not a lot of the men are brawny. Intellectual types, mostly. Who's going to protect if things get rough? If the KKK decides to step in?"

Grossman waved his hand, "Ah – I'm not scared of these folks. They're mostly all talk and steam. I think their brains have been affected by too much heat and drinking from 'White Only' fountains!" He laughed at his own joke. "They still fancy themselves to be plantation owners – ignorant bunch! – even the officials," he finished with a note of disdain, pushing his plate from him.

Emanuel took a drink from his iced tea and grimaced. "They sure make it sweet down here," he noted, then added, "Too bad it doesn't affect their temperament."

"Squeeze the lemon," Grossman offered, from his own experience. "Anyway,"

Emanuel went on as he gave his lemon a squeeze, "keep up with the newscast. They've got a television in the lobby, and I'll be interested in the noon broadcast. I'm sure the locals will want to smear us the best they can, wherever they can. If they carry the national news, I also want to hear the update on the China attack on Formosa."

"Right, well, we're the Communist invasion here, haven't you heard?" Grossman picked out one of the papers in a stack on the desk and read, "The Jackson Daily News asks," He read in a mocking tone, 'Why the hell go to Korea to shoot Communists when the hunting is good on home grounds?" Grossman caught the sober look on Emmanuel's face, who was in no mood for joking about it, and so conceded. "All right, I'll watch what news I can, but after that I'll be meeting with a delegation from Virginia that's coming in," he reminded and looked at his watch. "Maybe we'll try the hotel's restaurant, for a lunch with the delegates. I hear it is known for the fine Southern cooking," He grinned while attempting a Southern accent.

Emanuel gathered papers for his briefcase and relied with a smile and raised brows, "Maybe you want to come back for a more relaxed vacation soon."

"Ha!" Grossman returned, as Bloch walked out the door, "Yeah – and some of that good ole Southern hospitality!

Grossman was right. Despite a thorough review by Poole, Bloch and Abzug of the failings of the trial process, and the contention and threat of mob violence they faced, McGehee and the other justices with him listened, but appeared unmoved. When it was suggested that the prosecutrix gave false testimony, the justices stirred with contempt at the audacious claim. Later, when Bella brought up the fact that no white man had ever been executed for rape in Mississippi and contended that McGee's conviction was due to racial prejudice, the tense uneasiness became tangible. She was much too bold a woman than they were accustomed to. The Prosecution attorneys presented a counter-affidavit and coolly denied that the Defense had any real evidence that they were under any threat, or that the proceedings did not offer them every opportunity to plead their case.

Refraining from using accusatory language, with reporters present, Deavours and Schwartzfager delivered their claims as if to make Poole look contentious and highly emotional, to the point of delusion. McGehee dryly announced that he would consider all that was said and announce his disposition the following morning by 11:00 a.m.

Reporters caught them for comments after the hearing." Mr. Poole, what will you do if Judge McGehee does not grant your appeal?" Cameras flashed, catching the stately Mr. Bloch and the picturesque Bella alongside.

"We plan to take our appeal either to the U. S. District Court or to the U. S. Supreme Court," he answered with brevity.

"You don't have much time!" the reporter laughed, then added quickly, "Mr. Bloch, Miss Abzug – We've heard that the Governor is not letting the Civil Rights Congress have their demonstration here today, what do you think of that"

"No comment," they both said in concert as they hurried to get in their cars, not wanting to give additional fodder to the media at this point in time. Bella was picked up by a group of women who were here for the delegation and craved an "hour or so" with her before their meeting that night. They left in a flurry of excitement.

"McGehee is planning to give us his answer just at the time Grossman will be going into the hearing with the Governor!" Emmanuel declared as they made their way out of the parking lot past a curious bunch of bystanders. "Tell me that's not a sinister pact!"

"If it's the decision I suspect, it will be to dash any hopes of success in the hearing," John admitted, but then added, "However, I believe Justice McGehee is a fair man. I think he will consider what we have said, despite the climate in town. I don't know how much he is going to let the Prosecution affect his decision, but the threat of Communistic influence may. By the way," he added in a lower voice, "I've been told by a tip from a relative that the Klan is making some underground moves. The heads are fighting for who is the top dog, and any show of 'protection from the Communists' will give rise to the victor. They're itching for some action. We need to warn Grossman of that."

Emmanuel shook his head and said, "I'm afraid it will only increase his acrimony. He is engendering a vile hatred for the traditions of this area."

John glanced soberly at Bloch as the car headed slowly down Capitol Street towards the hotel. His silence spoke of thoughts that dared not find expression, and he let out a deep sigh. From the window they saw a group of people gathered on the corner, talking earnestly with one another and dressed in their finest. A more plainly dressed mother and child stood some distance from them staring.

"Delegates," Emmanuel noted, "You can spot them a mile off around here." He then cocked his head towards John and asked, "Have you lived here all your life?"

"Yes, I have," he returned, and after a moment added, "and there are some very good people in Mississippi, some of the most gracious and deeply thoughtful people you'd ever want to meet." He added with a slight smile, "You may not have met them in this visit."

Emmanuel was thinking on his earlier statement, however, and said, "That's right, that writer, William Faulkner, is from around these parts, isn't he?"

John answered affirmatively and added, "There have been many great writers that have come from Mississippi. Many great thinkers, artists, musicians; Mississippi is rich with culture and genuine hospitality. There **is** another side to the South that isn't so apparent at the present time, I'm sorry to say." He pulled the car up in front of the hotel and stopped, finishing with, "To be clear, there are a lot of ingrained ideas here that I vehemently disagree with, and I'm not proud of, believe me! But there is a rich culture here that goes beyond this present racial issue." Emmanuel was listening intently, so he went on." Despite the climate against my work at present, I love Mississippi and her people, and I wouldn't want to live anywhere else." It was spoken genuinely, and he was glad to be able to express it.

Emmanuel nodded thoughtfully. He then put on his hat, gathered his things, and opened the car door, but before leaving he smiled, saying, "Thank you, John. I'm glad to have met a true Southern gentleman," and tipped his hat. He then turned to walk into the Heidelberg, pausing briefly for two wide-brimmed hatted ladies to walk in before him. A call was heard from down the street, "Filthy Commies, go home!"

CHAPTER THIRTY-SEVEN

DIE SILENT

"I'm going back there tonight," Mrs. Rosalee McGee said. A reporter from the Daily Worker busily jotted down the comments Rosalee made while cameras flashed. It was two days before Willie was scheduled to sit in Mississippi's portable electric chair and don the "cap of death" that two jailers had earlier suggested, smiling, that Rosalee put on herself, "to see what it felt like" when her cousin was on death row. Delegates from the Civil Rights Congress and Chairman Patterson listened with reverence to what sounded to them to be a declaration of sacrifice. Rosalee now wanted to go back to the dangerous waters in Laurel, Mississippi after having been "succored by the likes of Communists" in New York. The crowd stood and cheered her, and people lined up to give her encouraging words to take with her. The reporter was moved as he wrote his piece, seeing Rosalee McGee in a great line of other notable black personages who had suffered for the cause of freedom.

"Frederick Douglass, head battered and arm broken, picks himself up and carries on his Abolitionist work; Sojourner Truth, warned of a lynch mob comingto burn down the hall where she is speaking, replies calmly, 'If they burn down the building, I shall speak from its ashes.' ; Harriet Tubman returns to the South time and time again, and leads scores of slaves to liberty; Charles Caldwell, Mississippi State Senator, wounded, addresses a lynch mob in 1875 and tells them 'to watch how a man dies, without begging and with his mouth shut.' Peter Poyar lifts himself from a pool of blood in a Charleston jail in 1822 and tells a comrade weakening under torture, 'Die silent, as you shall see me do!' And to the day on July 25, 1950, when Rosalee McGee, warm, tender and beautiful, Rosalee McGee, says calmly, 'I'm going back there tonight,' as though she were going to a resort."

Rosalee wouldn't read the article until tomorrow but was now sitting next to Bessie on the bus, watching her stare out the window at the swiftly passing trees. They were both mostly silent, except when one or the other let out a deep sigh. Bessie's thoughts had drifted back to the time she had first visited Willie in jail, when the lawyers had told her that Willie had signed a confession to the crime.

"Willie," she had said, aghast, "Willie, why did you sign such a thing when you were innocent?" She had told one of the New York gatherings this story, and many heads wagged, just as hers had. Mothers, who had been with their children when they had gotten in trouble, who hated the day and cursed the bad act that brought it. Bessie recalled their faces when she had lowered her voice to relate what Willie had said in return, "Mother, I had to sign so that I would be living when you came. When I get to the trial, I will tell the truth." The crowd, wide-eyed and emotional, was encouraged with the tale, but at the next scene, became overcome with disgust. "He couldn't tell the story at the next trial," she had begun, then with emotion cracking her voice she finished, "he was so beat up or drugged, or both that he just mumbled like an idiot – like he was crazy!" Her voice rose with the emotion. "They did that to my boy because they would not stand for the fact that he might tell the truth – that he had been framed!" She was ashamed of that part. She wasn't ready to tell them about an affair, and besides, the Congress had advised that it not be brought out just yet. People would be more likely to support a cause of a totally innocent man than one who had his pleasure fulfilled in a white woman's bed.

Regardless, she had to fight the shame when she saw the crowds stand and applaud her, shouting encouragement and cheering their cause. She wasn't even sure what this 'Communism' was all about, anyway. She had just been glad somebody was helping her, but was now feeling nauseous thinking about it, or was it the bus ride? She adjusted herself in her chair and asked Rosalee for a stick of gum, which she always carried now to keep her breath fresh, with the spending money the Congress gave her.

"What we gonna do first when we get home, Momma?" Rosalee asked, mostly out of politeness. She knew what she was going to do. Make calls, get involved, check on the children. She would talk to Willie, somehow, too, although she secretly dreaded it.

"I'm gonna try to see my boy," she said simply. No other plans emerged. "We can ask the church to gather for a vigil," Rosalee offered. "Pray for those lawyers and for those judges. Mr. Patterson called and told the lady that's the head of that Woman's Commission that they're about to start another Civil War over this thing, because they're scared of Communism coming in and taking away their 'rights' as a State." She looked at Bessie, who was still staring out the window, and continued, "I heard that they were trying to get the church to ask Mr. and Mrs. Hawkins to come and talk with them there. If theys all talk together, maybe they could get them to see that they should do the right thing and at least tell the judge they don't know if it was Willie that came in that night."

Bessie looked at her, thinking she was crazed. Communists going to church?

Besides, Willie was there that night, he had said. What kind of "truth" were they going to come to together in a church with Communists and the Hawkins? She thought this but thought it better to remain silent. No use arguing with Rosalee. Sides, she was doing what she thought was best, maybe it would help.

"I don't know, Rosie, I jes don't know," was all she said, and looked out the window again.

Bessie started thinking again, trying to fix her mind around just what Communism was. She had been scared of it, too, when she was younger and sure didn't think it would ever have anything to do with any church. She hadn't really taken any time to ponder it so much in later years. Her father had told her tales of a heartless, big, government that didn't really care about the people, except just the power they could get over them. He had warned her not to be fooled by it, when it seemed she was much too young to care about such things and was much more interested in how to make a fellow's head turn your way. "They just wants you to follow a carrot, like a dumb mule," he said, "'till they gets you where they wants you, then BAM! They got you in their pen again – just like the white man always wants to do with black folk – just keep em fed and watered, so they can use em. Only the government wants everbody – white, black, red, – everbody!" She hadn't really understood, but she just wanted to ask her Dad what was she gonna do with this fix, only he was long gone now.

Rosalee was torn between being put off by Bessie's silence, and still trying to understand what this would be like for a mother. She and Willie hadn't really known each other for a long time, but she was fired up about the cause for all of her people, now. She kept her caring for Willie at arm's length. She didn't want the agony of being the other half of him, but consoled her conscience with the fact that she was doing all she could to fight for his chance at a real trial, and for the rights of so many other black people in the South. She liked this new stage of her life where she was able to see what the rest of the world was like. The women at the Commission had taken her in like she was one of their own, and even more, treated her like a celebrity, of sorts. She felt she could do her best work for her people with the help of these Communists. They couldn't be so bad, wanting black people to be on the same footing as white people. She was proud to be a part of the group, and she would make sure Willie would join the group with her, if he got out. If he got out. The thought brought chills to her spine and she shivered, despite the temperature. She folded her arms tightly to her chest and stared to the front of the bus as it was rolling to a stop. "Holly Springs," the driver announced. "We can take a break here. Colored restrooms are 'round back."

"We don't have far now, Momma," Rosalee said to Bessie as she patted her arm.

In Jackson, Dr. Tucker, the pastor of the First Presbyterian church, who had been approached by the "arrogant men and women of the Delegation of Communists," as the papers said, came to witness the "invasion" upon the Governor. He was interested to see the Rev. R. H. Harris, a negro minister of the Dallas Congress, who had said he would bring his delegation to join with "at least 1,000 others that would converge on Jackson from nearly every state in the union." He was further quoted as saying, "This is not just a fight for the life of one negro, but a fight for the lives of 15,000,000 negroes in the United States!" The Governor in return was reported to say, "We will not tolerate a wild-eyed, howling mob of Communists and sympathizers, gathered by the Civil Rights Congress to stage a demonstration in Mississippi," and he promised to "expose this gang at the proper time and prove they tried to mislead the people and create a false impression of the administration of justice in Mississippi."

Now was the day, and throngs of people gathered outside the Capitol Building to witness it, the day Communists had their time to talk with the Governor of Mississippi. There were mixed comments in the crowd – some fearful, some angry, most very curious. Serious discussions were fomenting stances where there really had been none. "States' Rights" was something many were being educated on. It wasn't just this trial, or the racial situation in general that was in jeopardy. The right of local people to set their own laws and standards was a stake – the 10th Amendment to the Constitution. The U. S. Supreme Court had turned the trial back to Mississippi, hadn't they? It concluded, in some minds that it had been seen that the judicial system had acted fairly.

"You must bear in mind that if the niggahs were in control here, it'd be a helluva time for the whites," one man was overheard saying. The woman behind him agreed, saying, "It would be no time before they would want every privilege a white person had."

"Our children would be forced to go to school with them!" another said.

One older man in the crowd said, but not very loudly, "If Communists have their way, it will be more than mixing with the Negroes that will cause our belly-aching."

A young boy was listening to it all and asked his mother, "Mom, what is a Communist?"

She laughed nervously, looking to see who had heard him as she avoided the task of defining it in the moment. "Well, now, that's a big question, and we'll talk about it at dinner tonight."

A taller man looked down at him and said, "All you need to know now is that we don't want them taking over our town!" He ruffled the boy's hair, who looked earnestly at him, still not satisfied.

"Here they come!" came the announcement, as a stream of well-dressed men and women poured through the crowd. People gave way as if they didn't want to be touched by the red river. It was a spectacle to behold, but a symbolic warning came through a messenger who was sent by the Governor to proclaim that only ten would be allowed in, or else the hearing would be canceled.

Grossman said, "We have been made aware of that. These ten have been selected to go in, and we request police protection."

A scattered group of policemen chose three to set their watch between the foreigners and the locals. One lady delegate whispered to another, as she glanced at the hardened eyes locked on them, "Remember, they've been told by the Jackson Daily News that it is open season for shooting the varmints." The other chided her with a sharp, "Hush!"

Once inside, Grossman and the petitioners were led to what they thought would be a private conference room. Instead, the doors opened to the Congressional Assembly Chambers. The huge, semi-circular hall's seats were packed with people, who were staunch State's Rights backers. Almost a third of them were Legionnaires, adorned with hats and medals ontheir coats. A sharp intake of breath was heard from one of the female delegates, as she saw several white ties on some who eyed them with warning as they took their places in the front of the assembly. This was all Aubrey Grossman needed to fortify his fighting spirit against this "backwards" crowd of people. He told the reporter from Chicago, a Mr. Ordower, to sit next to him and whispered intensely for to him to get "every word." A Correspondent for the "Compass," in New York, also sat nearby, nodding his head in affirmation. Bolstered with the knowledge that the nation would soon know all the details, and blocking out the present danger, Grossman approached the Governor.

Governor Wright gave an opening statement to say, almost apologetically, that he had granted this hearing for the duration of two hours. He wove into his introduction, "Justice McGeehee, who sits beside me, has just announced to me the disposition of his hearing from yesterday on the appeal of this case, State of Mississippi vs. Willie McGee, in which he gave audience to both Counsel for the Prosecution and Counsel for the Defense, and he does today tell me that disposition." He paused for effect to a deeply silent audience. "Justice McGeehee of the Supreme Court of the State of Mississippi denies the Writ of Error Coram Nobis," pronouncing the words slowly with a note of sarcasm, "and any appeal of the Willie McGee case." Comments rumbled through the crowd until the Governor spoke again, saying sharply, "Mr. Grossman, you may state your position."

"Governor Wright," he began, not able to actually stomach the words, 'Your Honor,' which was noted by all who knew the proper protocol, "I am Aubrey Grossman and these are delegates representing the thousands of members of the Civil Rights Congress and other human rights organizations. We are here today to ask for clemency for Mr. Willie McGee." A murmur was heard at the mention of "Mr. McGee." He kept his eyes forward as he continued, "Mr. Willie McGee, a man who has been condemned to die in just one day from now, and who we believe has not had the chance to have witnesses on his behalf, nor have his attorneys had ample time to prepare their defense, and so we believe Mr. McGee has not had the opportunity for a fair trial."

The Governor replied, "Yes, yes, I know why you have come. Why, just this morning, I got 1,215 telegrams and letters from the likes of you." He peered over his glasses to add, "One of them was in a foreign language – must've been Russian." He lifted his eyebrows with meaning to the congregation. He then leaned back and focused his eyes on Grossman again saying tersely, "You have two hours with which to present your testimony, and we have offered you this venue to express your side. Let's have it." He clasped his hands and rubbed them together with elbows on the desk, looking as if a vulture considering its prey.

Grossman began to elucidate the basic stance of the delegates gathered, "We believe that the rights of a person should not be prejudiced by his race, color or religion, and that this case set before us has been determined based upon a long-held system of prejudice against the Negro. It is well known that no white man in Mississippi has been charged with death for the crime of rape in many years. Please do not misunderstand our presence. We have not come with ill intent, but rather, to come to an understanding of the changing of times. I have many here who would like to offer their own insights into this, as well, and will give them the chance to express their perspectives as representative of many others who could not be here."

He then offered in turn the microphone to the other delegates. It was expressed that this was an appeal to the democratic process, and fairness between people interested in upholding the laws of the judicialsystem.

One man declared earnestly that "This is not a question of the North against the South. We've got to work together. We've got to have real democracy."

He was interrupted by Justice McGeeHee, who felt personally the jab of any mention of a fair judicial system and one lacking 'real democracy. ' "Just answer me this, what was the Nigra doing there at four in the morning?" Laughs and comments of approval came from the audience. It was evident that the man knew little more than the interpretation of the case from the "Daily Worker's" point of view and had not himself studied the facts.

Another man, wearing a Veteran of Foreign War's hat spoke next, saying, "Millions of people are watching what you do. We are fighting for democracy. It hurts us all over the world, what we're doing to the colored people."

Governor Wright lashed out, "You mean we should break the sovereign law of Mississippi, just because it would be bad propaganda in a lot of foreign countries?" The Legionnaires applauded and laughed, as the man sat in disgust.

Another speaker had only begun his protest before he was interrupted by McGeehee to question his knowledge of the actual facts of the case. It again became apparent that the delegates were not prepared for recreating the argument of the trial but had just planned to give a human rights appeal. Grossman angrily interrupted and said, "Let me make this clear. We feel positively, definitely, strongly! That Willie McGee is innocent, and an innocent man should not die. The evidence, excluding the confession which we believe was coerced, is meaningless. As time passes, facts will come out to show Willie McGee is innocent." The tenor of Grossman's speech said more than his words. He was already positioned for a brawl and his words became hostile as he continued, "This gathering is indicative of a 'fair hearing' in the State of Mississippi, where justice is shaped by your prejudices." He pointed and wagged his finger at McGeeHee. "Your 'Jim Crow' laws that segregate this population treat the Negro, cruelly, as if he is an animal! Your lynchings, and your 'legal lynchings' are abhorrent to the rest of the nation. As the crowd began to throw back shouts to his comments, Grossman became louder. "It's no accident that this case happened in the home state of Representative John Rankin, whose ideas are totally false!"

Governor Wright had held up his hand to McGeeHee to keep his peace, wanting the hearing to come to the pitch it did, but now hit the gavel for silence and snapped back, "I assumed that your group came in good faith to present reasons why I should stay the execution of Willie McGee. Instead, you have criticized everything, including the administration of justice in the State of Mississippi. I'm not going to have any more criticisms of our courts, of our customs. Stick to this case!"

Grossman, wiping the sweat from his brow, motioned for others to come to the microphone. Another veteran stepped up and began, "I will admit that I don't know all the facts of this case, but a new trial should be allowed in a court where there isn't a mob yelling outside!" He looked around at some of the Legionnaires and white ties and continued to speak about the intimidation that prevented those who would testify.

Sidney Ordower, stepped up to the microphone and made some brief comments and admitted, "I, too, have not actually read the entire transcript of this case, but just knowing the basics of the case," he shook his head and added, "any thinking person would understand that the evidence is inadequate." It was well noted by a nod of the head or a lifted chin by those in the audience that this was an indisputable slap to the face of the intelligence of the officials of the State, which should be revenged.

McGeeHee spoke up, asking him what he really knew about the "basics of the case." Did he know about the vine that had been bruised by a foot, the electrical wire that had been cut? Did he know anything about the position of the parked truck that several had witnessed to?

Ordower sputtered, "Everything – every so-called piece of evidence produced by the prosecution was very circumstantial. The confession itself was not voluntary." He hoped it would be sweeping enough to be correct in some sense. He burned inside, wishing he had read more about the evidence before coming to this meeting. He heard McGeeHee saying, "Don't you understand, Mr. Ordower, that it is a judge who decides whether or not a confession is free and voluntary after he is presented with testimony?"

Ordower felt the crowd's thoughts pressing in on him, but knew he answered according to his conscience. Just how moving his answer was, he wasn't sure. How could he express a hunch of an evil cover-up with no hard evidence himself? He went back to taking notes of the others.

Next, a modest looking woman, her hair parted down the center, was led to the microphone. She was a scientist, one who studied anthropology. If any had read her books, they may be appalled at her ideas concerning the "Races of Man." Acting as if she meant to merely present her scientific point of separate cultures not understanding one another, she slid in her prejudice that the customs and background of the South make it impossible to be rational when it came to a black man being with a white woman. "Your stresses and anxieties don't permit for objectivity," she said matter-of-factly in a smooth tone and continued, "Life is precious, as is the life of any man. Consider well what you do…I have come to cast a doubt in your mind."

Wright finally interrupted her, "Is it your opinion that there should be no death penalty for rape?"

She held back her opinion, but asked with straightened neck, "Do you know how many places in the world rape is punished by death?" She was hoping to offer her research of "backward" countries.

Wright, perceiving the implication, replied quickly, "No, I don't, but I'm not interested." He returned her cool stare and tone adding, "I'm interested only in Mississippi law."

"Has a white man ever been condemned to death for rape in Mississippi?" She asked, ready with the answer.

Wright conclusively cut it off saying, "I don't know, but it wouldn't make any difference to this case."

Another sweet-talking woman took the microphone to say in a high voice, "I am Mrs. Winifred Feise of New Orleans. I'm a mother and have two children. I want to speak to you as a woman, a Southern white woman." She looked straightly at the governor, "I want to talk about rape."

The atmosphere became tense as this innocent looking woman who boldly began talking about her consideration of what she would have done, had she been in Mrs. Hawkin's shoes. No one really wanted to hear it, but she went on to state openly, "Would I submit, as that woman says she did, with a child sleeping alongside her in the bed. Well, I might, at the point of a gun, but nobody says that Willie McGee had a gun." No one interrupted to tell another person who hadn't read the facts that he was supposed to have had a knife, threatening to slit her throat. She continued, blissfully ignorant of the thoughts of others, "If I submitted then, it would not be rape, I would have permitted it." Although women in the congregation were blushing, turning away from such talk and hiding their faces in their handkerchiefs, she continued undeterred, "Is it possible that I would discuss menstrual problems with a rapist? That woman says she did." The women slowly began to sink in their seats. "I speak frankly, as a woman. I cannot believe her story." As she continued to speak of the woman's point of view, to the amusement of the Governor and the others sitting near him, who winked to one another, she began to speak about Rosalee, and what she had said regarding Mrs. Hawkins, but the Governor wasn't going to let her go any further.

"If you are getting your information from this 'Rosalee,' I don't believe this is credible evidence to offer here. I have read the stories in your "Compass," newspaper and it sounds to me like a pack of lies by a so-called wife of McGee," he waved his hand in demonstration, "who just showed up, by the way, and generated by the Civil Rights Congress to prejudice the Nation against Mississippi's ruling." He straightened in his seat to declare, almost growling, "If it wasn't for the Civil Rights Congress this whole thing would have been over years ago."

Grossman stood up and shouted, pointing his finger again, "Yes! If it wasn't for the Civil Rights Congress, Mr. McGee would be dead!" He lost himself in his fervor, leaning forward threateningly. "McGee's trials here had mobs howling for his blood outside, how could that be a fair venue? And the judge," he stopped himself midstream to choose his words, "No judge, however honest, stands above the people. He carries his prejudice inside of him just like the rest of us!"

McGeeHee sat up straight in his seat, infuriated, "You mean to say he didn't get fair treatment? Why the boy has had three trials in over four years!"

Grossman attempted to control his temper, giving his best appeal to human rationale. "I am asking you, Governor, to issue a stay for Willie McGee." He paused and swallowed, continuing with his appeal, "I'm saying to you, Governor, unless you have some interest in putting McGee to death immediately, what human hurt can be done to delay it, so people throughout the world will never say you refused to grant a stay when McGee's attorneys assure you they have new evidence to present? I ask only for a stay so the evidence can be presented, and the issue proved."

However moving and logical his words were, Governor Wright had only heard the implication of "lyncher!" and wasn't about to soften. He couldn't risk continuing what may sway opinion even in the South. He stood and declared, "Our time is up. Meeting adjourned!" Wright quickly turned to walk out, his blood pressure at a pitch. Justice McGeeHee followed behind, more somberly. Realizing the room had been left to its own devices as to how to manage crowd conflict, no one was quick to react. Grossman looked around, assessing the situation and took the lead, gathering his flock, as if undefeated, to leave the room. Overheard comments as they passed were snarly. "Arguing and shaking fingers at the governor in public!" "Brazen women!" And more ominously, "They'll know soon enough what Mississippi Justice is like!"

They left with eyes burning on their backs. Once outside, rain began to trickle onto their fine clothing, as they marched towards the hotel. A car of detectives with smirked faces kept pace with them. "Just keep walking, "Aubrey encouraged. Small groups from the crowd of people followed them on either side. Hearts beat inside their chests as fast as the rain began to pelt their hats. On the street in front of the hotel a group of men were gathered. "Kill the bastards," one slurred, while another suggested, "I've got some rope!" The delegates rushed into their hotels, whispering to one another, "Where do we go?" "We're not safe here!"

Aubrey assured them that he would call and demand police protection, and that he would call Ted Thackrey, the publisher of the Compass in New York, to make him aware of the mood of the people and to send a telegram demanding protection, as well. Semi-assured and drenched delegates filed down the hallway to the safety of their closed doors.

Grossman smoothed his own ruffled feathers in the hotel room, feeling restless and unnerved. He dialed the rotary phone with the numbers he read from the "Emergency" section of the card in his room and asked for the Chief of Police.

"Yall ah connected now," the operator said in a Southern tone, which Grossman was tired of hearing at this point.

"This is the Chief," came the voice through the crackled connection.

Grossman said in a pressured tone, "I need protection for myself and the delegates who are staying here in Jackson. We have had threats to our lives, and I have women here who are panicky."

"Now, what are you all so afraid of," he drawled, "Nothing's going to happen to your group here if you don't call it on yourselves."

"Are you, or are you not, going to furnish us with protection?" Grossman demanded, panting.

"Well, let's just see if we need it, first," The Chief said tersely. "All you've told me so far is that you've heard some talk. This is going to blow over if you just plan on leaving town soon enough."

Grossman made his second call right away to Thackery, who promised to send the telegram that night. He sighed deeply after hanging up and ruffled his hair. The atmosphere of threat had been tangible after he had blurted his accusations – he realized it had been mostly his fault. His anger had stirred up more and had endangered the others. Still, the matter was unfinished, and he was going to see it through. He was glad to be alone with his thoughts to sort them through. He determined to further wage his battle by pen and would have to just have room service tonight and write down his recollections of the episode for the "Worker." He called for a menu and sat at the desk to write.

John and Emmanuel had just had their own meeting with denial in Biloxi, after a contested hearing with Judge Mize of the District Federal Court of Appeals. The prosecution team had countered their every move as in the previous hearing, and there was again a lack of hard evidence of the introduction of new witnesses or facts. They drove back to Jackson, discussing their final game plan after talking with Bella by phone, who was now in Washington preparing for the hearing with the U.S. Supreme Court to once again ask for a stay and new trial.

"I've not yet heard from Aubrey but received a call from one of the newsmen that the Governor denied clemency," she had said. "It doesn't sound pretty. Watch out for yourselves there," she warned. They determined that Emmanuel would stay in town for now with the delegation, while John took off again on a plane to Washington to assist Bella in the plea.

"I have a friend you can stay with, if at any time you feel you need more anonymity," John offered as he stopped the car to let him off at the Heidelberg, and jotted down the name and phone number on a pad. He tore it off and handed it to him as he said, "This hotel is not really the safest place right now."

"Thanks, you may be right," Bloch answered, sticking the note in his pocket, and wishing him a safe trip. Once home again, John made a call to Gerry and told her he wouldn't be back until the next day; that he had to fly into Washington for the final appeal. Yes, he still had some clean clothes. No, he wasn't scared of anything, really. Yes, he had the news about the hearing.

"I heard people talk, John," she said, holding the receiver to the phone as if it were his face. "They are so angry, and I think really, they're scared. They think we're going to be taken over by Communists, and the…" she stopped, choking on the words, "…the Klan, I think they're up to no good."

"Gerry, the Klan hasn't been active in years, other than burning a cross here or there. I'm not worried about them. You just keep yourself and my girls safe inside until I get back, you hear me?"

Gerry made an "Unhmm" noise in response, realizing that the first part of his sentence didn't agree with the last half. She could tell he was worried, too. She tried to remember how brave she had felt in the beginning of this whole mess, as she hung up the phone and whispered a prayer.

John peeked in at Perry to see how he was doing, and said, "Hang in there, buddy, they'll be back soon." Perry only twittered, sounding scared himself.

Back in the car, John waited with the car running outside another hotel for Sidney Ordower, who wanted to hitch a ride to the airport with him, as he was going back to Chicago. As Sidney with his suitcase in hand passed through a group of men standing just outside the hotel, he noticed that they turned to watch him get into the car. John asked as they slowly drove away, "What do you think about my calling a cab to get us to the airport?"

"I think that might be a good idea," Ordower breathed.

They stopped to call from a service station down the road, whose owner had always been friendly towards John, and promised to keep his car hidden in the garage until he got back.

Bloch, meanwhile, had met with some of the delegates who complained that they were too nervous to stay in the hotel and had called the number John had given him to see if they could find refuge. They traveled together and accepted with much thanks the kind invitation to dinner and a bed.

The cab driver had been talkative, asking where they were headed from the airport even though John and Sidney were trying to keep their quieted conversation to themselves. A crackle came through his speaker, diverting him to answer how far he was and when he would be available again. He replied in a lowered, inaudible tone.

John took the opportunity to tell Sidney about his previous visit to the airport and the hallway they could take when inside if they needed it. As they pulled into the airport, however, the hair on their necks rose up, seeing eight to ten men all dressed in white sports shirts.

"No, don't pull up here," John yelled to the driver, but it was too late. The door was thrown open, Sidney was pulled from the car and with punches forced to the ground.

John fled through the other door and around the car to attempt to stop it. "No, no!" he yelled, ducking a punch intended for himself. "No! Stop it," he cried, hearing lurching sounds fromevery punch. He boldly threw his body through the huddle, reaching for Sidney, and trying to wrench the men off. John felt someone grabbing him by the jacket to throw him sideways, nearly ripping it from his back, as he saw the kick to Sidney's side and his howl of pain. The noise alerted the guards on duty at the airport, who came running out, causing the white shirted men to scatter like wolves into the dark.

John called Aubrey after Sidney had been cared for inside the airport. Both men still planned to get on the flights, but Sidney managed to say between groans, as he held the ice pack to his side, that he would call the U. S. Attorney's office in Jackson to file charges. Aubrey agreed to follow up and would demand that federal action be taken and arrests be made. He hung up the phone and paced.

He couldn't concentrate, nor could he get to sleep until late into the night.

The sun was shining brightly through the window, before Aubrey rose and rubbed his eyes, shaking off the nights' anxieties. He had just showered, gotten into his clothes for the day, and was combing his hair when a knock came at the door. He looked at his watch, wondering who would be here at this time of the day. Lunch wasn't for another two hours. He opened the door with a shock to find Governor Wright, himself, along with the Chief of Police and the Chief of the Highway Patrol standing at the door, looking very serious.

Wright waved the telegram in his face arrogantly saying, "Just what is all this about? Why do you send for help from "up North" thinking you need protection in our fine State when we have been so cordial to you and your group?"

Grossman laughed and returned, "Well, It looks like I'm the most protected man in Jackson right now!"

Wright flared his nostrils and said through tight lips, "We are offering you and your fellow gang of Communists protection right now to leave and go back where you came from."

"I'm not ready to leave," Grossman returned with a set jaw. "I have legal business to attend to. I am staying until Willie McGee is given a stay or executed, and I demand protection while I do my job." He pointed his finger threateningly towards the Chief, causing the Chief to put his hand on his gun.

Wright lifted his brows and opened his hands, as if to absolve himself, "Well, then, I have to tell you, Mr. Grossman, you're on your own. Let's go, fellows" He turned and walked down the hall, adding, "We're not needed here." The Chief looked at Grossman and half-smiled ominously, as he tipped his hat and said, "Enjoy your stay," and turned with the other officer to follow the Governor's languid walk.

Grossman had seen this kind of antagonistic behavior before, but never from top officials. He shook his head and closed the door, then turned to his desk to add this to his writing, for what was sure to be a hot story. Room service did come with a brunch menu, and he ordered eggs and toast. He wrote, paced and stretched, and finally opened the door at the knock to receive his meal from a unusually nervous young black attendant. He tipped him with a bit of concern for his state, but let it go and went back to his writing, chewing bites of his breakfast in between. Another knock at the door puzzled him. He rose and walked slowly with heightened alert to the door to say, "Who's there?"

"Western Union," came the reply.

"Ah, Thacker, I'll bet," he thought, relaxed and opened the door, but reeled back as he was struck in the head with a black-jack. He threw a fist waywardly at the gang of men who attacked him. Black-jacks swung and pummeled him right and left. He covered his head with his arms and heard himself yelling for help as he felt a warm liquid flowing down his face. A surge of anger caused him to rise to the struggle, as the beating continued. The well-dressed leader with a white tie and suit stood watching both the attack and the hallway in silence. Grossman managed to catch one of the blackjacks in his grasp and tore it away from his assailant, starting to swing it himself.

The men backed up and froze as one of them whipped out a gun and aimed it at Grossman's stomach. "Hand it back," the man said with crazed eyes, "Real nicely now." Grossman, trembling, slowly stuck it outwards for him to grab. The eerie quiet was disturbed by a rumbling in the elevator and the familiar ding of the ascent to the floor.

The leader suddenly said darkly, "That's enough." They all turned quickly and disappeared down the hallway. Grossman slammed the door and shakily managed to bolt it in place. He then turned and swaggered towards the bathroom to wash his wounds. A call to the desk from a nearby room brought the hotel manager with an attendant to the door, but Grossman, still on the alert, had a standing lamp in his hand for a weapon and blood dripping from his wounds as the door was opened with a master key. The manager rushed in to steady him while the attendant called for an ambulance.

CHAPTER THIRTY-EIGHT

"RUN FOR IT WILLIE!"

B y the time John made it to the Supreme Court with Bella, emotion was on his side,
even though they would not hear about Grossman's encounter until later, they had
heard about an additional beating of a man named Steve Fisher, who was a reporter
for The Compass, also trying to leave town that day. The hearing came before Justice
Burton, who was acting in the absence of the court which was in recess for the summer.
He read the written arguments of both sides and asked for oral arguments to be given.
The Assistant Attorney General from Mississippi had also flown in for the hearing to
counter the Defense with his own argument. He was no match for John, who dramatically related his saga, pointing to the bruises on his head, telling of the two reporter's
merciless beatings, and of threats towards all involved throughout the case with emotional impact. He told of the inflammatory articles in the Jackson Daily News, which
stoked fears and prejudices to a pitch. He argued that the intimidation of the witnesses
for the Defense prevented a fair trial. In turn, Bella argued that there was, indeed,
new evidence that would prove the prosecution had purposefully lied. She startled the
Attorney General by proclaiming that they would prove that the prosecutrix had previous relations with McGee. This would start a heightened volatility of the case, but it was
the trump she had to play, or all was lost.

Justice Burton tapped his pen after scratching down notes on his pad. He could
not, in good conscience, turn his back on all of this and speak for the whole court in
this matter. There was certainly enough evidence to create doubt, yet he was well aware
of the political implications of the case and the ramifications of any adverse publicity.
He worded his decision carefully. The call to the Mississippi Supreme Court was made
at 1:05 p.m., close to the time Grossman was being attacked in the Heidelberg Hotel.

"No criticism of the courts of Mississippi is intended by the decision I am about to make," he began, "but the ends of justice shall best be served by granting a stay of execution until the request for a writ certiorari is disposed of by this court."

The Daily Worker reported that Abzug and Poole were literally "dancing down the hallway," leaving the courthouse, as word traveled to the Laurel jailkeeper to release Willie back to the Jackson jail. It wouldn't be easy. The Leader would later publish that Willie's "...removal from jail here was the first time that he has actually faced death from mob violence."

The Sheriff parted the office blinds with his fingers to get a better look at the crowds gathered outside near the entrance to the jail.

"Sheeit!" he exclaimed. He turned to the Deputy Sheriff standing in front of his desk. "If we're going to move Willie, there's going to be a lot of hotheads out there that might want to enforce their own justice. The Deputy went to the window to look.

"Well, I'll Swannee!" he declared.

The Sheriff turned back to him and said in a lower tone, "Better use the catwalk to get McGee out of here. I'll call for backup." He lifted his phone receiver as the Deputy stared at him, wide-eyed. "Well, get going, Royals!"

At least a hundred men and some women gathered in small groups, bitterly talking about the news they had heard earlier that morning that another stay of execution had been granted.

"Go to Washington," one man said, "and tell them you are a member of the Communist Party and they'll give you the dome to the Capitol!"

"That mealy-mouthed idiot at the Supreme Court couldn't stand the red-hot heat!" another yelled.

"You know they probably bribed that fellow! Those Communists will stoop to anything to push their power!" The voice escalated, "They want to take over government everywhere!"

Another man exclaimed, "You know, those Feds are probably part of it all! There's no tellin how many Reds are in high places!"

One woman said loudly to the crowd, "My son is going off to fight in the Korean War to fight against this blasted Communism! We first need to fight Communism right here in our own home territory!"

That riled several men, to hear a mother's plea for action. Threats of taking justice in their own hands were voiced. One man said in a low tone to the woman, "Don't worry, mam, we brought what we need to take our rights back." He motioned his head towards a truck, where another man was waiting, going through the equipment piled in the truck's bed. She pursed her lips and nodded her head once sharply in acknowledgment.

"Look!" One man's hushed voice projected into the crowd. Several turned to see the four suited men get out of the car and walk hurriedly towards the hotel across the street. Several other cars drove up and surrounded the area of the courthouse and jail. The crowd began to murmur their suspicions.

Another man said, "You know, that Deputy just walked while go from the City Hall to the jailhouse – did you see him?" One other thought he had, but the interest of the crowd remained on the cars.

"Well, now, I'd say that seems to be the Mississippi Bureau of Investigation!" said a plumpish man as he rolled his cigarette through his teeth. Several agreed and the anticipation mounted that they would soon witness the release of McGee.

Meanwhile, Deputy Sherriff Royals was rattling the key inside the lock of Willie's cell." Well, I guess you've heard the good news by now."

"Yessuh," Willie said and added grinning, "They've done saved the some of the negroes in Martinsville from the chair, too!"

The Deputy frowned at the inference to the CRC's work but went back to the present task. "Well, now, yo're not safe yet. Let's see if we can get you to the Jackson jail in one piece. These fellows outside may just decide to forget what they heard this mawnin and see to it themselves." He released the barred door and looked again at Willie as he reached for the handcuffs. "You know, there's maybe about a hundred men out there on that lawn, up to no good."

Willie knew what he meant, although he had not used the word, "lynch," and began to sweat. The all-too familiar threat of death grabbed his stomach with nausea and caused his eyes to bulge. He allowed himself to be cuffed and followed the officer down the hall to the catwalk.

"Good luck, Willie!" came a call from one of the cells.

Royals stopped just before the long window over the catwalk, peered out at the crowds and turned back to McGee, saying in a hushed voice. "You're going to have to crawl with those cuffs, Willie. Think you can do it?" Willie nodded, dropped on his knees, and began to inch down the length of the window, making sure his backside didn't pop up too high as he grunted forward. The deputy crawling alongside him found he felt a strange bond with this man in his exigency and wondered at the feelings of compassion as he saw blood beginning to drip from Willie's hands. "Wait," he whispered, and struggled to take the keys out of his pocket to free the cramped red wrists. Willie took in the act of kindness, breathing hope back into his heart. They scrambled down the hall, still bent after the long crawl, quickly ran through the court where Willie had been condemned, and then down the marble stairs of the courthouse, past the wondering eyes of office staff. The deputy stopped suddenly and turned back around to cuff McGee, disregarding the expressions in the room. He then took him firmly by the arm, to lead him towards the outer framework of the doors, where he could look out the window from a hidden vantage point. He wiped his forehead as he declared, "We didn't fool them all!" He looked at Willie with urgency and said, "Are you ready, Willie?" All Willie could find within himself to do was nod his head vigorously. "Run for it, Willie!" He yelled as they both bolted out the door, heading for the parked car that was already running and waiting for them. The blow to Willie's head and the screamed threats caused him to momentarily stagger, but when he heard a shrill whistle that alerted the larger crowd to move to action, a force within himself steadied and propelled him on down the concrete path. Fists intended to knock McGee to the ground met with empty air as Royals and his prisoner flew into the opened automobile doors, guarded by armed police. The crowd was held back, with only their thrown protests for satisfaction as the car sped away towards Jackson.

Gerry read the report of the incident over the phone to John. "It says that 'If the blow had knocked the negro to the sidewalk, it appears almost certain that he would have died by lynching. Half an hour after the incident the crowd had thinned, but at nightfall was again gathering." She stopped to make a high-pitched groan.

"Go on, honey," John urged.

She gathered herself and continued, "Anger had mounted among the night throngs. Again, the Communist Party and the Civil Rights Congress were blasted.

There was talk, too, of a lynching party that would go to Jackson to get McGee. Soon the lawn of the courthouse was overrun, and it was necessary that the crowd gather in the courtroom. The story of that gathering is told in other columns of today's issue of the Leader-call."

She left from the reading to say, "John, the Governor is calling for meetings of people to stand against the Communists. Another article here says that there were 800 people at that meeting with the Governor and other top officials. They're calling for more meetings, too – weekly ones – and are calling themselves, 'The League of Citizens.'" She stopped, thinking of how to express her angst, "It-It's like a war is going on right here in Mississippi!" She paused for a moment to the silence on the other end of the line then said in a more hushed voice, "I'm scared for you to travel back right now."

John ignored the comment but asked, "Were there reports on Grossman's beating, and the others?" He had already heard of the attack from a phone call Bella received after the hearing.

Gerry shook the paper to look again and said, "Yes, but they are saying that the incidents were provoked by the propaganda effect. They think it was exaggerated and say that they have no way of finding out who did it, because nobody got a good enough look at them."

"I got a good look at the men who beat Ordower!" John claimed pointedly, "And I am going to press charges when I come back! What did they say about the hearing before the Governor?"

"Well, it does have just a snippet here about Mr. Grossman," she said, and began to read again. "Grossman, at Tuesday's clemency hearing, insulted every tradition of the South, every court, every judge and every officer of the State of Mississippi. He did it deliberately, provokingly."

"Does it relate any of his comments?" John said at the pause.

"Well, just about his attack, not about the hearing," Gerry said as she perused the rest of the article, then commented with a note of excitement, "It says here that there was a 400-person demonstration for McGee in Times Square in New York! Did you hear about that?"

John frowned, remembering that the affair was centered mostly around the fictional story of McGee's "wife." "Yeah, I heard," he said simply, then continued quickly, "I'm going to be coming home tonight, regardless. The longer I wait, the more time they have to think about cornering me again. Besides, I'm ready to rest from this whole thing. I want to put my arms around you and hold my baby girls again!"

Gerry gazed at the toys on the floor she had not yet put away after putting the babies to bed and sighed. "Well, we miss you, too," she conceded, but added, "Just be safe, honey, I was so scared when we heard of all this."

He assured her he would take all precautions, and with loving goodbyes and a laugh as they heard a squawked, "Goodbye, honey." coming from the background.

John placed the receiver back on its hook, lit a cigarette and poured a drink from a bottle he had bought to celebrate with, although he didn't feel much like celebrating anymore. He took off his shirt and lay back on the soft pillows of his hotel room, picking up the evening edition of the "Daily Worker" that lay nearby to reread the articles.

"John R. Poole, Willie McGee's lawyer, will fly back to Jackson, Mississippi to face disbarment and perhaps heightened mob violence for helping to save McGee's life." It quoted Bella, saying, "the attacks again Poole represent a denial of elementary justice because they sought to prevent vigorous defense of an accused man's cause. The persecution of a lawyer for acting with great courage in furtherance of the best traditions of the bar is a matter of concern to the whole bar and country. An increasing number of lawyers face disbarment proceedings because of the clients they represent with courage and vigor, or because of their own views. Such violence, threats and attempts at intimidation degrade the administration of justice for the strike at the essentials of a fair trial, the independence of the bar, and its right and duty to provide a vigorous advocacy of a client's cause." She maintained, "When it takes a hero to represent an accused Negro, the right to counsel is nearly destroyed. The McGee case is not untypical of such cases."

He lay the paper down, taking another drink to wash away the edge of uncertainty. Although he had felt jubilant earlier in the day over their victory and had just been called a hero by the woman who had earlier considered him incapable, he couldn't settle the nagging feeling he had inside, and rose to sit again on the edge of the bed, not ready yet to loose his stump from its yoke. So far in this case he had been focused on the release of an unjust condemnation of a man. He abhorred the racial prejudices of the South but was disturbed by what could be a sweeping condemnation of the South itself, or of State's rights to rule itself, as abhorrent as it was to him in this particular situation. He contemplated as he encircled himself with smoke, that the freedoms that had been given to individuals and to States were given specifically to protect from a dictatorship, regardless of any misuse of those freedoms. The progressive ideals he had once vigorously backed were now contaminated with the smiling demon of Communism, and he had found himself in its approving embrace. How did the two get mixed? How was it that he had joined himself to what he had before seen as the greater evil? He stood, and would have paced, but the late hour had caused his leg to have spent its endurance. He flinched, sat back down again, and picked up the phone to make another call.

"Hullo?" Al answered drowsily.

"You've been at it again, I can tell!" John joked.

"Heey, buddy! Hey, congratulations on that stay – heard it was rough for you on the way up!" Al woke a bit into sobriety, rubbed his eyes and said, "How are you?"

"Oh, they were out to get that reporter more than me. I just got a little of the backlash" John answered, dismissively, then quickly went on, "Say, I wanted to know what happened at that meeting with the Governor. What was said that got everybody so riled up against Grossman?"

"Yeah, he did get it the worst. I've heard it was the Klan. They're behind all the rough-housing, but they probably got the nod from Wright. Who knows if he wasn't one of them before he was elected? Did you hear he's organizing groups to…"

John interrupted, "Gerry told me about that, but do you know what Grossman said?"

Al rubbed his head, thinking, "Well, let's see, I heard he bashed McGeehee pretty good."

"What did he say?" John had respect for the Supreme Justice who he felt had been very fair and impartial in some of the cases he had the opportunity to hear or try himself in his court, even with Negro clients.

"Oh, he said he was so prejudiced that he couldn't render an impartial judicial opinion. Called him backward, too, and ignorant, I believe." Al clicked his fingers with memory and said, "Yes, and then he also berated the people of the South in general and their traditions that blind them and keep them from progressive thinking." He waved his hand dramatically for no one.

"Unhuh, progressive thinking," John responded. He was beginning to think that his own progressive thinking had been a blinding factor for himself. "Anything else?" "Well," Al picked up his glasses and put them on, "the paper doesn't say specifically, but from what I heard from other folks, Mr. Grossman might have well as spit in their faces, and didn't give a flip about procedure."

"And can you blame him?" John asked.

Al sat down and sighed, "No, no, I really can't." He paused briefly, then continued, "Look, I fully agree that there is a segment of bull-headed, and yes, ignorant people who are very stuck on white supremacy, but that's not everything that is at stake here."

"What do you think is at stake?" John asked.

"Well, you may know the real reasons I dropped out," Al paused for a response, feeling a bit vulnerable, but the alcohol had loosened his inhibitions.

"Go on," John encouraged.

Al searched for a moment for the words, then said, "The Jewish man and the black man share common ground – they both experience persecution most everywhere. It makes them prime bait for a flag of freedom to be waved over their heads like a carrot, but it's a false flag, I've learned. We can easily become pawns to be sacrificed for a greater power. No matter which way this case goes at this point, the Civil Rights Congress wins because of the national stir, and you know by now they are a front group for the Communist Party." He paused for recognition from John who just breathed deeply into the phone. Al continued, "If McGee fries, they have more fuel for their own fire. If he is freed, which he won't be after all this show, or the South would be ready for another Civil War, he would be a poster boy for the "benefits of the Communist party." Al let himself run with the thought, waving his glass in the air to no one, "Come, all you persecuted people, and Daddy Government will wipe away all your tears. Of course, we will own you then, but don't let that trouble you any, now." He took another drink, satisfied with his own exposition.

"They're also using this Rosalee, posing with her children as McGee's family," John added. "I don't like the fact that they are garnering support based on lies."

"But she's happy she's getting some bills paid, and food on the table. By the way, are you getting any bills paid?" Al asked pointedly.

"Bella told me a payment would be coming when they get the delegates' donations this month," he answered, feigning assuredness.

"Unhuh, those delegates who just spent all their money on traveling to Mississippi and Washington? You might be waiting awhile." Al paused thoughtfully and added, "I can send a case your way next month, I think." He paused, thinking of the probability that John would be disbarred, but without any consoling words coming to mind he remained silent.

John took a deep breath and answered, guessing his thoughts, "I guess I have some time to fight these disbarment proceedings before selling encyclopedias." It was meant to be a joke, but neither of them laughed. He shot down his drink and said, "Thanks, Al. I'll be back in the office next week."

"Okay, champ," Al said, trying to sound encouraging, "Have a safe trip, now."

John placed the receiver back on its hook and looked at it, as if he were looking at his loved ones from afar, then settled back again, this time pulling off his wooden leg, standing it beside the bed and covering himself with the blanket. He adjusted the pillow turned off the bedside lamp. This decision would be best to sleep on, he thought, and did finally drift off into a merciful and sound sleep.

CHAPTER THIRTY-NINE

A DEAD DRAW

Sullen's crass opinion regarding the events of the day before blasted the headlines with:

"THEY DESERVED IT – AND MORE"

The article that followed gave no apologies for his thoughts or any actions taken.

"The people of Mississippi have no regrets to express over the physical beatings administered to Aubrey Grossman, organizational secretary of the Civil Rights Congress, Sidney Ordower, who described himself as a radio commentator and Progressive candidate for United States Senator, and Steve Fischer, reporter for The Compass, a Communistic publication, who came to Jackson Tuesday to make pleas in behalf of Willie McGee, thrice-condemned rapist.

The only regret to be expressed is that they were not more roughly handled.

They were given a mighty small portion of what they richly deserved.

In their harangues before Gov. Wright, Grossman and Ordower insulted every tradition dear to Southern people, made slanderous charges against our court officials for which they did not have one word of proof, and conducted themselves like a pair of wild-eyed radicals who have no respect for the land they desecrate by living therein.

As for Fischer, the character of the story he writes for the newspaper he represents will fully reveal what sort of critter he is.

By their coming to Jackson, flouting disrespect for our laws and our courts, these men invited trouble, and it is just too damned bad that they didn't get larger doses of what they asked for."

Sullens may have seemed like a mad man to some, but he was, in fact, voicing the opinions of others who had gathered at the mass meeting the previous night. There had been several speeches given by businessmen and city officials who wanted to pass an ordinance that would mandate fines and or jail time for a known Communist to come into their borders.

"If Birmingham has the gall to do it, why don't we?" one said.

"If we don't do it now, it will be as good as offering them safe haven in Mississippi!" shouted another, adding, "Our children will grow up listening to their ideas and accepting them as rational! We know where these thoughts come from – we know what it will lead to!"

The Mayor acknowledged his approval of the ordinance but was so disturbed by the day's events that he didn't feel like speaking. He did, however, say that he would communicate with the Federal Bureau of Investigation to secure a speaker for another meeting, and added in response to Burton's ruling that, "They ought to let Stalin and his gang come over here for six months and let those goddamn Communists go over there for six months!

He turned to a news reporter to add, "And that's for publication, too!" The County Prosecutor, E. K. Collins spoke and said, "This is more than just the trial of Willie McGee. The Communists put pressure on the State Department. Write to your congressmen and to your senators to stand up for your State's Rights!"

Judge Collins was not at the meeting but had a prepared statement that said that he had not, himself, ordered the rapist to be removed from the Laurel jail and wrote in part that "...it is time for the people and the public officials of Mississippi and this area to gird themselves with sufficient courage to fight against communism and uphold the state's courts!"

"Mercy!" said Gerry's mother, Cecil, as she folded clothes and listened to her daughter read once again from the papers." Isn't there a Christian among them? This _is_ about one man's life and his guilt or innocence – not politics!"

John twirled the ice in his glass of tea, lazily recuperating from the trip and listening to Gerry speaking with candor, "John was fighting for that man's rights to a fair trial – he wasn't in it for the politics!"

"I know, dear, but it has certainly turned into a political matter." She turned to John and asked, "Do you agree with the politics of that...that Congress?" She waved her hand instead of searching for the words to properly address the group.

John took a long drink of tea, leaned back and stretched his legs out, clasping his hands over his belly.

Cecil said with some exasperation, "Well, do you?"

Dolphus, Gerry's father was sitting in a nearby chair, having already expressed his opinions more confidentially to John.

John took a deep breath and looked Cecil in the eyes to say, "I've decided to drop out of the case."

Gerry started at that, saying, "You're dropping out?" She searched for the words to say and sputtered, "after all we have been through to support this cause?"

"It's not our cause that's at the forefront right now, honey," he said, gently. "Your mother is right. It's turned political, and Willie's life is just a symbol on a flag for the dastardly battle of political will." Dolphus looked at him, giving him encouragement with a nod of his head. John continued, speaking slowly and deliberately, "I will not be a part of this masquerade they are carrying on nationwide, nor will I stand behind anyone who berates the whole of the State of Mississippi. This issue is a serious one, but it should not be the only perspective of the nation for our home state and all the people we care for. I've done my part to try and save McGee's life, but I am not in favor of a Communistic takeover, and this case will not be given any other chance in the future if that is the issue." He paused and looked down as he admitted, almost as to himself, "My staying in will not help McGee at this point."

He reworded his statement to the same reporter who had come to his door before and was now called back to report to the paper John's stance.

"In view of the circumstances that have arisen in the Willie McGee case in the past few weeks, I feel compelled to withdraw from the defense and to give a statement of my position in the matter.

This action is not taken because of a fear of reprisal, but because of my objection to the activities of the Civil Rights Congress, which is sponsoring the defense. During the first part of this year, I made a contract to represent McGee in what further proceedings that I considered necessary to give him the full benefit of all the law of the land. At that time, I did not know that the Civil Rights Congress would come to Jackson and stage the demonstration which they did. I was employed to represent McGee – not the Civil Rights Congress – and when this group did come to Mississippi, I found myself under a duty to fulfill my contract, even at the expense of jeopardizing my own name and reputation. I am not a member of the Civil Rights Congress, and I am not associated with it in any manner whatsoever. As a matter of fact, I strongly object to the actions of the members when they were in Jackson. I am informed that one of its members insulted the Chief Justice of our Supreme Court, Harvey McGehee, and accused him of being so prejudiced against members of the Negro race that he could not render an impartial judicial opinion. Such a statement is completely unfounded and untrue.

Our Supreme Court has simply demonstrated its desire to render justice regardless of a man's race, creed, or the popularity of his case. I am further informed that insulting remarks were made to our Governor and to the State of Mississippi in general, all of which were untrue. Certain other actions of members of the Civil Rights Congress indicate that they did not come to Jackson in good faith.

So, having completed my contract to represent McGee, and having considered the nature of the organization which is sponsoring his defense, I hereby announce that I have withdrawn from the case, and that I shall hereafter have no more to do with it."

The only part John felt contradicted over was including the Governor. He actually despised most of what the Governor stood for, but the office of the Governor he was willing to include with due respect.

"If he thinks that will save him, he's dead wrong!" Collins laughed, sitting at a table in a private conference room with Easterling, Swartzfager and Deavours.

"We have twelve attorneys that are willing to sign the petition for his disbarment," Deavours said, "they were literally knocking on my door to be a part of it!"

"He's dead in the water already, and damned well deserves to be!" Collins said, then laughed again saying in a mocking voice, "having considered the nature of the organization that is sponsoring the defense! Now, it took him just a little while to consider that nature, didn't it?"

"Maybe he needs to go back to high school and learn a little more about Stalin and Hitler!" Deavours laughed sardonically.

Easterling, who was the most inflamed over the Attorney General's report as to what he viewed as insults against Mississippi's judicial system that Poole and Abzug had themselves used to persuade the Federal Justice, said, "That statement is so full of holes, it will not even hold shucks! He knew damned well who he was dealing with. I'm going to make my own statement for the paper that says so! He charged us with perjury by saying what he did in Washington, and he has no damned proof one way or the other! Why, he had that goddamned Red lawyer with him the whole time he was in Laurel the second time. He didn't owe him anything in the way of a contract when he saw how Laurel's people were being harassed! No, I tell you, I'm going to see to it that this son of a bitch doesn't ever see a day in a courtroom again! If there was reason to disbar him before, even more so now because of these damned lies in his statement!"

Others at the table humored Easterling with Mmhuh's and chuckles, but he was so long-winded, no one really wanted to encourage him to go on.

The mood was antagonistic, but Swartzfager wasn't feeling it. After a few more caustic remarks were made over the morning's news, he interjected, "And so now we only have the attorneys from the Civil Rights Congress and over half the nation against us." The laughter dried up as they stared at him. He continued, "Poole was just their puppet. Our revenge on him makes no difference when it comes to the trying of this case."

Collins leaned forward and said between his teeth, "There will be no more trying of this case with those damned Communists." He wagged his finger and added, "Mark my words. We will have our execution by this time next year." He took a puff of his cigar and finished with, "At the latest."

Swartzfager battled in his mind for words to express what he was contradicted over. Recent gossip had spread concerning the affair, and he knew that the CRC planned to bring it up this time. He wanted the chance to prove it wasn't true – that McGee was indeed a vile thug. He felt unsettled with it and would have gladly entertained a chance in court to argue it – not with foreigners, but with another Mississippi attorney, even Poole – if he hadn't been stuck to the hip of those Communists. He shook his head, revealing his unsettled feelings. All he could offer at present to his cohorts was, "I hope you're right." He raised himself out of his chair and repeating it for emphasis before excusing himself.

Collins stopped him." You'll be at our Wednesday night meeting, won't you?

The crowd will want you to say a few words about your experience with what Communists are now trying to move this case along with – the affair, you know."

Swartzfager met his questioning eyes just long enough to say, "Sure, sure, a few words," and turned to walk out the door. He heard laughter start up again as he closed it behind him.

Schwartzfager did only have a few words of knowledge about the story of the affair, and really didn't have a clue as to what was going on behind the backdrop of the CRC. Abzug had heard the story of the affair from Rosalee this time, although she knew that Willie had not been married to her at the time.

Regardless, Rosalee told the story as if she had been Eliza and knew firsthand of what had happened to Willie during that time. In her telling of the tale, to which she signed a sworn affidavit, she related that Willie and Mr. Hawkins met when they were both working at the Masonite plant in Laurel. Hawkins talked to Willie about doing some yardwork for him and so he became a regular at the Hawkins' household. The affair started, she said, when Willette had a particular odd job for him. Once, Rosalee related, Willette even came to McGee's home while Willie was away and asked Rosalee to convey a message to him, that she wanted another chore done. When Willie heard it, he admitted to Rosalee that a chore was not what she wanted, and he told her everything that had happened to him. He had been afraid to say no, because she had told him she would say he had raped her if she ever got angry at him, and he must do as she wished. He claimed that he was more afraid she might just do it, because she was always "wired up" like she had emotional problems of some sort. Rosalee claimed that Willie went away to the army to try and break the hold Willette had on him, but it started up again when he came home. She said that Willie had even gone away to California to get away from it, but became homesick for his wife and children, who he couldn't afford to move out there with him, and so came back again. The affair picked up where it left off when Mrs. Hawkins found out he was back in town again. Rosalee thought that the night Willette had run out in the street half-naked, it was her own husband, Troy, who she was afraid of, because he had woken up and discovered what was going on. To keep her hide, and her place in society, she had claimed she had been raped. The sworn statement could be used as the reason Abzug needed a new trial. She presented her appeal to the U. S. Supreme Court on November 22, 1950, to reverse the refusal of the writ of error coram nobis, previously blocking the presenting of new evidence in the trial. She didn't yet present the affidavit, however, wanting to tidy up the facts a bit before exposing it in trial proceedings. It may have been the fatal mistake. Although discussions amongst the Justices were mixed, the claim that McGee and Hawkins had previously known each other through work and McGee's hired help should have been easy to prove. Why hadn't it been brought out before? Regardless, there was some support for having a full hearing. It turned out to be not enough support, however, as The Supreme Court denied the appeal on the 26th of March.

"Oh, Lord above, what does this mean?" Bessie was wailing after she read the news. She turned to Rosalee and asked in a pleading voice, as if she could tell her it wasn't true, "This isn't the end of Willie's hope, is it? Missus Abzug said she would try everything! She told us don't worry none cause of Mr. Poole's droppin' out, that she'd be able to take care of it all!"

Rosalee's lips didn't know how to form the right words, although she tried, she could only say, "I-I don't know, Momma, I just don't know!" They stared at each other for a moment before they both started crying. After a few moments, Rosalee couldn't stand it anymore, besides, the children were just outside playing, and she knew her boy could hear the crying. He didn't need to know just yet.

"Momma, quiet, now, listen to me," she started, patting her on the back, although she wasn't quite sure what she was going to say. Bessie wanted to hear any hope, and did quiet herself with big breaths in. "Now, you listen to me," Rosalee repeated, stalling for inspiration, then said, "I'm going to write up everything I've said in that affidavit I put my signature on. Miss Abzug didn't even use that yet." She did become inspired as she was talking and became convincingly fluent. "I can go back up North and make flyers and pass them out to all sorts of folks – You know that Governor Wright got thousands of letters and telegrams from people all over the place? They not going to let this thing drop!

We'll just make sure this whole nation presses on the State of Mississippi and force them to pop Willie right out of that jailhouse!" The picture she painted made both of them laugh with some relief, but it was dampened by the tear she had to wipe away that was rolling down her cheek. Bessie shoved aside her doubts and sighed to cover her raw heart with hope.

"You think it could be taken from the courts 'cause all the people want it?" she asked, sounding like a child asking her mother.

"Why, I'm sure it's been done before. Sides, these are new times! America is waking up to her colored children's voices. No telling what could happen. The stay of execution for them boys in Martinsville happened when nobody thought they had a chance, didn't it?"

Bessie nodded, thoughtfully. Then she lifted herself wearily from the table and began to walk to the living room." Momma, where are you going?" Rosalee asked, wonderingly.

"Going call Miss Abzug, rite now," she replied.

The trip to New York was planned, and Rosalee did write her testimony and delivered speeches to several audiences who were enthusiastic for the cause.

Rosalee wasn't the only one working hard. Members of the Civil Rights Congress and others wrote their own pieces and exhorted crowds to "Save Willie McGee!" A pamphlet written by a reporter for the Daily worker summarized the story for readers, quoting Rosalee as saying, "I told the children, the three girls, Della, Gracie and Mary and my little boy, Willie Earl, that I was coming up here so I could bring their father back to them. I just got to get Willie free. He never raped that white woman. I will go wherever I have to go. I will travel as far as I have to travel. Nothing will stop me. I am going to appeal everywhere for my husband, who has already suffered four deaths."

The writer even quoted Willie's daughter, Della as saying, "We need daddy.

He has been gone so long. Since my momma has been gone, people tell me my daddy will die in the hot seat. That's what the man told me at the store…Don't let him die!" It was a touching appeal. The fact that Willie's daughter Della was long gone to California with her mother, Eliza, didn't make a difference to anyone here.

The writing ended with an urgent appeal to set up committees, to write to President Truman to intervene under provisions of the Federal Civil Rights Act, and to call on their public officials to communicate with the President and with Governor Wright on behalf of McGee.

Although letters and telegrams again flooded Governor Wright's office, he refused to be moved, considering them all Red-bait propaganda.

Willie did his own fighting back, signing an affidavit that gave the account of the affair in explicit details, excluding the scheme to murder Troy. He didn't want to have another reason to be on trial.

The new execution date for May 8, kept on creeping closer and closer, however, with no real tangible way to arrest it, no matter how many protested far from the streets of Mississippi.

"Did you pay the utilities yet?" Gerry asked John, whose face was covered up by the paper he was reading "I put the bill on the dresser-top, oh, I don't know – last week? It was already behind, and I'm afraid they are going to get shut off by the first of the month if we haven't paid it."

"Damn!" John put the paper down, not wanting to read any further anyway, about the upcoming execution date. He didn't have anything else to say, though. The exclamation was not because he had forgotten, but because he had no money to pay it yet. Nor was there money to pay the mortgage for the second month in a row, but he wasn't going to tell Gerry that now.

"John," Gerry started, disturbed by his more frequent cussing and drinking, "did you pay it?" she managed to ask, even while fearing a reaction.

He looked at her with widened, accusing eyes, and demanded loudly, "With what money do you think I paid it with?" Crying ensued from the back room in response.

"Oh, John, you woke the girls!" Gerry threw her hands down in angered protest as she went, too quickly, back to the babies' bedroom, trying to fight back her own tears. She was in no mood to face the situation. They had borrowed money from her parents for too many bills already. She knew that John couldn't get work and had been ostracized by most of the community. Even those who had sympathy for him were afraid to be associated with him, and the cases Al could give him were too few and far between. Al had been ostracized, himself, from the mainstream, with only his Jewish community to keep him afloat. Disbarment proceedings would take time, but it was public knowledge that the documents had been filed. Gerry just wanted to pretend that life was still normal for them and found refuge in cooing her girls back to sleep.

John buried his forehead in his hands for a long moment, elbows propped on the table. He then reached for his pack of cigarettes to find one left. He lit it and after crunching the pack in his hand and tossing it in the nearby trash, resumed his position. He would have to tell her tonight they needed to move to Texas.

CHAPTER FORTY

FURTHER ALONG WE'LL UNDERSTAND WHY

"Let's go, Willie, we're taking another trip!" Jones County Deputy Sheriff Olmonn sighed loudly. They had stopped on their round-about trip to Laurel in a town called Raliegh, MS. They had gotten a call over the radio to stop somewhere and call the Attorney General, Coleman "Better get him out, I've heard more than I care from locals calling my office snitching on the lynch groups." At the protest he added, "If we're going to get this thing done right, we're going to have to find someone to pose as him driving into Laurel on the day of the execution – not before! I've heard word that we have more than one person that has access to the keys that would be more than willing to "lose" them." He looked into the phone and grimaced, "No, I'm not going to give you any names. Hell, it might be you I'm talking about!" At the audibly loud protest from the receiver, he responded even more loudly, "Just get him back to Hinds County with his head on, and you'll still have your job!" He hung up the phone and remarked to the officer sitting in his office, "Didn't want to tell them it was because of the Civil Rights folks. He might not have brought him back at all."

"Mmhumh…I think yore right about that," the officer said lazily.

The Clarion Ledger reporter had captured the start of the event. "Will you gentlemen just pose for one moment for me? There, you two on one side," he positioned the two black tied men on one side of McGee, "and you men on the other." Two officers of the law were to the left of McGee, who stared wide-eyed into the camera.

"Make it quick, this ain't Hollywood!" One officer complained. All of the others looked into the camera and slightly smiled for the photo. As they turned to leave for the drive back to Jackson, the reporter snuck in a quick question. "Willie, do you have anything to say?" The disdain from the surrounding men was tangible as Willie took the opportunity to say, as if he were speaking to the nation, "I ain't got nothing to say now, but I'll have plenty to say later on. That is, if you're there then." The reporter scribbled it down, looking once more at Willie's soulful eyes, wondering about the statement. Would he be present after an appeal was filed, or did he mean in the world to come? He got a chill up his spine as the group rustled out of the jail's hallway.

Earlier that day, with just three more days to go before the execution date, Mr. Coe, another Civil Rights attorney with Bella, had been pleading for clemency again today in front of Governor Wright and other state officials. An appeal had been filed asking for an injunction against McGee's execution, saying that the actions of the people in Mississippi had blocked McGee from his civil rights in the case, and there had been a hearing going on most of the morning. Bella heard the news by phone from a call she had gotten from a delegate of the CRC who had told her, "There were close to a hundred people who came from all over the nation to protest, but they were locked up almost right away by those Jackson police." He had exaggerated. There had only been forty-five, but he wanted to give this poor mother some assurance that there was hope.

"Locked up?" Bessie asked, doubtfully, "What are they gonna be able to do locked up?" Rosalee bothered Bessie at her side, trying to listen in. Bessie finally gave in and said, "You talk to him! It don't make no sense to me."

"Yes?" Rosalee asked with anticipation. She twirled the cord to the receiver as she was told that the hearing was still going on, and not only that, but there were "…people today in Washington D. C., both white and coloreds together, that have T-shirts made that say, "Free Willie McGee," and they are going to chain themselves to the Lincoln Memorial on Monday!"

"Chain themselves?" Rosalee asked wonderingly.

"Yes," he continued energetically, "They're chanting, 'Lincoln freed the slaves, Truman free McGee!" He repeated it as if he were chanting himself, then ended more solemnly with, "His life is a symbol to the nation of a million lives that have been taken unjustly."

Rosalee wiped a falling tear as she said, "Tell them we are so thankful for their support. Yes, please call us again if you hear any other word." She paused and pressed her lips together, tasting another stream of salty tears. "No," she answered to the unheard question as Bessie watched, hanging on every word she could hear. "They won't let us visit Willie until the night of the execution. That's right. Ok, then. Thank you, thanks so much." She hung up the phone and blew into a handkerchief before turning to Bessie's worried eyes and said, "All the nation is watching, Mom," she paused at the unexpected emotion and fought to hold back more tears, but they betrayed her, escaping to run down her cheeks in twin streams, "They're all fighting to free Willie." She managed a wet smile, as if she believed it would have an effect on the tidal wave rushing towards the execution date.

Bessie held her hands together and replied, "Mmhumh." She had no comforting tears. Her heart was dull and dry, and the lines in her forehead ached.

The protestors, who were largely well-dressed women from church groups, unions or progressive organizations, were packed into several jail cells talking loudly among themselves and to the guards. One woman cried, her floppy hat still in place, "Just wait until we get our lawyers to sue you for blocking our civil rights!" Another pitched in, "You know it is an American right to protest. Are we still in America?"

The several women began a chorus of "Doesn't seem so!" "No, I'd say not!" and "Where are we, anyway, in Hell?" "It feels like it!"

The guard seemed mildly amused at this large gathering of what he saw as a flock of foreign females. He wanted to ask where their husbands were, but imagined men figured they would have been more likely to have gotten a beating for their protests.

"Good Lord," came an exclamation from another, "I can't eat this slop!

Can't we send out for something?"

The guards looked at one another and their chuckles turned into louder laughter before seeing the deputy walk down the hall to take in the show.

On another floor, several serious looking black men, who were dressed in coats and ties, were talking quietly among themselves, watching with controlled fear the guardsmen who had earlier joked that they had "plenty for lynching now!" One who looked to be in charge said in a low voice, "Now, brothers, hear me. We share in the suffering of Willie McGee and our God hears our protest. He hears words from our soul, and he knows the soul of that Governor."

"Amen," was chorused by several. A younger man was comforted by a hand on his shoulder of an elder, who stole glances towards the guards as the group exchanged encouragements.

Everyone knew that Abzug and Coe had earlier pled that there was testimony and evidence that had never been heard. Although the word "affair" was never used, everyone present knew exactly what they were talking about. The Daily Worker subscription had been shared amongst all, along with the pamphlets that had been sent to them professing Rosalee's story of Mrs. Hawkin's harassment of her husband. In it also was Bessie's speech.

"Large numbers of the citizens of the Nation believe that my son, Willie McGee, is not deserving of the punishment which hangs over him," Bessie had argued with rare courage to a sea of faces. "Rightly or wrongly, and we do submit rightly, they feel that if he were a white man, he would not be doomed to die." The applause had sustained her shaking knees.

In a current gathering in Mississippi, Wright had his hands clasped together and elbows on the desk as he asked Bella, who was standing in front of him once again, "Are you asking for clemency for Willie McGee because he is innocent, or because you believe the sentence for rape is unfairly applied?"

Bella looked down for a moment to put words to her thoughts, then said into the microphone, "We submit there is some doubt, and as long as there is doubt, we believe there should be clemency."

Wright blasted back with, "Why didn't you take that same line when this case was painted to the world in the multitude of lies?"

Coe confronted Wright later in the hearing saying, "You should avoid putting yourself in the historical position of Pontius Pilate, which is exactly what would happen if you wash your hands," he demonstrated with the rubbing of his own, "and say, 'The courts did it, not I.'"

Wright's face reddened." When I make my decision, I'll assume full responsibility." Laurel's mayor, Carroll Gartin, who was also at the hearing, defended Mrs. Hawkins. "As though she has not already endured enough suffering at this man's bestial hands, his friends now try to cast a stench of dark suspicion about her." He continued, "The filth and foulness of such obscenity is a dastard insult to the name and honor of a Laurel wife and mother who is fine and noble and pure." He held his chin high towards the blasphemers. Their pleas were urgent, but filtered through Communist colored glasses, to court officials.

Coe eyed the still energetic Abzug and let out a deep breath. He had had enough, and told her so, earlier. This would be his last effort in this case. He already had to deal with the officials regarding the protestors.

"Let them be released, and I will see that they leave town immediately," he had asked the officials. They were compliant. They wanted neither the publicity nor the effort of keeping all these head-strong women captive for too long. They had reluctantly given the same opportunity to the black men, with side comments that warned what would happen to their necks if they had any ideas about staying anywhere near Mississippi.

Wright ended the hearing, announcing, "I will render my decision in this case on Monday morning. Good day, ladies and gentlemen." He turned and left Bella and Coe looking at one another.

McGee had heard bits and pieces about the stir in town but felt moved anyway to write once more to Rosalee. He should let her know, at every opportunity, how much he pined for her and was grateful for all she was doing for him. He could write to her more easily than to his mother. It rubbed his heart raw to write a letter to his mother, who he really longed to be comforted by, rather than to comfort. He also prepared a statement, which Miss Abzug had helped him with, and he read it through now to get a feel for how it would sound to the Judge this Monday. In part it read, "To charge as I did under oath, that there was actually no rape and that the prosecution knew it, that the complainant's story was not the truth.... that far from never having seen me in her life, as she testified, we knew each other intimately over a number of years, would have been beyond the power of someone like myself, imprisoned, terrorized by my jailers, and constantly under fear of lynching." "Hey Willie – you gonna go to church services in the mawnin?" The call came from a cell across the hall. Willie paused to answer, "You can count on me bein there!" He looked down again and continued to read, as the man called to someone else, "Ever body go to church in the mawnin! Gonna pray for brother Willie." "Amen!" "I'm there!"

"We'll be there with you, Willie!" the calls came.

Willie brushed away an errant tear and read on in silence, trying his best to just focus on the words and the truth they held for him, "My lawyers took the same attitude, making it plain that to interpose such a defense.... would be out of the question in Mississippi, and they could not see their way clear to present it in open court."

Lawyer Poole said something like that to him before, too. He wondered how he was doing – Lawyer Poole. He had heard that he was getting disbarred. He had asked what it meant. Miss Bella had told him it meant he couldn't be a lawyer anymore. He wished he could've just talked to him one more time. He was sad that his new baby might not be getting the food she needed if her Daddy couldn't work. It felt good to worry about somebody else, but before he got going on it too much, someone down the hall started singing a song.

"Everyday, everyday I have the blues!" He stood from his bench and begin to clap in time.

"Everyday, everyday I have the blues, ooh yeah."

"I know what you mean!" came from another cell. "When you see me worried woman it's you I hate to loo-ose. Nobody loves me, nobody seems to care."

"Oh, yeah," someone else chimed in.

"Yes nobody loves me, nobody seems to care...oh, no.... Speaking of words and trouble darling, you know I had my share."

"You know thas right!" cried another.

The rhythmic beating on the cell doors and benches got louder as others joined in on another verse. It made a smile come to Willie's lips and he stood, putting his paper down, and clung to his cell's bars to watch the hall come alive. He let himself feel comforted for the moment, as he listened.

"Everyday, everyday I have the blues, oh yeah! Everyday, everyday I have the blues, oh no…. When you see me worried woman, baby, it's you I hate to lose, unhuh."

In another city in Mississippi, a deputy was overseeing two negro workers loading the wooden electric chair into a large van that also held the generator that fed the electricity to it, when engaged. The straps of leg braces flapped morbidly as the men carried it.

"Careful not to bend the wire!" the deputy shouted. The cap with its attached wiring was fitted inside the seat for travel, but one of the men had to hold it in place with his hand to keep it from slipping. They managed to get it up the ramp and strapped into the van before they slammed the door. "Ok, now," the deputy said, "when you get to the courthouse, they want it set up in the courtroom plate-glass window, facing out." When the carrier looked puzzled, he added matter-of-factly, "You know, so that folks on the lawn can watch."

The carrier frowned, nodding consent, "Ok," he said simply.

The deputy continued, "Just make sure you've got it there by Monday morning." He paused to say with a grin, "They say this time it's gonna be put to use!" His laugh was cut short as it was met with grim expressions. He left them with, "You boys'll be paid once it's up and running," and turned to walk back to his office.

On Monday afternoon, Abzug and Coe argued again in a hearing in the Federal Court before Judge Mize this time, reiterating every plea that had already been made, and then some. This time they sought an amount of damages for violations of McGee's civil rights. Willie was scheduled to die tonight at midnight, and all the cards needed to be played.

However, Mississippi was not the only place where McGee's case was being pled. There were nation-wide marches and petitions signed, rallies and campus debates. The case of Willie McGee rose above the individual and whether or not he was guilty of the crime. It became a symbol of freedom from tyrannical rule, and not just Communistic or progressive people were irate. There had been statements given by William Faulkner, Einstein and other prominent people.

Common folk of all persuasions were stirred, as well. President Truman was inundated with telegrams and letters to free Willie McGee, not just from individuals, but from groups and organizations of all kinds. On the second of May, he had been sent a letter that was signed by ninety-one prominent people, including Uta Hagen, Oscar Hammerstein, Garson Kanin, Norman Mailer, Wallace Stegner and Sam Wanamaker. He even received letters from groups and individuals in foreign countries – Germany,

France, and China. In communistic societies news was spreading like wildfire how America treated its Negro population. Many letters pleaded with Truman to stop and study the facts.

Everyone seemed to be sure that McGee was not guilty from the bits and pieces of information they had about the case. Truman would not step in despite every legal attempt made, not wanting to tamper with State's rights himself. Judge Mize and Governor Wright of Mississippi ultimately held the life-or-death decision for McGee in their hands.

McGee had, himself, spent part of the afternoon talking with a reporter from "Life" Magazine. His hair was nicely groomed, and he was in a neat, white collared shirt. He had his picture taken from several different angles, all of which he met with drawn and somber face. He was allowed to smoke as he talked about his version of the affair, why it couldn't be acknowledged, and what it had been like for him to be a Negro in Mississippi. He mostly spoke as if in past tense, as if it hurt too much to acknowledge the present or the future. Then he quoted, as best he could remember, some of his prepared statements.

"Taking my life doesn't end such things as have been existing, will be existing till the end of the world. There is a lot more things that causes me not to get a fair decision about this – solely because I am a Negro; this is a white woman. A lot of folks, a lot of men, think they know a woman and don't. They find it hard to believe that Mrs. Hawkins would just hold on and not let the truth be known."

The reporter lingered, his questions abated, as he watched McGee sit and stare with distant eyes.

"Time to go, McGee," a jailer had stepped in quietly and delivered his message in a low voice. McGee took one last deep drag from his cigarette and slowly crushed it in the ashtray, noting that his hands were shaking involuntarily. He felt dizzy. His surroundings became surreal. He had made this trip before but had a different feeling about it this time. There was a heavy weight inside that would not be lifted.

Another jailer had gathered some personal belongings in a small box. He handed it to him along with a telegram." This came for you just now," he said.

Willie looked down at the writing and focused on it as he was being handcuffed in the front this time. It was from a man who called himself "Father Divine," a black evangelist from New York. As Willie read the words, he felt bolstered by a man he never knew who sent the message on behalf of his congregation and many others. "The Lord is my shepherd; I shall not want." The familiar psalm held deeper meaning and comfort than it ever had for him. "Yea, though I walk through the valley of the shadow of death, I will feel no evil; for thou art with me; thy rod and thy staff, they comfort me."

From inside him came a refreshing wave of peace. Oddly, it didn't stop his shaking, but he did not feel that he was his body anymore. He followed the men out to the waiting car, clasping the box tightly.

Once in the car, he grasped for a song to keep the feeling alive. He started in a weak but haunting voice, "Tempted and tried, we're oft made to wonder, why it should be thus, all the day looong." The deputy tried in vain to block out the familiar song he had also sung in church as a boy, by turning up the static just a bit on the patrol car radio. "Further along we'll know all about it. Further along, we'll understand whyy…" The sun was setting and rose and gold hues painted the evening sky.

CHAPTER FORTY-ONE

WHISKEY AND TRUTH

Abzug and other lawyers, whom she had associated with at the last phase of the case, were still hard at work to try every legal avenue possible. They asked a federal judge in New Orleans to grant a restraining order until the arguments could be heard. He refused. A last-minute desperate call to President Truman to intervene came to no good end. Finally, pleading once again to the U. S. Supreme Court. Perhaps it was because this was the third mercy call without solid evidence, or maybe it was the heightened national fear of an impending Communistic takeover that prevented another move to halt the execution. Whatever the reasons, all legal actions were exhausted by 10:25 p.m., and protestors gathered around the radio to hear the final news reports and console one another with promises of new battles on the horizon.

Earlier in Laurel, while the patrol car carrying McGee took a four-hour drive out of the way in order to avoid gangs intending to take justice into their own hands, the adolescent son of a deputy was putting on a wig and smearing black coal grease on his face. He laughed nervously, asking his Dad and his Dad's co-worker, "Do you think I make a good nigger?" The co-worker chuckled, but his Dad was more serious.

"You'd better look like the best nigger out there tonight, if this thing is going to work!" He was dressed in jail khakis and was about the size of McGee. He wiped the grease down his neck while his father fluffed the wig to resemble the coarse, curly, Negro hair.

"All right, then," he said, finally, looking at his watch. We'll get in the car and wait for the radio message that they are fifteen minutes from here before we leave. You hunch down in the back of the car. Don't be looking out at the crowds, you hear me?"

"Yes, sir," the son said as he gazed in the mirror at the odd transformation.

"It might be dangerous for you if you do. They might just be riled up enough to use you as the whipping boy! They won't be happy to find out they've been tricked." He turned his son to look him in the eyes. "Do as I say, son, and everything will be just fine, you hear?" He paused with concern and said, "Are you sure you want to do this?"

"Yes, sir, I do!" He tried to sound as enthusiastic as possible to not reveal the anxiety creeping in.

On the Laurel courthouse lawn, crowds had gathered early on. Mothers had brought picnic suppers in order to be there early enough to save their place.

Children were riding bicycles and the Fathers were talking amongst themselves. There was lighting set up that provided a stage-like atmosphere as the night wore on. Chairs had been arranged in rows just behind the van with the electric generator, where the older folks were given preference. The radio station host from Hattiesburg's WFOR was setting up and testing his equipment. There had been a ruckus just before dark when ready groups of younger men had attacked a patrol car, thinking that McGee was being delivered. They wanted to get in their own bruises on his face before he died. The Sheriff's deputy had called them off before they dragged his son through the broken window. Mothers gathered younger children in their laps, while older ones clammored to get a view.

In another part of Laurel, Pauly Schwartzfager was sitting in his home, trying to block out the looming event. Compassion and curiosity are often odd partners when a tragedy is at hand. It's hard to tell, sometimes, which one compels a bystander to move in to understand a victim's need. Though his conscience had not bothered him one inkling throughout the case, even when he had "arranged" the grand jury pick in order to secure an indictment, it showed its head now when the clock was ticking towards McGee's midnight execution.

He had just done his job, after all, he told himself. A damn good job – that won him many pats on the back from acquaintances, assurance from his constituents, and a compliment of high regard from the Judge. He had planned to bask in the satisfaction of the finality of the verdict, but instead became unexpectedly anxious and restless to such an extent that he needed, rather than wanted the third beer he took from the fridge.

Dinner was turned down in preference for another beer to take off the edge. As his thoughts became more freely flowing, the inebriation allowed the fears to surface. Images of McGee on the stand pointing at his scars, denying the charges, looking at him during cross-examination without the cower of guilt. It all came to him in a flood of memories.

Swartzfager knew what prejudices were capable of and what was most likely to be the truth about the way things were handled.

"Damn it all!" He said out loud, involuntarily, and finished off the last of the bottle as if to stop his tongue from betraying him. "What if you have committed an innocent man to death," he finally questioned himself in a lucid thought. He looked at the clock whose second hand seemed to race. Then, in what seemed to be a brilliant revelation, it came to him that a man under the influence of alcohol will usually let the truth come to the forefront. If he were to offer a dying man the solace of alcohol, he may just get the truth. It wouldn't profit a dying man to lie, and the truth may possibly put both their consciences to rest. He grabbed his coat, opened a desk drawer that had a pistol in it and checked to make sure it was loaded. If Willie was saved from execution again, a riot might break out, and he wanted to be ready. He made a hurried excuse to his wife's worried expression, and got in his car, headed for the store across the river that sold liquor from the back entrance. Once there, he cut his lights, but kept the motor running, spewing tell-tale exhaust into the night air, as the dark figure approached his car. He thought for a moment to purchase a cheap brand – what would it matter?

Thinking twice after looking at the large eyes that peered from the face as black as the night, he said, "Get me some Jack Daniels, will you? Black label." He handed him a bill along with some change.

"Yes suh, thank you suh."

It seemed too much time was passing as he sat there, and he snapped on the radio. News of the crowd gathering in the courtyard, and reviews of the Willie McGee case were being covered.

"Dammit!" He said again, just as he caught sight of his purchase being brought to him in a brown paper bag. His car threw dust out of the gravel driveway, and he turned his lights back on as he sped down the country road. When he finally reached the town, he saw the lights from the courtyard and took a deep breath in as he took in the fact that there was a crowd of hundreds of people already gathered. He pulled around to the less crowded back entrance to the jail. He walked through the gate, nodding to the officer guarding, but offered no explanation of the bag when he asked for entrance to the room where McGee was being kept. The police officer obligingly kept his eyes focused upward as he led him to the room.

Willie had just finished having his last meal and saying prayers with his mother and her pastor, who were told that they would need to sit out in the hall for a spell.

Bessie was unable to contain her grief, and Swartsfager pressed his eyelids together as she passed with a handkerchief, barely holding back the sound of her graveled groans. The pastor glanced at him, not ignoring the held purchase, but nodded his consent.

After they passed, Pauly stepped into the almost shockingly bright atmosphere of the room that held the remains of deep prayer.

McGee was standing with fingers rested lightly on the pages of the Bible on the table beside him. He acknowledged the bulky man before him without emotion.

"Hello, Willie," Pauly said in as sober a voice as he could manage.

Willie looked at him with eyes that penetrated the façade. He felt no need to return the greeting.

Swartzfager presented the bag with some ceremony as he explained, "I've brought something that may help your wait."

Willie thought momentarily as he considered accepting any form of gift from the man who was as responsible for his coming death as the one who would pull the switch of the generator. Having just received his peace from God, the liquor paled in comparison. Still, the opportunity to taste the pleasure of life once again and be numbed to the present reality which could soon shake that peace, in itself seemed to be a result of the Grace of prayer. He picked up his water glass from the table, drank the last bit and shoved it towards the gift of the brown bag. "I'll take some now," he proclaimed, and sat down.

Shwartzfager pulled up a chair and poured whiskey into the glass, filling it a fourth of the way. Willie shot it down and savored the feeling of the burning in the back of his throat. He placed his glass back down in front of the bottle.

Shwartzfager eyed him with caution and curiosity, then filled it again, this time pushing the whole bottle towards him as McGee downed the second drink.

"Whooey!" McGee couldn't help himself as he felt the rush of fire not only burn his throat but helped to loosen the bands of nervous fear. Shwartzfager smiled with a gulp of unexpected emotion and cleared his own throat to hide it.

"That's Black Jack," he offered, intending to impress with the quality, then realizing the irony of the name, he caught himself from saying anything further at the moment and nervously looked away to examine the room. His eyes fixated on the Bible that lay open on a nearby table. Willie looked on his benefactor now with some curiosity himself. Feeling emboldened not only by the drink, but also by his feeling of connection with eternity which exacted no rules for skin color, Willie asked simply, "Why are you here?" He took the bottle, poured another drink, and looked again at the man with slumped shoulders that sat across from him. Willie wondered for a moment if he had just imagined that he had been so intimidating before. In this moment he looked defeated and frightened. He then focused on the glass in his hand and twirled the liquor in it before drinking it down.

"I thought I might offer something that would ease the pain," Shwartzfager finally said and raised himself to look into the eyes of the condemned man who did not flinch, nor offer relief from reality. He offered McGee a cigarette and lit it for him as he took it. They sat in silence for a spell, then Pauly attempted some fragmented statements as conversation, telling him about the crowds outside.

McGee told him about the long ride he had getting in. The liquor began to affect him, and he had alternating spells of wanting to talk and wanting this man out of his space of contemplation. He wasn't sure, though, that he wanted to torture his mother anymore.

Pauly searched Willie's eyes as he had drunk about half of the bottle then said, "Willie, before I leave, I did just want to hear one thing from you." McGee looked at him as steadily as he could. Schwartzfager leaned back in his chair, wiped his hand from his forehead down his nose and covered his mouth for a moment, then crossed his arms over his chest as if garnering strength or for protection to ward off the answer as he finally asked, "I just want to know – did you do it?"

McGee took in the state of the man in front of him, then looked away for a moment with a far-away look in his eyes. He pressed his lips together before taking a deep breath and raising his eyes again to more solidly meet his adversary's with truth.

"Yessir, I did it," he paused and added, "but she was just as guilty as I was."

Shwartzfager nodded as if in understanding, as if he already knew. His eyes were wide, and his lips pursed. "I see," he said, "I see." He leaned forward slowly to say something but reconsidered, and just kept nodding. He eased his elbows onto his knees, wrung his hands as if to wipe off the guilt, then held his heavy forehead in them and stared at the ground as Willie threw another shot of whiskey back in his throat. The night would haunt Pauly for the rest of his life.

At 11:00, Mr. and Mrs. Hawkins were ushered into the packed courtroom and found their seats in the front row. There was a mixture of people who had been selected to be in the courtroom, along with those who were excited that they had managed to slip in through an acquaintance. All reasoned among themselves that it was a unique experience to be able to witness such severe consequences of judgment. One college-aged man recollected studying the gatherings that watched the guillotine executions. It was commonplace then, he said, too loudly. All temporarily hushed their conversations after the Hawkins sat down.

Outside the radio announcer was on air, describing the gathering, but downplaying the circus-like atmosphere he saw before him, not relating that cold drinks were being sold. He assured the radio listeners that this was for those who were not able to travel to be here and that no one was celebrating a man's death, but that it was being recorded for history.

"Time is rapidly running out for McGee," the announcer said, "And down here, right below us, they are opening the truck, getting it all set, ready to turn it on, so that the juice will be funneled up through these cables that are running from the truck to the chair, and will of course, provide the power that will give Willie McGee the execution."

John had the thought of turning the blasted thing off. He could hear the tenor of the crowd and imagined the conversations. Instead, he steadied his glass to pour himself another drink of Black Jack, while clenching his cigarette between his lips. Gerry was quietly washing up some dishes, not wanting to sit too near the box that was broadcasting at Death's doors, even though they had both stayed up to hear it. The station didn't come in too well, anyway. It was easier for her to busy her mind about other things for a while. She had begun to pack the house, saving everything of any value just in case they might need to sell something later on.

This made her feel a little concerned, though, that their friends might not have space for them to move in all those boxes. She considered selling things ahead of time, maybe Mother would help.

At the same time, Willie was led through the catwalk by a jailer, who had asked to do the duty. He was one that Willie had said had shown him kindnesses. He held Willie's upper arm gently and listened to his gasped prayers as he walked and stumbled towards the heavy wooden door that led to the courtroom. Willie's head had been shaved just before midnight, and it had sobered him up. He had told the barber that he wasn't worried at all, that he had made his peace with the Lord and that, "Willie is ready to go."

The stumbling was due to the fact that it was no longer him that was walking. He was watching serenely from just above – the shell of his body being led through the ominous courthouse gathering and placed in the hard wooden chair. He watched as his legs were being strapped in and the morbid domed cap was placed on his head. He came to himself to ask, "Is Reverend Patterson here?" He heard the words, "Yes, he is Willie, he is right here." He then could see the blazing lights coming through the window in front of him, and heard a mixture of loud, confusing noises. He thought of his mother, and his eyes flashed as he prayed silently that she be comforted.

Gerry's thoughts were interrupted by the broadcaster's louder announcement, "Here it goes!" and the sounds of the revving engine penetrated through the static. She couldn't help but cry, "Oh, how awful!" She grabbed her face with both hands and let herself sob the pent-up emotion.

It caused John to release his own stream of tears, and to say with anguish, "Oh, Lord have mercy!"

The sound of the generator's "whoosh" with each of the three powerful electrical charges caused the crowd outside to let out war-whoops, as they simultaneously witnessed Willie's body shaking with the jolts. The satisfaction that those in the courtroom were looking for came in the form of a noxious smell of burnt flesh that caused a speedy exit to commence.

Outside, a young boy had shimmied up a nearby pole to get a better look and was included in the picture that was taken of the wild-eyed crowd that appeared on the front page of the next issue of "Life" magazine. Their eerie smiles were incongruent with the topic of the inside article that read, "The End of Willie McGee." It claimed that Willie McGee had been a pawn of the Communistic agenda, saying that "… as the Communists moved in, such groups as the NAACP drew back." That part was true, the groups normally supporting the black man did not want to be associated with such a "red flag". The coverage painted a picture of the interest of the CRC being only for their agenda, and "…who came to Laurel to capitalize on his plight, and later wandered off, looking for some new symbol."

The Clarion Ledger showed less dramatic pictures of the crowd milling about, and painted the picture as more reasonable. The caption read that it was "The return of Willie McGee to the scene of his crime to pay with his life in the state's portable electric chair attracted hundreds of people to Laurel…" It showed a smiling, almost jubilant picture of McGee, bizarrely placed, that said he had "…jauntily sat in his jail cell and smoked a cigar as his head was being shaved." It did not mention that he reeked of alcohol.

Newspapers in the North that were more sympathetic to the cause of saving McGee ran a copy of his last letter to Rosalee. She hadn't been in Mississippi at the time, but was still in Detroit, attending a rally. She sat reading the letter with other women supporters in the room, who were waiting with her until the end.

"Dear Rosalee, they are planning here to kill me and I don't know if you and the people will be able to save me. If I have to die, I want you to say goodbye to my mother and the children and all the people who no it is wrong to kill a man because of his color. You no I am innocent. Tell the people again and again I never did commit this crime. Tell them that the real reason they are going to take my life is to keep the Negro down in the south. They can't do this if you and the children keep on fighting. Never forget to tell them why they killed their Daddy. I no you won't fail me. Tell the people to keep on fighting."

CHAPTER FORTY-TWO

THE OASIS OF HOPE

The car radio was playing, "…But the Yellow Rose of Texas is the only girl for me!" Gerry had asked for it to be turned up so that she could sing it along with the Mitch Miller band. The three girls in the back seat of the new family Ford listened, singing along with a phrase here and there, since it had been a theme song of their stay in Texas, but were distracted by the more interesting scenes out the window. One thing in particular that captured their amazement was the wet spots on the road that would shine in the distance but disappear as you came up to them. At the insistence of the girls to have their dad explain why this was so, he turned down the radio. "Those aren't really wet spots, they are called mirages," he explained." They appear to be an oasis on a hot day."

"What's an o-a-sis?" Beverly asked.

"It's a place in the desert where there is actually a small body of water that may have a palm tree by it, where a thirsty traveler can refresh himself with a drink and rest in the shade."

"But they're not real?" Carolyn asked, trying to figure out the phenomenon. "Well, these that you see on the road are not, you're right!" he commended. "It's a <u>mir</u>-age," Gerry repeated for her.

"Mir-age," came the chorus from the back seat.

"That's right," John continued, "The sun is reflecting the heat waves on the road, just like it does in the desert, and it tricks the wanderer to chase after them."

"Oh!" came the acceptance of the explanation, and all the girls watched out the window with fascination at the "mirages" that came and went, pointing out each one and following it to reveal the charlatan in the end with laughter at their discovery.

John turned up the radio again to hear the news of the continuing bus boycott in Montgomery, Alabama. "I think they're going to win this thing in the end," he said to Gerry as the girls giggled in the back seat.

"Now sit back!" Gerry directed the girls, then turned back to say, "It's been a long time coming."

"Yes, it has," John agreed, and became lost in thought once again. He was looking forward to meeting again with the groups that were supporting integration. He had read with great interest the reports on the plight of those who were instigating the bus boycott. He had told his friend, who the family had stayed with while they were in Texas, "I think this man, Martin Luther King, Jr., is going to make some break-throughs. I'm going to keep my eye on him!"

He adjusted his rear-view mirror and caught a glance of his four-year-old daughter, who was continuing to peer out the window in scientific study of the vanishing mirages. How long would it be before she attended an integrated school, he wondered. Shortly after she was born, he realized he would need to eat some humble pie and plead his way back to the Mississippi Bar. He had represented himself, and in his defense had once again disavowed any link to Communism. He didn't mention that he was even more interested, however, in supporting the integration of the black population into the mainstream of society. He would let this be known later, after a year or two back in the field. They seemed to be more impressed by the fact that he had rehabilitated himself from his drinking. It hadn't been so hard to do when his family didn't have even enough money for food. Gerry liked to tell the story to the girls that, "Daddy even gave up cigarettes one week when we had to eat eggs for breakfast, lunch and dinner every day." They would now stay in the duplex that Gerry's mother and father owned and lived in. It would be so good to be back with family again, she had declared, and John had said he would be glad to not have to sell another blasted encyclopedia. Al had told him that business had picked up, and the Willie McGee case was now water under the bridge. He had said that he had an overflow of clients, and that he believed work would pick up quickly for John. John was determined to also represent the black population who couldn't afford a lawyer, as a life-long commitment to payback for the one he wasn't able to win.

"Daddy!" Carolyn said sharply, with amazement. "What?" John looked back, hoping nothing was wrong.

"I think that one was real water!" came the delighted reply.

"Don't scare your Daddy like that when he's driving," Gerry chided. "But it was! I think it was real water! It's an oasis!"

John looked back in the rear-view mirror and saw a city truck washing the streets, and slopping water from its brushes.

He laughed and said, "I think you're right, honey, that one was a real oasis." The yellow car sped down the highway with its crew, past the "Welcome to Mississippi" sign, to which they all gave a hearty cheer.

EPILOGUE

In compiling this intricate story that involves so many perspectives, I realize there will be some who will take issue with this interpretation of history. To all who do, I first offer my apology for any offense. This is meant to be a historical narrative and not an explicit historical rendering. Please know that I have attempted to stay true to facts that I have taken from newspapers, trial transcript, research of my own and that which was borrowed from Alex Heard in his book by Harper Collins, "The Eyes of Willie McGee," and from stories I have been told by my father and his friends. I took poetic license to interweave these where I believed they would have occurred chronologically and gave life to them in the form of a narrative. The meeting of Paul Schwartzfager and Willie McGee on the night of his execution was inspired by the story Jon Schwartzfager told me of his father. Jon has spent his career attempting to free those who are on death row unjustly.

Bridgette McGee, Willie McGee's granddaughter, helped to verify the story of her family's flight to the West Coast and the conjured-up story of Rosalee. We all benefitted in our lives from the experiences of our fathers and predecessors and the uncovering of this story, which is my hope for all who read "Pawn."

My intent is not to stir up further animosity in race relations. My desire in writing this book is to not only give honor to those who were involved in standing up for what they believed to be a just cause, but to also shine light on the individual human experience of us all – from every perspective. The more we can understand the impulses, misunderstandings and fears that cause irrational thought against others different from us, I believe the more we can evolve in our acceptance and compassion for one another. Evil is not claimed by any one culture, or any era of human history. Humility shows us that we often project it from ourselves on others, becoming astonished in the reflection.

My father and mother loved their home in Mississippi, as did I, and I was reluctant many times in the writing to expose – yet again – the sordid history of race relations in the South. If I didn't believe bringing the truth to light would not be healing in the long run, I would have not attempted the task. I would encourage the reader to also reflect on the many beautiful aspects of the Southern people and their culture that are often overlooked when the focus is solely on past prejudices.

John Poole went on to use his genius to become what some entitled him, "the lawyer's lawyer." He did not forget his beginnings, however, and continued to serve the black population with little recompense, as mentioned earlier. He often brought home canned goods, bags of tomatoes and other gifts home that we suspected may have been the only payment he received. One man, whose son he had defended, sent him a Christmas gift every year. Although we experienced borderline poverty growing up, looking back, we are proud that we were part of the struggle, and that our parents raised us to see all races as equal.

Thank you for reading, and may God bless us all in these days.

Made in the USA
Columbia, SC
01 August 2022

64351503R00204